D0871265

A COLERIDGE COMPANION

A COLERIDGE COMPANION

An Introduction to the Major Poems
and the *Biographia Literaria*

JOHN SPENCER HILL

MACMILLAN PUBLISHING COMPANY
NEW YORK

First published in the United States 1984 by
MACMILLAN PUBLISHING COMPANY
866 Third Avenue
New York, NY 10022

Library of Congress Catalog Card Number 83-82622
ISBN 0-02-914110-9

Typeset in Great Britain by
Scarborough Typesetting Services
and printed in Hong Kong

For Boyd R. Buttsworth

ὁ τοῦ βιοῦ στέφανος φιλία ἐστιν

Contents

List of Plates

18   Coleridge's 'Bed- and Book-room' in the attic of No. 3, The
     Grove, Highgate, from a lithograph by George Scharf the
     Elder (Revd Nicholas F. D. Coleridge)

List of Maps

Preface

Like Tristram Shandy, this book can trace its conception to a particular event and point in time. It began in March 1976 from a colleague's stricken lament, as he was going off to lecture on Coleridge, that it is impossible for a non-specialist to teach Coleridge well because so many of his critics take too much for granted and tend to disappear without warning into impenetrable, swirling mists of aesthetic theory or metaphysics or theology. Somebody, he said, should explain their explanations.

The chapters which follow are an attempt to provide a readable distillation of Coleridge scholarship and to make the general reader aware of the major problems and major lines of analysis associated with the most frequently studied of Coleridge's works. Each chapter begins with a detailed account of the composition and publication history of the poem (or prose work) under consideration, followed by sections that take up specific questions of criticism (e.g. is 'Kubla Khan' a 'fragment'?) or of relevant background information (e.g. Coleridge, Wordsworth and the Supernatural), and concludes with a summary of the various interpretative approaches to the work. It has been necessary, of course, to be selective and to arbitrate between various critical views, but I have tried to be both fair and comprehensive within reason. The book is not a descriptive bibliography but is rather, in intention at least, a work of genial criticism in which the reader is guided through the primary texts and secondary materials in an orderly, illuminating fashion.

Initially I proposed, naïvely enough, to cover 'all' of Coleridge, with chapters not only on the major poems and *Biographia Literaria* but also on the dramas, minor poetry and remaining prose works, and on Coleridge's philosophy, theology, politics and literary criticism. It did not take me long to see the impracticality of attempting so much in one short book and the necessity of limiting myself to the major writings. As the book progressed, numerous other compromises were forced upon me by considerations of length. Undoubtedly the most regrettable of these is the omission of 'Christabel', which, had more space been available, would most certainly have been included.

My greatest debt in writing this book is to the many Coleridge scholars whose industry and insights have made it both possible and necessary. Their names appear throughout the text and in the notes at the end of the volume. Other debts are more personal in nature. I am profoundly grateful to my wife and our three children for their patience, encouragement and understanding; it has not always been easy, but they were more than equal to the task. The book is dedicated with great affection to Dr Boyd Buttsworth, physician and friend, whose concern and advice made the work possible. A simple dedication, however grateful and sincere, is no adequate recompense for so much kindness, generosity, wisdom and friendship. But it is at least a beginning.

Ottawa,   J. S. H.
Canada

List of Abbreviations

AP	*Anima Poetae, from the Unpublished Notebooks of Samuel Taylor Coleridge*, ed. E. H. Coleridge (London, 1895)
BL	S. T. Coleridge, *Biographia Literaria . . . with the Aesthetical Essays*, ed. J. Shawcross, 2 vols (London and New York, 1907; corrected edition 1954)
BL [W]	S. T. Coleridge, *Biographia Literaria*, ed. George Watson (London and New York, 1965; repr. 1975)
CC	*The Collected Works of Samuel Taylor Coleridge*, general editor Kathleen Coburn, 16 vols and index (London and Princeton, NJ, 1967)
CL	*Collected Letters of Samuel Taylor Coleridge*, ed. E. L. Griggs, 6 vols (London and New York, 1956–71)
CN	*The Notebooks of Samuel Taylor Coleridge*, ed. Kathleen Coburn, 5 vols and index (London and New York, 1957)
CPW	*The Complete Poetical Works of Samuel Taylor Coleridge*, ed. E. H. Coleridge, 2 vols (London and New York, 1912)
E&S	*Essays and Studies by Members of the English Association*
EIC	*Essays in Criticism*
ELH	*A Journal of English Literary History*
HCR	*Henry Crabb Robinson on Books and their Writers*, ed. E. J. Morley, 3 vols (London, 1938)
IS	*Inquiring Spirit: A New Presentation of Coleridge from his Published and Unpublished Prose Writings*, ed. Kathleen Coburn (London, New York and Toronto, 1951; repr. London and Toronto, 1979)
JDW	*Journals of Dorothy Wordsworth*, ed. Mary Moorman, 2nd edn (London and New York, 1971; repr. 1976)

JEGP	*Journal of English and Germanic Philology*
LL	*The Letters of Charles and Mary Anne Lamb*, ed. E. W. Marrs, Jr, 5 vols (Ithaca, NY, and London, 1975)
LW: EY	*The Letters of William and Dorothy Wordsworth: The Early Years, 1787–1805*, ed. E. de Selincourt and Chester L. Shaver, 2nd edn (Oxford, 1967)
MC	*Coleridge's Miscellaneous Criticism*, ed. T. M. Raysor (London, 1936)
MLN	*Modern Language Notes*
MLQ	*Modern Language Quarterly*
MP	*Modern Philology*
N&Q	*Notes and Queries*
PAPS	*Proceedings of the American Philosophical Society*
PMLA	*Publications of the Modern Language Association*
PQ	*Philological Quarterly*
PWW	*The Prose Works of William Wordsworth*, ed. W. J. B. Owen and J. W. Smyser, 3 vols (Oxford, 1974)
PWW [G]	*The Prose Works of William Wordsworth*, ed. A. B. Grosart, 3 vols (London, 1876; repr. New York, 1967)
REL	*Review of English Literature*
RES	*Review of English Studies*
SC	*Coleridge's Shakespearean Criticism*, ed. T. M. Raysor, 2 vols (London, 1930; revised and slightly abridged, London, 1960)
SEL	*Studies in English Literature* (Rice University)
SIB	*Studies in Bibliography*
SIP	*Studies in Philology*
SIR	*Studies in Romanticism*
TLS	*The Times Literary Supplement*
TSE	*Tulane Studies in English*
TT	*The Table Talk and Omniana of Samuel Taylor Coleridge*, ed. H. N. Coleridge (London and New York, 1917)
TWC	*The Wordsworth Circle*
UTQ	*University of Toronto Quarterly*
WPW	*The Poetical Works of William Wordsworth*, ed. E. de Selincourt and H. Darbishire, 5 vols (Oxford, 1940–9; repr. 1967)

WW   Mary Moorman, *William Wordsworth: A Biography*,
             2 vols (London, Oxford and New York, 1957; repr.
             1968)

References to the above books and periodicals are by page only
(e.g. *LW: EY*, p. 188), volume and page (e.g. *CL*, I 357; *ELH*,
XXVI 525–6), or by volume and entry number (e.g. *CN*, I no.
1575). For other books and periodicals, the system is parallel.

Most references to individual poems are by line only, or by book
and line (e.g. *The Task*, IV 286–310).

References to classical works follow the appropriate tradition.

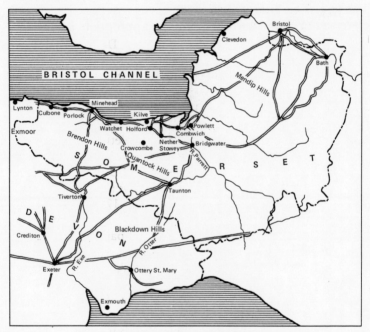

Map 1   Somerset and Devon

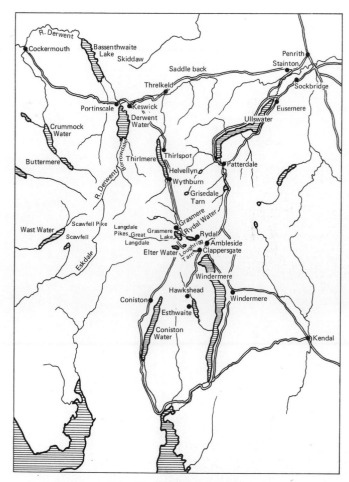

Map 2   The Lake District

1 Coleridge: a Biographical Sketch[1]

Samuel Taylor Coleridge was born on 21 October 1772 in Ottery St Mary, a market-town of some 2500 souls situated on the banks of the little river Otter in south-east Devon. Christened Samuel Taylor in honour of his godfather, he was the youngest of nine sons and one daughter born to John Coleridge and his second wife, Ann (*née* Bowden). John Coleridge, well advanced into middle age when his last son was born, had been since 1760 the vicar of the parish and master of the local grammar-school; he was, as Coleridge fondly remembered, a good albeit slightly eccentric man, an Israelite without guile − 'in learning, good-heartedness, absentness of mind, & excessive ignorance of the world, he was a perfect *Parson Adams'* (*CL*, I 310). Of Coleridge's mother little is known, and Coleridge himself has left scant impression of her, except to say that she was an admirable household economist and was concerned for her family's social well-being.[2]

As the youngest in a large family, Coleridge was spoiled by both his parents and, as a consequence, suffered at the hands of his older brothers, especially Frank, the second youngest. Being by nature a timorous child, he responded to the taunts and torments of his brothers, and later of fellow schoolboys, by retreating into passivity and the privacy of the world of books. From an early age he was an avid reader of fairy-stories and such works as *Robinson Crusoe* and the *Arabian Nights*; and often, among the weathered gravestones in the Ottery churchyard (Plate 1), the 'spirits used to come upon me suddenly, & in a flood − and then I was accustomed to run up and down . . . and act over all I had been reading' (*CL*, I 347). But he was also resourceful in his retreat, for he quickly acquired abilities beyond his years and so gained admiring approval in a sphere elevated well above the arenas of fraternal

1

and schoolyard rivalry: 'because I could read & spell, & had, I may
truly say, a memory & understanding forced into almost an unnatural ripeness, I was flattered & wondered at by all the old women
– & so I became very vain, and despised most of the boys, that were
at all near my own age – and before I was eight years old, I was a
character' (*CL*, I 347–8). The complexity and contradiction in his
personality were thus established early in life: on the one hand, a
morbid fear of rejection and disapproval that prompted apologetic
self-abasement and a neurotic sense of insecurity; on the other
hand, an impetuous and articulate brilliance, especially in conversation, that pulled astonished auditors helplessly along in its wake.
His early compulsion to omnivorous reading, moreover, while
originally a refuge from insecurity and the trials of childhood, also
laid a firm foundation for his later convictions about the nature of
perception and the validity of imaginative experience. His mind, as
he told Thomas Poole, had been 'habituated *to the Vast*' from his
early reading of fairy-stories and romances – '& I never regarded
my senses in any way as the criteria of my belief. I regulated all my
creeds by my conceptions not by my *sight* – even at that age' (*CL*,
I 354). This platonising intuition, confirmed and developed by his
early reading, and later given conceptual form and a framework
after his discovery of German metaphysics, lies at the root of much
that is most characteristic and valued in Coleridge's mature
thought, including his theory of imagination.[3]

Coleridge's formal schooling began in 1778 when he entered his
father's grammar-school at Ottery. In October 1781, however, only
three weeks before Coleridge's ninth birthday, his father, at the age
of sixty-one, died of a sudden and unexpected heart attack. For a
few months Coleridge remained at the Ottery school as a day
scholar under Parson Warren, his father's successor, who, according to the son loyal to his father's memory, was 'a booby'. Through
the good offices of Judge Buller, a former Ottery student, he was
enrolled in the Christ's Hospital preparatory school at Hertford in
July 1792, and six weeks later 'was drafted up to the great school at
London' (*CL*, I 388). Life for the bluecoat boys of Christ's Hospital
was not easy: the food was monotonous and meagre ('Our appetites
were *damped* never satisfied'), freedoms were few and selective,
and school discipline was harsh and frequent, as Charles Lamb
remembered with a shudder in his vivid account of 'Christ's Hospital Five and Thirty Years Ago' (1820). But there were compensations, too, for the spartan conditions – compensations at least

for the talented and dedicated. Under the able preceptorship of the Revds Matthew Field and James Boyer, masters of the Lower and Upper Grammar Schools respectively, hard work and academic achievement were prized and rewarded, and intelligence not only accepted but celebrated. In these circumstances Coleridge not surprisingly blossomed. He was praised by his teachers, grew in self-confidence, and was regarded as a prodigy by his peers. In the school cloisters (Plate 2), according to the idolatrous Lamb, his eloquence held chance passers-by entranced with admiration as they listened to 'the young Mirandula . . . unfold . . . the mysteries of Jamblichus, or Plotinus . . . , or reciting Homer in his Greek, or Pindar − while the walls of the old Grey Friars re-echoed to the accents of the *inspired charity-boy*!'[4]

In February 1791 Coleridge matriculated at Jesus College, Cambridge, and took up residence at the college in October of that year, five days before his twentieth birthday. Despite an auspicious beginning, however, Cambridge was far from a happy experience. Mounting debts, academic disappointments, and a new-found intoxication with radical politics which diverted him from his studies created problems with which he was temperamentally unequipped to cope − and his instinctive response was to flee. In December 1793 he impetuously enlisted in the 15th Light Dragoons and, having given his name as Silas Tomkyn Comberbache, was duly sworn in at Reading as a trooper. After a good deal of time and trouble, his release from the Dragoons was secured by his brothers, and Coleridge, temporarily chastened and filled with new resolution, was permitted to return to Cambridge in April 1794. But the mood did not last, and he eventually left the university in December 1794 without obtaining a degree.

During his last months of nominal residence at Cambridge, Coleridge was in fact seldom at the university. In June he set off on a pedestrian tour of Wales. The route took him through Oxford, where he was introduced to Robert Southey, two years his junior and a student at Balliol. Southey, who was reading Plato's *Republic*, was toying in a desultory way with the attractions of emigrating to America and setting up an ideal society along the lines of Plato's imaginary state. Coleridge found the idea irresistible and was swept immediately away by the happy prospect of transforming dream into reality, waxed eloquent on the practicability of such a scheme, and within a few weeks had convinced Southey and several other newly acquired friends, including

Tom Poole of Nether Stowey, of its feasibility. The plan, christened 'Pantisocracy' (i.e. equal government by all), called for twelve educated men to establish a settlement on the banks of the euphonious Susquehanna River in Pennsylvania, where there were no hostile Indians and where the mosquitoes were not as bad as English gnats. Three or four hours of manual labour a day would supply the frugal needs of the settlement, leaving the remainder of the day for philosophic discussion, meditation, and literary composition. Wives were necessary, of course, to look after household duties and to ensure the colony's growth and future. In August, Southey became engaged to Edith Fricker of Bristol, the third in a family of five daughters living with their widowed mother and supporting themselves with their needles. The second daughter, Mary, was already married to a young Quaker poet named Robert Lovell: both convinced Pantisocrats. And in an impetuous moment of enthusiasm Coleridge found that he had himself proposed to, and been accepted by, Sara Fricker — the eldest of the five sisters. In September he returned to Cambridge, preaching Pantisocracy to everyone he met, with a dawning but not yet daunting sense of the implications of his acts: 'My God! how tumultuous are the movements of my Heart — Since I quitted this room what and how important Events have been evolved! America! Southey! Miss Fricker! —' (*CL*, I 103).

Just after Christmas, Coleridge confessed to Southey that he did not love Sara Fricker. 'O Southey!' he pleaded, 'bear with my weakness. Love makes all things pure and heavenly like itself: — but to marry a woman whom I do *not* love . . .' (*CL*, I 145). It was a cry for help and understanding. During the two months preceding his letter, Coleridge had attempted to forget the past and stave off the future by ignoring them. Although expected in Bristol, he remained in Cambridge and then moved on to London, where he penned a series of political sonnets for the *Morning Chronicle* and spent convivial evenings in the Salutation and Cat with Charles Lamb and other friends. He also began to compose 'Religious Musings'. 'Mark you, Southey!' he declared from his safe and distant London refuge, '*I will do my Duty*.' But Southey had seen enough to doubt this resolution and, toward the end of January 1795, he appeared in London, tracked the stray sheep to the Angel Inn, and escorted him back to Bristol and his patient fiancée. He joined Southey and George Burnett in the latter's lodgings in College Street, where Southey could keep an eye on him, and over the next six months delivered a number of lectures on public affairs and on 'revealed religion', which earned him some notoriety as a democrat.[5] During these months of lecturing, however, a serious rift began to open between Coleridge and Southey over the Pantisocracy scheme. Coleridge was still devoted to the plan, but Southey, who was having second thoughts, suggested that the American venture was too drastic a start and that the scheme should first be tested in a modified experiment on a farm in Wales. Coleridge was outraged: 'Your private resources', he told Southey in scornful rebuke, 'were to remain your individual property, and every thing to be separate except on five or six acres. In short, we were to commence Partners in a petty Farming Trade. This was the Mouse of which the Mountain Pantisocracy was at last safely delivered!' (*CL*, I 165). The quarrel caused a breach between the two men that, while not permanent, was to take many months to heal over. 'You have left a large Void in my Heart', said Coleridge; 'I know no man big enough to fill it' (*CL*, I 173).

Ironically enough, however, although Coleridge did not know it at the time, he had just met the man who was more than big enough to fill the void left by Southey — for in September 1795 William Wordsworth had swum into his ken. Almost nothing is known about this first encounter between Wordsworth and Coleridge, except that it took place in Bristol (*LW: EY*, p. 153) and that their mutual admiration led in the following months to an exchange of letters. In March 1796 Joseph Cottle, the Bristol bookseller and future publisher of *Lyrical Ballads*, transmitted a manuscript copy of Wordsworth's 'Guilt and Sorrow' to Coleridge, who (according to Azariah Pinney) read the poem 'with considerable attention' and 'interleaved it with white paper to mark down whatever may strike him as worthy [Wordsworth's] notice' (*CL*, I 216n.). And by mid May Coleridge was calling Wordsworth 'A very dear friend of mine, who is in my opinion the best poet of the age' (*CL*, I 215). But, despite the intimacy and warmth of such remarks, the two young poets had no personal contact between their first meeting in September 1795 and the occasion of Wordsworth's visit to Nether Stowey in March 1797 which inaugurated the period of close and productive friendship.

Shortly after the break with Southey, Coleridge took a decisive step. On 4 October 1795, in St Mary Redcliffe ('poor Chatterton's Church'), he was united in marriage to Sara Fricker, 'the woman, whom I love best of all created Beings' (*CL*, I 160). He may be convicted of short-sightedness but not of insincerity in this union. Although an ill-matched pair by temperament and abilities, Coleridge and his bride were genuinely in love. What had started as an engagement of Pantisocratic convenience had blossomed, over the months of close contact in Bristol in 1795, into a deep and unfeigned attachment: 'my addresses to Sara, which I at first payed from Principle not Feeling, from Feeling & from Principle I renewed: and I met a reward more than proportionate to the greatness of the Effort. I love and I am beloved, and I am happy!' (*CL*, I 164). The couple settled in Clevedon, in a myrtle- and jasmine-covered cottage overlooking the Bristol Channel – an idyllic setting described in 'The Eolian Harp', the finest poem that Coleridge had so far composed.

But the Clevedon idyll was short-lived. The imperatives of bread and cheese soon turned Coleridge's attention to the necessity of his earning a living. He proposed to do so by his pen. In December 1795 he published *Conciones ad Populum*, a collection of political writings incorporating some of his Bristol lectures of the previous spring, and he laid the plans for a political periodical devoted to current affairs but containing as well some poetry and book-reviews. In order to drum up subscriptions for this periodical, to be called *The Watchman* since its function was to watch over and preserve 'Freedom and her Friends' from the meddling depre-dations of the Pitt government, Coleridge embarked on an exten-sive tour of the Midlands, advertising his magazine in impassioned harangues to gatherings of men of liberal political sentiments in Birmingham, Sheffield, Manchester and Liverpool.[6] Along the way he preached in Unitarian chapels – on one occasion to a congregation of 1400 people – in spirited political sermons which, he gleefully declared, 'spread a sort of sanctity over my *Sedition*' (*CL*, I 179). He returned to Bristol, whither his wife had moved to be with her mother during his absence, with nearly a thousand names on the subscription-list for *The Watchman*. It was an auspicious beginning – but it did not last. The first number, which made its appearance on 1 March 1796, was followed by nine later issues at intervals of roughly eight days; but in the second number (9 March) Coleridge published a flippant 'Essay on Fasts' with an offensive motto from Isaiah ('Wherefore my Bowels shall sound like an Harp'), which cost him, he said later, 'near five hundred of my subscribers at one blow' (*BL*, I 120). While there were other reasons as well for the periodical's demise, it is certainly true that the 'Essay on Fasts' offered subscribers a convenient excuse to withdraw, and *The Watchman*, having watched in vain, spoke for the last time on Friday, 13 May 1796.

With the termination of *The Watchman*, Coleridge's finances were ruined. Only the timely generosity of his numerous friends saved him from going to prison for debt and provided him with a meagre allowance to meet his immediate needs. It was imperative that he should find security and a means of livelihood. In April Cottle had published Coleridge's *Poems on Various Subjects*, but he could hardly expect poetry to supply his daily bread. Other possibilities suggested themselves — a translation of Schiller's works, preaching for hire as a Dissenting minister, writing for the *Morning Chronicle* in London, or serving as a live-in tutor to educate the sons of a wealthy widow, Mrs Evans of Darley, near Derby — but all proved themselves either impracticable or impossible for one reason or another. As summer ripened into autumn, still with no solution in sight, Coleridge's responsibilities increased: on 19 September, while Coleridge was away in Birmingham arranging to tutor Charles Lloyd,[7] Sara was safely delivered, somewhat prematurely, of a son — their first child, subsequently christened 'David Hartley Coleridge, in honor of the great Master of Christian Philosophy' (*CL*, I 247). With the birth of Hartley and the arrival of Charles Lloyd, life in the Frickers' house on Redcliffe Hill in Bristol, strained at the best of times, became intolerable. Coleridge's health declined, and early in November he was taking twenty-five drops of laudanum every four hours to check a violent attack of neuralgia.

At length Thomas Poole, not without misgivings, came to the rescue. Poole located a tiny cottage in Lime Street, Nether Stowey (Plates 4 and 5) into which the Coleridges moved on 31 December 1796. The yearly rent was only £7. Despite the fact that the house was draughty and mouse-ridden, Coleridge was blissfully happy:

Our House is better than we expected — there is a comfortable bedroom & sitting room for C. Lloyd,[8] & another for us — a room for Nanny, a kitchen, and outhouse. Before our door a clear brook runs of very soft water; and in the back yard is a nice *Well* of fine spring water. We have a very pretty garden, and large enough to find us vegetables & employment. And I am already an expert Gardener — & both my Hands can exhibit a callum, as testimonials of their Industry. We have likewise a sweet Orchard; & at the end of it T. Poole has made a gate, which leads into his garden . . . . (*CL*, I 301)

Peace of mind and physical exercise led to a spectacular recovery of health, and returning health prompted and sustained renewed intellectual efforts – he wrote magazine reviews, prepared his poems for a second edition, and at the request of Richard Brinsley Sheridan began to compose a tragedy (*Osorio*) which, he had reason to hope, would be produced at Drury Lane. All in all, the joy and security of Nether Stowey, with its mixture of manual and mental labours sweetened with modest social pleasures, were the fulfilment of his Pantisocratic dreams. He described his daily routine to John Thelwall in February 1797:

> I never go to Bristol – from seven to half past eight I work in my garden; from breakfast to 12 I read & compose; then work again – feed the pigs, poultry &c, till two o'clock – after dinner work again till Tea – from Tea till supper *review*. So jogs the day; & I am happy. I have society – my *friend*, T. Poole and as many acquaintances as I can dispense with – there are a number of very pretty young women in Stowey, all musical – & I am an immense favorite: for I pun, conundrumize, *listen*, & dance. The last is a recent acquirement – . We are *very* happy – & my little David Hartley grows a sweet boy – & has high health – he laughs at us till he makes us weep for very fondness. – You would smile to see my eye rolling up to the ceiling in a Lyric fury, and on my knee a *Diaper* pinned, to warm. (*CL*, I 308)

Clearly he had found his Susquehanna not in far-off America but in a humbler stream much nearer home, his 'dear Gutter of Stowey'.

It was into this world of rural society and simple domestic joys that Wordsworth burst like a comet in the spring of 1797. In the last days of March, Wordsworth, returning to Racedown in north Dorset from a business trip to Bristol, paid a short visit to Coleridge at Nether Stowey. A little over two months later Coleridge reciprocated by spending three weeks with the Wordsworths at Racedown in June. His arrival at Racedown, when he left the high road, leaped over a gate and bounded across a pathless field to greet the waiting Wordsworths, was a scene never forgotten by William and Dorothy – and it serves, also, as a vivid emblem of the impetuous delight and unrestrained optimism with which Coleridge precipitated himself into the most important and productive friendship of his life. The two young poets talked poetry, discussed the tragedies that each was engaged in writing (Wordsworth *The Borderers* and Coleridge *Osorio*), and recited some of their compositions to each other. Dorothy listened, made suggestions, offered earnest praise. A stream of letters spread word of the excitement and admiration stimulated among the trio during these first weeks of their intimate association. Dorothy Wordsworth, who had not met Coleridge until his visit to Racedown, at first thought him very plain, 'that is, for about three minutes', after which she was utterly captivated by him: 'He is a wonderful man. His conversation teems with soul, mind, and spirit' (*LW: EY*, p. 188). Coleridge, for his part, was equally enthusiastic: Wordsworth, he announced, was 'a great man' beside whom 'I feel myself a *little man* . . . & yet do not think myself the less man, than I formerly thought myself' (*CL*, I 325); and Wordsworth's 'exquisite Sister' struck him as a paradigm of intellectual (if not physical) beauty, whose 'taste', he declared, was 'a perfect electrometer − it bends, protrudes, and draws in, at subtlest beauties & most recondite faults' (*CL*, I 331).

When Coleridge left Racedown toward the end of June, he took with him a resolve to establish his new friends in the vicinity of Stowey. He was not long in accomplishing his purpose. By a combination of cajoling enquiries, local influence and simple good luck, he managed in less than a month's time to secure for the Wordsworths a year's lease on Alfoxden House (Plate 6), and by mid July he had settled his friends in their new home. It was an ideal setting: close to Stowey, surrounded by natural beauty, the house and grounds large and private. To Robert Southey (with whom he had renewed his friendship) Coleridge sent an enthusiastic report of Alfoxden:

a gentleman's seat, with a park & woods, elegantly & completely *furnished* − with 9 *lodging rooms*, three parlours & a Hall − in a most beautiful & romantic situation by the sea side − 4 miles from Stowey − this we have got for Wordsworth at the rent of 23£ *a year, taxes included*!! − The park and woods are *his* for all purposes *he* wants them − i.e. he may walk, ride, & keep a horse in them − & the very large gardens are altogether & entirely his. (*CL*, I 334)

From the day the Wordsworths took possession, Alfoxden House became Coleridge's second home — the scene of animated discussions of literature and literary theory, the place where visiting friends such as Charles Lamb and the radical John Thelwall were entertained with lavish country hospitality, and the point of departure for countless walking-trips across the Quantock Hills and along the Bristol Channel where schemes for poems such as 'The Ancient Mariner' were born.

Under the fostering influence of 'the god Wordsworth', Coleridge's insecure Muse was encouraged to sing with a fluency and power she had never known before. From the summer of 1797 to the spring of 1798 Coleridge experienced the most sustained and successful burst of poetic creativity that he was ever to enjoy. Beginning with 'This Lime-Tree Bower' in July, he composed during this period of just under a year the majority of those poems on which his poetic reputation largely depends: 'The Ancient Mariner', 'Frost at Midnight', 'The Nightingale', part I of 'Christabel', and probably 'Kubla Khan' as well.[9] In addition, he finished his tragedy *Osorio* (although it was rejected by Drury Lane) and saw through the press the second edition of his *Poems* (October 1797). And in the spring of 1798 long and animated discussions with Wordsworth about the role of the natural and the supernatural in poetry led to the plan of *Lyrical Ballads*, which was subsequently published by Joseph Cottle in September 1798.

It would be a serious error, however, to suppose that 1797–8 was a period of uninterrupted bliss and lotus-like indulgence in Apollo's golden realms. While poetry consumed much of Coleridge's time and interest, the urgent importunities of the everyday world claimed a good deal of his attention as well. The foremost consideration was, as always, that of bread and cheese. Coleridge's writing brought in little money and, however much he dreamed of self-sufficiency through his garden and few domesticated fowl, he was neither dedicated nor competent enough to supply his family's needs by working the land. Clearly he needed to be gainfully employed in some secure position. In January 1798 such an opportunity presented itself: the Unitarian ministry at Shrewsbury, with an annual salary of £150 and a manse included, had fallen vacant and Coleridge was invited to preach a sermon 'preparatory to an offer'. The young William Hazlitt, whose father was the Unitarian minister in the nearby village of Wem, was present 'to hear this celebrated person preach' and has left a vivid account of the powerful effect of Coleridge's person and sermon on the Shrewsbury congregation.[10] The post was his if he chose to accept it. Within a few days of his sermon, however, Coleridge received a letter from Josiah Wedgwood offering him 'an annuity for life of £150 . . . no condition whatsoever being annexed to it' (*CL*, I 374). The purpose of this generous gift was to permit Coleridge to devote himself to literature, free of financial anxiety and unshackled by the time-consuming demands of any regular profession. It was an irresistible offer, and he accepted it quickly and gratefully, to the great disappointment of the Shrewsbury congregation.

In the early spring of 1798 it became clear that the Wordsworths, whose strange and solitary behaviour bred deep suspicion among their conservative country neighbours, would not be able to renew their lease on Alfoxden House.[11] Coleridge, at about this same time, had determined to travel to Germany in order to learn German and to experience at first hand the revolution in philosophical and scientific thinking that was taking place in the German universities. When no suitable accommodation could be found in the vicinity of Stowey for the Wordsworths, it was decided that they would accompany Coleridge into Germany. Mrs Coleridge, whose domestic burdens had increased with the birth in May 1798 of a second son, was to remain in Stowey under the protecting eye of Tom Poole. On 16 September Coleridge, the Wordsworths and John Chester[12] set sail from Yarmouth for Hamburg on a North Sea crossing recounted by Coleridge in a spirited series of letters later published as 'Satyrane's Letters' at the end of the *Biographia Literaria*. Germany was a happy and stimulating experience for Coleridge. Soon separating from the Wordsworths (who spent the long lonely winter in Goslar pining for England), Coleridge and the faithful Chester travelled to Ratzeburg to practise their German and then, in February 1799, on to Göttingen, where Coleridge enrolled at the university and threw himself into the exciting intellectual life of contemporary German thought. He attended J. F. Blumenbach's lectures on physiology and natural history, became acquainted with J. G. Eichhorn, who was among the foremost of German Biblical scholars, studied Gothic and Old High German under the supervision of T. C. Tychsen, an eminent linguist, devoted himself to acquiring a thorough grounding in the history of German literature, and assiduously collected materials for the critical biography of Lessing that he proposed to write as the first-fruits of his German labours. 'For these last 4 months,' he wrote to Josiah Wedgwood in May 1799, 'I have worked harder than, I trust in God Almighty, I shall ever have occasion to work again' (*CL*, I 519).

At the end of July 1799 Coleridge returned to Stowey after an absence of eleven months. Much had changed in the interval. The Wordsworths, no longer nearby, had settled in the north of England. Coleridge's second son, Berkeley, had died of complications from an inoculation for smallpox while his father was in Germany. The draughty Lime Street cottage, after a year abroad, was intolerably cramped; and routine domestic life and the mundane conversation of his wife, after the soaring intellectual flight of the German academy, was a burden and terrible anticlimax. Unable to adjust to his return to quotidian existence, Coleridge spent much of the next twelve months away from home. In September he was with Southey on a walking-tour through Devon; in October he was in Bristol, where he made the acquaintance of Humphry Davy, who was experimenting with nitrous oxide at Dr Beddoes' Pneumatic Institute; and for most of November he was in the North with Wordsworth, touring the Lake District and enjoying the conviviality of life in the family of Thomas Hutchinson, who lived, with his brother and three sisters, on a farm at Sockburn, near Durham. The Hutchinsons were distant relations and childhood friends of the Wordsworths and, when they had returned from Germany in May, William and Dorothy had been taken in by them while they looked for a suitable home and considered their future plans. Wordsworth was eventually to marry Tom Hutchinson's eldest sister, Mary; and Coleridge, who first met and fell in love with Sara, the middle of the three Hutchinson sisters, during the autumn of 1799 (*CN*, I no. 1575), was destined to be tortured by his hopeless passion for her for the next ten years.[13]

In the last week of November Coleridge left the North bound, not for Stowey, but for London. Daniel Stuart, the proprietor of the *Morning Post*, had offered him a salaried post as leader-writer for the newspaper. Taking up lodgings in Buckingham Street, the Strand, where his wife and three-year-old son soon joined him, Coleridge divided his time over the following four and a half months between political journalism and an ambitious translation of Schiller's dramatic trilogy, *Wallenstein*. But he was not cut out to sit for long with his wings furled: regular employment became tedious and, in any case, all of his friends and he himself expected more of his talents than that they should be squandered on such ephemera as hack journalism and translations from the German. He needed to make a new beginning, to devote himself to more noble literary and philosophic pursuits, to leave London. But where should he settle? In April he visited the Wordsworths, who had found a cottage at Grasmere in the Lake District. In May and June he was in the West Country, visiting friends in Bristol and Tom Poole at Nether Stowey. But the lure of the North, and Wordsworth, was overpowering. On 24 July 1800 the Coleridges took up their abode at Greta Hall, Keswick, a newly completed house overlooking Derwentwater and the mountains of Borrow-dale (Plates 12 and 13) — and only twelve miles distant from Wordsworth's cottage at Grasmere. 'Our house', he told Poole, 'is a delightful residence, something less than half a mile from the Lake of Keswick, & something more than a furlong from the town. It commands both that Lake, & the Lake Bassenthwaite — Skid-daw is behind us — to the left, the right, & in front, Mountains of all shapes & sizes — the waterfall of Lodore is distinctly visible' (*CL*, i 618). It was indeed a beautiful and romantic prospect, with the promise of hope and inspiration and renewed creativity. But it was not to be.

The move to Keswick marks the beginning of the bleakest and most terrible period of Coleridge's life — a period that was to last for fifteen long and harrowing years. It began happily enough with the continuation of 'Christabel' and the birth in mid September of a son, whom Coleridge somewhat playfully named Derwent after the local river and lake. But the mood soon changed. With the cold winds of winter blowing down from Skiddaw came physical illness, at first in the form of eye trouble and excruciating boils, which kept him from work and made mere existence a trial almost beyond endurance. As his health declined over the next three years, he took increasingly large doses of laudanum; but, com-pletely unaware of opium's addictive properties (about which contemporary medical science knew virtually nothing), he un-wittingly made his cure a major cause of his suffering. Laudanum did not bring relief but produced hallucinations and frightful nightmares from which he was awakened by his own screams[14] — and the evils of the drug were intensified, not alleviated, by attempts to reduce his dosage. He was bound upon a wheel of fire and, baffled, knew not where to turn or what to do. Nor was opium the only problem. Sara Coleridge, whose family and friends

were all in the South, was not happy at Keswick; and marital
tensions, a serious factor since Coleridge's return from Germany,
grew more pronounced and moved inexorably toward open hostility and a separation. Blame may be assessed on both sides. Mrs
Coleridge, ill at ease with the Wordsworths and their circle,
complained with justice that her husband spent more time at
Grasmere than at Greta Hall and that he neglected his domestic
responsibilities in order to cultivate his friendships. Coleridge, for
his part, finding neither physical comfort nor intellectual companionship at home, turned more and more to the sympathetic
and discerning audience at Dove Cottage to provide him with the
understanding and stimulation and enthusiastic acceptance that
he so desperately required. And then, of course, there was Sara
Hutchinson. Coleridge's love for her, deep and dependent, fuelled
a terrible guilt that he could neither control nor assuage. And
there was another neurotic guilt, even more profound and debilitating, resulting from his inability to progress with anything that
he regarded as really important. He could complete nothing he
started — 'Christabel' was still a fragment, for example, and his
'Life of Lessing' no more than a reiterated promise — and he
became increasingly convinced that his Muse (if not indeed a
chimera) had been suffocated and forever silenced by his abstruse
philosophical studies. Endowed with great gifts and abilities, he
had produced nothing commensurate with his own or his friends'
expectations of him. At the age of twenty-nine his life had fallen
into the sere and yellow leaf, and he began to think of himself as a
mental voyager shipwrecked in infinity: 'Mind, shipwrecked by
storms of doubt, now mastless, rudderless, shattered, — pulling in
the dead swell of a dark & windless Sea' (*CN*, I no. 932). On the
night of 4 April 1802, as the mountain winds rose and howled
outside his study window, Coleridge poured out his anguish and
fears about his domestic troubles, his sense of atrophied accomplishment, and his struggles with sickness and opiates and despair,
in a long and poignant verse-letter to Sara Hutchinson — a verse-
letter which evolved, through a number of redactions, into 'Dejection: An Ode'.[15]
The paralysis of hope and effort that spread through him at
Keswick led eventually to a determinate act. On 9 April 1804 he
sailed from Portsmouth aboard the merchantman *Speedwell*
bound for Malta, where he hoped to rediscover his health and
redirect into productive channels the dammed-up currents of his

intellectual life. It was a voyage in vain.[16] After more than two years abroad in Malta and Italy, he returned to England as ill and as unhappy as he had left; still he had produced nothing worthy of his potential, still he was wrapped in the endless coils of the serpent Opium, still he was hopelessly in love with Sara Hutchinson. Lingering in London for two months while he worked up his resolve, he finally set out for the North in October 1806. By the end of the year he had separated from his wife and was living with the Wordsworths at Coleorton in Leicestershire in a farmhouse lent to them by Sir George Beaumont. Here, in January 1807, Wordsworth recited *The Prelude* to him — a poem whose sweeping grandeur and accomplishment drove painfully home his own sense of frustration and failure.[17] In April, when the Wordsworths (and Sara Hutchinson) left Coleorton for London, Coleridge trailed along. But he was a man without a home, adrift on the wide wide sea, and he lodged aimlessly with various friends in Bristol and London for several months, until at length he took up a six-month stand in rooms at the *Courier* office in the Strand (January–June 1808), where he attempted to earn a living by returning to journalism and by delivering a series of lectures on poetry and the principles of taste at the Royal Institution. By June, however, he was on the wing again — first to the Clarksons at Bury St Edmunds, then to Bristol, Leeds and Keswick, and finally coming to roost at Allan Bank (the Wordsworths' new house at Grasmere), where he sheltered for the best part of a year and a half (December 1808– May 1810). He was now on at least cordial terms with his wife, who visited him at Allan Bank, and his return to the Lakes reinvigorated him to the point that he was able, almost single-handedly, to compose and prepare for the press twenty-seven numbers of a new periodical venture which he entitled *The Friend: A Literary, Moral, and Political Weekly Paper*. Given his by now abject slavery to opium, his industry and dedication to this demanding enterprise over a period of eleven solid months is little short of miraculous.

In October 1810, after an extended visit to Greta Hall, Coleridge set off with Basil Montagu for London, intending to seek medical help for his opium habit. In a moment of rash anger Montagu reported that Wordsworth had declared Coleridge's case to be hopeless, had said he was a '*rotten drunkard*' who was 'rotting out his entrails by intemperance', and had asserted that 'for years past [Coleridge] had been an ABSOLUTE NUISANCE in the Family' (*CL*, III 296). In all probability some exaggeration is involved, either on Montagu's or on Coleridge's part. But the words struck deep. For eighteen months there was stony silence between the two principals. Living wretchedly in London with 'the never-closing, festering Wound of Wordsworth & his Family' forever before him, Coleridge resumed his on-and-off journalistic career with Daniel Stuart's *Courier* and delivered, when his health permitted, several series of lectures on literature and on Shakespeare in particular. At length, through the mediation of Lamb and Henry Crabb Robinson, a superficial reconciliation with Wordsworth was effected in May 1812, but the fire had gone out of their friendship: 'A Reconciliation has taken place – ', Coleridge told Tom Poole almost a year later, 'but the *Feeling*, which I had previous to that moment, when the . . . Calumny burst like a Thunder-storm from a blue Sky on my Soul – after 15 years of such religious, almost superstitious, Idolatry & Self-sacrifice – O no! no! that I fear, never can return' (*CL*, III 437).

The story of the years 1812–16 is largely that of a struggle with opium. Placing himself under the care of a succession of physicians, Coleridge tried to conquer his habit, but without success. Through sheer force of will he managed to complete some work: lectures on Shakespeare in London and Bristol, three essays 'On the Principles of Genial Criticism Concerning the Fine Arts' published in *Felix Farley's Bristol Journal* (August–September 1814), and most significantly the composition of *Biographia Literaria* from June to September 1815.[18] On 15 April 1816, after a nearly fatal collapse, Coleridge presented himself at the front door of Moreton House on Highgate Hill, the home of James Gillman and his wife Anne. It had been determined that Coleridge's case was not hopeless but that, if he were to survive, he would require retirement and strict medical supervision. It was not enough to consult physicians; he needed to be under a trained and watchful eye day and night. James Gillman, whose practice was in Highgate, agreed to take him in as a patient and house-mate – for a month. In fact he was destined to spend the remaining eighteen years of his life in the fair haven of the Gillman household. At Moreton House there was, of course, no miraculous cure; but the Gillmans provided Coleridge with a sympathy, attentive care and profound admiration that restored his self-esteem and his faith in his own potential. Moreover, although Coleridge contrived within a week or two of his arrival to have laudanum smuggled in to him, Gillman managed to regulate his habit sufficiently to enable him to produce a substantial body of work in the following years. Shortly after his arrival at Highgate 'Christabel' and 'Kubla Khan' were published, at the instigation of Lord Byron, by the London house of John Murray, Byron's own publisher. Other important works followed in rapid succession: in December 1816 and April 1817 the first two of a projected series of three 'Lay Sermons', in July 1817 (after frustrating delay) the *Biographia Literaria* and a collective edition of Coleridge's poems entitled *Sibylline Leaves*, and in November 1817 his play *Zapolya*. A long and thoughtful 'Treatise on Method', commissioned originally for the *Encyclopaedia Metropolitana*, led to a revised and expanded three-volume edition of *The Friend* in November 1818; and from December 1818 to March 1819 Coleridge delivered two series of lectures, one on the history of philosophy and another on literature. Never before had he accomplished so much or worked with such sustained energy over so long a period.

By November 1823, when the Gillmans and their permanent house-guest moved into No. 3, The Grove (Plate 17), Coleridge had become both a national figure and a national *character* − 'The Sage of Highgate', as Thomas Carlyle described him with a mixture of malice and sincere respect, ensconced on the brow of Highgate Hill 'as a kind of *Magus*, girt in mystery and enigma; his Dodona oak-grove (Mr Gillman's house at Highgate) whispering strange things, uncertain whether oracles or jargon'.[19] For his 'Bed- and Book-room' (Plate 18) at The Grove, Coleridge chose an attic room with a commanding view 'over Southampton Farm, Kenn Wood, & Hampstead not surpassed within a hundred miles of London' (*CL*, v 335); and here, protected and encouraged by the faithful Gillmans, he wrote *Aids to Reflection* (1825) and *On the Constitution of the Church and State* (1829). He also made plans and notes for a theological *opus maximum* which, although never completed, was the great hope of his declining years and consumed most of his intellectual energies during the last ten years of his life. In the Gillmans' parlour two floors below his attic study or in the garden behind The Grove, he entertained his visitors and admirers, some of whom, such as Emerson, who paid a visit in August 1833, had travelled considerable distances to meet him. When he was well enough, he accepted dinner invitations in London. But most of the time he spent close to home, talking to those who came to him, immersed in his own theological and philosophic thoughts, or in recollections of the past, or in prayer. The end for this high-aspiring

and much-suffering man came peacefully in the early morning of
25 June 1834. The funeral took place on 2 August. The deepest
mourner was Charles Lamb, who could not bring himself to
attend: 'His great and dear spirit haunts me. . . . Never saw I his
likeness, nor probably the world can see again. I seem to love the
house he died in more passionately than when he lived. . . . What
was his mansion is consecrated to me a chapel.'[20]

2 The Conversation Poems

'The Nightingale', which appeared in *Lyrical Ballads* (1798) with the subtitle 'a Conversational Poem', is the only one of his poems to which Coleridge himself ever applied this particular epithet. However, following a suggestion made in 1925 by G. M. Harper,[1] twentieth-century readers have generally grouped together six poems composed between 1795 and 1798 as Coleridge's Conversation Poems: 'The Eolian Harp', 'Reflections on Having Left a Place of Retirement', 'This Lime-Tree Bower my Prison', 'Frost at Midnight', 'Fears in Solitude' and 'The Nightingale'. Although arguments have sometimes been made to extend the canon to include other poems – notably, 'Lines Written at Shurton Bars' (1795), 'Dejection: An Ode' (1802), and 'To William Wordsworth' (1807)[2] – majority opinion has resisted any such extension.

The six Conversation Poems are linked by a number of striking stylistic and structural similarities.[3] All, for example, speak in a muted voice that is benevolent, confiding, familiar, and often colloquial – a voice utterly distinct from the other voices, whether stridently polemical or hauntingly supernatural, that are heard in the verse of Coleridge's Somerset years. The Conversation Poems also share a common metrical form: a fluent and relaxed blank-verse measure (arranged in apparently loose verse-paragraphs) that recalls, at least superficially, William Cowper's technique in *The Task* (1784) or the natural, conversational rhythms of some of the Elizabethan dramatists, particularly Philip Massinger.

Yet perhaps the most important shared characteristic of the Conversation Poems is their tripartite rondo structure. Each begins by establishing the physical setting, a particular place which is described in vivid, concrete detail; in the second section of each poem, the immediate setting and situation give way to a meditation or *rêverie* inspired by the scene; and finally, in the closing movement, the poet returns with a deepened insight to the

physical location from which he had begun.[4] Although some of the
poems are structurally quite complex, this basic rondo pattern lies
at the heart of each and represents an important tenet of Coleridge's poetic credo: 'The common end of all *narrative*,' he wrote in
1815, 'nay, of *all*, Poems is to convert a *series* into a *Whole*: to
make those events, which in real or imagined History move on in a
strait Line, assume to our Understandings a *circular* motion — the
snake with it's Tail in it's Mouth' (*CL*, IV 545).[5]

In form, the Conversation Poems may best be described as
dramatic monologues — a generic term which stresses the dynamic interaction that exists in these poems between the speaker
and the person, whether present or imagined as present, to whom
the speaker is addressing himself. They must be sharply distinguished, however, from the dramatic monologues of such later
writers as Robert Browning and T. S. Eliot, which explore the
ironic self-revelation of character and in which the narrative 'I' is
distinct from the poet himself. Coleridge's poems are not ironic,
and they are intensely subjective. In terms of narrative point-of-
view and dramatic self-exploration perhaps the closest things to
them in English are certain of Donne's dramatic lyrics (e.g. 'A
Valediction: forbidding Mourning') or some of the lyric meditations — overheard colloquies between the self and God — of
later Metaphysicals such as Herbert and Vaughan.

The centre of each Conversation Poem is dominated, as Humphry House has said, by 'the Ego, the "I" — the seeing, remember-
ing, projecting mind' of Coleridge himself.[6] But this 'egotism' is
not self-regarding indulgence, not an end in itself. Rather, it treats
the poet's self as the necessary point of departure for exploration of
the universe and as the necessary terminus to which, the exploration completed, to return. Such egotism proves, indeed, to be
self-revelatory: the self that eventually comes home to itself is
invariably a self transformed and deepened by its experience.

Solipsism is avoided in these poems partly by the mind's encounter with other minds, and partly by its encounter with the
objective reality of the external world. On the one hand, the
presence of other minds — the poet's wife, Charles Lamb, the
Wordsworths, the infant Hartley — is therapeutic or at least
corrective in that it provides a second consciousness that prevents
the poet from slipping into total self-absorption. Occasionally the
felt presence of these bystanders is intrusive (as in 'The Eolian
Harp'), but for the most part it is salutary and can serve, as in

'This Lime-Tree Bower' or 'Frost at Midnight', as the powerful catalyst of visionary insight. On the other hand, solipsistic tendencies are countered by the dynamic interaction established between the poet's intelligence (his thoughts, feelings and memories) and the objects of the external world that trigger and sustain his meditation. The products of this imaginative blending of thoughts and things, this interpenetration of mind and nature, are what Coleridge later called *symbols*. On a hazy April night on Malta in 1805, he was palpably struck by the manner in which the internal and the external were dovetailing creatively in his mind:

> In looking at objects of Nature while I am thinking, as at yonder moon dim-glimmering thro' the dewy window-pane, I seem rather to be seeking, as it were *asking*, a symbolical language for something within me that already and forever exists, than observing any thing new. Even when that latter is the case, yet still I have always an obscure feeling as if that new phænomenon were the dim Awaking of a forgotten or hidden Truth of my inner Nature   (*CN*, II no. 2546)

The Conversation Poems are poetic counterparts of this statement, developing the interchange dramatically and directly in symbols. 'Nature' in these poems has a double aspect: it is both realistic and symbolic, its function both sensuously descriptive and subtly analogical. Landscape, that is to say, is also inscape − for the natural settings detailed so vividly and minutely serve to describe the geography of the poet's soul as well as the external topography of his situation.

Coleridge's Conversation Poems do not, of course, spring forth fully formed and without antecedents, like the mythical spawn of Oeucalion and Pyrrha raised from stones thrown blindly behind them. The form evolved slowly and its development was assisted by a variety of influences, both personal[7] and literary. Among the literary influences, the most significant is the debt to the popular eighteenth-century tradition of loco-descriptive poetry, a subgenre succinctly defined by Dr Johnson as 'a species of composition that may be denominated *local poetry*, of which the fundamental subject is some particular landscape, to be poetically described, with the addition of such embellishments as may be supplied by historical retrospection, or incidental meditation'.[8] The tradition of Augustan local poetry, originating from Denham's 'Cooper's

Hill' (1642), was lyricised in the sonnets (1789) of William Lisle Bowles and began, as M. H. Abrams has shown conclusively,[9] to develop in a rudimentary but unambiguous fashion certain characteristic features of a Coleridgean Conversation Poem. The evidence for direct influence is clear and beyond doubt: like such later works as Wordsworth's 'Tintern Abbey' and Keats's odes, Coleridge's Conversation Poems 'evolved from the descriptive—meditative structure of the eighteenth-century local poem, primarily through the intermediate stage of Bowles's sequence of sonnets'.[10]

Despite such influences and other debts, however, the Conversation Poems remain essentially original compositions. From Cowper and others Coleridge learned the technique of writing conversational blank verse. From Augustan local poetry and from Bowles he learned to unite description and meditation in poems rooted firmly in a localised natural setting. From the traditions of English and Continental Neoplatonism he learned to read Nature's mystic book both reverently and analogically, discerning in the external world both the hand of the Creator and subtle correspondences to aspects of his own inner being. Yet Coleridge's poems are unique in their achievement of a conversational seriousness and in their particular synthesis of man and nature, a fusion of self and non-self that lies at the heart of Coleridge's visionary realism — and effected, through him, much of the tone and substance of the entire Romantic Movement. The Conversation Poems provide clear instances of the fruitful conjunction of tradition and the individual talent, in which an established genre of loco-descriptive verse is transformed and blended with other traditions in order to adapt it to the needs of a new age. They are, in their quiet and modest way, the prophetic heralds of the Romantic revolution.

'THE EOLIAN HARP'

'The Eolian Harp' has attracted a good deal of scholarly attention. Much of this interest stems from the fact that the poem is a complex and perplexing document which was greatly revised over a period of twenty-three years. No one would claim that it is an unqualified success or that it shows no trace of the file.

The first draft is a mere seventeen lines in length and, since the manuscript is dated 'Clevedon, August 20th, 1795', it was apparently composed when Coleridge and his bride-to-be visited Clevedon to rent the cottage in which they were to spend their first months of marriage. This earliest version — called an 'Effusion', that is, a spontaneous outpouring of personal sentiment — is little more than a pastoral description of the cottage and its setting, although the poet does propose (with playfully erotic overtones) to set an Aeolian harp in the casement:

> In the half-closed window we will place the Harp,
> Which by the desultory Breeze caress'd,
> Like some coy maid half willing to be woo'd,
> Utters such sweet upbraidings as, perforce,
> Tempt to repeat the wrong!
>
> (*CPW*, ii 1021)

When the poem appeared for the first time in print in Coleridge's *Poems on Various Subjects* (1796), it was portentously entitled 'Effusion XXXV' and had grown to fifty-six lines, in which the original 1795 version had been incorporated, with variant readings, as the first sixteen and a half lines. No longer a simple descriptive idyll, this newly expanded version is clearly an artful construction. Taking the original lines as a point of departure, it develops the image of the harp's music in fanciful analogies and posits a second centre of focus in the poet's memory of past times when he has been receptive, like a kind of human harp, to unbidden thoughts that traversed his 'indolent and passive brain'. Such memories suggest the metaphysical speculation, expressed as a question, that all living things may be merely 'organic Harps' activated by 'one intellectual breeze' that is the soul of each and God of all. But from such pantheistic conjectures he is peremptorily recalled to orthodoxy by pious Sara, whose watchful eye darts 'mild Reproof' to check such dangerous 'Shapings of the unregen'rate Soul'.

The expanded 1796 text was reprinted in Coleridge's *Poems* of 1797. In the third edition (*Poems*, 1803), however, Coleridge made a number of significant changes. He omitted a total of seven lines (i.e. lines 5, 8, 13 and 21–5 in the 1796 text) and he added a new quatrain, in place of the deleted lines 21–5, so that after 'soft floating witchery of sound' the poem continued,

> Methinks, it should have been impossible
> Not to love all things in a World like this,
> Where e'en the Breezes of the simple Air
> Possess the power and Spirit of Melody![11]

Fourteen years later, when he prepared the poem for inclusion in *Sibylline Leaves* (1817), the first collective edition of his poetry, Coleridge again reworked his Clevedon 'Effusion'. In this revision he restored to the poem, now entitled for the first time 'The Eolian Harp', all of the lines deleted in 1803, and expanded the new quatrain added in 1803 (quoted above) from four to eight lines:

> O! the one Life, within us and abroad,
> Which meets all Motion and becomes its soul,
> A light in Sound, a sound-like power in Light,
> Rhythm in all Thought, and Joyance every where —
> Methinks, it should have been impossible
> Not to love all things in a world so fill'd,
> Where the breeze warbles and the mute still Air
> Is Music slumbering on its instrument![12]

In *Sibylline Leaves* (1817) these eight lines appeared, not in the text itself, but in the Errata; and when they were moved (with one small change[13]) from the Errata into the body of the poem itself in the 1828 edition of Coleridge's poems, we arrive at last at the *textus receptus* of 'The Eolian Harp'. (The 1828 text was reprinted without changes in the 1829 and 1834 editions of Coleridge's *Poems*.)

The complex evolution[14] of 'The Eolian Harp' between 1795 and 1828 has important implications for the interpretation and intended meaning of the poem. In the first place, it is really several quite separate poems which must be variously interpreted depending on which version one is reading. M. H. Abrams summarises the poem's changing meaning in this way:

> In its first short form [of 1795] 'The Eolian Harp' had been a love-poem which assimilated the relation of the wind and the strings of the harp to the dalliance, the 'wooings and retirings', of the human lovers. It had next [in *Poems* (1796)] been developed into a marriage poem, and also expanded into a metaphysical speculation about 'all of animated nature'. In its final

form [1817 – 1828] it is still a love-poem, but a cosmic love-poem, in which the love between the poet and his bride becomes the exponent of a universal relationship – the 'union of the individual with the Universe' which, Coleridge said, occurs 'through love'. It is still a marriage-poem, too, but one in which the human union becomes an exponent of the primal union in which 'all other marriages are celebrated inclusively'. For in the lines added in 1817 the poet breaks through sensation into vision. . . .[15]

In the second place, there is the problem of Coleridge's use of the Aeolian harp itself as a symbol. In 1795–6, when Coleridge was still a Necessitarian (*CL*, I 213) under the spell of the empirical philosophy of Locke and Hartley, the Aeolian harp was a convenient image for the human mind as a passively receptive instrument stirred only by external forces, responding (like the wind harp) only when acted upon by stimuli *ab extra*. After 1800, however, as Coleridge evolved the essentials of his 'dynamic philosophy' where the mind is active in perception, the Aeolian harp became progressively less adequate as a metaphor and was ultimately rejected altogether: 'The mind does not resemble an Aeolian Harp, nor even a barrel-organ turned by a stream of water, conceive as many tunes mechanized in it as you like, but rather as far as objects are concerned a violin or other instrument of few strings yet vast compass, played on by a musician of genius.'[16] In Coleridge's writings after 1800, as John Beer has said, the wind-harp image loses 'its dominating position as a primary symbol, and remains only as a useful symbol for certain permanent elements in human experience'.[17]

While the complexity of the poem's evolution and the changes in Coleridge's philosophy between 1795 and 1828 preclude the possibility of any easy interpretation, it is still possible, using the *textus receptus* of 1828, to make some general interpretative comments about 'The Eolian Harp'.

Like the Conversation Poems which follow, 'The Eolian Harp' takes us on a circular journey from the Clevedon cottage out into the cosmos and back to the cottage again. But this simple pattern, as Abrams has argued, is deceptive – for within the rondo framework lies the more complex structure of a double helix.[18] The first movement (lines 1–33), setting out from the Clevedon cottage, spirals upward to a visionary insight into the 'one Life within us and abroad'. The second movement (lines 34–64), which is much less successful, rises from remembered experience into speculation – only to sink back, bathetically, into the arms of orthodoxy.

In the opening twelve lines the situation and setting are vividly established in a rustic tableau:

> most soothing sweet it is
> To sit beside our Cot, our Cot o'ergrown
> With white-flower'd Jasmin. . . .
>   (2–4)

The scene is not merely languorously pastoral. It is clearly paradisiacal. The tranquil lovers by their cottage overgrown with luxuriant vegetation recalls the prelapsarian bower of Adam and Eve in *Paradise Lost*, IV 690–703 – an echo reinforced both by the references to jasmine and myrtle (plants mentioned by Milton) and by Coleridge's effort to allegorise these flowers as Edenic emblems of Innocence and Love (line 5). In lines 6–12, where the scene expands out from the cottage into the surrounding landscape, there is a subtle balancing of inertia and activity: the emblematic stasis of the evening star is coupled with almost imperceptible transformations in the 'slow saddening' clouds, and the scents of a bean-field are 'snatched' from a world at rest. The alternation of activity and passivity fosters a mood of hushed expectancy, brought brilliantly to a climax in lines 11–12 in the contrapuntal conjunction of expiring sibilants and assertive 's'-alliterations in the ocean's distant voice: 'The stilly murmur of the distant Sea / Tells us of silence.' Passively receptive to external sensation, the poet waits in an atmosphere charged with anticipation.

A quick systolic contraction in the middle of line 12, marked by a new verse paragraph, recalls him to his immediate situation as the breeze strikes the harp in the window beside him. Silence blossoms into sound, and the lute's harmonious tones, symbolic of their human love, prompt an analogising response from the poet. In a series of two similies – the first (lines 15–17) playfully erotic, the second (lines 20–5) developing the Edenic implications of the poem's opening lines – the poet is led to a sudden insight into the harmonious unity of all existence: 'O! the one Life within us and abroad. . . .'

There are two structural patterns at work in this passage (lines 12–33). First, there is a widening of vision, a diastolic expansion that takes the poet from his cottage into the cosmos, from his immediate physical situation into a metaphysical perception of unity in multeity. Second, there is a movement from simile to metaphor — a movement, that is, from fanciful approximation to full imaginative participation in the One Life within and around him. What is particularly remarkable is the way in which these two patterns are interwoven and the way in which the imagery becomes, paradoxically, more sensuous as it becomes more dematerialised. There is a playful distance in the coy dalliance of the initial simile of the maid 'half yielding to her lover' (line 15); in the second simile, however, the lute's delicious surges of sound lift us out of reality into a sensuous fairy-land of honey-dropping flowers and hovering birds of paradise; and finally, in the metaphoric conclusion (lines 26–33), there is a coadunation of experience and its elements in a rich imaginative vision, in which perception is presented synaesthetically: 'A light in sound, a sound-like power in light' (28). It is no longer the harp but the breeze itself that warbles (32) and even the 'mute still air' is potential harmony, is 'Music slumbering on her instrument' (33). From particular love (his relationship with Sara) the poet has ascended in lines 12–33 to a participation in universal 'joyance',[19] and the shift from simile to metaphor — or from fancy to imagination — marks the progression of Coleridge's growth into visionary insight.

At the beginning of the second helix in line 34 a swift systolic beat brings him back to Sara and present reality. And this time it is memory that serves as the catalyst of inspiration. He remembers times when, receptive to external sensation and trains of internal association, he had stretched himself on a sunny hillside. In this posture, where he was passive and resembled in his very stance the harp that is the central image of his poem, his 'indolent' brain was traversed by 'many idle flitting phantasies' (40) that moved him outward into tentative metaphysical speculation:

> And what if all of animated nature
> Be but organic Harps diversely fram'd,
> That tremble into thought, as o'er them sweeps
> Plastic and vast, one intellectual breeze,
> At once the Soul of each, and God of all?
>
> (44–8)

But the speculation, however hesitantly advanced, is short-lived. The lines which follow (49–64) constitute a palinode in which metaphysics is rejected in favour of orthodox fideism. Overwhelmed by a conviction of original sin (cf. *CL*, I 396) and daunted by his wife's reproving eye, he descends timorously and thankfully back to Sara and their pastoral cottage. These closing lines, which Coleridge doubtless intended to be climactic, are felt by most readers to be a decided blot upon the poem. They have been much discussed, and there are two major difficulties associated with them: first, the dramatic function of the poet's wife, and, second, the problem of what precisely is being rejected in these lines, and why.

Poor Sara has generally been roughly treated. Humphry House describes her as 'an extremely narrow and governessy orthodox Christian'; and George Watson insists on the 'blunt fact . . . that Sara is merely a nuisance in the poem, which ought to have closed on the penultimate paragraph'.[20] Although Sara's presence in the closing verse-paragraph is dramatically intrusive, she none the less represents (as recent commentators have argued[21]) an important facet of Coleridge's own mind, and her presence allows him to dramatise an internal confrontation between metaphysics and faith, from which the latter emerges victorious because Coleridge distrusted, perhaps even feared, his own speculative reason. 'The Eolian Harp' thus establishes, as Harold Bloom has said, 'a dialectic between two Coleridges, the imaginative and intellectually daring poet, and the timidly orthodox young husband, glad to submit to the mildly reproving eye of his "Meek daughter in the family of Christ!"'[22]

The second problem is to determine exactly what is being repudiated. Most readers would agree that the palinode applies to the hypothesis (tentatively enough advanced) of all animated nature being diversely framed harps (lines 44–8). But what is there that is dangerous in such vague Neoplatonic speculation? As John Beer says, 'the conception of a plastic spirit, "at once the Soul of each, and God of all" is not necessarily unattractive even to orthodox Christians, who might easily find ways of subsuming it to their own beliefs'.[23] The answer lies, it seems, partly in the pantheist drift of the analogy and partly in Coleridge's suspicion of mere cerebration. On the one hand, the radical identification of God, man and nature which might be inferred from these lines comes perilously close to pantheism, a doctrine from which Coleridge recoiled and which he branded as a sophisticated form of atheism: 'How is it', he wrote in March 1796, 'that Dr Priestley is not an atheist? − He asserts in three different Places, that God not only *does*, but *is*, every thing. − But if God *be* every Thing, every Thing is God −: which is all, the Atheists assert' (*CL*, ɪ 192). On the other hand, while faith and philosophy may coexist and co-operate, there is always the danger (especially in theories of mechanistic association) of intellectual activity being divorced from feeling and becoming an end in itself: 'Believe me, Southey!' he said in 1803, 'a metaphysical Solution, that does not instantly *tell* for something in the Heart, is grievously to be suspected as apocryphal' (*CL*, ɪɪ 961). The retreat into fideism is an evasion which, if poetically inopportune, is none the less theologically defensible; and Sara, in recalling Samuel from his 'idle flitting phantasies' to humility and a 'Faith that inly *feels*', plays the valuable role of Raphael to her husband's Adam by exhorting him to be lowly wise and not to solicit his thought with hidden matters.

'The Eolian Harp', then, is a qualified success. The first movement of the poem (lines 1−33) is a finely executed poetic statement ascending from natural description, to fanciful analogy, to imaginative participation. The second movement (lines 34−64), however, after dabbling with a potentially dangerous metaphor, sinks lamely and tamely back into orthodoxy. Moreover, as Humphry House has pointed out, 'the late grafting on of lines 26−33 [on the One Life], which follow admirably from the beginning, has immensely improved the poem up to that point; but it has completely thrown out its balance as a whole, and virtually made nonsense of the unaltered ending'.[24] The difficulty, essentially, is that the ending denies the possibility of an imaginative probing and metaphysical insight that has already occurred in the One Life passage; it shuts the gate after Pegasus has bolted.

'REFLECTIONS ON HAVING LEFT A PLACE OF RETIREMENT'

When this poem, which was (probably) composed late in 1795, was first published in the *Monthly Magazine* for October 1796, it was entitled 'Reflections on entering into active life. A Poem which affects not to be Poetry'. A year later it appeared in the second edition (1797) of Coleridge's poems with the title 'Reflections on Having Left a Place of Retirement' and the Horatian motto

Sermoni propriora[25] added. Keeping its 1797 title and motto, the poem was reprinted (with some minor changes) in all later editions of Coleridge's poetry.

Both the 1796 subtitle and the self-deprecating motto of 1797 constitute apologies for the poem — apologies for which there is some considerable justification. 'Reflections' is composed of four verse-paragraphs of unequal length and uneven execution. The first section (lines 1–26) describes the Clevedon cottage and introduces, in swaggering verse, a 'wealthy son of Commerce' from Bristol who declares the cottage and its environs to be a 'Blessèd Place'. In the second section (lines 26–42) the scene shifts abruptly and without adequate transition to a 'stony Mount' from whose height the poet can see the Bristol Channel and the distant coast of Wales. The third section (lines 43–62), which returns briefly to the pastoral cottage, quickly becomes political in subject-matter and highly rhetorical in style. The idyllic isolation of the Clevedon setting is renounced as an evasion of duty; and the poet, having indulged his guilt at dreaming away 'the entrusted hours / On rose-leaf beds' while his countrymen are toiling and bleeding in the war with France, resolves with self-conscious bravado to

> go, and join head, heart, and hand,
> Active and firm, to fight the bloodless fight
> Of Science, Freedom, and the Truth in Christ.
>
> (60–2)

The renunciation of retirement in favour of humanitarian activity leads in the short conclusion (lines 63–71) to proleptic nostalgia, in lines which are close enough to the Wordsworth of 'Tintern Abbey' to make the reader blink:

> Yet oft when after honourable toil
> Rests the tir'd mind, and waking loves to dream,
> My spirit shall revisit thee, dear Cot!

'Reflections' is spoiled not only by its obtrusive polemics and aggressively self-assertive tone[26] but also — and perhaps pre-eminently — by its structural weaknesses. Although the poem does illustrate the 'rondo' device by beginning and then returning to the Clevedon cottage, it is torn internally between the opposing claims of visionary and ethical idealism. The first two verse-paragraphs

extol the virtues of rustic retirement, and they rise in the second
paragraph to a visionary climax, a moment of *extasis*, in which
landscape and seascape are seen transformed:

> But the time, when first
> From that low Dell, steep up the stony Mount
> I climb'd with perilous toil and reach'd the top,
> Oh! what a goodly scene! *Here* the bleak mount,
> The bare bleak mountain speckled thin with sheep;
> Grey clouds, that shadowing spot the sunny fields;
> And river, now with bushy rocks o'er-brow'd,
> Now winding bright and full, with naked banks;
> And seats, and lawns, the Abbey and the wood,
> And cots, and hamlets, and faint city-spire;
> The Channel *there*, the Islands and white sails,
> Dim coasts, and cloud-like hills, and shoreless Ocean —
> It seem'd like Omnipresence! God, methought,
> Had built him there a Temple: the whole World
> Seem'd *imag'd* in its vast circumference:
> No *wish* profan'd my overwhelméd heart.
> Blest hour! It was a luxury, — to be!
>
> (26–42)

The passage is invested with an almost allegorical significance. It is
an early (and theistic) Romantic rendering of the mind's road to
God:[27] stumbling up the bleak and stony mountain of life, the poet
is rewarded with the visionary spectacle of earth counterfeiting
infinity.

Unfortunately, however, the imaginatively realised mountain
sequence (which is the one instance of fine writing in the poem) is
only tenuously connected to the opening verse-paragraph and is
disastrously severed from the paragraphs which follow it. In the
last two sections, having voluntarily cast aside his visionary
mantle, Coleridge enters the arena of public action; and in this
world, as Richard Haven points out, 'the visionary moment seems
unreal or unimportant': 'the remembered moment has no . . .
ethical content to carry over and enrich the public and the practical. The ethical order which he accepts derives from other
sources, from other kinds of thought, and he has as yet no single
language which can reconcile the two.'[28]

In the final analysis, then, the poem is broken on the unresolved opposition of what a former age would have called the *vita activa* and the *vita contemplativa*. Indeed, the poem's dilemma is mirrored in its two titles: 'Reflections on entering into active life' (1796) and 'Reflections on Having Left a Place of Retirement' (1797). It fails because visionary and ethical experience are seen as mutually exclusive and because the poet's heart and intellect are held in solution and loose mixture rather than being intimately combined and unified. Much of the poem is, in truth, *sermoni propriora* — 'proper for a sermon'.

'THIS LIME-TREE BOWER MY PRISON'

Early in July 1797, shortly after Coleridge had settled the Wordsworths at Alfoxden, Charles Lamb paid a long-postponed visit to Nether Stowey. Coleridge had eagerly looked forward to his arrival, anticipating the pleasure he would have in showing his friend the beauties of the Quantock countryside on extended walking-tours. He was, however, denied this pleasure by an unfortunate accident, laconically reported later that month in a letter to Southey: 'dear Sara accidentally emptied a skillet of boiling milk on my foot, which confined me during the whole time of C. Lamb's stay & still prevents me from all *walks* longer than a furlong'. The letter continues: 'While Wordsworth, his Sister, & C. Lamb were out one evening; / sitting in the arbour of T. Poole's garden, which communicates with mine, I wrote these lines, with which I am pleased' (*CL*, I 334), and there follows the earliest version of 'This Lime-Tree Bower',[29] beginning,

> Well — they are gone: and here must I remain,
> Lam'd by the scathe of fire, lonely & faint,
> This lime-tree bower my prison.

This manuscript draft is fifty-five lines in length and differs from the final text (seventy-six lines long) chiefly in that the latter expands the description of the 'roaring dell' and adds the passage, immediately following, in which his friends 'emerge / Beneath the wide wide Heaven'. These major changes are confined to the opening twenty-eight lines of the *textus receptus*.[30] The poem, fittingly addressed to Charles Lamb, was first published in Southey's *Annual Anthology* for 1800; apart from minor variants, the 1800 text is that of the final version. In 1810 the poem was reprinted in Mylius's *Poetical Classbook*; and from 1817, when it was published in *Sibylline Leaves*, it has appeared in all editions of Coleridge's poetry.

'This Lime-Tree Bower' is perhaps the most genial and engaging poem Coleridge ever wrote. It is, as Michael Schmidt says, 'one of our great poems, a personal poem of shared joy, momentary optimism, sincere generosity of impulse'.[31] While these features of openness and selfless friendship need to be stressed, one must see as well that beneath the poem's relaxed exterior there lies a tightly-knit structure which is the vehicle of a deeply felt imaginative vision.

The poem is based on the rondo pattern characteristic of the Conversation Poems: from the lime-tree bower to which he has been confined the poet ranges out in imagination and then returns to the bower again. But here for the first time Coleridge integrates this emotional and experiential curve into a unified poetic structure. In 'The Eolian Harp' speculative thought had been repudiated in the palinode at the end of the poem, and in 'Reflections' visionary experience had been rejected in favour of ethical activity; in 'This Lime-Tree Bower', however, vision and imagination are wholly assimilated and form the core both of stucture and of meaning. The poem is divided into three verse-paragraphs, which trace the poet's growth into vision: in the first section (lines 1–20) Coleridge finds himself alone and isolated, imprisoned in Poole's arbour and unable, except in imagination, to share the sights and sounds that his friends (Lamb and the two Wordsworths) are enjoying on their walk; in the second paragraph (lines 20–43), as he imagines the trio emerging from a dark and wooded dell into bright fields and meadows, he calls spontaneously on Nature to reveal her beauties fully to Lamb, who, living in London, has been cut off from such experience; and then in the last section (lines 43–76) he returns to the lime-tree bower to find it transformed and to discover that it is sometimes well 'to be bereft of promis'd good, / That we may lift the soul, and contemplate / With lively joy the joys we cannot share' (66–8). The movement of the poem, then, is from egotism to cathartic altruism and from confinement to liberation. It is both an epiphany and a record of spiritual growth. As Donald Davie has pointed out,

> when the poet thought all had been said, it turned out that nothing had been said; in calling to mind the pleasures he cannot share, his imagination permits him to share them. This refers back to the paradox which gives the poem its title. How can a bower of lime-trees be a prison? And, even as he begins to show how this can be, he proves that it cannot be, since the imagination cannot be imprisoned; and the poet goes on to acknowledge, at the end of the poem, that the prison is no prison, and the loss no loss.[32]

The nature of the poem's spiritual and imaginative parabola will be clearer if we look at each of its three sections in more detail.

The poem begins on a note of querulous egotism. The first five lines are dominated by the presence of the narrative 'I' — fixed, incarcerated, peevish, self-pitying, and entirely self-centred. At the end of line 5 the focus shifts to Lamb and the Wordsworths, but their fraternity and gladness establish a dissonant counter-point to the poet's loneliness and sense of loss — a contrast set up, with hollow self-consolation, in the opening line: 'Well, *they* are gone, and here must *I* remain'. The obtrusive narrative voice is skilfully faded in lines 6—9 (where it is oblique rather than direct and aggressive), but it is never lost sight of: 'whom I never more may meet' (6), 'of which I told' (9). And the reader is thus subtly prepared for the descent into the dank and sunless dell with its solitary 'branchless ash' as a pictorial symbol of Coleridge's own mood and predicament. Like the bower of lime-trees, the dell is a confining enclosure — an image of the enclosed world of the self.

> The roaring dell, o'erwooded, narrow, deep,
> And only speckled by the mid-day sun;
> Where its slim trunk the ash from rock to rock
> Flings arching like a bridge; — that branchless ash,
> Unsunn'd and damp, whose few poor yellow leaves
> Ne'er tremble in the gale. . . .
>
> 　　　　　　　　　　　(10—15)

The poet has projected his own sense of lost happiness into the scene: landscape is also inscape. But the dell is not static and lifeless: the ash 'flings' itself from rock to rock and the motion of the waterfall fans a long file of Adder's Tongue that nods and drips in sympathetic response. Gradually the poet, too, under the sway of imagination begins to respond to a correspondent breeze within and to participate in the vision; he is no longer separated from his friends, but seems to be actually present, describing, pointing, directing their attention to specific phenomena: 'the dark green file of long lank weeds, / That all at once (a most fantastic sight!) / Still nod and drip . . .'. This, in Coleridge's own words, 'is *creation* rather than *painting*'.[33] The image of the dell, which begins as an analogue of isolation and confinement, becomes the vehicle of liberation and imaginative freedom.

Nevertheless, the dell is an ambivalent symbol. Despite its life and motion, it remains claustrophobic − a dark enclosure cut off from the larger world. Its movement is self-contained and self-generated, an image still of egotism; and the poet's eye is led down the *scala naturae* from the branchless ash straining toward the light, to the file of long lank weeds in the dark interior, to the completely inanimate 'blue clay-stone' given the appearance of life by the water dripping from its edge. And this last image, which draws attention to itself by its three heavy stresses, admirably summarises the ambiguous nature of the description as a whole: while the stone is itself lifeless and inert, it is still '*blue* clay-stone' − blue being the traditional colour both of hope and spiritual insight.[34]

In the second section of the poem (lines 20−43) the imaginative energy that has been building through the opening lines is released, and the poet is catapulted out of the restricting enclosure of the dell and shakes himself completely free of the selfish egotism implied (though partly transcended) in the earlier lines:

> Now, my friends emerge
> Beneath the wide wide Heaven − and view again
> The many-steepled tract magnificent
> Of hilly fields and meadows, and the sea,
> With some fair bark, perhaps, whose sails light up
> The slip of smooth clear blue betwixt two Isles
> Of purple shadow! Yes! they wander on
> In gladness all. . . .

(20−7)

Here the imagination is set free and the poet shares vicariously the joy of his friends. The centripetal activity of the first movement, where Nature is made a projection of the poet's self-centred isolation, gives way in the second movement to a centrifugal activity in which Ego is left behind and the poet selflessly participates in the experience of others. The distance between *they* and *I* (gradually faded in the first movement) is entirely obliterated here; the threatening solipsism of the dell yields place to generosity of impulse: 'Yes! they wander on / In gladness all' – a joy that the poet, in empathetic love, experiences too. For, as R. A. Durr points out, 'from his soul has issued forth a light and glory enveloping and informing the scene, and it is all active now: the sails *emit* light, the heath-flowers *shine*, the clouds *burn*, the groves *live* in the yellow light, the ocean *kindles*. The poet's soul is aglow in the fervor of life and love, and so, then, does he know Nature aglow.'[35] Instrumental in this centrifugal identification is Coleridge's relationship with Lamb, whose experience is an analogue of his own. As Lamb, long in 'the great City pent', has had to win his way through evil and strange calamity[36] with patient soul, so too Coleridge, imprisoned in self-pity, has had to work his way through a descent to light – from the lime-tree bower, through the dark and narrow dell, to the open landscape stretching beneath the wide wide heaven. And it is his warm feeling for Lamb, his vicarious participation in his friend's joy, that is the motivating factor in this spiritual growth.

It should be noticed, as well, that this second movement of the poem is expressed in specifically religious language. Lamb and the Wordsworths are imagined to emerge, not merely beneath the sky, but beneath the wide *heaven*; and the prospect that greets them (in a fine Miltonic inversion) is invested with religious significance: 'The many-steepled tract magnificent / Of hilly fields and meadows.' They are in Nature's cathedral. And the rich Miltonic invocations of lines 32–7 are the prelude to a moment of epiphanic communion in which Lamb, like Coleridge before him, discourses with the Almighty Spirit through the forms of external nature. This visionary insight is neither pantheistic nor wholly mystic: 'Nature *is* not the Almighty Spirit; it simply veils Him; He is shining in and through Nature, which thus partakes of the Reality which it renders intelligible.'[37] In other words, Nature is *symbolic* (as it has been throughout the poem) and it is here *perceived symbolically* as the light of sense goes out and the observer sees into the life of things.

In the concluding section of the poem (lines 43—76) the poet returns to the bower and discovers the spiritual distance that he has travelled. The bower, no longer oppressive and confining, has become a microcosm of his larger vision:

> A delight
> Comes sudden on my heart, and I am glad
> As I myself were there! Nor in this bower,
> This little lime-tree bower, have I not mark'd
> Much that has sooth'd me. Pale beneath the blaze
> Hung the transparent foliage; and I watch'd
> Some broad and sunny leaf, and lov'd to see
> The shadow of the leaf and stem above
> Dappling its sunshine![38] And that walnut-tree
> Was richly ting'd, and a deep radiance lay
> Full on the ancient ivy, which usurps
> Those fronting elms, and now, with blackest mass
> Makes their dark branches gleam a lighter hue
> Through the late twilight. . . .
>
> (43—56)

With 'sudden' delight he realises that the beauty of which he felt deprived when the poem began and which he had later experienced vicariously with Lamb has, in fact, been all about him in the bower all along. With new appreciation, as though he were seeing it for the first time, he details the minute glories of the arbour in the sunlight, moving effortlessly from noon to evening — from the transparent foliage beneath the midday blaze to the twilight chiaroscuro of ivy-leaves against the dark elm branches — in the space of ten lines (47—56). The shift from past tense ('*Hung* the transparent foliage') to present tense ('and *now*, with blackest mass / *Makes* their dark branches') is almost imperceptible, but it subtly underscores the poet's spiritual growth during these few hours and prepares the way for the 'moral' (lines 59—67) that revelation is potentially present in all created nature so long as there is an eye to see it and an ear to hear it. Then in the last nine lines (68—76) this moral statement is given concrete expression in the symbol of the homeward flying rook.

These closing lines accomplish a number of things. They bring to a climax, as the rook's black wing vanishes in the light of the setting sun, the light-dark imagery that has run through the poem as a visual *leitmotiv*. They mark also the culmination of the poem's dual spatial focus, for the separate worlds of Coleridge in his bower and Lamb on the Quantock hillside — that is, of the poet's *actual* and his *imaginative* experience — are fused and blended in the light of a sunset common to both and the creeking flight of a bird that bridges the experiential gap between them. Moreover, the act of blessing the rook, analogous to that of the Ancient Mariner in blessing the water snakes, symbolises the full extent of Coleridge's growth from isolated loneliness to participation in the One Life within him and abroad: 'The poet, being blessed in the condition of grace, is able to bless.'[39] And finally, the closing lines reaffirm the moral of lines 59–67 by transferring to Lamb the lesson that Coleridge himself has learned, namely, that 'No sound is dissonant which tells of Life' (76).

'FROST AT MIDNIGHT'

'Frost at Midnight', which many regard as the most successful of the Conversation Poems, was written in February 1798, when Coleridge was still working on 'The Ancient Mariner'. Surprisingly, despite its air of mystery and the supernatural, the poem was not published in *Lyrical Ballads*, nor is there any evidence that it was ever considered for inclusion in that volume. In mid September 1798, shortly before he left for Germany, Coleridge was in London and arranged that it should be published in a quarto pamphlet along with two other of his poems; the pamphlet, under the imprint of the London bookseller Joseph Johnson, appeared later that year with the title *Fears in Solitude, Written in 1798, during the Alarum of an Invasion. To which are added, France, an Ode; and Frost at Midnight*. After he returned from Germany, Coleridge suggested to Southey in December 1799 that, if 'Johnson should mean to do nothing more' (*CL*, I 550) with the three poems, they might find a place in Southey's projected *Annual Anthology*. Southey was interested, and Coleridge wrote back five days later: 'I will speak to Johnson about the Fears in Solitude — if he give them up, they are your's' (*CL*, I 552). Johnson, however, would not relinquish his right to the poems, and in February 1800 Coleridge told Southey that 'The fears in Solitude, I fear, is not my Property — & I have no encouragement to think, it will be given up' (*CL*, I 573). The three poems were later published together in the *Poetical Register* for 1808—9, and also appeared in 1812 as a separate publication, under the imprint of Law and Gilbert. 'Frost at Midnight' was finally separated from its two 'companion' pieces in Coleridge's *Sibylline Leaves* (1817), where it was included with a number of the other Conversation Poems in a section entitled 'Meditative Poems in Blank Verse'. Thereafter similarly grouped, it was published in all the lifetime editions — 1828, 1829 and 1834 — of Coleridge's poetry.

Like most of Coleridge's poems 'Frost at Midnight' underwent substantial revision over a number of years. While there are a number of minor variants, the major changes may be limited to two. First, the quarto edition of 1798 had included a six-line coda, so that the original ending of the poem read,

> Or whether the secret ministery of cold
> Shall hang them up in silent icicles,
> Quietly shining to the quiet moon,
> Like those, my babe! which ere tomorrow's warmth
> Have capp'd their sharp keen points with pendulous drops,
> Will catch thine eye, and with their novelty
> Suspend thy little soul; then make thee shout,
> And stretch and flutter from thy mother's arms
> As thou wouldst fly for very eagerness.

When Coleridge offered the poem to Southey in 1799, he noted that it could stand 'a little Trimming' (*CL*, I 552). Perhaps even that early he had these six concluding lines in mind, for they were omitted in all later editions because (as Coleridge said in a marginal note) they 'destroy the rondo, and return upon itself of the Poem'.[40] In any event, it is easy to assent to Humphry House's judgement that the decision to drop these lines 'was one of the best artistic decisions Coleridge ever made'.[41]

The second major revision centres on lines 19—25 of the final version. This section, in the 1798 quarto edition, contains ten lines: unlike the final version, where the film on the grate is a 'companionable form' because it echoes the mind's own mood, the 1798 lines stress the activity of 'the self-watching subtilizing mind' that anthropomorphises lifeless external things by transfusing into them the mind's 'own delights, / Its own volition, sometimes with deep faith / And sometimes with fantastic playfulness'. Later, when the poem was published in the *Poetical Register*, this same section was expanded to fourteen lines, which make even more explicit the opposition between 'common sense' responses to phenomena and such fanciful self-projection ('these wild reliques of our childish Thought').[42] The conceptual (or philosophic) problem with both these versions is that creative perception is distrusted and, as well, no allowance is made for a reciprocal interchange of action from without and from within in the act of perception.[43] Moreover, Fancy dominates Imagination: the mind, rather than participating imaginatively in the unity of all life, simply imposes fanciful meanings and associations on external phenomena. In *Sibylline Leaves* and in the 1828 version of the poem, although the fourteen lines are compressed into fewer lines, the same difficulties remain:

> To which the living spirit in our frame,
> That loves not to behold a lifeless thing,
> Transfuses its own pleasures, its own will.

It was not, finally, until the revisions for the 1829 edition that the passage assumed its final form, in which the 'idling Spirit' finds an 'Echo or mirror seeking of itself' in the objects of its contemplation.

Although the primary 'source' of 'Frost at Midnight' is undoubtedly Coleridge's own experience on a cold February night in 1798, it is impossible (as Humphry House has pointed out) not to believe that the poet had a passage from William Cowper's *The Task* in mind as he wrote:

> Me oft has fancy ludicrous and wild
> Sooth'd with a waking dream of houses, tow'rs,
> Trees, churches, and strange visages express'd
> In the red cinders, while with poring eye
> I gazed, myself creating what I saw.
> Nor less amused have I quiescent watch'd
> The sooty films that play upon the bars
> Pendulous, and foreboding in the view
> Of superstition prophesying still
> Though still deceived, some stranger's near approach.
> 'Tis thus the understanding takes repose
> In indolent vacuity of thought,
> And sleeps and is refresh'd. Meanwhile the face

Conceals the mood lethargic with a mask
Of deep deliberation, as the man
Were task'd to his full strength, absorb'd and lost.
Thus oft reclin'd at east, I lose an hour
At evening, till at length the freezing blast
That sweeps the bolted shutter, summons home
The recollected powers, and snapping short
The glassy threads with which the fancy weaves
Her brittle toys, restores me to myself.
How calm is my recess, and how the frost
Raging abroad, and the rough wind, endear
The silence and the warmth enjoy'd within.
              (*The Task*, IV 286–310; 1785 edn)

While the parallels in situation and imagery, together with a
number of verbal echoes ('films', 'pendulous', 'toys', etc.), would
seem to preclude the possibility of coincidence, Coleridge has
utterly transformed the passage in adapting it to suit his own
purpose. Indeed, the contrasts are much more remarkable than
the similarities. The case is well put by House:

> Cowper emphasises the utter indolence, the insignificance, of
> his mood and the quite false appearance of 'deep deliberation'
> which he gives to others; and the verse in which he gives ex-
> pression to this is, strictly, desultory and unshaped. . . . But in
> Coleridge's poem there is no question of deceit or of a lost hour;
> his thought acquires serious content as it moves, and the man is
> really tasked to his full strength. What makes 'Frost at Midnight'
> an achieved artistic whole is the design, the organisation, in the
> movement of the thought.[44]

It may be added — though this is to speculate — that Coleridge's
difficulties with revising lines 19–25 may stem ultimately from the
fact that Cowper's fanciful vision, in which the poet 'gazed, myself
creating what I saw', was *too* much present to him and that Coleridge (perhaps without ever being consciously aware of it) found it
hard to shake himself free of the influence of Cowper's projection-
ist view of mental activity.

What makes 'Frost at Midnight' an artistic success, as House
points out, is its tightly knit organisation. As in 'This Lime-Tree
Bower', the poet begins with a sense of his own separation and

alienation from the world around him but then rises, as egotism yields to altruism, to a vicarious participation in natural beauty through the imagined responses of his infant son. The poet's spiritual growth is developed, not only in the characteristic 'rondo' device which takes him from his Stowey cottage into strange seas of thought and then returns him to the cottage again, but also in an intricately structured temporal sequence in three movements: from his present situation he is led, by memory, into the past and then projected forward, in imagination, to a visionary future which both recaptures the past and returns him to his present situation.

The first movement (lines 1–23) opens with the frost's 'secret ministry', which contrasts sharply in its silent operation with the poet's vexed desire to know and explain such mysteries. His restless mood, which is out of tune with the universal 'hush of nature' around him, finds (or seems to find) an analogue in the fluttering film playing over the grate in the fireplace:

> The Frost performs its secret ministry,
> Unhelped by any wind. The owlet's cry
> Came loud — and hark, again! loud as before.
> The inmates of my cottage, all at rest,
> Have left me to that solitude, which suits
> Abstruser musings: save that at my side
> My cradled infant slumbers peacefully.
> 'Tis calm indeed! so calm, that it disturbs
> And vexes meditation with its strange
> And extreme silentless. Sea, hill, and wood,
> This populous village! Sea, and hill, and wood,
> With all the numberless goings-on of life,
> Inaudible as dreams! the thin blue flame
> Lies on my low-burnt fire, and quivers not;
> Only that film, which fluttered on the grate,
> Still flutters there, the sole unquiet thing.
> Methinks, its motion in this hush of nature
> Gives it dim sympathies with me who live,
> Making it a companionable form,
> Whose puny flaps and freaks the idling Spirit
> By its own moods interprets, every where
> Echo or mirror seeking of itself,
> And makes a toy of Thought.

These lines develop a distinction between solitude and isolation; they establish a tension between the serenity of nature and the agitation of the poet — and the gap between them widens as the passage progresses. On the one hand, there is the calm of external nature; but this 'extreme silentness' is somewhat illusory, for it is full of activity — the frost performing its secret ministry, the owlet's cry, the baby's peaceful breathing, the 'numberless goings-on of life' throughout the village and the world beyond. If one is to attune oneself with this activity, however, and understand this mysterious language of silence, then one must listen with the heart as well as with the ear. On the other hand, in dissonant counter-point to the unity of life around him, there is the poet's oppressive sense of isolation and the increasingly frantic attempts of his probing intelligence to penetrate the mysterious veil of silence. He discovers that the 'solitude' to which he has been left is not a solace; indeed, it is disquieting and produces an opposite effect in him: 'it disturbs / And vexes meditation with its strange / And extreme silentness'. He attempts to define the calm by cataloguing its components — 'Sea, hill, and wood, / This populous village!' — but enumeration, even when repeated like an incantation, does not bring revelation. The 'numberless goings-on of life' are in-accessible to him: 'Inaudible as dreams!' His Stowey parlour (a symbol, like Poole's lime-tree bower in an earlier poem, of the enclosed world of self) becomes a prison in which he is cut off from the life of the larger world. Unable to communicate with that world, he looks about for something to which he can relate and finds (he thinks) a 'companionable form' in the film fluttering on the grate — 'the sole unquiet thing', an analogue of his own rest-lessness. But the film, like the roaring dell in 'This Lime-Tree Bower', is an ambivalent symbol: it is a companionable reflection of the poet's mood and mind, but at the same time its 'puny flaps and freaks' mock his efforts at intellectual activity, making 'a toy of Thought'.

In the second movement (lines 23–43) intellection gives way to *rêverie* and the present yields place to the past. The transition is a smooth one, for the image of the fluttering film (and the popular superstition attached to it[45]) provides a bridge from actual to remembered experience:

> But O! how oft,
> How oft, at school, with most believing mind,

Presageful, have I gazed upon the bars,
To watch that fluttering *stranger*! and as oft
With unclosed lids, already had I dreamt
Of my sweet birth-place, and the old church-tower,
Whose bells, the poor man's only music, rang
From morn to evening, all the hot Fair-day,
So sweetly, that they stirred and haunted me
With a wild pleasure, falling on mine ear
Most like articulate sounds of things to come!
So gazed I, till the soothing things, I dreamt,
Lulled me to sleep, and sleep prolonged my dreams!
And so I brooded all the following morn,
Awed by the stern preceptor's face, mine eye
Fixed with mock study on my swimming book:
Save if the door half opened, and I snatched
A hasty glance, and still my heart leaped up,
For still I hoped to see the *stranger's* face,
Townsman, or aunt, or sister more beloved,
My play-mate when we both were clothed alike!

In these lines, as Frederick Garber says, the poet 'has moved from
being a spectator of his current working consciousness into staring
at himself as a child; and what he was doing then as a child is
exactly what he is doing now as an adult, playing spectator to an
earlier acting self. . . . The mind which had sought for a likeness
outside of itself goes one step further and finds one within itself as
well.'[46] In fact, the movement inward is an extremely important
one, for the poet's analogising consciousness is more open and
responsive to memory than to his present circumstances and search
for companionable forms in the world outside himself. In this
section two biographical memories are superimposed on one
another in a kind of poetic double-exposure: the poet relives those
times at Christ's Hospital when, unhappy and alone, the fluttering
stranger had reminded him of his happy childhood in Ottery St
Mary, and he recalls how the vision of his 'sweet birth-place' had
lingered with him during school-hours and superstitiously
prompted him to hope that the schoolroom door would open to
reveal this glad past in the shape of an Ottery townsman or his aunt
or his beloved sister Anne (who had died in March 1791 during his
last term at Christ's Hospital).[47]

    This second section, with its overlaid presentation of two former selves, is pivotal. On the one hand, the image of the lonely dreaming schoolboy imprisoned beneath the stern preceptor's gaze gathers up and refocuses the restless alienation, the oppressive sense of solitude, explored in the opening movement. On the other hand, however, the joyous Ottery memories — dominated by the haunting music of the church-bells — look forward to the third section of the poem and the 'natural' education that his son will experience under the benevolent preceptorship of the 'Great universal Teacher', who reveals 'Himself in all, and all things in himself'. Janus-like, then, the second movement has a double aspect; it is both a recapitulation and an anticipation. The door that opens on the past leads also to the future; and the 'presageful' stranger does in fact arrive when the poet glances up from himself to see his son standing, as it were, in the door 'half opened' by reflection and reminiscence.

In the third section (lines 44–74) the contrapuntal exploration of self is further developed in the contrast between the poet's past when he was 'pent 'mid cloisters dim' at Christ's Hospital and his son's projected education amid the beauties of the natural world. The infant's gentle breathing, which interrupts the 'abstruser musings' and train of associated memories, returns Coleridge momentarily to the present and then sends him forward to an altruistic benediction in which he transcends self by rediscovering it in and through his son:

> Dear Babe, that sleepest cradled by my side,
> Whose gentle breathings, heard in this deep calm,
> Fill up the interspersèd vacancies
> And momentary pauses of the thought!
> My babe so beautiful! it thrills my heart
> With tender gladness, thus to look at thee,
> And think that thou shalt learn far other lore,
> And in far other scenes! For I was reared
> In the great city, pent 'mid cloisters dim,
> And saw nought lovely but the sky and stars.
> But *thou*, my babe! shalt wander like a breeze
> By lakes and sandy shores, beneath the crags
> Of ancient mountain, and beneath the clouds,
> Which image in their bulk both lakes and shores
> And mountain crags: so shalt thou see and hear
> The lovely shapes and sounds intelligible

> Of that eternal language, which thy God
> Utters, who from eternity doth teach
> Himself in all, and all things in himself.
> Great universal Teacher! he shall mould
> Thy spirit, and by giving make it ask.
>
>   Therefore all seasons shall be sweet to thee,
> Whether the summer clothe the general earth
> With greenness, or the redbreast sit and sing
> Betwixt the tufts of snow on the bare branch
> Of mossy apple-tree, while the nigh thatch
> Smokes in the sun-thaw;[48] whether the eave-drops fall
> Heard only in the trances of the blast,
> Or if the secret ministry of frost
> Shall hang them up in silent icicles,
> Quietly shining to the quiet Moon.

The 'deep calm' around him that had originally pressured him into perplexity is no longer vexing or alien, nor is it inaccessible to him. Sound and silence coexist symbiotically: the water-drops heard falling from the eaves or being hung in silent icicles, the blowing wind and the secret ministry of frost, are all parts and portions of one wondrous whole; they are now, as the poet listens with his heart as well as with his ear, the *intelligible* sounds of one eternal language. And, as his thought turns from himself to his sleeping child, he realises — in Max Schulz's words — that 'the beneficent and awesome processes of life taking place outside in nature and inside the cottage . . . are identical'.[49] The eave-drops heard 'in the trances of the blast' are analogous to the baby's gentle breathings, and the robin imagined as pouring out its soul on the snow-tufted boughs of the apple-tree has its counterpart in the poet who, having carried 'the feelings of childhood into the powers of manhood',[50] sings now in full-throated ease. Understanding, insight and reconciliation have come to him through childhood — his own and that of his son. In this instance at least, then, the child truly is the father of the man.

    'Frost at Midnight' is the record of an epiphany. It dramatises a movement 'from the willful and superstitious solipsism of a depressed sensibility, toying with a companionable form, to the apprehension of a regenerate companionship, based not on superstition but on substantial belief'.[51] (Significantly, the revelation — or self-revelation — occurs at *midnight*; that is, at the transitional moment between the end of the old and the beginning of a new day.) It is a religious poem which describes the attainment through the visible world of an insight into the invisible world beyond. The poem begins and ends with the 'secret ministry' of frost — a mystery which is explored but never explained. 'The meaning of the poem', as Robert Langbaum has succinctly expressed it, 'is in all that has accrued since the original vision, in the gain in perception. But the gain is rather in the intensity of understanding than in what is understood', for (as in 'Tintern Abbey') 'the revelation is not a formulated idea that dispels mystery, but a perception that advances in intensity to a deeper and wider, a more inclusive, mystery'.[52] At the heart of this mystery lies the blending, the balanced reconciliation, of the familiar and the strange — a mystery that is perhaps best described, not by a literary critic, but by another poet, in a little quatrain that Coleridge himself might have written:

> That shining moon — watched by that one faint star:
> Sure now am I, beyond the fear of change,
> The lovely in life is the familiar,
> And only the lovelier for continuing strange.[53]

'FEARS IN SOLITUDE'

The publication history of 'Fears in Solitude' parallels that of 'Frost at Midnight' (see above, pp. 38–9). While Coleridge, as was his custom, made a number of minor alterations in phrasing each time the poem was republished, there is only one important change that need be noted here. As the result of 'dissatisfaction with organized utilitarian life' after the Battle of Waterloo,[54] he added lines 54–8, which first appeared in the version printed in *Sibylline Leaves* (1817) and are perhaps the worst lines in the poem:

> All individual dignity and power
> Engulfed in Courts, Committees, Institutions,
> Associations and Societies,
> A vain, speech-mouthing, speech-reporting Guild,
> One Benefit-Club for mutual flattery. . . .

Like the other poems in the Conversation group 'Fears in Solitude' is an occasional poem. Coleridge dated the manuscript precisely ('NETHER STOWEY, *April* 20, 1798) and the poem was published with the subtitle 'Written, April 1798, during the Alarms of an Invasion'. As E. P. Thompson has shown, the threat of a French invasion caused considerable excitement and 'March and April, 1798, saw the greatest *levée* of the Volunteers in the whole decade.'[55] The North Petherton Corps (which drew on the residents of Nether Stowey) was founded in April 1798 with considerable oratorical flourish: 'England was never in more imminent danger of being invaded', declared the Somerset justices, 'and by an enemy the most barbarous, sanguinary and destructive, than at this present moment, an enemy that has spread desolation, that has been guilty of every enormity, that has spared no one of whatever way of thinking or acting from rapacity and plunder. . . . It behoves us therefore as Britons . . . to arm.'[56] This call to arms put Coleridge (and Wordsworth) in an awkward position. Both poets were regarded with suspicion and a measure of fear by their country neighbours. In the eyes of simple country-folk the odd behaviour of the two men − their long walks, even at night, and their intense discussions of Lord knew what all − was sinister and (it seemed certain) seditious. Their political opinions were well known; they had openly entertained John Thelwall, perhaps the most notorious Jacobin in England, in July 1797; they had spoken out against the war with France, and a government agent had been sent − at the request of local residents − to report on their activities. Although Wordsworth was largely indifferent to local opinion, Coleridge was not; he was well and happily settled in Stowey and intended to stay, even after Wordsworth (in March 1798) had been refused renewed tenancy of Alfoxden. Both men − but Coleridge in particular − must have known that the calling up of the Militia and their response to it would be regarded by their Somerset neighbours as a test of their loyalty and patriotism. '*The heat was on*', as Professor Thompson puts it; 'You did not volunteer or not-volunteer, according to fancy. Every gentleman, every professional man, was under scrutiny.'[57] Tom Poole joined up − but neither Coleridge nor Wordsworth did. Instead, Coleridge wrote 'Fears in Solitude', a private and public declaration of his own political sentiments in which he expressed his patriotic feeling but, at the same time, made plain his opposition to Pitt's administration. And, if it is true that in going to Germany in the autumn of 1798 Coleridge and Wordsworth 'were hopping the draft', it is equally true that their departure was 'a withdrawal from the vortex of an unbearable political con- flict'.[58] Coleridge had already in 'France: An Ode' (published in the *Morning Post* on 16 April 1798) publicly recanted his earlier enthusiasm for the French and led the retreat to the right among the intellectual liberals in England, but he could not support Pitt's handling of the French war or his ruthless suppression of the Irish Rebellion in the spring and summer of 1798.

'Fears in Solitude' treads a careful path between censure and eulogy. Beginning in a low key with the description of 'A green and silent spot, amid the hills, / A small and silent dell' (lines 1–28), it passes quickly to an indictment of his fellow-countrymen for their callous inhumanity and their insensitivity to the suffering of others (lines 29–129):

> Boys and girls,
> And women, that would groan to see a child
> Pull off an insect's leg, all read of war,
> The best amusement for our morning meal! . . .
> And all our dainty terms for fratricide;
> Terms which we trundle smoothly o'er our tongues
> Like mere abstractions, empty sounds to which
> We join no feeling and attach no form!
> As if the soldier died without a wound. . . .
> (104–7, 113–17)

The passage concludes with a Miltonic commination of divine retribution. Then, quite suddenly, in the middle of line 129 the poet calls upon his countrymen to stand forth against the French, to 'repel an impious foe, / Impious and false, a light yet cruel race, / Who laugh away all virtue, mingling mirth / With deeds of murder' (139–42). But this exhortation is immediately followed, in lines which look back to the earlier condemnation of his countrymen, with an earnest plea that the English may return from battle not only victorious but chastened:

> And oh! may we return
> Not with a drunken triumph, but with fear,
> Repenting of the wrongs with which we stung
> So fierce a foe to frenzy!
> (150–3)

Having told this 'bitter truth, but without bitterness' (155), Coleridge proceeds to a eulogy of his 'native Britain' and the hope that
she will prove a regenerate nation purged by trial (lines 176—202).
In the closing verse-paragraph (lines 203—32) we are returned to
the dell of the opening scene and to the poet's beloved Stowey:

> And now, belovéd Stowey! I behold
> Thy church-tower, and, methinks, the four huge elms
> Clustering, which mark the mansion of my friend;
> And close behind them, hidden from my view,
> Is my own lowly cottage, where my babe
> And my babe's mother dwell in peace!
>
> (221—6)

This 'return' is not forced. The peace of dell and cottage is precisely what is at stake, precisely what is threatened by invasion
from abroad and arrogant self-delusion at home.

In general, 'Fears in Solitude' has fared badly at the hands of
critics. C. L. Moody, who reviewed the poem for the *Monthly
Review* (May 1799), while he found much to praise in the poem's
balanced political statement, was nevertheless 'forced to censure
some of [the] lines as very prosaic'; the anonymous reviewer in the
British Critic (June 1799), on the other hand, could do no more
than lament Coleridge's 'absurd and preposterous prejudices
against his country'.[59] Modern readers, when they have bothered
to discuss the poem, have scarcely been more generous. Max F.
Schulz thinks it to be marred by an 'incongruous mixture of styles';
George Watson, who finds the poem 'a shameless return' to
Coleridge's 'older, effusive manner', tartly declares that 'it is only
by stretching charity that it can be considered a conversation poem
at all'; and Reginald Watters, who feels that Coleridge 'loses his
touch' when he turns to his public theme, concludes, 'The cold
truth remains that this is very poor verse and that it is only when he
is considering and recreating the landscape that the poem lives.'[60]
The adverse criticism, it may be added, begins with Coleridge
himself: in 1799 he dismissed 'Fears in Solitude' as a 'dull ode' (*CL*,
I 552) and later, in a marginal comment, he declared that the
poem was 'perhaps not Poetry, — but rather a sort of middle thing
between Poetry and Oratory — sermoni propriora. — Some parts
are, I am conscious, too tame even for animated prose' (*CPW*,
I 257).[61]

The poem, however, is just not *that* bad, and these judgements are, in the main, far too severe. 'Fears in Solitude' is a qualified success. It is not a complete success, for it is marred by flat, prosaic passages and passages of bombastic rhetoric; but neither is it a total failure. Its strengths become apparent when it is set beside such a poem as 'Reflections on Having Left a Place of Retirement', which *is* a failure both stylistically and structurally. 'Reflections' is spoiled by fatuous and pompous declamation and by the fact that it is little more than a series of loosely related scenes; it is also, as suggested above (see pp. 30–2), torn between the ethical claims of the *vita activa* and the visionary claims of the *vita contemplativa*. In marked contrast, 'Fears in Solitude' is a carefully constructed artistic whole: the realms of nature and politics are intimately related, not hopelessly severed from one another. The logic of the poem moves in an artful parabola from nature to politics and back to nature, in such a way that the solitude of the 'green and silent spot, amid the hills' becomes more meaningful and more precious. The 'return' is not gratuitous embroidery; it is integral to the poem's structure and argument.

I must dissent, too, from the usual views that the only successful passages are those of lyrical natural description and that the poem's political sections are a 'shameless return' to Coleridge's early 'effusive manner'. Indeed, quite the reverse seems to me to be true. The tone of 'Fears in Solitude' is neither hysterical nor (like 'Reflections') histrionic and posturing in its political statements; its blank verse moves with ease for the most part and its texture is richer than that in any of the pre-1798 political verse; and, apart from the 'owlet Atheism' (line 82), the poem is virtually free of the obtrusive and stilted personified abstractions that clog many of Coleridge's early poems. The style, if not strictly conversational, is at least (as Carl Woodring says) 'a middle thing between a torrential effusion like *Religious Musings* and a "conversation poem"'.[62] Moreover, there is much in the political sections of the poem that is finely imagined and finely phrased — a point which may be illustrated by the fine lines about the tramping boots and confused alarums that drown the singing of the unseen skylark:

> What uproar and what strife may now be stirring
> This way or that way o'er these silent hills —
> Invasion, and the thunder and the shout,

> And all the crash of onset; fear and rage,
> And undetermined conflict. . . .
>
> (34–8)

This is an effective counterpoint to the passage of natural description preceding it, a well-executed incursion into the peaceful solitude of the poet's (and the reader's) security and complacent sense of well-being. The object of the poem, after all, is to prompt the age to quit their clogs, to prize liberty and eschew licence; and it *is* possible – even for Coleridge – to be both Miltonic and successful.

'THE NIGHTINGALE'

'The Nightingale' was composed in April 1798, the same month as 'Fears in Solitude'. With the subtitle 'a Conversational Poem' it was published in *Lyrical Ballads* (1798); it was one of Coleridge's four contributions to the volume and was substituted at the last moment for 'Lewti', which, since it had been previously published, might have compromised the anonymity of *Lyrical Ballads*.[63] It was republished in the second edition (1800) of *Lyrical Ballads*, where Coleridge dropped the subtitle and deleted lines 64–9 (see *CL*, I 594). The poem reappeared in the two later editions (1802 and 1805) of *Lyrical Ballads* with these same omissions. In *Sibylline Leaves* (1817) both the subtitle 'a Conversation Poem' and lines 64–9 were restored; and this version was reprinted in Coleridge's *Political Works* of 1828, 1829 and 1834. There are a few minor textual variants (listed in the notes in *CPW*), but they are of no real consequence and the only major alterations are those (mentioned above) concerning the subtitle and lines 64–9.

Of all the Conversation Poems 'The Nightingale' is the most perplexing. The poem has not been much discussed by Coleridge's critics, and those who have discussed it have generally been careful in their praise. The anonymous reviewer in the *British Critic* of October 1799, for example, declared left-handedly that 'The Poem on the Nightingale, which is . . . styled "a conversational Poem", is very good; but we do not perceive it to be more conversational than Cowper's "Task", which is the best poem in that style that our language possesses'.[64] The ambivalent response of this early reviewer is shared by many modern readers, although perhaps for other reasons. On the one hand, there is much fine writing in the poem and, as George Watson observes, 'it comes near, at moments, to seeming one of the most considerable of Coleridge's poems'.[65] On the other hand, however, there are a number of problems with the poem's structure, theme and tone. That Coleridge himself was aware of some of these difficulties is apparent from the doggerel verse-letter which he sent to Wordsworth together with a copy of the poem on 10 May 1798 (*CL*, I 406):

> In stale blank verse a subject stale
> I send *per post* my *Nightingale*;
> And like an honest bard, dear Wordsworth,
> You'll tell me what you think, my Bird's worth.
> My own opinion's briefly this —
> His *bill* he opens not amiss;
> And when he has sung a stave or so,
> His breast, & some small space below,
> So throbs & swells, that you might swear
> No vulgar music's working there.
> So far, so good; but then, 'od rot him!
> There's something falls off at his bottom.
> Yet, sure, no wonder it should breed,
> That my Bird's Tail's a tail indeed
> And makes it's own inglorious harmony
> Æolio crepitû, non carmine.

The poem's structure is tripartite and employs (though in a different way) the rondo device characteristic of this group of poems. The opening section (lines 1–49) establishes the natural setting — Coleridge and the Wordsworths standing, at night, on an 'old mossy bridge' and listening to the song of a nightingale — and establishes a contrast between literal and literary Nature. The poet censures the literary tradition that has caused the nightingale's song to be interpreted as melancholy and rebukes those 'youths and maidens most poetical, / Who lose the deepening twilights of the spring / In ball-rooms and hot theatres', for their sentimentality and artificiality in heaving 'their sighs / O'er Philomela's pity-pleading strains' (35–9). Against this false artifice Coleridge opposes the 'different lore' that he and the Wordsworths have learned by going out into the natural world itself, where the nightingale's song, far from being sad, is full of love and joy: "Tis the merry Nightingale / That crowds, and hurries and precipitates / With fast thick warble his delicious notes' (43–5).[66] In the second section of the poem (lines 49–86) the scene shifts abruptly to a wild grove 'hard by a castle huge' — a grove full of nightingales who 'answer and provoke each other's song' (58) — and to the account of 'a Lady vowed and dedicate / To something more than Nature in the grove' (72–3) who knows all the notes of the nightingales and who glides through the grove's pathways at night to hear their songs. It is impossible not to catch a glimpse of 'Christabel' in this Gothic setting and night-wandering maid. Then, in the final section (lines 87–110), the poet returns briefly to the initial scene in order to bid goodnight to the Wordsworths ('We have been loitering long and pleasantly, / And now for our dear homes') — and then promptly digresses (or does he?) to describe how his little son Hartley would respond to the renewed strain of the nightingale and to relate the 'father's tale' (which seems to derive from an incident recorded in a Notebook entry of late 1797 or early 1798[67]) of how Hartley had wakened crying from 'an infant's dream' and been soothed by the beneficent influence of the moon. The poem concludes with the vow that Hartley 'shall grow up / Familiar with these songs, that with the night / He may associate joy' (107–9), and with a final farewell to the nightingale and to the Wordsworths.

From a structural point of view the question must be put as to whether or not these three sections are successfully integrated into a single artistic whole. What relationship is there between Coleridge and the Wordsworths on the mossy bridge, the 'gentle Maid' in the grove against a Gothic backdrop, and the domestic excursus on Hartley Coleridge? Is the poem a unified poetic construction, or a digressive series of heterogeneous incidents and anecdotes? The answers to such questions are by no means easy, and Coleridge's critics are far from unanimous in their answers. Max F. Schulz, while conceding that 'The Nightingale' is 'the least overtly unified of the conversation group', concludes that 'Coleridge, the lady, the birds, and Hartley all hear "the voice of vernal hours" and respond rapturously. It is this substantiation of the idea that "in nature there is nothing melancholy" which gives oneness to the multiplicity of their experiences and unity to the diverse episodes of the poem'.[68] For George Watson, however, the poem is not a structural success and 'wander[s] off in its last two stanzas to describe "a most gentle maid" who has loved the nightingales, and to tell a sentimental "father's tale" of the infant Hartley's reaction to their song. The final address to William and Dorothy . . . is too perfunctory to pull the poem back into shape.'[69]

It seems to me that what rescues the poem, in spite of its episodic manner, is the intricate way in which image-patterns are developed and interwoven. Imagery of sound and silence, for example, runs as a unifying *leitmotiv* throughout the poem and is subtly blended with the imagery of starlight and moonlight in such a way that the whole cluster of images gathers significance and deepens as the poem progresses. The opening movement establishes a dialectic between two sorts of response to the nightingale's song — that is, between those who listen with the heart and are receptive to the sound and those who impose their own egotism on the song and so pervert it. The latter category is illustrated by the 'night-wandering man' (and his *précieuse coterie* of imitators and admirers) who has projected his own unhappiness into the nightingale's song and so 'filled all things with himself, / And made all gentle sounds tell back the tale / Of his own sorrow' (19–21). Against this sort of individual, however, is placed another class — represented by Coleridge and the Wordsworths — who do not 'profane / Nature's sweet voices, always full of love / And joyance' (41–3) and who, comfortable in the presence of mystery, are alert to Nature's eternal language without needing to interpret every word precisely:

> Come, we will rest on this old mossy bridge!
> You see the glimmer of the stream beneath,
> But hear no murmuring: it flows silently,
> O'er its soft bed of verdure. All is still,
> A balmy night! and though the stars be dim,
> Yet let us think upon the vernal showers
> That gladden the green earth, and we shall find
> A pleasure in the dimness of the stars.
> And hark! the Nightingale begins its song. . . .
>   (4–12)

In the second movement of the poem the theme of willing and receptive exposure to nature is further developed, not directly (through the poet and his friends), but indirectly and distanced, in the figure of the 'gentle Maid' who glides through the grove near the castle.[70] But she is not quite an ordinary maiden; she is, rather, 'like a Lady vowed and dedicate / To something more than Nature in the grove' (72–3). Her Eleusinian aura, her presentation as a kind of priestess, imparts a sacramental significance to the scene over which she presides and paves the way for a bolder and more dramatic use of the image-cluster centred on sound–silence and light–darkness:

> she knows all their notes,
> That gentle Maid! and oft, a moment's space,
> What time the moon was lost behind a cloud,
> Hath heard a pause of silence; till the moon
> Emerging, hath awakened earth and sky
> With one sensation, and those wakeful birds
> Have all burst forth in choral minstrelsy,
> As if some sudden gale had swept at once
> A hundred airy harps!
>
> (74–82)

For a fleeting second, somewhere between the breathless 'pause of silence' and the sudden shower of light and song as the moon reappears, we have seen into the One Life and experienced (without being able to explain it) the universal 'joyance' to which the throng of nightingales gives vent. There has been a moment of revelation, an epiphany — but the mystery itself remains intact. Then, in the final movement, this imaginative vision is reiterated and, as it were, domesticated in the anecdotes about Hartley. In the days of his angel-infancy (a theme that Wordsworth was to develop in his 'Ode: Intimations of Immortality') the child responds intuitively both to the nightingale's song —

> How he would place his hand beside his ear,
> His little hand, the small forefinger up,
> And bid us listen!
>
> (94–6)

— and to the calming influence of the moon:

> And he beheld the moon, and, hushed at once,
> Suspends his sobs, and laughs most silently.
>
> (102–3)

But the final movement does not succeed, partly because the introduction of Hartley so late in the piece is both awkward and obtrusive, and partly because the descent from visionary insight to domestic detail — curiously reminiscent of the cancelled ending of 'Frost at Midnight' — involves an abrupt change of tone which, since we are not adequately prepared for it, is somewhat bathetic. It may be added, too, that the image-cluster we have been following, in which sound—silence and light—darkness have been so intricately interwoven in the earlier movements, begins to unravel in the last section, where sound and sight are assigned to two discrete incidents, one imagined (lines 91—5) and one remembered (lines 98—105). In any event, while the concluding section may make 'it's own inglorious harmony', it is difficult not to accept Coleridge's assessment in the verse-letter to Wordsworth that 'There's something falls off at [the] bottom' of the poem.

If the poem's structure (with some reservation about the conclusion) is defensible, its tone and treatment of its subject-matter are more difficult issues to resolve satisfactorily. There would seem to be two major problems here. First, from what has been said already, it would seem that Coleridge's purpose in 'The Nightingale' is serious. Wordsworth certainly took it seriously. Discussing his own 'Idiot Boy' in a letter of June 1802 to John Wilson, Wordsworth wrote,

> But a great Poet ought to do more than [faithfully reflect the feelings of human nature;] he ought to a certain degree to rectify men's feelings, to give them new compositions of feeling, to render their feelings more sane pure and permanent, in short, more consonant to nature, that is, to eternal nature, and the great moving spirit of things. He ought to travel before men occasionally as well as at their sides. I may illustrate this by a reference to natural objects. What false notions have prevailed from generation to generation as to the true character of the nightingale. As far as my Friend's Poem in the Lyrical Ballads, is read it will contribute greatly to rectify these.
>
> (*LW: EY*, pp. 355—6)

Was Coleridge's aim in writing the poem 'to rectify men's feelings' with respect to the nightingale? In part, no doubt, it was. But there is another factor too. The nightingale was 'one of the most approved subjects of popular poetry'[71] in the 1790s and there are

numerous examples of the theme in literary magazines of the
decade. That Coleridge knew himself to be writing within an
established 'tradition' is apparent from the opening lines of his
verse-letter to Wordsworth: 'In stale blank verse a subject stale / I
send *per post* my *Nightingale*'. Coleridge's poem, however, is far
from being simply another instance of the approved theme;
indeed, as R. H. Hopkins has persuasively argued, 'The Nightingale' parodies the Gothic and pseudo-Miltonic artificiality of late
eighteenth-century melancholy poetry. Does parody coexist comfortably with a serious philosophic treatment of the theme?
Hopkins believes that it does:

> Coleridge reverses the convention from a melancholy based on
> fancy to a characteristically Coleridgean theme of joy based on
> imagination. *The Nightingale* parodies subtly the convention
> by alluding to its worst excesses (yet without committing them)
> so that the ironic complexity of the poem depends on the reader
> recognizing what pitfalls are skirted.[72]

This is a valiant effort to improve the poem's image, and Hopkins
may well be right; yet, when one turns from his analysis to the
poem itself (especially the first verse-paragraph), one still feels
uneasy about the jarring conjunction of opposing tones. Too often
irony slips into a vein of patronising satire:

> 'Most musical, most melancholy' bird!
> A melancholy bird? Oh! idle thought!
> > (13—14)

> And youths and maidens most poetical . . .
> Full of meek sympathy must heave their sighs
> O'er Philomela's pity-pleading strains.
> > (35, 38—9)

The second major difficulty connected with the poem's treatment of its theme centres on the number of literary allusions. It is
surely odd that a poem which exhorts its readers to quit their books
and let nature be their teacher should be the most bookish of the
Conversation Poems. One obvious influence is that of Milton, as
has long been recognised: 'Miltonic, yet original' was the judgement of Charles Burney in the *Monthly Review* for June 1799.[73]

In addition to the direct quotation of line 62 of 'Il Penseroso' in line 13 of Coleridge's poem, there are a number of Miltonic echoes in 'The Nightingale': 'building up the rhyme' (24), for example, is a clear allusion to line 11 of 'Lycidas'; and Coleridge's view that the poet should be 'of his fame forgetful! so his fame / Should share in Nature's immortality' (30—1) seems likewise to derive from 'Lycidas' (lines 78—84). Alun Jones finds a 'strange echo' of *Comus* (lines 102—4) in Coleridge's 'tipsy Joy that reels with tossing head' (86) and points out that Coleridge is much indebted, not only to 'Il Penseroso', but also to Milton's *happy* nightingales in Sonnet I and in *Paradise Lost* (IV 602—4)[74] — and he might have added Elegy V, lines 25—6. Moreover, as George Watson says, the style of 'The Nightingale' is 'Miltonic in an infinity of ways — in the abundance of enjambement, in the inversions and suspensions of syntax'.[75] Milton's voice, while predominant, is not the only one we hear; there are (as other readers have pointed out) echoes of Chaucer and Spenser[76] — and perhaps as well a reminiscence in the description of the nightingale's 'swift jug jug' (60) of Trico's song in Act V, scene i, of John Lyly's *Alexander and Campaspe* (1584):[77]

> What bird so sings, yet so does wail?
> O! 'tis the ravished nightingale.
> Jug, Jug, Jug, Jug, Tereu, she cries,
> And still her woes at midnight rise.

Individually, these allusions mean little, but taken together they present a problem. 'The Nightingale' argues explicitly for the value of 'natural education'; yet the poet cannot make his case without resorting to books, thereby apparently undermining the position he would assert. How is it possible, without contradiction, to refute Milton and then to write a Miltonic poem? Is there not some confusion here? One may argue (as Watson does) that 'the relationship is alternately one of attraction and repulsion, an alternation of miltonizing and anti-miltonizing';[78] or, *vice versa*, one may argue that Coleridge echoes and imitates Milton (and others) consciously, that he wittily employs Milton to parody the poetic endeavours of eighteenth-century Miltonisers. I suspect, however, that there *is* some confusion, some unresolved and probably unconscious tension in Coleridge himself — and that Wordsworth is at the bottom of it. Wordsworthian poems such as 'Expostulation and Reply' and 'The Tables Turned' (both composed in the spring of 1798), and the method of educating young Basil Montagu,[79] leave no doubt about Wordsworth's strict adherence to Rousseauistic and Hartleian doctrines of natural education. Coleridge, on the other hand, prized book-learning and loved 'old folios'; both literature and nature were essential to him. It is inevitable then, that both should combine in his making of poems; and it is not surprising that 'The Nightingale', although it asserts a Wordsworthian view of natural education, should express that theory in a typically Coleridgean blending of observation and allusion.

'The Nightingale' is indeed a perplexing poem. It is certainly one of the most considerable of Coleridge's poems; yet one cannot praise it without reservations. Despite unifying strands of imagery, the poem's structure and tone remain problematical. At the root of these problems I am inclined to see a confusion between the related, yet distinct, aims of Coleridge and Wordsworth in their respective contributions to the *Lyrical Ballads*. Coleridge's endeavour, it will be remembered, was to 'be directed to persons and characters supernatural, or at least romantic', while Wordsworth's object was 'to give the charm of novelty to things of every day' (*BL*, II 6). 'The Nightingale', although not originally intended for the volume, seems somewhat uneasily suspended between these two modes. The opening section (lines 1—49) develops, albeit in a Coleridgean fashion, along Wordsworthian lines: it gives the charm of novelty to a hackneyed poetic subject and so awakens 'the mind's attention from the lethargy of custom, and [directs] it to the loveliness and the wonders of the world before us'. The second section (lines 49—86) with its Gothic hints and supernatural aura moves toward the romantic world of 'Christabel' and 'The Ancient Mariner' — but the transition is a reasonably smooth one. In the third section (lines 87—110), however, we are wrenched away without warning into the peculiarly Wordsworthian world of 'Anecdote for Fathers' and 'We Are Seven'. The change in tone and manner is disconcerting, and the reader is not prepared for this moment when Coleridge's nightingale begins to warble with so pronounced a Westmorland accent.

3 'Kubla Khan'

*If a man could pass thro' Paradise in a Dream, & have a
flower presented to him as a pledge that his Soul had
really been there, & found that flower in his hand when
he awoke − Aye! and what then?* (*CN*, III no. 4287)

'Kubla Khan' is a fascinating and exasperating poem. Almost
everyone has read it, almost everyone has been charmed by its
magic, almost everyone thinks he knows what it is about − and
almost everyone, it seems, has felt impelled to write about it. It
must surely be true that no poem of comparable length in English
or any other language has been the subject of so much critical
commentary. Its fifty-four lines have spawned thousands of pages
of discussion and analysis. 'Kubla Khan' is the sole or a major
subject in five book-length studies;[1] close to 150 articles and book-
chapters (doubtless I have missed some others) have been devoted
exclusively to it; and brief notes and incidental comments on it are
without number. Despite this deluge, however, there is no critical
unanimity and very little agreement on a number of important
issues connected with the poem: its date of composition, its 'meaning', its sources in Coleridge's reading and observation of nature,
its structural integrity (i.e. fragment *versus* complete poem), and
its relationship to the Preface by which Coleridge introduced it on
its first publication in 1816.

In a moment of rash optimism a notable scholar once began an
essay by declaring that 'We now know almost everything about
Coleridge's "Kubla Khan" except what the poem is about.'[2] The
truth of the matter, however, is that we know almost nothing conclusive about 'Kubla Khan', including what it is about. This flower
plucked in Paradise (or on Parnassus) and handed down to us by
Coleridge is, indeed, a miracle of rare device; but like all miracles
it is largely elusive.

Perhaps the strangest fact connected with this strange poem is the dearth of early references to it. Coleridge mentions 'Kubla Khan' on only three occasions: (1) in the endnote of the Crewe Manuscript (1810?) he gives a brief account of the poem's origin; (2) in the long Preface added to the poem in 1816 he provides a much fuller story of the composition of 'Kubla Khan', but the account in the 1816 Preface differs significantly from that in the Crewe endnote; and (3) in September 1830 he told Henry Nelson Coleridge that 'I wrote *Kubla Khan* in Brimstone Farm between Porlock and Ilfracombe – near Culbone.'[3] The rest is silence. Neither in his published works nor in his voluminous correspondence and notebooks (where he often quotes from his own poetry to illustrate some point) is there any reference to or quotation from 'Kubla Khan'. This frustrating silence, moreover, extends from Coleridge himself to his friends and acquaintances. Prior to its publication in 1816, there are (to my knowledge) only six references to 'Kubla Khan'[4] – and this is surely surprising when we remember that the poem was written at least sixteen years before it was eventually published.

Scholarship and historical criticism, then, have little evidence (solid or otherwise) on which to deploy their talents. Aye! and what then?

COMPOSITION, PUBLICATION HISTORY AND THE CREWE MANUSCRIPT

The date of 'Kubla Khan' has been much debated and, barring the unlikely discovery of definitive evidence, will doubtless always be a matter of conjecture. A number of dates – ranging from the summer of 1797 to the spring of 1800 – have been proposed. Coleridge himself stated on one occasion that he wrote the poem 'in the fall of the year, 1797' (Crewe MS) and on another that it was composed 'In the summer of the year 1797' (1816 Preface). Authorial statements of this sort are usually conclusive; however, the discrepancy (however slight) between 'summer' and 'fall' 1797, coupled with Coleridge's unreliability over dates and with some other factors, has led certain scholars to propose a later date. Nevertheless, while dating arguments for 1798 and 1799–1800 must be taken seriously, most Coleridge scholars in recent years have come to accept the fall of 1797 as the probable date of composition.

Before looking in detail at the various dating-arguments, we need to pause briefly over two early pieces of evidence that have an important bearing on the question of when 'Kubla Khan' was composed. The first of these is straightforward. In a poem entitled 'Mrs Robinson to the Poet Coleridge', Mary 'Perdita' Robinson praised Coleridge's genius in the following couplet:

> I'll mark thy "sunny dome," and view
> Thy "caves of ice," thy fields of dew![5]

These lines were written in October 1800; and, as the two phrases in quotation marks make plain, Mrs Robinson was alluding to 'Kubla Khan'. We can say with certainty, then, that 'Kubla Khan' was in existence by October 1800 and that 'Perdita' Robinson had seen it by then.

The second piece of evidence is earlier, but its significance is not so easily determined. At the end of her Hamburgh Journal (1798) Dorothy Wordsworth inserts a tantalising reference:

> [William] brought me his pockets full of apples . . . and some excellent bread. Upon these I breakfasted and carried *Kubla* to a fountain in the neighbouring market-place, where I drank some excellent water. It was on Saturday the 6th of October [1798] when we arrived at Goslar at between 5 and 6 in the evening.[6]

The most plausible explanation of this enigmatic allusion is that the Wordsworths in Germany had playfully named their drinking-*can* 'Kubla' in honour of Coleridge's poem.[7] If this is so, then it argues strongly that 'Kubla Khan' was written sometime before the Wordsworths and Coleridge set off for Germany in September 1798 – *unless* (as Elisabeth Schneider argues) Dorothy wrote up this section of her Hamburgh Journal between 1799 and 1802 after returning to England, in which case the reference to '*Kubla*' might involve a retrospective nicknaming of their German drinking-can.[8] On balance, however, although Dorothy's Journal entry is vague, it offers a serious obstacle to a post-1798 dating of 'Kubla Khan' and provides (to speak positively) strong circumstantial evidence that the poem was written before September 1798. And at this point we may turn to examine the various dating-arguments.

One suggestion, proposed initially by E. H. Coleridge and J. D. Campbell, places the composition of the poem in May–June 1798. The argument for this date was prompted by Coleridge's Notebook entry of 3 November 1810:

> If ever there was a time and circumstance in my life in which I behaved *perfectly* well, it was in that of C. Lloyd's mad quarrel & frantic ingratitude to me − He even wrote a letter to D[orothy] W[ordsworth], in which he not only called me a villain, but appealed to a conversation which had passed between him & *her*, as the grounds of it. . . . After this there succeeded on his side a series of wicked calumnies & irritations − infamous Lies to Southey & to poor dear Lamb − in short, a conduct which was not that of a friend, only because it was that of a madman / On my side, patience, gentleness, and good for evil − yet this supernatural effort injured me − what I did not suffer to act on my mind, preyed on my body − it prevented my finishing the Christabel − & at the retirement between Linton & Porlock was the first occasion of my having recourse to Opium. . . . (*CN*, III no. 4006)

In the 1816 Preface to 'Kubla Khan' Coleridge had written: 'In the summer of the year 1797, the Author, then in ill health, had retired to a lonely farm-house between Porlock and Linton, on the Exmoor confines of Somerset and Devonshire.' Taken together, these two statements led E. H. Coleridge to believe that 'Kubla Khan' was written during this retirement prompted by the mental and physical strain of the quarrel with Charles Lloyd and that, since the 'quarrel was at its height in May 1798', Coleridge 'should have written "the summer of 1798"' in the 1816 Preface (*CPW*, I 295). J. D. Campbell accepted this argument and extended it:

> Coleridge is generally unreliable in the matter of dates assigned to particular single events, but I think we may trust him when he synchronises. Besides, it seems far more probable that *Kubla Khan* was composed after *Christabel* (I.) and *The Ancient Mariner*, than that it was the first breathing on his magic flute.[9]

A 1798 dating for *Kubla Khan* is supported by Malcolm Elwin,[10] and also by Lawrence Hanson, who explores four possible periods in March–June 1798 when the 'retirement' might have taken place.[11]

Although a date in 1798 — specifically, May 1798 — is certainly possible, there are a number of difficulties with the arguments in its favour. First, while Coleridge connects opium with a 'retirement between Linton & Porlock' in his note of 3 November 1810, he says nothing about composing a poem then; he mentions the abandonment of 'Christabel' but not the composition of 'Kubla Khan' (or of anything else). Besides, the note is inaccurate in at least one respect, since May 1798 is demonstrably *not* 'the first occasion of [Coleridge's] having recourse to Opium'. One such lapse of memory might well lead one to suppose that there are others. Second, there is some doubt that Coleridge had sufficient opportunity in April or May 1798 for even a brief 'retirement' at Porlock. Both E. K. Chambers and Elisabeth Schneider, who have studied Coleridge's movements carefully during these months, conclude that he was probably at or close to Nether Stowey during this time.[12] Third, as Schneider points out, since the quarrel with Charles Lloyd was a matter which preyed on Coleridge for some years, 'E. H. Coleridge appears to have telescoped into a month or two events that had actually been spread over several years.'[13] And, finally, one must surely distrust the logic of arguing (as both J. D. Campbell and Lawrence Hanson do) that 'the perfection of the poem ['Kubla Khan'], and particularly . . . its metrical beauty, would suggest that it was the last and not the first of the three great poems'.[14] By analogy, we should find ourselves having to argue that Shakespeare must have written *Timon of Athens* before *King Lear* or that Coleridge must have composed 'The Nightingale' before 'Frost at Midnight' because the latter are more perfect and beautiful works.

Another solution to the dating-riddle is proposed by Elisabeth Schneider, who devotes a ninety-page chapter to the problem in her book *Coleridge, Opium and 'Kubla Khan'*. She offers two possible dates — October 1799 or May–June 1800 — and concludes that 'The date of October, 1799, seems to me slightly more likely than that of the following May or June, but either would appear possible.'[15] Why 1799 or 1800? The argument is too elaborate to permit any easy summary; however, it may be said that, in broad outline, it involves five major observations. (1) The major influence on 'Kubla Khan' is Milton, especially *Paradise Lost*, and 'I know of no other such Miltonic months in Coleridge's life as those running, roughly, from August, 1799, to the spring of 1800.'[16] (2) There are in 'Kubla Khan' numerous echoes of and tonal parallels with two other poems, Landor's *Gebir* and Southey's *Thalaba*, which Coleridge read in 1799–1800. (3) The imagery of 'Kubla Khan' seems to have been influenced by the scenery which Coleridge saw in Germany (especially in the Harz Mountains) in late 1798 and in 1799 – and these impressions were reinforced by the rugged scenery of the West and North of England which he explored with Southey and Wordsworth in August–November 1799 after returning from Germany. (4) Having explored the connections between 'Kubla Khan' and Southey's *Thalaba*, Miss Schneider quotes at length a letter of December 1799 (*LW: EY*, pp. 279–80) from Wordsworth to Coleridge, which recalls some of the imagery of Coleridge's poem, and concludes that between May and December 1799 'there was a concentration of interest among Wordsworth, Coleridge, and Southey upon many of the images, ideas, and words that we find in "Kubla Khan"'.[17] (5) Internal poetic evidence also supports a 1799–1800 date:

> No verse . . . distinctly resembling that of the 'dream'-fragment appears among the poems known to have been written in 1797 or 1798. In 1799 and 1800, the 'Ode to Georgiana' and the several others of a like sort were a conscious departure from Coleridge's recent metrical forms, and 'Kubla Khan' most closely resembles these.[18]

Miss Schneider's arguments have not met with much success among other scholars.[19] This is due, in part, to the awkward necessity of having to explain away a damaging piece of (apparently) solid evidence for a pre-1799 dating – namely, the reference to 'Kubla' in Dorothy Wordsworth's Hamburgh Journal for October 1798. As Miss Schneider herself says, 'Uncertainty must remain about any date after 1798 because of Dorothy Wordsworth's word "Kubla".'[20] In part, too, there is the problem of the strained and inferential nature of the case. For example, Coleridge knew Milton's poetry *well* long before 1799 and Milton is arguably the most important poetic influence on Coleridge from the beginning of his career. Similarly, the impact of German scenery and the scattered echoes of Landor and Southey can be easily paralleled, usually much more persuasively, in the Somerset scenery and the literary works in which Coleridge was immersed while living at Nether Stowey in 1797–8. Finally, the appeal to internal poetic evidence is a double-edged sword: there is nothing in Coleridge's 1799—1800 verse that comes as close in imagery and tone to the spirit of 'Kubla Khan' as the 'o'erwooded, narrow, deep' and 'roaring dell' of 'This Lime-Tree Bower' (July 1797) or certain wild and 'romantic' passages in his drama *Osorio* (March—October 1797).

The third, and most widely accepted, date for 'Kubla Khan' is October or November 1797. Until the discovery of the Crewe Manuscript in 1934, the only evidence from Coleridge himself about the poem's composition was to be found in the 1816 Preface, where the date given is 'the summer of the year 1797'. But that date has never seemed reasonable because Coleridge was too busy and his movements in July—August 1797 are too well documented to make a 'retirement' near Porlock possible in the summer of that year. In the Crewe Manuscript endnote, however, Coleridge says of 'Kubla Khan',

> This fragment with a good deal more, not recoverable, composed in a sort of Reverie brought on by two grains of Opium, taken to check a dysentery, at a Farm House between Porlock and Linton, a quarter of a mile from Culbone Church, in the fall of the year, 1797.

I shall return later to the Crewe Manuscript and the discrepancies between its account of the poem and that given in the 1816 Preface; for the moment it is enough to notice that the date given for the composition of 'Kubla Khan' in the Crewe endnote is, not the summer, but 'the fall of the year, 1797'. On the basis of this change of season Alice Snyder, who first reported the discovery of the Crewe Manuscript, suggested that the dating question — which had been resolved in favour of May 1798 — should be reopened with this new evidence in mind.[21]

The question was reopened. E. K. Chambers, who had been a vigorous supporter of a May 1798 date, undertook to re-examine the evidence in his biography (1938) of Coleridge. His conclusion was that 'Kubla Khan' was, in all probability, composed in the fall of 1797 — and he thought it possible to date it even more precisely. On 14 October 1797 Coleridge had written a letter to John Thelwall, in which he excused his delay in replying to Thelwall by saying that he had 'been absent a day or two' from Stowey; and in this same letter he went on to say: 'My mind feels as if it ached to behold & know something *great* — something *one & indivisible* — and it is only in the faith of this that rocks or waterfalls, mountains or caverns give me the sense of sublimity or majesty!' (*CL*, I 349). Coleridge's absence from Stowey, coupled with the reference to 'rocks or waterfalls, mountains or caverns' (which recalls the imagery of 'Kubla Khan'), led Chambers to believe that the poem was written in October 1797, a few days before the letter to Thelwall.[22] A number of later scholars have been led to the same conclusion.[23]

But even more attractive than Chambers's October 1797 dating is the possibility that 'Kubla Khan' was written in the following month, November 1797, while Coleridge was on a walking-tour with the Wordsworths — a tour which took the trio to Porlock and then on (as Dorothy records[24]) to Lynmouth and the Valley of the Rocks (or Valley of Stones) near Lynton. Initially suggested (almost as an aside) by H. M. Margoliouth in 1953, the case for supposing 'Kubla Khan' to have been written on this walking-trip with the Wordsworths in early November 1797 has been argued convincingly by Mark Reed:

> it makes sense to suppose that STC should have retired to a farm 'between Porlock and Linton' on this trip, for he was certainly (which cannot be said of the early Oct date) in that neighbourhood. If his illness involved dysentery from the onset, an immediate retirement would have been necessary. Nothing whatever is known of STC's movements during his absence of 'a day or two' in early Oct, and it is hard to perceive why he would have traveled so far — well over twenty miles — merely to sequestrate himself for such a brief time if sickness was the cause of his leaving Stowey — least of all if his sickness was actually dysentery.[25]

This is a persuasive argument, and it agrees perfectly with Coleridge's own account in the Crewe endnote. John Beer, who has also been persuaded by Reed's case, offers a hypothetical reconstruction (adding a conjecture about the man from Porlock) of the 'retirement' during which 'Kubla Khan' was composed: 'while returning from the Valley [of the Rocks], Coleridge was taken ill and forced to retire to the lonely farmhouse, while William and Dorothy Wordsworth continued on their way back (on their way possibly, despatching the "person on business from Porlock" to bring supplies of some sort to Coleridge)'.[26] All in all, while other dates remain possible, a November 1797 dating of 'Kubla Khan' is the most attractive possibility and makes the best use of the scanty evidence.

As a kind of footnote to the dating-discussion, it may be added that there have been attempts to identify the very farmhouse to which Coleridge retired and wrote 'Kubla Khan'. There have been two suggestions. Wylie Sypher, noting that there are only ten houses in the whole parish of Culbone and that only three farmhouses have ever been built within a mile of Culbone Church, settled on Ash Farm, 'a squat, tidy cottage of gray stone' which still stands today.[27] Morchard Bishop, on the other hand, basing his argument on Coleridge's statement (1830) that 'I wrote *Kubla Khan* in Brimstone Farm between Porlock and Ilfracombe — near Culbone', identified the house as Broomstreet Farm, 'since there is no record . . . of any farm in the neighbourhood that goes by the name of Brimstone'.[28] Since Ash Farm is much closer to being 'a quarter of a mile from Culbone Church' (Crewe endnote) than is Broomstreet Farm, most scholars have preferred the former and have argued that 'Coleridge, if he did confuse the real name of the farm long after the event, could have turned *Ash* into *Brimstone* as easily [as] *Broomstreet* into *Brimstone*.'[29] However, J. H. Goodland (who agrees with Bishop) points out that 'the local dialect could account for a mishearing; "Broomstreet" is still pronounced "Brimson" in the locality' (*CN*, III no. 4006n). Once again, then, there is no consensus — nor does a definitive conclusion seem possible.

The history of 'Kubla Khan' from its composition to its publication in May 1816 is almost a complete enigma. Although Coleridge alludes briefly to the Tartar emperor Kublai Khan in two Notebook entries of 1802 and 1804 (*CN*, I nos 1281 and 1840), he never mentions 'Kubla Khan'; and the Notebook entries seem unrelated to the poem. A Notebook entry of October 1806 (*CN*, II no. 2882) concerned with Pindar may, Miss Coburn suggests, be linked with an attempt to continue 'Kubla Khan', but the poem is not mentioned and the connection between the two is a mere guess. Potentially more interesting is another Notebook entry, belonging to May–August 1811, which echoes the imagery of lines 25–7 of 'Kubla Khan': 'Channels riverless — 5 mile deep' (*CN*, III no. 4094); but, again, it is difficult to see how these cryptic phrases might be linked meaningfully with the poem. And these dark hints (if, indeed, they have any relevance at all) are all that Coleridge's Notebooks yield on the poem's history between the time of its composition and the time of its publication. Coleridge's letters (apart from one of March 1798 to which I shall return) are no more enlightening. It is not known where he kept the poem, or whether he revised it much between 1797 and 1816, or why he delayed so long in publishing it. It *is* known that he recited it occasionally: John Payne Collier records that in a conversation (c. 1811–12) Coleridge recited 'some lines he had written many years ago upon the building of a Dream-palace by Kubla-Khan'; and Leigh Hunt, probably in early April 1816, was almost present at another recital: 'He recited his *Kubla Khan* one morning to Lord Byron, in his lordship's house in Piccadilly, when I happened to be in another room. I remember the other's coming away from him, highly struck with his poem, and saying how wonderfully he talked.'[30]

It was this recital of 'Kubla Khan' just missed by Leigh Hunt that resulted, in fact, in the poem's publication. At Byron's insti-gation, the publisher John Murray visited Coleridge in April 1816 and offered to publish both the incomplete 'Christabel' and 'Kubla Khan'. In the final bargain Coleridge received £80 for the former and £20 for the latter. On 25 May 1816 Murray published an octavo pamphlet of sixty-four pages entitled *Christabel; Kubla Khan, a Vision; The Pains of Sleep*, which ran through three editions in the course of the year. In the Preface by which Coler-idge introduced 'Kubla Khan', he acknowledged his debt to Lord Byron: 'The following fragment', the Preface begins, 'is here published at the request of a poet of great and deserved celeb-rity. . . .'

The remainder of the 1816 Preface is given over to an explan-ation of how 'Kubla Khan' came to be written. It is a story that everyone now knows. The poet, in ill health, had retired to a lonely farmhouse; as the result of a 'slight indisposition', he had taken an 'anodyne' and fallen asleep while reading about Kubla Khan's palace in Purchas's *Pilgrimage*. Continuing 'for about three hours in a profound sleep', his dreaming mind (triggered by what he had been reading in Purchas) was swept up into a poetic vision of some 300 lines – a vision so powerful and immediate that 'all the images rose up before him as *things*'. Upon awaking he eagerly set about transcribing his dream-vision, when, unfortunately, he was 'called out by a person on business from Porlock, and detained by him above an hour'. Returning to his room, he discovered to his great dismay that, 'though he still retained some vague and dim recollection of the general purport of the vision, yet, with the exception of some eight or ten scattered lines and images, all the rest had passed away like the images on the surface of a stream into which a stone has been cast, but, alas! without the after restoration of the latter!' Nevertheless, 'from the still surviving recollections in his mind', he has often proposed to finish for himself 'what had been originally, as it were, given to him'. And he closed the account with a motto from Theocritus: 'Tomorrow I'll sing a sweeter song.'

For more than one hundred years this account of the poem's composition, together with the text of the poem published in 1816 (and subsequently reprinted in Coleridge's collected poems of 1828, 1829 and 1834), were all that scholars had of 'Kubla Khan'. No transcriptions of the poem (assuming there ever were any) had survived, and no manuscript of the poem was known to exist. But in 1934, in the Lamb and Coleridge Centenary Exhibition held in the National Portrait Gallery, there suddenly appeared an autograph manuscript of 'Kubla Khan', loaned to the exhibition by the Marquess of Crewe. The significance of the Crewe Manuscript is that it contains a number of variants, most but not all of them fairly minor, from the text of the poem as published in 1816; and, more important, it provides an alternative and much shorter account of the poem's birth − an account which differs in significant respects from that given in the 1816 Preface.

The Crewe Manuscript (Plates 8 and 9) is a holograph in Coleridge's handwriting on both sides of a single sheet. Attempts to date the manuscript have been unsuccessful, although it is universally believed that, while not the original version of the poem, it predates the text published in 1816, probably by some years. T. C. Skeat has managed, with some guesswork, to trace the history of the Crewe Manuscript:

The only possible clue to its origin is a faint pencilled note at the end of the manuscript: 'Sent by Mrs Southey,[31] as an Autograph of Coleridge.' From this we may conjecture that the manuscript was originally sent by Coleridge to Southey, passed into Mrs Southey's possession after the latter's death in 1843, and was subsequently given by her to some private autograph collector. It subsequently appeared in the sale-room of Messrs Puttick & Simpson on 28 April 1859, when, as lot 109, it was knocked down to Monckton Milnes, owner of a noted collection of autographs, for the modest sum of £1. 15s. From him it descended to his son, afterwards Marquess of Crewe, so the history of the manuscript from 1859 onwards is established.[32]

It need only be added that in 1962 the manuscript was acquired from the Marchioness of Crewe by the British Museum, where it now resides as Additional MS 50847.

Since the Crewe Manuscript is an earlier text than the version of 'Kubla Khan' published in 1816, the variants give us a glimpse, as it were, into the poet's workshop. Sometimes a variant shows how a passable line is improved by slight revision, as, for example, in line 17 when 'From forth this Chasm with hideous Turmoil seething' (Crewe MS) is changed to 'And from this chasm, with ceaseless turmoil seething' (1816 text). Sometimes, however, seemingly minor alterations are more important and revealing. There are two such instances. First, lines 6–7 in the two versions are as follows:

> So twice six miles of fertile ground
> With Walls and Towers were compass'd round.
> (Crewe MS)

> So twice five miles of fertile ground
> With walls and towers were girdled round.
> (1816 text)

The changes from 'six' to 'five' and from 'compass'd' to 'girdled' show how Coleridge gradually refined on what he found in *Purchas his Pilgrimage*, where he read that Kubla built his palace by '*encompassing sixteene* miles of plaine ground with a wall' (emphasis added). Many suggestions, including a number of Freudian ones, have been made to account for these changes. The second important alteration occurs in line 41, where the Abyssinian maid is 'Singing of Mount Abora' (1816 text). John Livingston Lowes had sifted through countless volumes looking for Mount Abora and had come up empty-handed. The reason for his failure to locate it became apparent when the Crewe Manuscript came to light, for Coleridge had there written 'Mount Amora' and then changed that (with a stroke of the pen) to 'Mount Amara'. Now, whatever may be said of 'Mount Amora' (a slip of the pen? a Freudian slip?), 'Mount Amara' leads us straight to Coleridge's source in Milton's *Paradise Lost*: 'Nor where *Abassin* Kings thir issue Guard, / Mount *Amara*, though this by some suppos'd / True Paradise . . .' (IV 280–2). Why Coleridge subsequently changed 'Amara' to 'Abora' in the 1816 text has been a matter of heated scholarly debate and need not detain us here; all we need notice for the moment is that Crewe Manuscript variants lead directly to the two major influences on 'Kubla Khan', namely, *Purchas his Pilgrimage* and Milton's *Paradise Lost*. All of the other variants in 'Kubla Khan' are minor and have been listed and described by a number of scholars.[33]

The issue of the 1816 Preface is, however, another matter. In the Crewe Manuscript there is no preface; there is only a brief endnote (quoted above, p. 67) in which Coleridge describes, tersely and succinctly, how 'Kubla Khan' came to be written. At times, the account of the poem's composition in the Crewe endnote throws useful light on the 1816 Preface and makes precise things which are there left vague: thus, the 'slight indisposition' and the unnamed 'anodyne' of the 1816 Preface are identified specifically in the Crewe endnote as 'dysentery' and 'two grains of Opium'. At times, the two accounts flatly disagree, as we have already seen on the question of when the poem was written: 'in the fall of the year, 1797' (Crewe MS) *or* 'In the summer of the year 1797' (1816 Preface). Scholarship has shown that the information in the Crewe endnote is reliable and that, where the two accounts overlap (as on the question of the date of the poem's composition), the Crewe version is to be preferred. But the Crewe endnote is short and omits much that is included – indeed, much that is most memorable – in the 1816 Preface. How much of the elaborate account in the 1816 Preface should we believe? Is it substantially true? or an embellishment of the truth? Or is it, as has often been suggested, a fabrication and a Coleridgean excuse for another incompleted work, which we should dismiss out-of-hand? The reliability and general worth of the 1816 Preface to 'Kubla Khan' has been, since the discovery of the Crewe Manuscript, perhaps the most hotly debated issue in Coleridge studies – and for this reason I have set aside a later section of this chapter to discuss the matter.

OPIUM AND THE 'DREAM' OF 'KUBLA KHAN'

Coleridge's use of opium has long been a topic of fascination, and the grouping of Coleridge, opium and 'Kubla Khan' formed an

inevitable triad long before Elisabeth Schneider combined them in
the title of her book. It is tempting on a subject of such instrinsic
interest to say more than is necessary for the purpose in hand, and
I shall do my best to resist temptation by exploring only four of the
most obvious and essential aspects of it: (1) the contemporary view
of opium in the late eighteenth century; (2) the extent of Coleridge's use and reliance on opiates in the late 1790s; (3) myths and
medical evidence about the relationship between opium and the
poetic imagination; and (4) 'Kubla Khan' as an 'opium dream'.

The most striking features about opium in the eighteenth and
early nineteenth centuries are the contradictory facts that, while it
was widely used and easily available, almost nothing was known
about it. Medical knowledge of the drug's properties was scanty
and unreliable: few people realised, for example, that opium was
addictive, and no one understood that withdrawal symptoms were
the result of discontinuation or diminished dosages. Indeed, everything that was known about it seemed positive and beneficial.
Laudanum (i.e. the simple alcoholic tincture of opium) was freely
dispensed to relieve pain in cases as different as toothache and
cholera; similarly, opium was used as a 'cure' for a host of emotional and psychological disorders; and, in such seemingly innocent patent-medicines as Godfrey's Cordial, it served as a
soothing syrup to quieten restless babies, often permanently. In
Coleridge's day, as Alethea Hayter has pointed out, 'most doctors
and patients still thought of opium not as a dangerous addictive
drug but mainly as a useful analgesic and tranquillizer of which
every household should have a supply, for minor ailments and
nervous crises of all kinds, much as aspirin is used today'.[34]

Since the medicinal use of opium was so common and widespread, it is not surprising to learn that its use involved neither
legal penalties nor public stigma. All of the Romantic poets
(except Wordsworth) are known to have used it, as did many other
prominent contemporaries. Supplies were readily available: in
1830, for instance, Britain imported 22,000 pounds of raw opium.
Many Englishmen, like the eminently respectable poet–parson
George Crabbe, who took opium in regular but moderate quantity
for nearly forty years, were addicts in ignorance, and led stable
and productive lives despite their habit. By and large, opium was
taken for granted; and it was only the terrible experiences of such
articulate addicts as Coleridge and DeQuincey that eventually
began to bring the horrors of the drug to public attention.

Coleridge's case is a particularly sad and instructive one. He had used opium as early as 1791 (see *CL*, I 18) and continued to use it occasionally, on medical advice, to alleviate pain from a series of physical and nervous ailments. 'I am seriously ill', he wrote to Joseph Cottle in November 1796; 'The complaint, my medical attendant says, is nervous — and originating in *mental* causes. I have a Blister under my right-ear — & I take Laudanum every four hours, 25 drops each dose' (*CL*, I 248–9). The evidence of Coleridge's letters argues that during the period 1791–1800 he used opium only occasionally and almost always for medical reasons. The turning-point, as E. L. Griggs has shown,[35] may be traced to the winter and spring of Coleridge's first year at Greta Hall, Keswick, in 1800–1. During this period a prolonged and debilitating succession of illnesses, which Coleridge blamed on the raw, wet climate of the Lake District, caused him to use regular and increasingly larger doses of laudanum in an effort to assuage the torments of what he described as an 'irregular Gout combined with frequent nephritic attacks'. But the opium cure proved ultimately to be more devastating in its effects than the troubles it was intended to treat, for such large quantities taken over so many months seduced him unwittingly into slavery to the drug. And his life between 1801 and 1806 (when he returned from Malta) is a sombre illustration of a growing and, finally, a hopeless bondage to opium.

By the time he realised he was addicted, however, it was too late. He consulted a variety of physicians; he attempted more than once (with nearly fatal results) to break off his use of opium all at once; and, at last, in 1816, when he submitted his case to James Gillman (in whose house he was to spend the rest of his life), he was able to control his habit and reduce his doses, although he was never able to emancipate himself entirely. Contemporary medical science, it must be remembered, concerned itself largely with opium as a panacea and was almost powerless (owing to ignorance) to provide meaningful assistance to those who became victims of its prescriptions. In this light, Coleridge's struggle with his addiction must be seen as heroic and experimental; and it should be added that his experience of addiction led not only (as is sometimes asserted) to sloth and self-pity, but more characteristically to a dearly purchased and altruistic desire to keep others out of the black pit into which he had fallen. 'If I entirely recover', he wrote to T. G. Street in 1808,

I shall deem it a sacred Duty to publish my Case, tho' without
my name — for the practice of taking Opium is dreadfully
spread. — Throughout Lancashire & Yorkshire it is the common Dram of the lower orders of People — in the small Town of
Thorpe the Druggist informed me, that he commonly sold on
market days two or three Pound of Opium, & a Gallon of
Laudanum — all among the labouring Classes. Surely, this
demands legislative Interference. . . .   (*CL*, III 125−6)

But to return to the 1790s: what can we say about Coleridge's
experience of opium at the time of composing 'Kubla Khan'?
Despite some dissent,[36] the majority of recent scholars agree with
E. L. Griggs that, until 1800−1, Coleridge was an occasional user
of opium (usually for medicinable purposes, but sometimes for the
pleasurable sensations which the drug induced) and that he was
not, in any proper sense of the term, an opium-addict before this
time. It is not surprising to find, then, that in the late 1790s Coleridge's opium experiences were essentially pleasurable; it was only
in later years, when his slavery was firmly rooted, that the evil of
opium manifested itself in the corrosive nightmares described in
'The Pains of Sleep' (1803) and when the sunny pleasure-domes of
early addiction darkened into gloomy and constricting vaults like
those depicted by Piranesi in his *Carceri d'Invenzione* (Plate 15).[37]
The effects produced by opium in the early stages were soothing
and seductive: 'Laudanum', he wrote his brother George in March
1798 (in terms which recall the imagery of 'Kubla Khan'), 'gave me
repose, not sleep: but YOU, I believe, know how divine that repose
is — what a spot of inchantment, a green spot of fountains, &
flowers & trees, in the very heart of a waste of Sands!' (*CL*, I 394).[38]
Opium, it seems (to cite an earlier letter, of October 1797, which
may well be describing a drug experience), tended to 'raise & spiri-
tualize' his intellect, so that he could, like the Indian Vishnu, 'float
about along an infinite ocean cradled in the flower of the Lotos'
(*CL*, I 350). Such an experience and such a mood are reflected in
'Kubla Khan'.

As we know from the Crewe endnote, Coleridge took 'two grains
of Opium' before he wrote 'Kubla Khan'; and this fact naturally
raises the issue of the drug's effect on the poet's creative imagination. Early critics, guided by Coleridge's statements in the 1816
Preface, assumed that there was a direct and immediate corre-
lation between opium and imagination. In 1897 J. M. Robertson

could not bring himself to doubt that 'the special quality of this felicitous work ['Kubla Khan'] is to be attributed to its being all conceived and composed under the influence of opium'; and in 1934 M. H. Abrams declared that the 'great gift of opium' to men like Coleridge and DeQuincey 'was access to a new world as different from this as Mars may be; and one which ordinary mortals, hindered by terrestrial conceptions, can never, from mere description, quite comprehend'.[39] More recent criticism, however, grounded on modern medical studies, controverts such conclusions decisively. According to Elisabeth Schneider, 'it is widely agreed now that persons of unstable psychological makeup are much more likely to become addicted to opiates than are normal ones' and that, among such neurotic users of opium, 'the intensity of the pleasure' produced by the drug seems (on the evidence of medical case-studies) 'to be in direct proportion to the degree of instability'. The explanation (she continues) of the supposed creative powers of opium lies in the euphoria that it produces:

> The relaxation of tension and conflict, accompanied by a sense of pleasant ease, occasionally helps to release for a time the neurotic person's natural powers of thought or imagination or (rarely) of action, though it does not give him powers that he did not have or change the character of his normal powers. . . . With some unstable temperaments the euphoria may be intense. Its effect is usually to increase the person's satisfaction with his inner state of well-being, to turn his attention inward upon himself while diminishing his attention to external stimuli. Thus it sometimes encourages the mood in which daydreaming occurs. The narcosis of opium has been popularly described as having the effect of heightening and intensifying the acuteness of the senses. This it quite definitely does not do. If anything, the effect is the reverse.[40]

Alethea Hayter, although she wishes to avoid the 'extremes' of the positions of Abrams and Schneider, nevertheless comes much closer in her conclusions to the latter than to the former. Opium, she argues, can only work 'On what is already there in a man's mind and memory', and, 'if he already has a creative imagination and a tendency to rêverie, dreams and hypnagogic visions', then opium may intensify and focus his perceptions. Her final verdict − which 'can be no more than a hypothesis' − is that 'the action of opium, though it can never be a substitute for innate imagination, can uncover that imagination while it is at work in a way which might enable an exceptionally gifted and self-aware writer to observe and learn from his own mental processes'.[41] The most reasonable conclusion to be drawn from these various explorations of the relationship between opium and the operation of the creative imagination is that, while 'Kubla Khan' might well not have been produced without opium, it most assuredly would never have been born except for the powerfully and innately imaginative mind of Samuel Taylor Coleridge.

And, that established, we come to a more difficult problem: the 'dream' of 'Kubla Khan'. The poem, according to Coleridge's account in his 1816 Preface, resulted from a vision in which the poet 'continued for about three hours in a profound sleep, at least of the external senses', during which time the images of the poem 'rose up before him as *things*, with a parallel production of the correspondent expressions'. On the strength of this statement generations of readers accepted without question that 'Kubla Khan' is, in Lawrence Hanson's words, 'the supreme example in English literature of the workings of the creative subconscious, unhelped − or unhindered − by conscious composition'.[42] The most vigorous exponent of this view is John Livingston Lowes in *The Road to Xanadu*:

> The dream, it is evident, was the unchecked subliminal flow of blending images, and the dreamer merely the detached and unsolicitous spectator. And so the sole factor that determined the form and sequence which the dissolving phantasmagoria assumed, was the subtle potency of the associative links. There was this time [in contrast to 'The Ancient Mariner'] no inter-vention of a waking intelligence intent upon a plan, to obliterate or blur them.

'Nobody in his waking senses', Lowes exclaims of the last section of 'Kubla Khan', 'could have fabricated those amazing eighteen lines.'[43] Many critics − even quite recent ones − would agree. F. W. Bateson, for example, asserts that in 'Kubla Khan' 'the process of creative composition [is] almost wholly unconscious or subconscious' − and he hastens to support the contention by quot-ing Wordsworth's comment of 19 December 1830 that 'Kubla Khan' 'was actually composed in a dream, certainly Coleridge believes so'.[44]

Not everyone, however, would agree. Scepticism concerning the poem's dream composition began as early as 1818: 'It is extremely probable', said Thomas Love Peacock with witty understatement, 'that Mr Coleridge, being a very visionary gentleman, has somewhat deceived himself respecting the origin of "Kubla Khan"; and . . . the story of its having been composed in his sleep must necessarily, by all who are acquainted with his manner of narrating matter of fact, be received with a certain degree of scepticism.'[45] Elisabeth Schneider is much less oblique: she argues that the weight of medical and psychological evidence 'is against the notion of "Kubla Khan" as any kind of special "opium dream"', and she concludes bluntly that, while the 'poem is no doubt "inspired", . . . the breath that entered it is of neither sleep nor opium'.[46] And George Watson, 'taking heart from the medical evidence', is quick to concur: 'we may surely dismiss one troublesome possibility at once: "Kubla Khan" is not a dream-poem'.[47]

Nevertheless, despite the apparently clear-cut alternatives of Lowes and Hanson *versus* Schneider and Watson − alternatives, it seems, which insist *either* on faith in the mysterious ways of the creative imagination (with or without help from opium) *or* on solid empirical and medical evidence − the case of the 'dream' of 'Kubla Khan' is not so easily to be resolved. To begin with, Coleridge's own accounts are contradictory: in the 1816 Preface he declares the poem to have originated during 'a profound sleep', but in the Crewe endnote it is said to have been 'composed in a sort of Reverie'. Now, a *rêverie* of any sort is not the same as a *profound sleep*, as many critics have pointed out; and we must surely distinguish between daydreaming (if that is what 'a sort of Reverie' means) where some measure of conscious control and direction is implied, and dreams occurring in sleep where the conscious mind is in abeyance. In general, as we have seen on the question of dating 'Kubla Khan', the Crewe endnote is more reliable than the 1816 Preface; and, if that is true also in the present case, then the poem is hardly the record of 'A Vision in a Dream' (as Coleridge's subtitle claims) in which the words and images rose up, unhindered and unbidden, as *things*. In short, if we accept the Crewe endnote's state of 'Reverie' as the mood in which the poem was written, then we must reject the notion that 'Kubla Khan' is an instance of 'automatic' or unconscious composition. Moreover, as Norman Fruman and others have pointed out, the variants between the Crewe and 1816 texts of the poem prove beyond question that Coleridge was 'romancing' when he said that 'the words here preserved' [1816 Preface] were the words he had written in the farmhouse. . . . It was also untrue to say that 'Kubla Khan', at least as he published it, had been composed 'without any sensation or consciousness of effort', since many changes were made *after* he wrote the document now known as the Crewe MS. And may not this text be a re-worked draft of perhaps many early attempts?[48]

Most readers are reluctant to accept Coleridge's account of the miraculous conception of 'Kubla Khan' provided in the 1816 Preface; yet, most accept, too, that the poem did originate in a dream or, more probably, a daydream[49] — and that 'Kubla Khan' is an inspired but consciously wrought artifact reproducing (at least in part) an actual semi-conscious experience in which day-dreaming, Coleridge's reading, and opium all had a part to play. 'What we may feel inclined to accept', according to Molly Lefe-bure, 'is that certain glimpses, or snatches, of "Kubla Khan" possibly derive from that dream . . . and [that the remembered fragments of that dream], at some unspecified date, he welded together, using all his incredible skill to produce a magical song, a miracle of vision-like verse'.[50] The most sophisticated and (I think) the most satisfying explanation of the 'dream' composition of 'Kubla Khan' is provided by John Beer in *Coleridge the Visionary*. There is substantial evidence, as Beer points out, to support the 'idea that very intricate mental processes can take place in states of imperfect consciousness', and hence to support Coleridge's claim in the Crewe endnote that 'Kubla Khan' was 'composed in a sort of Reverie'. After citing instances of similar phenomena recorded in modern psychological studies, Beer explores a parallel case in Coleridge's own writings — namely, his attempt in *The Friend* (no. 8, 5 Oct 1809) to offer a psychological explanation of Luther's celebrated vision of the Devil. Baffled in his attempts to under-stand a passage in the Hebrew Bible, and unhelped by either the Vulgate or Septuagint translations, Luther,

ceasing to *think*, yet continuing his brain on the stretch, in solicitation of a Thought, . . . sinks, without perceiving it, into a Trance of Slumber: during which his brain retains its' waking energies, excepting that what would have been mere *Thoughts* before, now . . . shape and condense themselves into *Things*, into Realities! Repeatedly half-wakening, and his eyelids as often re-closing, the objects which really surround him form the place and scenery of his Dream. All at once he sees the Arch-fiend coming forth on the Wall of the Room . . . [and] he *imagines* that he hurls [his ink-stand] at the Intruder, or not improbably in the first instant of awakening, while yet both his imagination and his eyes are possessed by the Dream, he *actually* hurls it! Some weeks after . . . he discovers the dark spot on his Wall, and receives it as a sign and pledge vouchsafed to him of the Event having actually taken place.   (*CC*, II ii 120)

As Beer shows, the circumstances in which Coleridge places Luther correspond in significant ways with Coleridge's own situation and state of mind at the time of composing 'Kubla Khan'. And such evidence, he concludes, tends to confirm Coleridge's statements about the poem's dream composition and to suggest that 'Kubla Khan' may well be the concrete resolution of 'a series of images which had been up till then the subject of intense thought on Coleridge's part': 'If so, it might be possible to trace a coherent and logical shape there, instead of merely the "unchecked subliminal flow of images" which Lowes found.'[51]

THE 1816 PREFACE AND 'KUBLA KHAN' AS A 'FRAGMENT'

> . . . *for any understanding knoweth the skill of each artificer standeth in that IDEA or fore-conceit of the work, and not in the work itself.*
> (Sir Philip Sidney, *Apologie for Poetrie*, 1595)

The Preface by which Coleridge introduced 'Kubla Khan' to the public in 1816 is a vexing document, and no aspect of it has proved to be more nettlesome than its reiterated insistence that 'Kubla Khan' is but a fragment of a much longer poem. While the 1816 Preface raises a number of important critical issues, there are two matters that require special attention: (1) the general worth and reliability of the Preface, and (2) the question of whether or not 'Kubla Khan' is a fragment.

Since the discovery of the Crewe Manuscript, the issue of the reliability of the 1816 Preface has been much debated. One school of thought maintains that it is untrustworthy and should be dismissed as a fabrication intended only to apologise for the publication of a fragment. 'As a whole', argues Elisabeth Schneider, 'the preface of 1816 sounds a good deal like the self-justifying memory of Coleridge on other occasions' — and, in this particular case, 'a marvellous origin and the man from Porlock could bear the blame and serve as a natural shield against criticism, while Lord Byron's admiration and the description of the fragment as a "psychological curiosity" might justify its publication'.[52] Warren Ober tartly dismisses it as 'a Coleridgean hoax, albeit a harmless one',[53] and Norman Fruman points out that the prefatory 'claim made for "Kubla Khan" was but one of a long series made by Coleridge concerning spontaneous composition'.[54] Walter Jackson Bate, more generously, sees Coleridge as trying to excuse the tardy publication of a difficult poem by escorting it, 'as he was to escort so much by [1816], with a cloud of apology'.[55] With the exception of Bate, it may be noted, all the critics who read the Preface as an elaborate fiction also assume that 'Kubla Khan' is not a finished piece but a fragment of a longer work. The relationship between the poem and its preface, on this view, is succinctly stated by Edward Bostetter:

> Why then did he write so extravagant a preface for *Kubla Khan?*
> . . . It is one of his apologies for uncompleted work: an attempt to forestall harsh criticism or ridicule by emphasizing that the poem is being published 'rather as a psychological curiosity than on the grounds of any supposed poetic merits'. . . . Opium is presented as a benign anodyne, responsible for the dream; and the man from Porlock rather than sloth or procrastination interrupts the composition.[56]

A second group of critics, instead of dismissing the 1816 Preface as a hoax or an instance of Coleridge's 'self-justifying memory', prefers to regard it as a prose parallel or analogue of 'Kubla Khan' itself — on the theory that 'to ignore the Preface may be to ignore Coleridge's abilities as a literary critic'.[57] The critics of this group all agree that 'Kubla Khan' is a poem about poetry and the poetic process, and they maintain that the Preface (whether or not its *facts* are actually true) confronts the same issues. Bernard Breyer interprets 'Kubla Khan' as 'a kind of allegory of the poem, an essay

on the *product* of the creative imagination' and argues that,
similarly, the Preface of 1816 should be seen as 'an allegory of the
creative *process* and the perennial difficulties that beset it: the
place of retirement between two towns, the ecstasy, the vision, the
attempt to reproduce the vision, the interruption from the outside
world, the dissipation of the dream'.[58] Indeed, many recent critics
have adopted the view that the 1816 Preface must be seen as the
prose counterpart of the poem it introduces.[59] The most vigorous
and convincing exponent of this approach is Irene Chayes, who
attempts to show that, 'If . . . the 1816 headnote to "Kubla Khan"
is understood as largely a prose imitation of the poem it introduces, also serving in part as argument and gloss, the long-
standing problems of unity, completeness, overall structure, and
ultimate "meaning" are set in a new perspective.'[60] On this reading, the 1816 Preface is neither an elaborate excuse nor an excrescence; it is rather, at least potentially, an invaluable key into the
enchanted *hortus conclusus* of Coleridge's Xanadu.

Until the discovery of the Crewe Manuscript (1934) and Elisabeth
Schneider's subsequent attack (1945)[61] on the veracity of the 1816
Preface, scholars accepted Coleridge's account of the poem's mysterious origin without serious reservation. Since Miss Schneider's
'exposure' of the 1816 Preface, however, it has been fashionable to
dismiss Coleridge's preface almost out-of-hand. Nevertheless, there
has always been a small group of critics (whose voice, in recent
years, has grown in strength and confidence) who have argued for
the essential truth of what Coleridge says about 'Kubla Khan' in the
1816 Preface. After all, as John Beer has said, 'the accumulation of
various pieces of evidence has tended to confirm many features of
it'.[62] E. S. Shaffer in her study of Coleridge's place in the 'mythological school' of Biblical criticism argues at length that experiences
of 'secular inspiration' (as she terms it) 'were in one form or another
so persistent with Coleridge, and figure so largely in his theory of the
imagination, that his account of the writing of "Kubla" should not
be dismissed as a figment', for

it is perfectly possible that he should have dreamed the whole in
this vivid compressed form in which all the major images are
concentrated and blent, and the action concentrated at the
point most pregnant with its own significance: the creation of
the holy city threatened with destruction and promised its
recreation. The prefatory 'Vision in a Dream' becomes a kind of

authentication of the poet's right to present [such a] prophetic lay.[63]

What both Beer and Shaffer are claiming, though their aims and ends are quite different, is that the 1816 Preface is essentially factual — although the facts are dressed up in a peculiarly Coleridgean manner. The same may be said of psychological critics such as James Hoyle, who, arguing for the 'essential truth' of the 1816 Preface, believes that Coleridge was driven by the lack of scientific testimony and established psychological terminology to express his experience in what (to modern eyes) appear to be fantastic and purely fictional terms.[64]

It may be said, then, in conclusion, that recent studies make it more difficult to dismiss the 1816 Preface as pure fiction or as a cloud of Coleridgean apology or as a disingenuous document intended to deflect adverse criticism. If we are to be fair to Coleridge, then we must be prepared to entertain seriously the possibility (perhaps, indeed, the probability) that the 1816 Preface contains a largely factual account of how 'Kubla Khan' came to be written.

The question of whether or not 'Kubla Khan' is a fragment is closely related to the issue of the reliability of the 1816 Preface, for it is in that preface that Coleridge declares with 'the most vivid confidence' that the poem as originally envisioned 'could not have been composed [in] less than from two to three hundred lines' but that when he started to write it down he was interrupted by the man from Porlock. It is important to note that Coleridge *always* referred to 'Kubla Khan' as a fragment. In the editions of 1816, 1828 and 1829 the poem bears the title 'Of the Fragment of Kubla Khan', and in the 1834 edition the title reads, 'Kubla Khan: Or, A Vision in a Dream. A Fragment.' Even the Crewe endnote corroborates the story: 'This fragment with a good deal more, not recoverable . . .', it begins. Moreover, the Coleridge circle accepted that the poem was incomplete; thus, Mrs Coleridge, for example, speaks of 'his fragments of "Christabel" & "Koula-Khan"'.[65]

Despite these repeated asseverations, however, many readers have flatly refused to believe that 'Kubla Khan' is merely the fragment of a longer poem. 'My contention', announced E. H. W. Meyerstein (in words later echoed by Humphry House), 'is that there is nothing in the least fragmentary about "Kubla Khan" and, were it not for Coleridge's preface, . . . nobody would ever have dreamt of thinking that there was.'[66] Similarly, Walter Jackson Bate argues that, 'without Coleridge's note, written so long afterwards, few readers would think "Kubla Khan" a fragment. In its self-sufficiency it differs from all of Coleridge's other poems that we actually know to be fragments.'[67] For Meyerstein, House, Bate and many other readers as well,[68] Coleridge's 1816 Preface is the main culprit — a red herring that leads us away from the organic unity and wholeness of the poem. It has also been argued that Coleridge called 'Kubla Khan' a 'fragment', not because it is incomplete, but because the 'fragment' is a legitimate artistic device and a peculiarly Romantic sub-genre.[69] And this view would support the sophisticated argument of R. H. Fogle that 'Kubla Khan is in the most essential sense a completed work, in that it symbolizes and comprehends the basic Romantic dilemma, a crucial problem of art' — for (Fogle contends) 'in good Romantic poetry there is a continuous tension, compacted of the sense of the immense potentialities of his theme set off against the knowledge that they can only partially be realized'. Thus, in 'the truest sense' 'Kubla Khan' is a completed work: 'In a more obvious sense it is clearly unfinished: as a narrative it barely commences, and it shifts abruptly with the Abyssinian maid from objective to subjective. Considered as lyric, however, it is self-contained and whole.'[70] Finally, still another critical approach to 'Kubla Khan' has involved exploring in detail its formal structure and metrical pattern: Alan Purves has done so and concludes confidently that 'We can be sure . . . that the "Kubla Khan" we have is a complete and carefully wrought poem: any expansion or continuation would have to have been different in theme and form.'[71]

It will perhaps have been noticed that, among the critical positions outlined in the preceding paragraph, there are two quite distinct attitudes concerning Coleridge's description of 'Kubla Khan' as a fragment. For critics such as Meyerstein and House (and most of those listed in n. 68), Coleridge was either wrong or lying in calling the poem a 'fragment'. For readers such as Fogle and Purves, however, Coleridge's probity is not in question: their position is that, while the poet may have called his work a fragment (for whatever reason), the poem nevertheless has a total meaning that is not fragmentary.[72]

But many critics would argue that 'Kubla Khan' is a fragment plain and simple. Some are only too happy to take Coleridge at his word and to assert, as T. S. Eliot does, that

> The imagery of that fragment, certainly, whatever its origins in Coleridge's reading, sank to the depths of Coleridge's feeling, was saturated, transformed there − 'those are pearls that were his eyes' − and brought up into daylight again. But it is not *used*: the poem has not been written. A single verse is not poetry unless it is a one-verse poem; and even the finest line draws its life from its context. Organisation is necessary as well as 'inspiration'.[73]

Most readers, however, are not so severe or so sceptical of the 'inspiration' which, according to Eliot, is responsible for the poem's 'exaggerated repute'. Rather, the majority of those who accept that 'Kubla Khan' is a fragment also agree that it is a miniature masterpiece.[74] Foremost among the supporters of this view are Elisabeth Schneider and John Beer, both of whom (despite their opposing views of the worth of the 1816 Preface) argue that Coleridge's assertion that 'Kubla Khan' is unfinished is sincere and that the poem 'must surely be thought of as a fragment that has been brought to a close of sorts but not wrought into a poetic whole − perhaps, more exactly, as a fragment with a poetic postscript':

> Coleridge himself called the poem a 'fragment'; and, haunted as he was by the ghosts of his many unfinished works, I should think it unlikely that he would have added by a deliberate falsehood to the number of that congregation in limbo. . . . The most likely explanation of the actual form of the poem would seem to be also the most natural. As it stands, it clearly consists of two parts, the description of Kubla's Paradise gardens and an explanation of why the poet could not after all finish what he had begun, or, to speak within the framework of the dream, why he could not re-create the vision he had seen. The whole reads like a fragment with a postscript added at some later time when it has become obvious to the poet that he cannot finish the piece. The postscript is skilfully linked with the rest by the recurrence of the dome and caves of ice; but these and other devices do not conceal, and I imagine were not meant to conceal, the actually disparate parts. If a man begins a poem, gets

stuck, and then adds the comment, 'I cannot finish this', even though he versify his comment to match his fragment, he is not likely to produce a whole in the poetic or aesthetic sense, though he does bring his piece to an end beyond which it could not be continued.[75]

SOURCES AND INFLUENCES

Although source-hunting has fallen into disrepute in recent years, the figure of the scholar-sleuth thumbing old folios in search of Coleridge's 'sources' has long bedevilled the critical history of 'Kubla Khan'. The major origin of this approach to the poem may be traced to a single, extremely influential book: John Livingston Lowes's *The Road to Xanadu*. Dedicated to the proposition that the images of 'Kubla Khan' represent a pastiche of subconscious recollection drawn from Coleridge's extensive reading, Lowes set out to track down the exact sources of particular images; and he concentrated his efforts on a painstaking survey of the travel-literature about Tartary, North America, and expeditions to discover the source of the Nile in Africa – literature with which Coleridge was familiar and which he certainly used in composing 'The Ancient Mariner'. The reader of Lowes's book is taken on a fascinating trip through William Bartram's *Travels through North and South Carolina*, Thomas Maurice's *History of Hindostan*, and a hundred other travel-books from Pausanius and Strabo to Athanasius Kircher and Major James Rennell. In each case Professor Lowes – affable, garrulous and excited – points out scenes and topographical features, domes and rivers and caves and mountains that remind one of this or that line in 'Kubla Khan' and lead inevitably (in Lowes's mind) to the conclusion that the 'hooked atoms' of images stored in the poet's memory, once set in motion, 'streamed up spontaneously, combining as they came'.[76] Some of Lowes's parallels are compelling, some are strained with ingenuity, and some are products of intoxicated special pleading. There are discoveries and insights, certainly; but the enterprise as a whole is doomed by its guiding assumptions – namely, that precise sources for particular images may be located if only one knows where to look in Coleridge's reading and that 'Kubla Khan' illustrates how the 'streaming continuum of *passive* association' bubbles up from the deep well of the poet's subconscious mind. It is not difficult to conceive how Coleridge, even in 1797, would have responded to the notion that the imaginative process is essentially associative and aggregative.

Following the road first charted by Lowes, subsequent scholars have toiled through two millennia of European literature in pursuit of Coleridge, clambering over obstacles and plunging into tangled thickets in order to map unnoticed byways to Xanadu. Sources for 'Kubla Khan' have been discovered in the Bible,[77] in Greek and Roman literature (Plato, Pausanias, Horace), in continental literature (Dante, Wieland), in English poetry (Spenser, Shakespeare, Milton, Akenside, Collins, Goldsmith, Erasmus Darwin, etc.), and in a host of more arcane and recondite volumes both in prose and verse. Despite this proliferation, however, the gains have been small and little of significance has been added to the list of sources proposed by Lowes. Moreover, there is a lamentable tendency among the post-Lowesian source-hunters to indulge in uncontrolled conjecture and to ignore even the most basic rules of evidence. Since Coleridge 'read everything', declares one critic, 'who can doubt that [he] knew Hesiod's *Theogony*?'; or, consider the shameless logic of a recent article on the influence of *Beowulf* on 'Kubla Khan': 'since *Beowulf* is a noted achievement in the history of the race it could have filtered down into Coleridge's mind via some inspirational afflatus from on high. At any rate, if dreamers are not always the authors of their own dreams, does it matter whether Coleridge had read *Beowulf*?'[78] *De rebus non apparentibus et non existentibus eadem est ratio*, the rule is the same both for things which do not appear and those which do not exist.

Not all source-studies, of course, involve the specious reasoning and special pleading of those just cited. Indeed, some of the arguments for influence are substantive, plausible and carefully argued. And yet, while this is true, there are two perennial problems associated with even the best of such analyses. In the first place, source-studies (including that of Lowes) generally do little to enhance our understanding or appreciation of 'Kubla Khan'. They treat the poem as a means rather than an end and devote their energies, not to interpretation, but to an often mechanical inventory of verbal parallels and apparent echoes from earlier literature. 'Kubla Khan' itself serves as a starting-place, almost a pretext, and the roads lead out from Xanadu, never to return.

In the second place, it is both fruitless and impractical to attempt to pinpoint *exact* sources for the imagery of 'Kubla Khan'. An example will make the reasons for this assertion clear.

One of the most widely accepted arguments for influence is Robert F. Fleissner's suggestion that the 'source' for the general topography of Coleridge's Xanadu may be traced to the picturesque description of Squire Allworthy's estate in Fielding's *Tom Jones*:[79]

> In the midst of the grove was a fine lawn, sloping down towards the house, near the summit of which rose a plentiful spring, gushing out of a rock covered with firs, and forming a constant cascade of about thirty feet, not carried down a regular flight of steps, but tumbling in a natural fall over the broken and mossy stones, till it came to the bottom of the rock; then running off in a pebbly channel, that with many lesser falls winded along, till it fell into a lake. . . . Out of this lake, which filled the centre of a beautiful plain, embellished with groups of beeches and elms, and fed with sheep, issued a river, that for several miles was seen to meander through an amazing variety of meadows and woods, till it emptied itself into the sea, with a large arm of which, and an island beyond it, the prospect was closed.

At first glance, when the reader's eye is alive only to the correspondences, the similarities between the two works are striking. Fielding's description offers, it seems, a close parallel to Coleridge's green hill with its transverse cedarn cover, his mighty fountain, his sacred river meandering for five miles through wood and dale before sinking into the ocean. On reflection, however, a number of dissimilarities emerge more and more prominently: Fielding's cultured Gothic and neo-pastoral landscape, complete with sloping lawns and grazing sheep, is, for example, a long way from the primitive energy of Coleridge's savage chasm, seething fountain, and sacred river that tumbles through measureless caverns and sinks in tumult to a lifeless ocean. While Claude Lorrain or John Constable might have given visual expression to the Allworthy estate, the scenery of 'Kubla Khan' belongs to the more troubled and brooding worlds of such painters as John Turner and Caspar David Friedrich — an observation that may be tested on the pulses by comparing Friedrich's *Höhle mit Grabmal* (Plate 7) with Coleridge's lines

> But oh! that deep romantic chasm which slanted
> Down the green hill athwart a cedarn cover!
> A savage place! as holy and enchanted
> As e'er beneath a waning moon was haunted
> By woman wailing for her demon-lover!

Moreover, even the closest parallels (verbal and visual alike) between the *Tom Jones* passage and 'Kubla Khan' cannot be said to constitute a case for direct influence, for they are by no means unique. Susan M. Passler, for instance, has discovered a sentence in Arthur Murphy's 'Essay on the Life and Genius of Henry Fielding, Esq' (1762) that provides as close an analogue to the imagery of 'Kubla Khan' as anything in *Tom Jones*: Fielding's creative genius, says Murphy, may be likened to 'a river, which, in its progress, foams amongst fragments of rocks, and for a while seems pent up by unsurmountable oppositions; then angrily dashes for a while, then plunges under ground into caverns, and runs a subterraneous course, till at length it breaks out again, meanders round the country, and with a clear placid stream flows gently into the ocean'.[80] It may be, then, that Arthur Murphy rather than Fielding himself lurks in Xanadu; it may be that they are both there — or that neither is. After all, as a number of critics have pointed out,[81] poets have eyes for more than books and do not compose only from reading. The rugged natural scenery of northern Somerset, with its cliffs and chasms, gushing springs and underground rivers, would have served, as well and perhaps better than bookish description, to inspire the imagery of 'Kubla Khan'. Indeed, Culbone Combe, a steep and wooded ravine within a mile or so of where Coleridge composed his poem, and the area immediately around it, supply more than a few Xanaduvian spectacles:

> The back of the cove is a noble amphitheatre of steep hills and rocks, which rise near six hundred feet above the church, and are covered with coppice woods to the tops. The trees . . . are oaks, beech, mountain ash, poplars, pines, and firs, mingled together in the most wanton variety. At the back ground of this cove, through a steep narrow winding glen, a fine rivulet rushes

down a narrow rocky channel overhung with wood, and passing
by the church, forms a succession of cascades in its descent down
the rocks into the sea. The spot is as truly romantick as any
perhaps which the kingdom can exhibit.[82]

The conclusion to be drawn from these examples is, of course,
that 'Kubla Khan' was shaped from a variety of influences both in
Coleridge's reading and in his observation of nature, but that it is
impossible to isolate unique 'sources' for individual images in the
poem. Only in two cases can we speak with any assurance about
direct influence: Purchas's *Pilgrimage* and Milton's *Paradise Lost*.
The opening section of 'Kubla Khan' (lines 1–11) is clearly
indebted to Samuel Purchas's description of Kubla Khan's pleasure-
house and palace-grounds in Book IV, chapter 13, of *Purchas his
Pilgrimage* (1613); and we have Coleridge's acknowledgement of
this influence, along with the relevant passage quoted from
Purchas, in the 1816 Preface to 'Kubla Khan'. Although there is
no authorial admission of indebtedness to *Paradise Lost*, there is
ample evidence (as numerous commentators have demonstrated[83])
to show that Milton's epic, whether consciously or subconsciously,
influenced the topography and imagery of Coleridge's poem – the
most relevant section of *Paradise Lost* being the description of
Eden in Book IV (lines 131–287), which contains the reference to
Mount Amara[84] and other verbal echoes and reminiscences.

Instead of searching for specific sources for 'Kubla Khan', however, a more profitable approach is to identify those traditions or
conventions which may be supposed to have influenced Coleridge.
Thus, one might show, for example, by citing *Tom Jones* as an
illustration rather than insisting on it as a source, that eighteenth-
century literary landscapes and the picturesque tradition in
general contributed to the landscape of Xanadu, or, similarly
(without pressing the specific claims of Culbone Combe or Wookey
Hole), that the ruggedly romantic scenery of northern Somerset
was likewise an important influence on the poet of 'Kubla Khan'.
A particularly instructive instance of the case for general influence (rather than for specific sources) is found in the concluding
lines of the poem:

> And all should cry, Beware! Beware!
> His flashing eyes, his floating hair!
> Weave a circle round him thrice,

And close your eyes with holy dread,
For he on honey-dew hath fed,
And drunk the milk of Paradise.

Now, John Livingston Lowes would have us believe that a source for these lines turns up in James Bruce's *Travels to Discover the Source of the Nile* (1790), in a passage describing the ruthless behaviour of Tecla Haimanout, king of Abyssinia, who capriciously ordered the execution of two of his civic officials.[85] This suggestion, however, which depends on the location in Abyssinia and one verbal parallel ('his long hair floating all around his face'), is neither probable nor necessary; and it offers, in any case, no insight into 'Kubla Khan'. Much more obvious and illuminating, although Lowes (in search of rarer game) does not mention it, is the traditional image of the inspired poet — a well-documented convention stretching from the Orphic cults of ancient Greece to the poet with his 'eye in a fine frenzy rolling' of *A Midsummer Night's Dream*, and beyond. The *locus classicus* is Plato's description of lyric poets who 'are not in their senses' when they are composing their poems and who 'are seized with the Bacchic transport and are possessed — as the bacchants, when possessed, draw milk and honey from the rivers, but not when in their senses' (*Ion*, 534a). This conception of poetic afflatus, as Elisabeth Schneider points out, was 'old even in Plato's day, and practically every detail used by Coleridge was a commonplace in it'.[86] Even apparent verbal echoes may easily be paralleled: the Platonic and Coleridgean conjunction of milk and honey, for example, turns up again in familiar analogues in Exodus 3: 8 and in Ovid's *Metamorphoses* (I, 111–12). With respect to influence and sources, then, the most that we can (or should) say is that the closing lines of 'Kubla Khan' provide a fine reformulation of the conventional description of the inspired poet, as found, *inter alia*, in Plato's account in the *Ion*. And what is true about the generalised nature of the sources for the concluding lines is also true (only Purchas and Milton excepted) for the earlier sections of the poem.

INTERPRETATIVE APPROACHES TO 'KUBLA KHAN'

There is an observation Never tell thy dreams, and I am almost afraid that Kubla Khan is an owl that wont bear

day light, I fear lest it should be discovered by the
lantern of typography & clear reducting to letters, no
better than nonsense or no sense. (Charles Lamb[87])

By far the most intriguing question about this most intriguing of
poems is 'What does it mean?' — if, indeed, it has or was ever
intended to have any particular meaning. For the overwhelming
majority of Coleridge's contemporaries, 'Kubla Khan' seemed (as
Lamb foresaw) to be no better than nonsense, and they dismissed
it contemptuously. 'The poem itself is below criticism', declared
the anonymous reviewer in the *Monthly Review* (Jan 1817); and
Thomas Moore, writing in the *Edinburgh Review* (Sep 1816),
tartly asserted that 'the thing now before us, is utterly destitute of
value' and defied 'any man to point out a passage of poetical merit'
in it.[88] While derisive asperity of this sort is the common fare of
most of the early reviews, there are, nevertheless, contemporary
readers whose response is both sympathetic and positive — even
though they value the poem for its rich and bewitching suggestiveness rather than for any discernible 'meaning' that it might possess.
Charles Lamb, for example, speaks fondly of hearing Coleridge
recite 'Kubla Khan' 'so enchantingly that it irradiates & brings
heaven & Elysian bowers into my parlour while he sings or says it';
and Leigh Hunt turns hopefully to analogies in music and painting
in an effort to describe the poem's haunting but indefinable effect:

> 'Kubla Khan' is a voice and a vision, an everlasting tune in our
> mouths, a dream fit for Cambuscan and all his poets, a dance of
> pictures such as Giotto or Cimabue, revived and re-inspired,
> would have made for a Storie of Old Tartarie, a piece of the
> invisible world made visible by a sun at midnight and sliding
> before our eyes.[89]

Throughout the nineteenth century and during the first quarter
of the twentieth century 'Kubla Khan' was considered, almost
universally, to be a poem in which sound overwhelms sense. With a
few exceptions (such as Lamb and Leigh Hunt), Romantic critics
— accustomed to poetry of statement and antipathetic to any
notion of *arts gratia artis* — summarily dismissed 'Kubla Khan' as
a meaningless farrago of sonorous phrases beneath the notice of
serious criticism. It only demonstrated, according to William
Hazlitt, that 'Mr Coleridge can write better *nonsense* verses than

any man in England' — and then he added, proleptically, 'It is not a poem, but a musical composition.'[90] For Victorian and Early Modern readers, on the other hand, 'Kubla Khan' was a poem not below but *beyond* the reach of criticism, and they adopted (without the irony) Hazlitt's perception that it must properly be appreciated as verbalised music. 'When it has been said', wrote Swinburne of 'Kubla Khan', 'that such melodies were never heard, such dreams never dreamed, such speech never spoken, the chief thing remains unsaid, and unspeakable. There is a charm upon [this poem] which can only be felt in silent submission of wonder.'[91] Even John Livingston Lowes — culpable, if ever anyone has been, of murdering to dissect — insisted on the elusive magic of Coleridge's dream vision: 'For "Kubla Khan" is as near enchantment, I suppose, as we are like to come in this dull world.' While one may track or attempt to track individual images to their sources, 'Kubla Khan' as a whole remains utterly inexplicable — a 'dissolving phantasmagoria' of highly charged images whose streaming pagent is, in the final analysis, 'as aimless as it is magnificent'.[92] The earth has bubbles as the water has, and this is of them.

During the past fifty years, however, criticism has been less and less willing to accept the view that 'Kubla Khan' defies rational analysis: the poem, it is widely assumed, must have a meaning, and the purpose of criticism is to discover what that meaning is, or might be. Yet despite this decisive shift in the critical temper, there remain some influential voices to argue for the mystery of 'Kubla Khan'. William Walsh, for example, maintains that it is 'an ecstatic spasm, a pure spurt of romantic inspiration'; and Lawrence Hanson treats it as an instance of 'pure lyricism — sound, picture, sensation — clothed in the sensuous beauty of imagery that none knew so well as its author how to evoke'.[93] Elisabeth Schneider, too, suggests that a good part of the poem's charm and power derives from the fact that it is invested with 'an *air of meaning* rather than meaning itself'.[94] Such opinions, while they are hardly fashionable in the current critical climate, ought not to be dismissed too lightly or seen to be no more than evasions of critical responsibility. On the contrary, they remind us that not everything about poetry is wholly explicable — especially in such poems as 'Kubla Khan', where 'meaning' is not a formulated idea and is, at best, only adumbrated through oblique and suggestive imagery. It may well be that more is meant in 'Kubla Khan' than meets the ear, but it is by no means easy to determine precisely what that meaning might be. And the impulse of literary critical professionalism to demystify, to reduce imaginative to merely rational statements, results too often in a kind of inversion of the alchemist's dream: it debases gold into lead by transforming complex symbols into simple allegories.

The first and, for over a hundred years, almost the only reader to insist on the intelligibility and coherence of 'Kubla Khan' was Shelley's novel-writing friend, Thomas Love Peacock: 'there are', he declared in 1818, 'very few specimens of lyrical poetry so plain, so consistent, so completely *simplex et unum* from first to last'.[95] Perhaps wisely, Peacock concluded his fragmentary essay with these words, thereby sparing himself the onerous task of explaining the consistency and meaning of so plain a poem as 'Kubla Khan'. More recent commentators, however, have been much bolder. In the criticism of the last fifty years one may distinguish, broadly, four major approaches to 'Kubla Khan': (1) interpretations of it as a poem about the poetic process; (2) readings of it as an exemplification of aspects of Coleridgean aesthetic theory; (3) Freudian analyses; and (4) Jungian interpretations. While recent critics concur in finding a symbolic substructure in 'Kubla Khan', there is little agreement among them as to how that symbolism should be interpreted. Critical approaches usually overlap, and individual critics often draw upon two, three or even all four of the above methods in formulating their particular explication of the poem's symbolic infrastructure. There are, in short, as many different interpretations of 'Kubla Khan' as there are critics who have written about it.

Generally speaking, however, the most popular view by far is that 'Kubla Khan' is concerned with the poetic process itself. 'What is "Kubla Khan" about? This is, or ought to be, an established fact of criticism: "Kubla Khan" is a poem about poetry.'[96] The Tartar prince Kubla Khan, who causes a pleasure-dome and elaborate gardens to be constructed in Xanadu, is often seen as a type of the artist, whose glorious creation, as the ancestral voices from the deep caverns warn, is a precariously balanced reconciliation of the natural and the artificial. The dream of Xanadu itself is an inspired vision which expresses dramatically the very nature of vision: the fountain that throws up its waters from an underground ocean and so gives birth to the sacred river that meanders five miles through Kubla's *hortus conclusus* before

sinking again into the subterraneous depths images the sudden
eruption of the subconscious into the realm of the conscious mind
and its eventual inevitable recession back into the deep well of the
unconscious. The artist's purpose is to capture such visions in
words, but in attempting to do so he encounters two serious
difficulties: first, language is an inadequate medium that permits
only an approximation of the visions it is used to record, and,
second, the visions themselves, by the time the poet comes to set
them down, have faded into the light of common day and must be
reconstructed from memory. Between the conception and the
execution falls the shadow. Coleridge confronts these problems
directly in lines 37–54 (the section beginning with the Abyssinian
maid), where he enters the poem as lyric poet *in propria persona*.
The vision of Kubla's Xanadu is replaced by that of a damsel
singing of Mount Abora – an experience more auditory than
visual and therefore less susceptible of description by mere words.
Moreover, it involves in an equivocal way a vision within a vision,
since the remembered dream of the Abyssinian maid is the cortex
of the lost vision of the content of her song. (Did Wordsworth,
perhaps, later recall these lines when he composed 'The Solitary
Reaper'?) If only, Coleridge laments, he could revive within him
the damsel's lost symphony and song, if only he could recapture
the whole of the original vision instead of just a portion of it, then
he would build 'in air' (i.e. find verbal music to express) the vision
he had experienced – and he would do so in such a way that wit-
nesses would declare him to be divinely inspired and form a circle
of worship around him.

  Such a reading of 'Kubla Khan', however, raises at least as many
problems as it solves. What, for example, ought we to make of
Kubla Khan and his enclosed garden? According to some
accounts, Xanadu is Paradise Regained and Kubla symbolises the
creative artist who gives concrete expression to the ideal forms of
truth and beauty;[97] according to other accounts, however, Kubla
is a self-indulgent materialist, a daemonic figure, who imposes his
tyrannical will upon the natural world and so produces a false
paradise of contrived artifice cut off from the realm of *natura
naturans* by man-made walls and towers.[98] The images of the
Abyssinian maid and the inspired poet in the closing section of the
poem also present serious difficulties in interpretation. The
problem is not so much that of the conjectured identification of
these figures (though this is often attempted) as of the overall

meaning and intention of the passage. Should we believe, as Humphry House and Irene Chayes have urged, that this final section must be read as a 'positive statement of the potentialities of poetry' and a 'prophecy of poetic triumph'? — or is Edward Bostetter correct in asserting that '*Kubla Khan* is a symbolic expression of [Coleridge's] inability to realize his power as a poet . . . and the last lines are a quite explicit statement of frustration'?[99] Scholarly disagreements such as these can be multiplied almost endlessly. In fact, the symbolic valency of virtually every image in the poem — the sacred river Alph, the substance and shadow of Kubla's pleasure-dome, the ancestral voices prophesying war, and so on — has proved a source of unresolved (and unresolvable) debate; and it is probably no exaggeration to say that no single interpretation of 'Kubla Khan' has ever wholly satisfied anyone except the person who proposed it. Despite the popularity of the view that 'Kubla Khan' is a poem about poetry, then, there is no consensus about just *what* is being said about the poetic process.

Another approach to 'Kubla Khan', which overlaps significantly with readings of it as a symbolic statement about poetry, centres on the use of Coleridge's own poetic theory in an effort to illuminate the poem. Four Coleridgean dicta are frequently invoked: pleasure, genius, the reconciliation of opposites, and fancy—imagination.[100] Such interpretations, however, while often instructive, are not without their problems. For example, although it is often pointed out that the imagery of 'Kubla Khan' contains numerous 'oppositions' (Kubla's cultivated gardens set against a savage romantic chasm, the sunny dome that contains caves of ice, etc.), it is by no means clear that the poem embodies the Coleridgean doctrine of the reconciliation of opposites. Indeed, as Elisabeth Schneider has said, there is ample reason to insist that such reconciliation is avoided and that, instead, the poem illustrates the very spirit of ambiguity and oscillation.[101] Even clearer, perhaps, as an illustration of the problems encountered in applying Coleridgean theory to 'Kubla Khan' is the diversity in interpretations of the poem as an embodiment of the fancy—imagination distinction. George Watson asserts dogmatically that 'Kubla Khan' is 'about two kinds of poem' and that 'there is no need to resist the conclusion' that Coleridge's intention was to contrast the *fanciful* (and therefore inferior) fixities and definites of Kubla's ornately palpable Xanadu (lines 1–36) with a programme of ideal *imaginative* creation (lines 37—54) that is hinted at but not actually realised in the poem as we have it.[102] For Alan Purves, however, Kubla Khan and Xanadu symbolise not Fancy but the Primary Imagination, while the inspired poet in the last section symbolises the Secondary or poetic Imagination.[103] And Irene Chayes offers yet another possible reading: the opening description of Kubla's palace and gardens (lines 1—11) illustrates the 'work of the arranging and ornamenting fancy'; the account of the erupting fountain and the course of the sacred river (lines 12—36) represents the 'autonomous and unconscious' operation of imagination — the fountain corresponding to Primary Imagination and the river to Secondary Imagination; and the final section, dealing with the Abyssinian maid and the inspired poet (lines 37—54), develops the symbolic representation of imagination by showing it to be, in its highest form, a willed and conscious activity: 'The last stanza . . . is concerned with a new creative process, governed by a purposive will, which would replace and correct the earlier process, autonomous and unconscious, or partially conscious, that was at work in the dream-vision.'[104]

Each of these interpretations, while compelling in its way, is ultimately unsatisfactory — not because it is 'wrong', but rather because it imposes too rigorously schematic a meaning on the poem and presupposes a theoretical precision beyond Coleridge's grasp in 1797. Since 'Kubla Khan' was composed well before Coleridge had worked out, even in outline, the major tenets of his critical theory, it is impossible to see how it can properly be interpreted as an illustration and symbolic embodiment of critical principles that had not yet been formulated. This is not to say, of course, that the poem is unrelated to the theory: it is only to insist that 'Kubla Khan', rather than being a material anticipation of later critical precepts, is a part of the process that leads eventually to the development and articulation of those ideas in a systematic way. And it is not surprising, therefore, that the 'meaning' of the poem should be obscure and ambiguous — for 'Kubla Khan' records an early, perhaps largely unconscious, exploration of critical perceptions united only loosely in an inchoate theory of literature.

A poem such as 'Kubla Khan' — so provokingly enigmatic and so deliciously suggestive — also provides an irresistibly fertile ground for psychological speculation, especially on the part of Freudian critics. When Coleridge called the poem a 'psychological curiosity' in his 1816 Preface and confessed that 'Kubla Khan' was the record of an actual dream, he unwittingly opened wide the door to analysts anxious to expound the latent psychological implications of his symphony and song. One of the earliest of the Freudian readings was offered in 1924 by Robert Graves, who proposed that 'Kubla Khan' expressed Coleridge's subconscious determination 'to shun the mazy complications of life by retreating to a bower of poetry, solitude and opium' — a serene refuge beyond the bitter reproaches of Mrs Coleridge (the woman wailing for her demon lover) and almost beyond the gloomy prophecies of addiction uttered by the 'ancestral voices' of Lamb and Charles Lloyd.[105] By comparison with recent Freudian interpretations, this is pretty tame stuff. Nevertheless, it was enough to alert I. A. Richards almost immediately to the chilling possibilities of such an approach: 'The reader acquainted with current methods of [psychological] analysis', he warned, 'can imagine the results of a thoroughgoing Freudian onslaught.'[106]

In general, the Freudians treat 'Kubla Khan' as an unconscious revelation of personal fantasies and repressed, usually erotic, urges; but there is little agreement about the precise nature of these subliminal drives. Douglas Angus argues that the poem illustrates a psychoneurotic pattern of narcissism that reflects Coleridge's abnormal need for love and sympathy; Eugene Sloane, however, is convinced that '*Kubla Khan* is an elaborate development of a birth dream', expressing an unconscious desire to return to the warmth and security of the womb (the hair in line 50, for example, is 'floating' in amniotic fluid); and Gerald Enscoe finds the core of the poem's meaning in the unresolved struggle between 'two conflicting attitudes toward the subject of erotic feeling', i.e. the 'attitude . . . that the sexual impulse is to be confined within a controlled system' is opposed to 'the anarchistic belief that the erotic neither should nor can be subjected to such control'.[107] Still other readers prefer to follow Robert Graves by concentrating on what the poem implies about Coleridge's experience with opium: James Bramwell reads 'Kubla Khan' as 'a dream-fable representing [Coleridge's] conscience in the act of casting him out, spiritually and bodily, from the paradise of his opium paradise'; and Eli Marcovitz, who sets out to 'treat [the poem] as we would a dream in our clinical practice', confidently concludes that 'Kubla Khan' is 'almost a chart of the psycho-sexual history' of a personality ineluctably embarked on the road to addiction:

It depicts the life of the poet — his infancy and early childhood, the pleasures and deprivations of the oral period, the stimulation and dread of his oedipal period, the reaction to the death of his father at nine, the fear of incest and genitality with the regression to passive-femininity and orality, and the attempt to cope with his life's problems by the appeal to the muse and to opium.[108]

Who would have supposed, without guidance, that so much meaning was compressed into only fifty-four lines?

Even this brief sampling illustrates clearly enough the limitations and liabilities of using Freudian keys to unlock the mysteries of 'Kubla Khan'. In the first place, of course, there is no received consensus (as we have just seen) about precisely what the poem reveals about Coleridge's subconscious mind. Nor is there agreement about the symbolic significance of the major images: is the stately pleasure-dome to be identified as the female breast (maternal or otherwise), or does it represent, as some think, the *mons veneris*? Similarly, what are we to make of the violent eructation of the fountain forced with ceaseless turmoil from the deep romantic chasm — the ejaculation of semen, or the throes of parturition? And then there is the hapless Abyssinian maid, who has been variously identified as Coleridge's muse, as his mother, as Mary Evans (an early flame), as Dorothy Wordsworth, and (since Abyssinian damsels are negroid) as the symbol of Coleridge's repressed impulse toward miscegenation.[109] A second and more serious problem with many Freudian readings, as the foregoing examples make clear, is a tendency to ignore basic rules of evidence and to indulge, as a consequence, in strained and unwarranted speculation. In one account, for example, we are asked (without irony) to believe that the last two lines of 'Kubla Khan' 'point by indirection to fellatio, cunnilingus and deep oral attachment to the mother'.[110] Another analyst, James F. Hoyle, interprets Coleridge's enforced 'retirement' to the farmhouse near Porlock as 'the neurotic person's "vegetative retreat" to parasympathetic preponderance with overstimulation of gastrointestinal functions, resulting in diarrhea' — and then, as if this were not enough, goes on to conclude that the 'costive opium' taken to check the attack of dysentery 'probably helped in converting depression to hypomania' and so was instrumental in transforming 'the diarrhea of [Coleridge's] failure in poetry and life to the logorrhea of *Kubla Khan*'.[111] A third problem with Freudian analysis is that, in general, it is more interested in the poet than in the poem and, in addition, often accords the 1816 Preface a stature at least equal to that of 'Kubla Khan' itself. As with the source-studies examined in the previous section, Freudian readings use the poem largely as a pretext for exploring extrapoetic matters: the roads of psychological criticism customarily lead away from Xanadu into the charted and uncharted realms of the poet's biography and subconscious psycho-sexual history.

Unlike the Freudians, who stress the psychological particularity of 'Kubla Khan', Jungian critics focus on the way in which the poem draws upon and perpetuates traditional images in which 'the age-long memoried self' is repeatedly embodied. Often the results of such an approach are illuminating and useful — largely because Jungian criticism, when it resists the reductivist temptation to explain away images with psychological tags, allows for ambiguities and the existence of half-seen truths. As Kathleen Raine points out in an engaging essay, 'Kubla Khan' was 'written in that exaltation of wonder which invariably accompanies moments of insight into the mystery upon whose surface we live'.[112]

The earliest (and still probably the best) Jungian interpretation of 'Kubla Khan' is to be found in Maud Bodkin's *Archetypal Patterns in Poetry* (1934). Her argument, in essence, is that Kubla's pleasant gardens and the forbidding caverns under them correspond 'in some degree to the traditional ideas of Paradise and Hades': 'the image of the watered garden and the mountain height show some persistent affinity [in Western literature as a whole] with the desire and imaginative enjoyment of supreme well-being, or divine bliss, while the cavern depth appears as the objectification of an imaginative fear'. In 'Kubla Khan' the heaven–hell pattern, presented as the vision of a poet inspired by the music of a mysterious maiden, evokes in the reader an 'organic response' (through the collective unconscious) to these atavistic emotional archetypes.[113] Subsequent Jungian critics have undertaken (with various degrees of success) to extend Bodkin's thesis — by developing the implications of the Edenic archetype,[114] by invoking Plato's doctrine of anamnesis or recollection,[115] and by analysing 'Kubla Khan' as a descriptive illustration of Jung's 'individuation process'.[116] There are, too, less respectably, some extreme Jungian (or pseudo-Jungian) interpretations: for example, Robert Fleissner's catachrestic argument for 'Kubla Khan' as an 'integrationist' poem.[117]

The summary of criticism in the preceding pages has not, of course, exhausted the diversity of approaches to 'Kubla Khan'. It has also been read as a landscape-poem[118] and as a poetical day-dream;[119] there are provocative interpretations of it as a political statement contrasting the profane power of the state with the sacred power of the poet;[120] and there are theological readings — quite important ones, in fact — which explore the visionary and apocalyptic theme of fallen man's yearning to recover the lost Paradise.[121] What, then, shall we say of 'Kubla Khan'? — that it has too much meaning, or too many meanings, or (perhaps) no meaning at all? *Grammatici certant et adhuc sub iudice lis est*: critics dispute, and the case is still before the courts (Horace, *Ars Poetica*, 78). In the circumstances, I will not presume to render a verdict, but merely to offer some advice. Literary criticism has more and more become a science of solutions. When a lurking mystery is discovered, analytical floodlights are trained upon it to dispel the shadows and open its dark recesses. But 'Kubla Khan', as Charles Lamb acutely perceived, is an owl that won't bear daylight. We must learn to take the poem on its own terms and, instead of attempting to salvage it by reducing it to a coherent substratum of symbols, we must reconcile ourselves to the fact that no single interpretation will ever resolve the complexities of so protean a product of the human imagination. Mystery and ambiguity, verisimilitude and teasing suggestiveness, are essential ingredients in 'Kubla Khan' — a poem which reflects, though darkly, Coleridge's largely subconscious ruminations on poetry, paradise, and the heights and depths of his own unfathomable intellectual and spiritual being. 'Kubla Khan' is one of those 'ethereal finger-pointings' so prized by Keats; it is a poem that has no palpable design upon us, and it provides at least one instance of an occasion on which Coleridge did *not* 'let go by a fine isolated verisimilitude caught from the Penetralium of mystery, from being incapable of remaining content with half knowledge'.[122]

4 'The Ancient Mariner'

COMPOSITION AND PUBLICATION HISTORY

> *That summer when on Quantock's grassy hills*
> *Far ranging, and among the sylvan combs,*
> *Thou in delicious words, with happy heart,*
> *Didst speak the vision of that Ancient Man,*
> *The bright-eyed Mariner. . . .*
> (Wordsworth, *The Prelude* (1805) XIII 393−7)

The evening of Monday, 13 November 1797, according to Dorothy
Wordsworth, was dark and cloudy.[1] At half past four in the afternoon Coleridge and the two Wordsworths set off in the thickening
dusk on a walking-tour, perhaps intending to retrace the path of a
walk earlier that same month along the rugged north Devon coast
to the eerie splendour of the Valley of the Rocks, west of Lynton.
Striking out from Alfoxden, where the Wordsworths had been
living since July, the trio headed north-west along a brown track
that led them over the bracken- and heather-covered tops of the
Quantocks. In all probability their destination for that night was
Watchet, a quaint old port some eight miles away on the Bristol
Channel. As they neared the coast, they would smell the sea and be
able to pick out on their right, across the grey waters of the Channel, faint pinpricks of cottage lights on the distant Welsh shore.

Trudging happily along in the gathering autumn darkness, the
two young poets talked with animation − and as they talked, a
plan began to form. In order to defray the expenses of their
present tour, they would collaborate on a poem[2] − in fact, a
ballad − which, they thought, might be offered for £5 to Richard
Phillips, the proprietor of the *Monthly Magazine*. The literary
ballad, as it happens, was much in vogue in the 1790s: Thomas
Percy's collection of early ballads, *Reliques of Ancient English*

Poetry (1765), had spawned a host of Augustan imitations; and, within a decade, the fast-paced narrative and rhythmic simplicity of the old ballad had been injected with the current Gothic fascination with charnel horrors and supernatural spectres calculated to thick man's blood with cold. The results were such popular thrillers as Gottfried August Bürger's 'Lenore' (which appeared in William Taylor's translation in the *Monthly Magazine* in 1796) and M. G. Lewis's 'Alonzo the Brave' (1796). In this climate it was reasonable to suppose, therefore, that a ballad along such lines would reap at least a modest monetary reward. Although 'The Ancient Mariner' would ultimately go well beyond the mere sensationalism of the Gothic horror-ballad, it is important to recognise that it was at first intended as simply another imitation, prompted by the fashionable success of this particular sub-genre and undertaken with only the limited expectation of procuring £5.

The germ of their joint ballad, recounted by Coleridge, was a strange dream of John Cruikshank (one of Coleridge's Stowey neighbours) in which a skeleton ship with figures in it had been a prominent — and suitably macabre — feature. Their central character (again Coleridge's contribution) was to be an Old Navigator; and, as they made their way through the evening mists along the road to Watchet, they plotted how this old sailor should, in his youth,[3] have committed a crime which had brought spectral persecution upon him and doomed him, like Cain and the Wandering Jew, to a life of eternal exile and wandering. Only a day or two before, Wordsworth had been reading Captain George Shelvocke's *Voyage round the World by the Way of the Great South Sea* (1726), and he remembered the episode in which one of the ship's officers, goaded by superstition, had shot an albatross that had been following the ship for several days.[4] 'Suppose', said Wordsworth, 'you represent him as having killed one of these birds on entering the South Sea, and that the tutelary Spirits of those regions take upon them to avenge the crime.'[5] The suggestion was quickly adopted, as was Wordsworth's further idea that the ship should be navigated by the dead sailors by whom the Mariner subsequently found himself surrounded. By the time they reached Watchet, the main outline of the tale had doubtless been decided upon and, in all probability, given (especially) Coleridge's facility in extemporising, the actual composition of the ballad was also under way.

In later years Wordsworth consistently maintained that 'much the greatest part' of the story was Coleridge's invention, but that he had suggested 'certain parts' himself. Wordsworth's self-effacement is commendable and, surprisingly, rather too diffident, for his contributions — the modified incident from Shelvocke and the sailing of the ship by dead men — are clearly essential features of the plot-line. Moreover, he contributed at least a handful of lines to the poem: for example,

> And listens like a three years' child:
> The Mariner hath his will
> (15—16; 1834 text)

and also, perhaps as a result of seeing the ribbed pattern of the sand at low tide as the trio walked west from Watchet along the coast the following morning, he provided two lines of the Wedding-Guest's description of the Mariner in Part IV:

> And thou art long, and lank, and brown,
> As is the ribbed sea-sand.
> (226—7; 1834 text)

Despite his enthusiasm for the project, however, and despite his substantial contributions to it, Wordsworth soon perceived that the attempt to collaborate on the ballad could not succeed. And so he voluntarily withdrew. In part, he was prompted to do so because, as he later said, his own and Coleridge's poetic styles were different, and also because 'we pulled different ways'[6] — a significant statement to which I shall return in the next section of this chapter. In part, too, no doubt, as had been the case with the proposal earlier that very month to collaborate in composing 'The Wanderings of Cain' (see *CPW*, I 285—7), Wordsworth's more cautiously laborious Muse was embarrassed by the astonishing fluency with which Coleridge could compose when the spirit was upon him. In any event it was clear to Wordsworth, within a day or two at the latest, that 'it would have been quite presumptuous in me to do anything but separate from an undertaking upon which I could only have been a clog'.[7] With that decision, the task of composing 'The Ancient Mariner' devolved upon Coleridge alone.

From Watchet, where the three friends probably spent the night, the course of their tour is largely unknown. Perhaps they wound their way along the coast, past Minehead, to Porlock or

Culbone. Perhaps they pressed on even further west, to Lynton and the Valley of the Rocks. All that is known for certain is that at some point they turned inland, for the return journey took them through Dulverton on the Somerset–Devon border. Neither is there any certainty about how long they were away from home, nor (unfortunately) about Coleridge's progress with 'The Ancient Mariner'. The next we hear of the poem, in fact, is Coleridge's laconic statement, sandwiched anonymously between comments on his translation of Wieland's *Oberon* and his growing proficiency in French and German, in a letter to Cottle written about 20 November 1797, 'I have written a ballad of about 300 lines' (*CL*, I 357).

The compositional history of 'The Ancient Mariner' between the end of November 1797 and the end of May 1798 (when it was sent to the printer) is largely obscure. Although the greatest part of the poem was written in the four months following Coleridge's return from the walking-tour with the Wordsworths, there are extant only three meagre references to it in the voluminous writings by the three friends during this period. On 6 January 1798 Coleridge was still planning to 'sell my ballad to Phillips' at the *Monthly Magazine*, 'who I doubt not will give me 5£ for it' (*CL*, I 368). A little over a month later he announced to Joseph Cottle that 'I have finished my ballad − it is 340 lines' (18 February 1798; *CL*, I 387). And finally, on 23 March, Dorothy Wordsworth recorded in her Alfoxden Journal: 'Coleridge dined with us. He brought his ballad finished. . . . A beautiful evening, very starry, the horned moon' (*JDW*, p. 11). These three short statements, however, raise some significant and perplexing issues. First, although Coleridge described the poem as 'finished' by 18 February, the Wordsworths did not see a 'finished' version until 23 March. Since there was almost daily intercourse between Stowey and Alfoxden during these five weeks, it is not reasonable to suppose that Coleridge completed 'The Ancient Mariner' over a month before the Wordsworths were made aware that it was finished. Second, there is the question of the poem's length. In November 1797 it was 'about 300 lines' and in February 1798 it was, more precisely, '340 lines' long − yet 'The Rime of the Ancyent Marinere', as it first appeared in *Lyrical Ballads* (1798), ran to 658 lines. In other words, it nearly doubled in length in the space of five weeks.

A satisfactory explanation, however, can be made to account

for these perplexing scraps of evidence. 'The Ancient Mariner' was originally conceived, it must be remembered, as a Gothic horror-ballad, inspired by the popularity of such works as Bürger's 'Lenore' and written with the intention of earning £5 from the *Monthly Magazine*. The few facts and many probabilities in the case argue strongly, moreover, that the idea of composing simply a fashionable supernatural ballad was the governing principle from the time of the November walking-tour all the way through to late February of the following year. According to the testimony of both poets, the original plan was for a tale of the supernatural replete with such Gothic machinery as a skeleton ship with figures in it, spectral persecution, and a ship sailed by dead men. In November 1797 this poem was about 300 lines long, and it had only grown by some forty lines when Coleridge mentioned it to Cottle in mid February 1798 — a circumstance which suggests that it was probably substantially the same poem on both dates. Moreover, while the 658-line 'Ancyent Marinere' of the *Lyrical Ballads* is much longer than contemporary readers would have expected a 'ballad' to be, a poem of 340 or so lines would have been within the parameters of the genre. (Bürger's 'Lenore', for example, runs to 260 lines in William Taylor's translation.) And then, too, there is the fact that Coleridge was still planning in January 1798 to sell his ballad to the *Monthly Magazine*, the same publication in which Taylor's version of 'Lenore' had appeared less than two years earlier. All of this suggests that the poem which Coleridge declared to be 'finished' on 18 February was the Gothic ballad that he had been polishing and adding bits to over the winter but that had been in existence in the form of a substantial draft since the end of the preceding November. If this is essentially correct, then the question naturally arises: what happened between 18 February and 23 March (when Dorothy Wordsworth saw the finished ballad) to prompt Coleridge to revise his poem — nearly doubling its length — and to transform a simple imitation of the Gothic ballad into the richly complex story of 'The Rime of the Ancyent Marinere'?

There is no simple answer to this question, and probably several factors combined to bring about the change. But there is *one* event of seminal importance that may be traced to this period of February–March 1798 — namely, the theoretical discussions which led to the 'plan' of the *Lyrical Ballads*. Although Wordsworth and Coleridge had contemplated a joint volume in November 1797 in which Coleridge's ballad was, in Dorothy's words, 'to be published with some pieces of William's' (*LW: EY*, p. 194), it is reasonably certain that nothing resembling the joint aesthetic plan, later described by Coleridge in the famous opening paragraphs of chapter 14 of *Biographia Literaria* and by Wordsworth in the Fenwick note to 'We Are Seven', was in the mind of either poet in the autumn of 1797.[8] During the winter of 1797–8 the two men saw very little of each other: Wordsworth was in London for the whole of December hoping to adapt his play, *The Borderers*, for the London stage; and, within a week of Wordsworth's return to Alfoxden, Coleridge left Stowey for a month's stay in Shrewsbury, where he delivered a series of Unitarian sermons – a visit immortalised by William Hazlitt in 'My First Acquaintance with Poets' (1823). Coleridge returned to Stowey in early February (probably the 9th), and for the next nine weeks was in almost daily contact with the Wordsworths, either at Alfoxden or at Coleridge's Lime Street cottage in Nether Stowey. It was, almost certainly, during these two months of close contact that 'the thought suggested itself' to the two poets 'that a series of poems might be composed of two sorts':

> In the one, the incidents and agents were to be, in part at least, supernatural. . . . For the second class, subjects were to be chosen from ordinary life; the characters and incidents were to be such, as will be found in every village and its vicinity. . . . In this idea originated the plan of the "Lyrical Ballads"; in which it was agreed, that my endeavours should be directed to persons and characters supernatural, or at least romantic; yet so as to transfer from our inward nature a human interest and a semblance of truth sufficient to procure for these shadows of imagination that willing suspension of disbelief for the moment, which constitutes poetic faith. Mr Wordsworth, on the other hand, was to propose to himself as his object, to give the charm of novelty to things of every day, and to excite a feeling analogous to the supernatural, by awakening the mind's attention from the lethargy of custom, and directing it to the loveliness and the wonders of the world before us.   (*BL*, ii 5–6)

To date the conception of the plan of *Lyrical Ballads* in February–March 1798 is to resolve a number of otherwise difficult problems. It explains, for example, why Wordsworth, who until the first week in March had been engaged entirely in blank-verse composition, should suddenly have turned his attention in March—May 1798 to the energetic production of a series of short ballad-like lyrics, such as 'Goody Blake and Harry Gill' and 'We Are Seven'. It explains too, of course, what happened to 'The Ancient Mariner': the untitled[9] ballad, designed originally for the *Monthly Magazine* and described as 'finished' on 18 February, was greatly expanded and heavily revised in the following five weeks in order to have it exemplify the aesthetic theory of the supernatural that it was Coleridge's task to embody in his contributions to *Lyrical Ballads*. While Wordsworth was engaged in making the familiar new and fresh, Coleridge was seeking to find concrete expression for those fantastic and frightening 'shadows of imagination' that haunt the peripheries of rational consciousness — and he began by reworking an existing ballad, begun with Wordsworth's help the previous autumn, into 'The Rime of the Ancyent Marinere'. And it was *this* poem that Dorothy Wordsworth described as 'finished' on 23 March 1798.

On the evidence of Coleridge's letters of March—May 1798 to Joseph Cottle and the evidence of Cottle's own *Reminiscences* (1847), it is clear that the contents of the joint Wordsworth—Coleridge volume, which Cottle was to publish, changed quite radically between mid March and the end of May 1798.[10] The first proposal, apparently suggested by Wordsworth, was for a two-volume work — the first of which was to contain only Coleridge's *Osorio* and Wordsworth's *Borderers* (*CL*, I 400). At the end of May, however, when Cottle came from Bristol on a week-long visit to Stowey and Alfoxden, the title of the work and some clear idea of its contents and the order of the poems had been decided upon. 'It was determined', writes Cottle, 'that the volume should be published under the title of "Lyrical ballads" . . . and that [it should] be published anonymously. It was to be begun immediately, and with the "Ancient Mariner"; which poem I brought with me to Bristol.'[11] Since it is unlikely that many of the poems ultimately included in the volume, with the important exception of 'Tintern Abbey' (composed in July 1798), were written after Cottle's visit, it is highly probable that he carried back to Bristol with him not only 'The Ancient Mariner' but most of the manuscript for *Lyrical Ballads* — on the understanding that the collection should begin with Coleridge's ballad and that the printing of the volume should be begun immediately.

When *Lyrical Ballads* finally appeared on London bookstalls in mid September 1798, neither of its authors was in England to witness the event. On 16 September, two days before the volume was published, Coleridge and the Wordsworths had set sail from Yarmouth for an extended visit to Germany. It was Coleridge's first sea voyage.

'The Rime of the Ancyent Marinere', the first poem in the 1798 *Lyrical Ballads*, differed markedly from the other poems in the collection and was utterly unlike any other ballad imitation that had hitherto appeared in English. What struck contemporary readers first was the strangeness of its style — its innovative and liberal use of obsolete words, archaic spellings, and sometimes awkward syntactic inversions:

> Never sadder tale was heard
>   By a man of woman born:
> The Marineres all return'd to work
>   As silent as beforne.
>
> The Marineres all 'gan pull the ropes,
>   But look at me they n'old:
> Thought I, I am as thin as air —
>   They cannot me behold.
>   (370–7)[12]

Wordsworth, sensing trouble, had taken the opportunity in his brief 'Advertisement' to *Lyrical Ballads* to declare that, while the poem had been 'professedly written in imitation of the *style*, as well as of the spirit of the elder poets', its language, 'with a few exceptions', had been 'equally intelligible for these three last centuries' (*PWW*, I 117). The earliest reviewers, however, were unconvinced: 'We are not pleased with it', said the *Analytical Review* in December 1798; 'in our opinion it has more of the extravagance of a mad german poet, than of the simplicity of our ancient ballad writers.'[13] But far more confusing and unsettling to contemporary readers than its style was the content of 'The Ancyent Marinere', which appeared wildly incoherent and unintelligible. No one had any idea what it was about; and, never having encountered a poem remotely like it, no one had any idea what to make of it. 'We do not sufficiently understand the story to analyse it', said Robert Southey; 'it is a Dutch attempt at German sublimity.' And Charles Burney dismissed it contemptuously as 'the strangest story of a cock and a bull that we ever saw on paper', although he did admit that 'there are in it poetical touches of an exquisite kind'.[14] These reactions are typical of the defensive perplexity into which 'The Ancyent Marinere' threw contemporary readers. While all the other poems in *Lyrical Ballads*, as Robert Mayo has shown, followed 'a more or less familiar course for 1798', 'The Ancyent Marinere' was 'definitely anomalous' and, as a result, critical 'opinion was confused as by no other poem in the volume'.[15]

Shortly after his return from Germany, Wordsworth in a letter to Cottle (24 June 1799) concluded that 'The Ancyent Mariner has upon the whole been an injury to the volume, I mean that the old words and the strangeness of it have deterred readers from going on'; and his initial response, therefore, was to propose that, if *Lyrical Ballads* were to come to a second edition, Coleridge's ballad should be excluded and replaced by 'some little things which would be more likely to suit the common taste' (*LW: EY*, p. 264). Coleridge, who did not return from Germany until mid or late July 1799, knew nothing of this decision at the time; and, in the event, 'The Ancient Mariner' was not dropped from the second edition (1800) of *Lyrical Ballads*, although it was very substantially revised. Pressured by Wordsworth and responsive to the reviewers' unanimous charges of obscurity and confusion, Coleridge attempted to make his ballad more palatable to contemporary tastes and clearer in meaning, by modernising some thirty or forty archaic words and by deleting forty-six lines of the 1798 text and adding seven new lines.[16] The heaviest revisions were in Parts V and VI, where Coleridge omitted forty-six of the original 263 lines and carefully altered another passage of twenty-two lines — revisions which were designed, it seems, to meet the objection of the anonymous reviewer in the *British Critic* (Oct 1799), who had found the poem's 'intermediate part . . . too long' and, as well, to have 'in some places, a kind of confusion of images, which loses all effect, from not being quite intelligible'.[17]

When the new and enlarged two-volume edition of *Lyrical Ballads* (dated 1800) finally made its appearance in January of 1801, it came forth neither anonymously nor as a joint production. It bore the title *Lyrical Ballads, by W. Wordsworth*. Coleridge's name was omitted from the title-page, and he was alluded to in the Preface merely as 'a Friend' who had been induced, 'for the sake of variety', to contribute 'the Poems of the ANCIENT MARINER, the FOSTER-MOTHER'S TALE, the NIGHTINGALE, the DUNGEON, and the Poem entitled LOVE' (*PWW*, I 118, 120). Almost certainly, as Mary Moorman has suggested, it was Coleridge who was mainly responsible for this curious arrangement, out of his reverential concern for Wordsworth's reputation: 'It was Wordsworth who was "the greatest poet since Milton", and he must become known' (*WW*, I 488). In addition, Coleridge allowed his 'Ancient Mariner', newly revised and with its archaisms expunged, to be removed from its original position at the beginning of *Lyrical Ballads* (1798) to the end of the first volume of the 1800 edition. In these changes, Coleridge acquiesced; indeed, he may have urged them in order to benefit his friend's literary reputation. But the matter does not end here — for Wordsworth attached to 'The Ancient Mariner' an insensitive and ungracious note of which, there is reason to believe, Coleridge remained ignorant until he saw the published volumes of *Lyrical Ballads* (1800).[18] This note deserves to be quoted in full:

> I cannot refuse myself the gratification of informing such Readers as may have been pleased with this Poem, or with any part of it, that they owe their pleasure in some sort to me; as the Author was himself very desirous that it should be suppressed. This wish had arisen from a consciousness of the defects of the Poem, and from a knowledge that many persons had been much displeased with it. The Poem of my Friend has indeed great defects; first, that the principal person has no distinct character, either in his profession of Mariner, or as a human being who having been long under the control of supernatural impressions might be supposed himself to partake of something supernatural: secondly, that he does not act, but is continually acted upon: thirdly, that the events having no necessary connection do not produce each other; and lastly, that the imagery is somewhat too laboriously accumulated. Yet the Poem contains many delicate touches of passion, and indeed the passion is every where true to nature; a great number of the stanzas present beautiful images, and are expressed with unusual felicity of language; and the versification, though the metre is itself unfit for long poems, is harmonious and artfully varied, exhibiting the utmost powers of that metre, and every variety of which it is capable. It therefore appeared to me that these several merits (the first of which, namely that of the passion, is

of the highest kind,) gave to the Poem a value which is not often possessed by better Poems. On this account I requested of my Friend to permit me to republish it.[19]

These mean-spirited remarks on 'The Ancient Mariner' must, even if he knew about them in advance, have been painful to Coleridge. For his part, Wordsworth never reprinted the note in any subsequent edition of his poems. Perhaps he was ashamed of it.

In addition to the revisions already discussed, Coleridge made two other changes to 'The Ancient Mariner' for the second edition (1800) of *Lyrical Ballads*. First, in response to the reviewers' charge of obscurity, he reworked the 'Argument' prefixed to the poem in an effort to make the meaning of the ballad clearer. While the 1798 'Argument' was confined to geographical description, that of 1800 put emphasis on the nature of the Mariner's crime and its repercussions:

How a Ship having passed the Line was driven by storms to the cold Country towards the South Pole; and how from thence she made her course to the tropical Latitude of the Great Pacific Ocean; and of the strange things that befell; and in what manner the Ancyent Marinere came back to his own Country.
(1798)

How a Ship, having first sailed to the Equator, was driven by Storms to the cold Country towards the South Pole; how the Ancient Mariner cruelly and in contempt of the laws of hospitality killed a Sea-bird and how he was followed by many and strange Judgements: and in what manner he came back to his own Country.   (1800)
(*CPW*, I 186)

Second, he called his poem 'A Poet's Reverie' — an unfortunate subtitle which, as Charles Lamb acutely observed, 'is as bad as Bottom the Weaver's declaration that he is not a Lion but only the scenical representation of a Lion. What new idea is gained by this Title, but one subversive of all credit, which the Tale should force upon us, of its truth?' (*LL*, I 266). The subtitle, in fact, although it has occasioned some critical discussion,[20] seems neither helpful nor substantive; and it is best to dismiss it as a Coleridgean evasion — an awkward apology for a difficult poem and an unnecessary (and misleading) concession to adverse criticism. Coleridge himself omitted it from all versions of the poem published after 1805.[21]

The much-revised 1800 text of 'The Ancient Mariner' was reprinted virtually unaltered in the third (1802) and fourth (1805) editions of *Lyrical Ballads*. (The only change was the omission of the prefatory prose 'Argument'.) Up to this point, then, Coleridge had not published 'The Ancient Mariner' under his own name: it had appeared anonymously in the first edition (1798) of *Lyrical Ballads*; and, in the editions of 1800, 1802 and 1805, where only Wordsworth's name appeared on the title-page, it was described simply as one of the contributions made by an unnamed 'Friend'. Indeed, it was not until 1817, by which time Coleridge was widely known to be its author, that he published 'The Ancient Mariner' under his own name in *Sibylline Leaves*. And for this occasion he again reworked his poem. The revisions of 1817, which cannot be dated with any degree of certainty and which probably evolved gradually over the period 1803–17, are particularly significant however, for they result in what is virtually the final version of the poem, and they are, as well, more creative (e.g. the addition of the prose gloss) than the revisions of 1800 had been.

As Kathleen Coburn and Patricia Adair have conclusively demonstrated,[22] the roots of the 1817 revisions may be traced back to Coleridge's Notebook entries of 1803–4. The Old Navigator born in Coleridge's fertile imagination and given form in 1797–8 proved in many ways to be a prophetic anticipation of his creator's own later experience of isolation and loneliness. In Coleridge's biography the years from 1800 onward were years of escalating personal suffering, deepening insecurity, and progressive estrangement from family and friends: ill health, opium addiction, the impairment of his poetic powers, marital incompatibility, a hopeless and guilt-ridden love for Sara Hutchinson, and increasing tensions in his relationship with Wordsworth — all were factors contributing to a growing sense of alienation and neurotic self-recrimination. By the summer of 1803 Coleridge had begun, tentatively and largely unconsciously, to identify himself with the lonely fictional wanderer of his youthful imagination (*CN*, I no. 1473n): on an unhappy tour of Scotland in August–September 1803, in the course of which he separated querulously from the Wordsworths and continued the journey on his own, he meditated an ode to solitude and felt himself fated 'to wander on the winds, a blessed Ghost' (*CN*, I no. 1504). Several months later (April–May 1804) on a sea passage to Malta – a self-imposed exile undertaken in the hope of physical and emotional restoration – his kinship with the Ancient Mariner was confirmed in actual experience and emerged clearly into consciousness. 'Like his Mariner', writes Miss Adair, 'he was "alone on a wide wide sea". Unhappiness deepened his natural tendency to introspection, and the notebooks of the Malta voyage reveal the poet himself enduring not only the Mariner's physical experience but also, half-consciously, identified with his guilt and fear and terrible isolation. Coleridge lives out his own poem.'[23]

'The Ancient Mariner' certainly was much in Coleridge's thoughts during his voyage to Malta. A number of Notebook entries contain echoes of the poem or quotations from it (*CN*, II nos 1996, 2002, 2060, 2087; also *CL*, II 1125), and on two occasions the ballad is mentioned by name:

> Edridge & his Warts cured by rubbing them with the hand of his Sister's dead Infant / knew a man who cured one on his Eye by rubbing it with the dead Hand of his Brother's – Comments on Ancient Mariner / – Our Captn 'Damn me! I have no superstition, I had as soon sail on Friday as on Saturday; but this I must say, that Sunday is really a lucky day to sail on / indeed to begin any sort of business upon /'. . . . (*CN*, II no. 2048)

> Plenty of Bonitos leaping up / likewise Porpoises, with a noise of rushing, like that of a Vessel dashing on by steam or other power within itself, thro' the Calm, & making the Billows & the Breeze, which it did not find / Ancient Mariner. . . .
>
> (*CN*, II no. 2052)

Since the Malta voyage was Coleridge's first extended experience of ocean travel, he was using the opportunity to discover what he could at first hand about such things as nautical superstition and the sights and sounds of life aboard a ship – and these observations would play an important part in the revision of 'The Ancient Mariner' for *Sibylline Leaves* of 1817. Although is it usually not possible except in a general way to trace specific revisions to Coleridge's Malta voyage, there is one exception, which is of considerable interest both because it permits us a glimpse into the poet's workshop and because it indicates clearly

how shipboard observation influenced later revisions in the poem.
In both the 1798 and 1800 versions of 'The Ancient Mariner' the
disappearance of the spectre-bark in Part III is described cursorily:

> With never a whisper in the Sea
>   Off darts the Spectre-ship;
> While clombe above the Eastern bar
> The horned Moon with one bright Star
>   Almost atween the tips.
>   (199–203; 1798 text)

In the 1817 version, however, this stanza is expanded into two and
the episode is rendered poignantly dramatic by the addition of
descriptive detail and the terrified response of the Ancient Mariner and his shipmates:

> The Sun's rim dips; the stars rush out:
> At one stride comes the dark;
> With far-heard whisper, o'er the sea,
> Off shot the spectre-bark.
>
> We listened and looked sideways up!
> Fear at my heart, as at a cup,
> My life-blood seemed to sip!
> The stars were dim, and thick the night,
> The steersman's face by his lamp gleamed white;
> From the sails the dews did drip –
> Till clombe above the eastern bar
> The hornéd Moon, with one bright star
> Within the nether tip.
>   (199–211; 1817 text)

A number of details in this highly effective passage may be traced
to observations made on the Malta voyage (see, for example, *CN*,
II no. 2086n), and in one case – the image of the steersman's face
gleaming white in the lamplight – experience is transformed into
poetic form. On the night of 12 April 1804, as the *Speedwell* made
her way south off the coast of France, Coleridge was on deck under
a canopy of stars, preyed upon by jealous thoughts of Wordsworth
and Sara Hutchinson and imagining that he himself 'died looking
at the stars above the top mast; & when found dead, these Stars

were sinking in the Horizon / – a large Star? a road of dim Light?
– Light of the Compass & rudderman's Lamp reflected with
forms on the Main Sail' (*CN*, II no. 2001). Within six months of his
return to England, Coleridge began to weave this or a similar
memory into the fabric of his poem, for a rough draft of lines
199–211 exists in a Notebook entry belonging probably to October
1806:

> (And) We look'd round & we look'd up
> And Fear at our hearts as at a Cup
>   The Life-blood seem'd to sip
> The sky was dull & dark the Night,
> The Helmsman's Face by his lamp gleam'd bright,
>   From the Sails the Dews did drip /
>   (*CN*, II no. 2880)

Sometime in 1815–16, when he was collecting and revising his
poems for *Sibylline Leaves*, Coleridge thoroughly reworked 'The
Ancient Mariner'[24] and announced, as well, that he intended to
prefix the poem with an essay 'on the employment of the Supernatural in Poetry and the Laws which regulate it' (*CL*, IV 561; also
BL, I 202). This introductory essay was, unfortunately, never
written; however, the textual revisions, together with the addition
of a motto from Thomas Burnet's *Archaeologiae Philosophicae*
and Coleridge's marginal gloss (which differs in details and in
emphasis from the narrative of the poem), supply at least some
idea of the principles that would have been enunciated in such an
essay.[25]

In the text of the poem Coleridge's revisions, while not sweeping, were certainly substantial: he added eighteen lines, deleted
nine, and polished another twenty or so lines. The most significant
revisions centre on (a) the role of the Wedding-Guest and (b) the
description of the spectre-bark and its two lurid occupants. In the
versions of both 1798 and 1800 there were disturbing elements of
low comedy in the depiction of the Wedding-Guest, particularly
near the beginning of Part I:

> But still he holds the wedding-guest –
>   'There was a Ship,' quoth he –
> 'Nay, if thou'st got a laughsome tale,
>   Mariner! come with me.'

> He holds him with his skinny hand,
>   Quoth he, 'There was a Ship — '
> Now get thee hence, thou gray-beard Loon!
>   Or my staff shall make thee skip.'
>   (9–16; 1800 text)

The colloquial burlesque tone of these lines, which is disruptive and seriously at odds with the strange tale that follows, was dropped in the new version, where Coleridge deleted the first and reworked the second of these early stanzas:

> He holds him with his skinny hand,
> 'There was a ship,' quoth he.
> 'Hold off! unhand me, grey-beard loon!'
> Eftsoons his hand dropt he.
>   (9–12; 1817 text)

The most extensive revisions, however, took place in Part III, where, both by addition and omission, the episode of the spectre-bark is made more powerful and sinister. The major addition to this section has already been mentioned (above, p. 116); the main omission is the deletion of the description of Death from a heavily revised passage of twenty-two lines. In the 1800 version the spectre-bark and its ghastly crew were presented thus:

> Are those *her* Ribs, through which the Sun
>   Did peer, as through a grate?
> And are those two all, all her crew,
>   That Woman, and her Mate?
>
> *His* bones were black with many a crack,
>   All black and bare, I ween;
> Jet-black and bare, save where with rust
> Of mouldy damps and charnel crust
>   They were patched with purple and green.
>
> *Her* lips were red, *her* looks were free,
>   *Her* locks were yellow as gold:
> Her skin was as white as leprosy,
> And she was far liker Death than he;
>   Her flesh made the still air cold.

The naked Hulk alongside came
  And the Twain were playing dice;
'The Game is done! I've won, I've won!'
  Quoth she, and whistled thrice.

A gust of wind sterte up behind
  And whistled through his bones;
Thro' the holes of his eyes and the hole of his mouth
  Half-whistles and half-groans.
                                        (179—200)

By dropping the detailed yet conventionally horrific description of
Death (stanzas 2 and 5 above), Coleridge shifted the emphasis in
the 1817 version to the figure of Life-in-Death, which is appropriate and desirable since it is she, not Death, who wins the
Ancient Mariner in the dice-game:

Are those *her* ribs through which the Sun
Did peer, as through a grate?
And is that Woman all her crew?
Is that a Death? and are there two?
Is Death that woman's mate?

Her lips were red, *her* looks were free,
Her locks were yellow as gold:
Her skin was as white as leprosy,
The Night-mare Life-in-Death was she,
Who thicks man's blood with cold.

The naked hulk alongside came,
And the twain were casting dice;
'The game is done! I've won! I've won!'
Quoth she, and whistles thrice.
                                        (185—98)

The effect of these stanzas is more controlled, more sinister — and
yet less tangible — than that of the earlier version. There is a
mounting tension in the hysterical half-perceptions of the staccato
questions in the first stanza, which is intensified in the vivid but
impressionistic presentation of the 'Night-mare Life-in-Death . . .
Who thicks man's blood with cold' (lines added in 1817) and is

brought to a sudden climax in the shrill 'I've won! I've won!' of the following stanza. By omitting the Gothic figure of Death, one of those 'unmeaning miracles' to which Lamb objected (*LL*, I 142), and by concentrating the terror in the unconventional figure of Life-in-Death, Coleridge succeeded in moving 'The Ancient Mariner' one step further away from the traditional Gothic horror-ballad and one step closer toward his object of employing supernatural agents as symbols of those frightening aspects of 'our inward nature' that haunt the fringes of rational consciousness (*BL*, II 6). Doubtless these revisions were prompted by those 'laws of the supernatural' that were to have been set down in the promised but unwritten essay intended to introduce 'The Ancient Mariner' in *Sibylline Leaves*.

In addition to the revision of the text of the poem itself, Coleridge made two other important changes. First, in place of the Arguments that had prefaced the poem in 1798 and 1800, he substituted a Latin quotation from a seventeenth-century Neoplatonic treatise, Thomas Burnet's *Archaeologiae Philosophicae* (1692). As J. R. Barth observes, the original intention of this motto was to serve as a 'direction-signal' for contemporary readers baffled by the poem's mysterious complexity — 'a kind of general warning about the conditions of the road, the terrain, and the weather ahead'.[26] But the motto is also important because it stresses, like the poem itself, the vital interaction between the realms of the natural and the supernatural, and because it exists *verbatim* in a Notebook entry (*CN*, I no. 1000H) which dates from 1801 or 1802 — that is, from over fifteen years earlier than the publication of *Sibylline Leaves*.[27] Much more significant than the motto from Burnet, however, was Coleridge's other alteration: the addition of the marginal prose gloss.

In 1843 Wordsworth told Miss Fenwick that the marginal gloss was not a part of the original plan for 'The Ancient Mariner' and that it was, therefore, 'no doubt . . . a gratuitous after-thought' (*WPW*, I 361). Although the gloss was, indeed, an afterthought (though by no means a gratuitous one), it is impossible to say just how much of an afterthought it really was. It might have been composed at any time between 1800 and 1817, and there is a good deal of evidence to suggest that it existed, in some form, at a relatively early date. Coleridge's Notebooks between 1804 and 1812, for example, contain a number of parallels to the gloss (*CN*, II nos 2293, 2610, 2727; III nos 4041, 4166), and these may be either anticipations of the gloss or, possibly, echoes of it. More-over, as R. C. Bald has noted, some early annotations by Coleridge in a copy of *Lyrical Ballads* (1800) support the conjecture that the gloss was written 'comparatively soon after the original com-position of the poem'.[28]

For the most part, the gloss provides a running commentary and summary of the poem's narrative action; it is essentially, that is, an artistic restatement of what is obvious in the text, a translation of the poem's substance into prose. At certain points in the super-natural parts of the story, however, the gloss adds details that are not in the poem itself. Thus, the gloss asserts that the Ancient Mariner's shipmates 'make themselves accomplices in the crime' (opposite line 101), that the Polar Spirit moves the ship 'in obedi-ence to the angelic troop' (opposite line 381), and that the Mari-ner's penance is exacted after a bargain is struck between the Polar Spirit and the angelic host (opposite line 393). Similarly, the gloss on the dice-game in Part III (lines 195-8) makes the meaning of the episode explicit in a way that the poem does not:

> Death and
> Life-in-Death
> have diced for
> the ship's
> crew, and she
> (the latter)
> winneth the
> ancient
> Mariner.

> The naked hulk alongside came,
> And the twain were casting dice;
> 'The game is done! I've won! I've won!'
> Quoth she, and whistles thrice.

These glossarial additions serve, as B. R. McElderry observes, both to strengthen the poem's 'moral' theme of crime and punishment and to give Coleridge an opportunity to explain certain obscure or ambiguous incidents in the poetic narrative: 'It is as if an artist drew a sketch from his own finished picture. As he sketches he follows the main design of his subject, but here and there he strengthens a line and adds a detail.'[29] While most readers have accepted McElderry's view that the 1817 gloss is not an artistic flaw (the poem and the gloss constitute, 'not one "true" story, but two versions, related, yet independent', of the same story) and that the gloss provides useful clues to Coleridge's ethical intentions in composing 'The Ancient Mariner', there is a dissenting minority of recent critics − spearheaded by William Empson − who regard the gloss as a 'parasitic growth' that must be removed before the poem can be properly appreciated or understood.[30]

McElderry's argument for the artistic integrity of the gloss is supported and extended by Huntington Brown in an interesting analysis of the dramatic relationship between poem and gloss. While the poem is clearly intended to be the work of an imaginary medieval minstrel, the style and the particular kind of learning displayed in the gloss mark it out as belonging to a later period: 'the minstrel is not meant to be the author of the gloss. The gloss can only be the work of an imaginary editor', whose prose style and learning declare him to be 'a scholar, modern rather than medieval, but distinctly old-fashioned, therefore an early and bookish antiquarian'.[31] In this view, the gloss achieves a semi-autonomous status and functions dramatically as a kind of choric commentary on the poetic narrative. By refracting the credulous medieval minstrel's supernatural tale through the pious understanding of an imaginary Renaissance editor–glossator, Coleridge was able (according to Brown) both to emphasise the remoteness of his story and to make it more acceptable to 'enlightened' contemporary readers.

In July 1817, after two years of difficulties and delays, Coleridge's collected poems, revised and rearranged, appeared under the title *Sibylline Leaves*. 'The Rime of the Ancient Mariner' with its learned epigraph from Thomas Burnet and its 800-word marginal gloss was the first poem in the volume – restored, after a long exile in the back pages of Wordsworth's *Lyrical Ballads*, to rightful pride-of-place as the opening poem in Coleridge's own collective edition. With only minor revisions and corrections the 1817 version of 'The Ancient Mariner' was reprinted in all later lifetime editions of Coleridge's poems (1828, 1829, 1834); and, although the 1834 version has become the *textus receptus*, the 1817 text was the last to incorporate significant alterations and so stands effectively as the final redaction in a complex series of revisions and rewritings stretching over nearly two decades.

COLERIDGE, WORDSWORTH, AND THE SUPERNATURAL

We tried the poem conjointly for a day or two, but we pulled different ways, and only a few lines of it are mine.
(Wordsworth in 1844, *PWW*[G], III 442)

The intellectual symbiosis of Coleridge and Wordsworth, especially in the period 1797–1804, has scarcely any parallel in literary history. 'It is almost impossible', as Thomas McFarland has said, 'to bring to mind any other two figures, so important each in his own right, but also so dependent each upon the other during his richest intellectual years.'[32] As poets and poetic theorists, both men blossomed together, each making profound contributions to the other's development, each a fostering sun for the other. In their differences as in their similarities they left indelible imprints upon one another – and 'The Ancient Mariner', begun as a joint composition, marks a crucial stage in the growth of their literary relationship and in their separate but mutually assisting search for an individual poetic theme and voice. At one time it was fashionable either to denigrate Wordsworth's contribution to 'The Ancient Mariner' or, conversely, to argue that Coleridge's ballad is, in essence, merely a restatement of the Wordsworthian philosophy of Nature's 'holy plan' and the consequences attendant upon those who violate it.[33] Each of these positions, of course, is extreme; and each ignores the subtle tracery of intersecting influence that lies behind the conception and composition of 'The Ancient Mariner'.

Before the period of close personal intimacy when they were neighbours in northern Somerset, both Coleridge and Wordsworth had been engaged in writing poetic dramas concerned with crime and the psychology of remorse and repentance. In the winter of 1796–7 Wordsworth, who had already dealt with the theme of criminal guilt and sorrow in his Salisbury Plain poems, returned to it again in *The Borderers* – a tediously didactic study of two contrasting responses to acts of wickedness. Marmaduke, the leader of a troop of noble-hearted outlaws on the borders of England and Scotland, is tricked by his lieutenant, the depraved and Iago-like Oswald, into causing the death of the blind and innocent Baron Herbert, who, he wrongly supposes, intends to sell the beautiful Idonea into infamy. While Oswald revels in evil deeds and plunges recklessly into a career of deliberate wickedness, the gentle-souled Marmaduke, once he learns of his terrible mistake, is overcome with remorse and prescribes as penance for his crime a life of perpetual exile from human society:

> a wanderer *must I* go,
> The Spectre of that innocent Man, my guide.

No human ear shall ever hear me speak;
No human dwelling ever give me food,
Or sleep, or rest: but over waste and wild,
In search of nothing that this earth can give,
But expiation, will I wander on –
A Man by pain and thought compelled to live,
Yet loathing life – till anger is appeased
In Heaven, and Mercy gives me leave to die.
                                        (2344–53)

While Wordsworth was polishing the draft of *The Borderers* in the spring of 1797, Coleridge too, at the invitation of Richard Brinsley Sheridan (*CL*, I 304), was sketching out his own verse drama on the psychology of criminal guilt. Drawing freely from the Sicilian's tale in Schiller's *Der Geisterseher* and also from M. G. Lewis's Gothic novel *The Monk*, Coleridge's *Osorio* is, like Wordsworth's play, a tale of crime, punishment and repentance: Osorio attempts to murder his older brother, Albert; the attempt fails, although Osorio thinks it has succeeded, and the intended victim returns in disguise to attempt to bring his brother to a sense of remorse and hence to effect his regeneration. Despite parallels in theme and characterisation, *Osorio* and *The Borderers* seem to have arisen quite independently: it was by coincidence and not by design that both poets chose to explore the currently popular theme of crime and remorse.[34] In view of what was to follow, however, the coincidence is a particularly interesting one, for the themes of crime, guilt, wandering and repentance are central motifs in a number of poems, including 'The Ancient Mariner' and 'Peter Bell', composed by Coleridge and Wordsworth in 1797–8.

'The Three Graves', a ballad begun by Wordsworth in 1796, adds a further dimension to the thematic interests shared by the two poets at this time – namely, the laying on of a curse. In the case of 'The Three Graves' the plot centres around the curse of a mother on her own daughter (with whose affianced lover the mother is herself in love) and the disastrous consequences of this curse upon the daughter and her lover. Coleridge, steeped in the literature of curses from his reading and reviewing of Gothic romances in the spring of 1797 (*CL*, I 318), was much attracted by 'The Three Graves', and, as a result, Wordsworth turned the completion of the poem over to his friend in June or July of 1797. It was their first attempt at collaboration.[35]

Five months later, in November 1797, the themes explored in *The Borderers*, *Osorio* and 'The Three Graves' led to two further attempts at collaboration — 'The Wanderings of Cain' and 'The Ancient Mariner'. After a visit to the Valley of the Rocks early in the month, Coleridge and Wordsworth began a prose tale, in the vein of Salomon Gessner's *Der Tod Abels* ('The Death of Abel') and using the desolate backdrop of the Valley of the Rocks as its setting, on the subject of the archetypal crime of man against man, Cain's murder of his innocent brother Abel. 'The Wanderings of Cain' was to have been, like *Osorio* and *The Borderers*, a study of criminal psychology: cursed by God for his evil deed and doomed to a life of eternal wandering, Cain struggles with the spirit within him and is consumed by an agony of remorse. Both the subject and the plot-line were supplied by Coleridge, who had long been interested in the 'Origin of Evil', on which he had contemplated writing an epic poem (*CN*, I no. 161), and the original plan called for a tale in three cantos which they proposed to finish in just one night: Wordsworth 'undertook the first canto: I the second: and which ever had *done first*, was to set about the third'. Having 'despatched my own portion of the task at full finger-speed', Coleridge gathered up his manuscript and hastened to see how Wordsworth was progressing — only to find that the latter sat idle, with a 'look of humorous despondency fixed on his almost blank sheet of paper', so that the whole scheme 'broke up in a laugh: and the Ancient Mariner was written instead' (*CPW*, I 286–7). Now, this account is not quite accurate, for 'The Ancient Mariner' was begun, perhaps two weeks later, during a second walking-tour along the Bristol Channel in November 1797. Nevertheless, it is not difficult to understand why Coleridge, whose account dates from 1828, should have conflated these two events: both 'The Wanderings of Cain' and 'The Ancient Mariner' began in the same month as collaborative attempts with Wordsworth, and both were stories of crime, curses, wandering and remorse.

'The Ancient Mariner', then, is the culmination of a developing cluster of related themes that can be traced with remarkable consistency through earlier works by both poets. Wordsworth's 'Salisbury Plain' and *The Borderers*, Coleridge's *Osorio*, and their efforts at joint authorship in 'The Three Graves', 'The Wanderings of Cain' and 'The Ancient Mariner' form related parts of a comprehensive theme which Charles Smith summarises as follows: 'a man commits a crime; the crime sets in motion the machinery of justice and punishment; it also calls down a curse upon his head; the criminal suffers severe pangs of remorse; and finally, through remorse, he finds regeneration and salvation'.[36] But this raises an interesting problem. If the subject and general theme of 'The Ancient Mariner' were ostensibly so congenial to Wordsworth, so closely linked to his own current interest in the psychology of criminal guilt and repentance, then why did he withdraw from collaboration on the ballad, especially when he had contributed so much to the elaboration of its plot? In part, no doubt, as had been the case a fortnight earlier with 'The Wanderings of Cain', Wordsworth's slow endeavouring art could not keep pace with the voluble facility of an inspired Coleridge in the white heat of creativity; and so he graciously resigned his claim, feeling that his continued participation could only be 'a clog' on the project. But there is, too, another more important reason: 'We tried the poem conjointly for a day or two, *but we pulled different ways . . .*' (*PWW*[G], III 442; emphasis added). The significance of this remark may be gauged and its meaning elucidated by setting it beside Wordsworth's comment, recorded by Barron Field in 1839, about Coleridge's handling of 'The Three Graves':

> I gave him the subject of his Three Graves; but he made it too shocking and painful, and not sufficiently sweetened by any healing views. Not being able to dwell on or sanctify natural woes, he took to the supernatural, and hence his Ancient Mariner and Christabel, in which he shows great poetical power; but these things have not the hold on the heart which Nature gives, and will never be popular, like Goldsmith's or Burns's.[37]

In essence, Wordsworth's objection is that Coleridge ignored the morally curative power of Nature and 'took to the supernatural' instead.

Although Wordsworth's statement about 'The Three Graves' belongs to a much later date than the period under consideration, there are none the less some revealing corroborative hints in the poems of 1795–7 that point to the beginning of a disagreement between the two men on the subjects of supernatural agency and the role of Nature. In both 'Salisbury Plain' and *The Borderers*, for example, there is no element of the supernatural whatsoever, and objects in the natural world serve, in a rudimentary way, as external guides to moral understanding and the beginning of wisdom. In the opening two parts of 'The Three Graves', which Wordsworth had drafted before he passed the work over to Coleridge, there is a similar effort to invest a blossoming thorn-tree with some sort of moral significance, while according anything supernatural the status merely of a convenient simile:

> Fast rooted to the spot, you guess,
>   The wretched maiden stood,
> As pale as any ghost of night
>   That wanteth flesh and blood.
>   (82–5)

In Parts III and IV of 'The Three Graves', however, which were written by Coleridge in the spring of 1798, supernatural elements, although still enmeshed in a Wordsworthian fidelity to psychological realism, emerge more prominently — as in the closing lines of Part IV, where Edward dreams guiltily of murdering his evil mother-in-law:

> So they sat chatting, while bad thoughts
>   Were troubling Edward's rest;
> But soon they heard his hard quick pants,
>   And the thumping in his breast.
>
> 'A mother too!' these self-same words
>   Did Edward mutter plain;
> His face was drawn back on itself,
>   With horror and huge pain. . . .
>
> He sat upright; and ere the dream
>   Had had time to depart,
> 'O God, forgive me!' (he exclaimed)
>   'I have torn out her heart.'
>
> Then Ellen shrieked, and forthwith burst
>   Into ungentle laughter;
> And Mary shivered, where she sat,
>   And never she smiled after.
>   (518–37)

A more striking use of the supernatural occurs in 'The Wanderings of Cain', where Cain encounters the ghost of his murdered brother, Abel:

> But ere they had reached the rock they beheld a human shape: his back was towards them, and they were advancing unperceived, when they heard him smite his breast and cry aloud, 'Woe is me! woe is me! I must never die again, and yet I am perishing with thirst and hunger.'
>   Pallid, as the reflection of the sheeted lightning on the heavy-sailing night-cloud, became the face of Cain. . . . And the Shape shrieked, and turned round, and Cain beheld him, that his limbs and his face were those of his brother Abel whom he had killed! And Cain stood like one who struggles in his sleep because of the exceeding terribleness of a dream.
>
> (*CPW*, I 290)

Although spectral encounters are the common fare of Gothic horror-ballads and romances, Cain's confrontation with Abel's ghost moves beyond such mere sensationalism, for the apparition functions as a symbolic projection of the guilt and despair in Cain's own tormented soul. As in a nightmare, Cain, the fugitive and vagabond condemned to life by God's command, comes face to face with the image of his own fears. Similarly, in 'The Ancient Mariner' the daemons and phantoms whom the Mariner encounters are projections from the unconscious depths of his own troubled mind.

It is unlikely, for reasons already suggested (pp. 107–9), that in the autumn of 1797 either Coleridge or Wordsworth was aware of any serious difference in their respective attitudes to the natural and the supernatural. It is a fallacy of *a posteriori* reasoning to suppose that Wordsworth, in proposing the murder of the albatross and the revenge taken by tutelary spirits of the South Pole, intended 'The Ancient Mariner' to exemplify his own particular philosophy of Nature. After all, in 1797 this philosophy was still inchoate; and, besides, 'The Ancient Mariner', as *originally* proposed, was not meant to illustrate a specific doctrine or system of philosophico-literary ideas: it was intended, quite simply, as a means of exploiting the fashionable Gothic mode in the hope of earning £5 from the *Monthly Magazine*. Coleridge, who was more at home with supernatural themes than Wordsworth and more *au fait* with the genre, not surprisingly prospered to such a degree in the enterprise that Wordsworth felt obliged to withdraw from it at an early stage.

In the spring of 1798, however, a dramatic change took place. Apparently as the result of long and serious aesthetic discussions, the two poets became aware of some basic differences in their approaches to poetic style and the subjects most appropriate for contemporary poetry. The consequence of this discovery took the form of an agreement to write two different kinds of poems while remaining faithful to two cardinal principles of poetry — namely, 'a faithful adherence to the truth of nature' and 'the power of giving the interest of novelty by the modifying colors of imagination' (*BL*, II 5). It was Coleridge's task to produce poems in which 'the incidents and agents were to be, in part at least, supernatural' and in which a human interest was transferred from 'our inward nature' in such a way as 'to procure for these shadows of imagination that willing suspension of disbelief for the moment, which constitutes poetic faith' (*BL*, II 5—6). In other words, Coleridge was to employ the supernatural as an expressive medium, or symbol, for 'romantic' emotional states (fear, guilt, remorse, etc.) and to imitate these states with such psychological fidelity and dramatic force that the reader, in a version of Aristotelian anagnorisis, would momentarily recognise truths of his own inner being in the fictional incidents or characters represented. With this object in view he rewrote 'The Ancient Mariner' in February— March 1798, transforming a Gothic horror-ballad into a direct emotional evocation of a guilty man's spiritual voyage of self-discovery through the unseen moral universe that lies within and above us all. In addition, he began work on 'The Ballad of the Dark Ladié' and on 'Christabel', in which, he said later, he would 'have more nearly realized [his] ideal' than he had in 'The Ancient Mariner' (*BL*, II 6). While Coleridge was thus engaged in making the strange more familiar, Wordsworth set about composing poems of a different sort: his aim, according to Coleridge,[38] was to produce poems that would 'excite a feeling analogous to the supernatural' by stripping from everyday objects and situations the film of custom and familiarity that obscure from us 'the loveliness and the wonders of the world before us' (*BL*, II 6). To accomplish this end, Wordsworth wrote the series of poems, mostly new compositions but occasionally revisions of existing drafts, which ultimately made up his portion of *Lyrical Ballads* (1798).

Although the majority of the lyrics and ballad-like narrative poems composed by Wordsworth in March–May 1798 were written simply in fulfilment of his agreement to give 'the charm of novelty to things of every day' (*BL*, II 6), there are a certain number of poems from this period in which he moves beyond this mandate and seems, quite consciously, to be attempting to counter or even refute Coleridge's theory of the supernatural, especially as it is employed in 'The Ancient Mariner'. In 'Goody Blake and Harry Gill', for example, Wordsworth treats the themes of crime and curses from a purely psychological point of view, excluding any hint or element of the supernatural. Similarly 'The Thorn', a poem distinguished from 'The Ancient Mariner' in the 'Advertisement' to the 1798 *Lyrical Ballads* (*PWW*, I 117) and later buttressed by a long defensive note (*WPW*, II 512–13) perhaps alluding to Coleridge's poem,[39] is an attempt to deal with superstition and abnormal psychology in an aggressively naturalistic way.[40] But the most striking example is Wordsworth's 'Peter Bell', written immediately after 'The Thorn' and considered for inclusion in *Lyrical Ballads* (*CL*, I 411), which is, as many readers have pointed out, clearly a sort of 'answer' to 'The Ancient Mariner':[41]

Like the Mariner, it is the story of the redemption of a human soul. But, whereas the Mariner, for the one sin of his pride and callousness in shooting the albatross suffers adventures and 'spectral persecutions' that must set him apart among men for ever, 'Peter Bell the Potter' is an ordinary coarse brute of a sinner who is at last frightened into becoming 'a good and honest man' by a process of purely natural visitations – the instruments of his salvation being a dead man, an ass, a little boy, a withered leaf, a woman, and finally some Methodist hymn-singers. . . . Not only does ['Peter Bell'] reveal Wordsworth's intense interest in the workings of the human mind – in what we should call psychology – but it is also a testament to his central faith: that 'nature' is capable of influencing for good even one of her more rebellious and insensitive children.

(*WW*, I 392)

In the long verse Prologue with which 'Peter Bell' begins, the poet-narrator is borne aloft in a silver boat shaped like the crescent moon and carried high among the wheeling stars in the vault of heaven. But he soon tires of such afflatus and longs to return to 'that tiny grain, / That little Earth of ours' (lines 49–50); and when the loquacious sky-canoe tries to seduce him into viewing 'the realm of Faery' and other secret lands 'Where human foot did never stray', he graciously but firmly declines:

> 'Temptation lurks among your words;
> But, while these pleasures you're pursuing
> Without impediment or let,
> No wonder if you quite forget
> What on the earth is doing. . . .
>
> 'Go – (but the world's a sleepy world,
> And 'tis, I fear, an age too late)
> Take with you some ambitious Youth!
> For, restless Wanderer! I, in truth,
> Am all unfit to be your mate.
>
> 'Long have I loved what I behold,
> The night that calms, the day that cheers;
> The common growth of mother-earth
> Suffices me – her tears, her mirth,
> Her humblest mirth and tears.
>
> (116–35)

It is impossible not to read into this rebuke an implied criticism of Coleridge's supernatural world of dream and fantasy, and to find in the 'ambitious Youth' a wry (but perhaps not entirely amusing) dig at Coleridge himself. Twenty years later, when he eventually published 'Peter Bell' in 1819, Wordsworth was both less tactful and less oblique in his censure of Coleridge: 'The Poem of Peter Bell', he declared in the pointed dedication addressed to Southey,

as the Prologue will show, was composed under a belief that the Imagination not only does not require for its exercise the inter-vention of supernatural agency, but that, though such agency be excluded, the faculty may be called forth as imperiously, and for kindred results of pleasure, by incidents within the compass of poetic probability, in the humblest departments of daily life.

(*WPW*, II 331)

The tale of 'Peter Bell' itself contains a remarkable series of parallels with 'The Ancient Mariner'. Like Coleridge, Wordsworth begins his story *in medias res* and sets the main action within a frame story which, with forced humour intended (one supposes) to recall the interjections of Coleridge's Wedding-Guest, occasionally obtrudes itself on the narrative — as in the opening lines of Part I:

> All by the moonlight river-side
> Groaned the poor Beast — alas! in vain;
> The staff was raised to loftier height,
> And the blows fell with heavier weight
> As Peter struck — and struck again.
>
> 'Hold!' cried the Squire, 'against the rules
> Of common sense you're surely sinning;
> This leap is for us all too bold;
> Who Peter was, let that be told,
> And start from the beginning.'
>
> — 'A Potter, Sir, he was by trade,'
> Said I, becoming quite collected. . . .
> (191–202)

Although a hawker of earthenware rather than a sailor, Peter is, like the Ancient Mariner, a solitary wanderer (lines 206–45); and, again like his nautical counterpart, he is guilty of a wanton attack on an innocent animal — in Peter's case the unprovoked cudgelling of a forlorn donkey grieving for its drowned master — which precipitates a chain of cause and effect that leads, after suitable therapy by terror, to Peter's rehabilitation:

> And Peter Bell, who, till that night,
> Had been the wildest of his clan,
> Forsook his crimes, renounced his folly,
> And, after ten months' melancholy,
> Became a good and honest man.
> (1131–5)

Despite such parallels, however, 'Peter Bell' differs markedly from 'The Ancient Mariner' in tone and atmosphere. Unlike Coleridge,

who plunges the reader into a nightmare world populated by
sinister phantoms and submarine spirits, Wordsworth clings to a
terra firma where everything is literal and factual:

> A primrose by a river's brim
> A yellow primrose was to him,
> And it was nothing more.
>   (248–50)

While the Mariner is actually threatened by the supernatural,
Peter only *thinks* that he is: a 'startling sight' seen in a pool, for
instance, which causes Peter to utter a 'frightful shriek' and faint,
turns out to be, not a spectre, but only the poor ass's dead master —

> The man who had been four days dead,
> Head-foremost from the river's bed
> Uprises like a ghost!
>   (578–80)

Given these similarities and differences, it is not difficult to accept
the argument that 'Peter Bell' is, in Kathleen Coburn's words, 'an
attempt at what Wordsworth took to be the same theme as *The
Ancient Mariner*: a crime against nature, punished by the laws of
the universe, with restoration and reformation of a Methodistical
sort following on repentance, and all done "without supernatural
agency", as he said'.[42]
    The evidence of such poems as 'The Thorn' and 'Peter Bell',
taken together with later statements by Wordsworth,[43] makes it
tolerably plain (as Miss Coburn goes on to say) not only that
Wordsworth disapproved of Coleridge's treatment of the supernatural but that the idea of 'supernatural agency' held a quite
different meaning for him. What that meaning is may be deduced
in good part from 'Peter Bell' and from Wordsworth's discussion of
the 'grave defects' of 'The Ancient Mariner' in his 1800 note
(quoted above on p. 112) on Coleridge's poem. In this latter,
Wordsworth objects to the Mariner's lack of a 'distinct character'
and to the fact that 'he does not act, but is continually acted upon';
furthermore, events in the poem 'having no necessary connection
do not produce each other' and 'the imagery is somewhat too
laboriously accumulated'. What Wordsworth stresses here, as elsewhere, is the necessity of behavioural probability in character

development and of causality in poetic action. And in such a
climate the supernatural must inevitably have a hard empirical
edge, being a useful tool as metaphor but a dangerous practice as
symbol: 'Supernatural agencies had they occurred in ['Peter Bell']
would have had to come from a *deus ex machina*, concrete,
visible, specific as the yellow primrose.'[44] Wordsworth's difficulties
with 'The Ancient Mariner', then, spring largely from his constitu-
tional antipathy to unexplained actions, unmotivated behaviour,
and narrative poems in which there is a direct evocation of preter-
natural reality through incident and character. On the analogy of
'Peter Bell' we may speculate that, if Wordsworth rather than
Coleridge had written 'The Ancient Mariner' in the spring of 1798,
it would probably have been the overtly didactic story of a callous
(rather than a merely thoughtless) individual who, having committed a crime against Nature, is conducted by logic and circumstance, after a period of educative suffering, to admit the error of
his ways and find absolution in the pantheistic sanctity of Abraham's bosom. This is not, of course, how things worked out. Coleridge's Mariner, racked by remorse and only partially redeemed, a
restless Cain-like exile compulsively recounting his inscrutable
experiences, forces his way into our imaginations, not with sweet
reason, but with a breathless tale of crime and judgements half-
understood that holds us spellbound, compelling the suspension of
our disbelief. For his part, Wordsworth wrote 'Peter Bell' instead.
Eschewing the obscure and awesome terrors of the Mariner's
strange seas, he turned to a humble potter and the healing impulses from the vernal wood to illustrate his own more Aristotelian
and Godwinian version of natural supernaturalism.

Whatever its importance as a statement of Wordsworth's philosophy, 'Peter Bell' is not an easy poem to like. It flirts and struts with
pretentious abandon on the cliff-edge of bathos and absurdity —

> Only the Ass, with motion dull,
> Upon the pivot of his skull
> Turns round his long left ear
> (413–15)

— and it has always proved an easy mark for ridicule, even before
its publication in 1819, as the wittily mordant parodies by John
Hamilton Reynolds and by Shelley amply demonstrate.[45] It is a
serious injustice, however, to point derisively to 'Peter Bell' as the

measure of Wordsworth's attitude to the supernatural or his ability
to handle successfully the themes of guilt and superstition in
poetry. As an antidote to such a misconception, one need only
turn, for example, to the earliest version of *The Prelude* (1798–9)
to witness the haunting power of Wordsworth's moral supernaturalism. There is the account of how, as a boy, he stole wood-
cocks on occasion from traps which others had set:

> Sometimes strong desire,
> Resistless, overpowered me, and the bird
> Which was the captive of another's toils
> Became my prey; and when the deed was done
> I heard among the solitary hills
> Low breathings coming after me, and sounds
> Of undistinguishable motion, steps
> Almost as silent as the turf they trod.
>
> (42–9)[46]

And there is, too, that 'act of stealth / And troubled pleasure' –
the stolen-boat episode – that prompts a guilty conscience to
transform the very landscape itself into an avenging presence:

> I dipped my oars into the silent lake,
> And, as I rose upon the stroke, my Boat
> Went heaving through the water, like a swan –
> When from behind that rocky steep, till then
> The bound of the horizon, a huge Cliff,
> As if with voluntary power instinct,
> Upreared its head: I struck, and struck again,
> And, growing still in stature, the huge cliff
> Rose up between me and the stars, and still
> With measured motion, like a living thing,
> Strode after me. With trembling hands I turned,
> And through the silent water stole my way
> Back to the cavern of the willow-tree.
>
> (104–16)

The difference between Wordsworth's invocation of the supernatural in such passages as these and Coleridge's use of the supernatural in 'The Ancient Mariner' is succinctly expressed by
Patricia Adair, who observes that, while Wordsworth's technique

is to 'suggest the supernatural through the real world', Coleridge 'suspends our disbelief in the mystery which lies beyond the normal by appealing to our observation of natural things'.[47]

'THE ANCIENT MARINER' AS A BALLAD

Although it has occasionally been suggested that 'The Ancient Mariner' may profitably be read as a miniature epic or even a dramatic monologue,[48] there is no doubt that Coleridge's poem is, first and foremost, a ballad. It is, as W. P. Ker said long ago, 'the most notable modern result of Percy's *Reliques of Ancient English Poetry*'.[49] The success of Bishop Thomas Percy's *Reliques*, a collection of ballads, sonnets, historical songs and metrical romances, was truly astounding. Based on a seventeenth-century manuscript (now known as the 'Percy Folio'), the *Reliques*, first published in 1765, and revised and augmented in three subsequent editions before the end of the century (1767, 1775, 1794), was largely responsible for the eighteenth- and nineteenth-century revival of interest in older English and Scottish poetry. The highly charged dramatic simplicity and the 'romantic' flavour of such poems as 'The Ancient Ballad of Chevy Chase' fired the imaginations of generations of poets, from Chatterton and Shenstone to D. G. Rossetti, Swinburne, and beyond. During the Romantic period the 'popular' or 'traditional' ballad (as distinct from the 'broadside' ballad favoured by Wordsworth in the *Lyrical Ballads*) was very much in vogue — witness Sir Walter Scott's many imitations of the genre — and occasionally, as in 'The Ancient Mariner' and Keats's 'La Belle Dame Sans Merci', the traditional ballad-form is utterly transformed by the intensely individual melody of true genius. 'The Ancient Mariner', it should be added, is not Coleridge's only early attempt in the genre: in the spring and summer of 1798 he began work on 'The Three Graves', 'The Ballad of the Dark Ladié', and, as well, on 'Christabel', which, while not a ballad *per se*, was influenced considerably by the ballad of 'Sir Cauline' in Percy's *Reliques*.

Coleridge's achievement in 'The Ancient Mariner', in terms both of indebtedness to tradition and of departure from it, can properly be appreciated only when one has a clear idea of the narrative and metrical characteristics of the ballads from which he

drew his inspiration. Percy's ballad of 'Sir Patrick Spence', which
Coleridge later used in his epigraph to 'Dejection: An Ode' (1802),
is fortunately both representative and short enough to be given in
full:

> The king sits in Dumferling toune,
>   Drinking the blude-reid wine:
> O quhar will I get guid sailòr,
>   To sail this ship of mine?
>
> Up and spak an eldern knicht,
>   Sat at the kings richt kne:
> Sir Patrick Spence is the best sailòr,
>   That sails upon the se.
>
> The king has written a braid letter,
>   And signd it wi' his hand;
> And sent it to Sir Patrick Spence,
>   Was walking on the sand.
>
> The first line that Sir Patrick red,
>   A loud lauch lauched he:
> The next line that Sir Patrick red,
>   The teir blinded his ee.
>
> O quha is this has don this deid,
>   This ill deid don to me;
> To send me out this time o'the yeir,
>   To sail upon the se?
>
> Mak hast, mak haste, my mirry men all,
>   Our guid schip sails the morne.
> O say na sae, my master deir,
>   For I feir a deadlie storme.
>
> Late late yestreen I saw the new moone
>   Wi' the auld moone in hir arme;
> And I feir, I feir, my deir mastèr,
>   That we will com to harme.

> O our Scots nobles wer richt laith
>   To weet their cork-heild schoone;
> Bot lang owre a' the play wer playd,
>   Thair hats they swam aboone.
>
> O lang, lang, may thair ladies sit
>   Wi' thair fans into their hand,
> Or eir they se Sir Patrick Spence
>   Cum sailing to the land.
>
> O lang, lang, may the ladies stand
>   Wi' thair gold kems in their hair,
> Waiting for thair ain deir lords,
>   For they'll se thame na mair.
>
> Have owre, have owre to Aberdour,
>   It's fiftie fadom deip:
> And thair lies guid Sir Patrick Spence,
>   Wi' the Scots lords at his feit.

'Sir Patrick Spence' employs, without significant variation, the characteristic ballad-stanza throughout — that is, a four-line stanza in which the first and third lines are in iambic tetrameter, while the second and fourth lines (the only ones which rhyme) are in iambic trimeter. Further, although there is little internal rhyme (a useful mnemonic device in early oral ballads), alliteration is abundant and so is repetition — both *simple repetition* ('And I feir, I feir', 'O lang, lang', 'Have owre, have owre', etc.) and *incremental repetition*, in which a line or stanza is repeated (often several times) with some small but material substitution: for example,

(a)   *The first line that Sir Patrick red,*
        A loud lauch lauched he:
      The next line that Sir Patrick red,
        The teir blinded his ee.

(b)   O lang, lang, may *thair ladies sit*
        Wi' thair fans into their hand. . . . .

      O lang, lang, may *the ladies stand*
        Wi' thair gold kems in their hair. . . . .

As in most traditional ballads, the language is plain and formulaic, there is no effort to describe the setting or delineate the characters, or to probe their psychological motivation, and little or no attempt is made to connect individual scenes or to describe the catastrophe which is the climax of the action:

> The ballad's method of narration has been aptly compared to the film technique of montage: the story is advanced by a series of quick flashes, one distinct scene following another. There is no connecting tissue between the scenes, no explanation of events leading up to the crucial situation or following it.[50]

'Sir Patrick Spence', like most folk ballads, focuses on a single episode, narrated by a detached commentator with stark economy but high dramatic intensity and immediacy. Its view of life is decidedly unsentimental, almost deterministic; and it can convey in the briefest of strokes vivid moments of love or of tragic loss. More than most other kinds of poetry, the ballad is capable of fulfilling the Miltonic dictum that poetry should be simple, sensuous and passionate; and 'I must only caution the Reader', as Addison said of the ballad of 'Chevy Chase', 'not to let the Simplicity of the Stile, which one may well pardon in so old a Poet, prejudice him against the Greatness of the Thought.'[51]

One of the most prominent features of 'The Ancient Mariner', however, appears only sparingly in early ballads − namely, the supernatural. Although there are occasional ghosts in the folk ballads, they are harmless creatures, whose task is to admonish rather than to terrify the living. Certainly, there is nothing in traditional balladry to rival Coleridge's Polar Spirit or the graphic horror of such a nightmare spectre as Life-in-Death. The inspiration for such figures came from the literary horror-ballads of the eighteenth century, perhaps the best-known of which is Bürger's 'Lenore'. By comparison with 'The Ancient Mariner', Bürger's poem strikes the modern reader as tame and contrived; but there is no doubt that, in its time, it was sensational enough: 'Have you read the Balad call'd "Leonora"', enquired Lamb with horrified delight in July 1796, 'in the 2d No. of the "Monthly Magazine"? −. If you have − !!!!!!!!!!!!!!' (*LL*, i 41).

'Lenore', which appeared in no less than seven English versions (one of them by Walter Scott) in 1796 alone, is the tale of Lenore's immoderate grief over the death of her lover Wilhelm, of Wilhelm's

sudden appearance on horseback, and the elopement of the two
lovers on an unearthly midnight ride:

> 'Looke up; the moon is bright, and we
>   Outstride the earthly men:
> I'le take thee to the bridal bed,
>   And night shall end but then.'

> 'And where is then thy house, and home,
>   And bridal bed so meet?'
> ''Tis narrow, silent, chilly, low,
>   Six planks, one shrouding sheet.'

> 'And is there any room for me,
>   Wherein that I may creepe?'
> 'There's room enough for thee and me,
>   Wherein that we may sleepe.

> 'And as thou lyest upon thy couch,
>   Aryse, no longer stop;
> The wedding-guests thy coming wayte,
>   The chamber-door is ope.' . . .

> Tramp, tramp, across the land they speede;
>   Splash, splash, across the see:
> 'Hurrah! the dead can ride apace;
>   Dost fear to ride with me?

> 'The moon is bright, and blue the night;
>   Dost quake the blast to stem?
> Dost shudder, mayd, to seeke the dead?'
>   'No, no, but what of them?'
>   (125–60)[52]

Despite Wilhelm's broad hints about the prospective bridal bed
(lines 131–2) and about riding with the dead, the credulous and
love-blinded Lenore supposes her lover to be alive — until their
journey ends abruptly in a graveyard and Wilhelm reveals himself
to be a *revenant*:

> And when he from his steed alytte,
>   His armure, black as cinder,

Did moulder, moulder all awaye,
   As were it made of tinder.

His head became a naked skull;
   Nor hair nor eyne had he:
His body grew a skeleton,
   Whilome so blithe of ble.

And at his dry and boney heel
   No spur was left to bee;
And in his witherd hand you might
   The scythe and hour-glass see.

And lo! his steed did thin to smoke,
   And charnel-fires outbreathe;
And pal'd, and bleachde, then vanishde quite
   The mayd from underneathe.

And hollow howlings hung in air,
   And shrekes from vaults arose:
Then knewe the mayd she might no more
   Her living eyes unclose.

                (233–52)

There were many other ballads, both translated from the German and English originals, that exploited the contemporary fashion and taste for the supernatural. M. G. Lewis's 'Alonzo the Brave and Fair Imogine' (1796), a Gothic ballad which Coleridge both knew and admired, carried the horrific to bizarre heights:

The lady is silent: the stranger complies,
   His vizor he slowly unclosed:
Oh! then what a sight met Fair Imogine's eyes!
What words can express her dismay and surprise,
   When a skeleton's head was exposed!

All present then utter'd a terrified shout;
   All turn'd with disgust from the scene.
The worms they crept in, and the worms they crept out,
And sported his eyes and his temples about,
   While the spectre address'd Imogine. . . .

                (52–61)[53]

The poem concludes with a macabre midnight revel during the course of which a chorus of pale, shrieking ghosts toasts Alonzo and his consort by quaffing blood from 'skulls newly torn from the grave' (line 83). Despite its incongruous and rollicking anapaestic rhythm, which Coleridge later likened to the experience 'of galloping over a paved road in a German stage-waggon without springs' (*BL*, II 24), 'Alonzo the Brave and Fair Imogine' was immensely influential in popularising Gothic supernaturalism and intoxicating the febrile imaginations of contemporary readers and poets alike.

Like Bürger's 'Lenore' and Lewis's 'Alonzo the Brave', 'The Ancient Mariner' is an imitation, with Gothic additions, of the traditional folk-ballad. At one level, then, it is admittedly derivative, drawing consciously upon earlier models — especially the ballads in Percy's *Reliques* — for much that is characteristic in its form and flavour. It owes a good deal, too, to the contemporary imitations of Bürger, Lewis and others: supernatural machinery, frequent use of internal rhyme, antiquated spelling and archaic diction, and so on. Whatever its debts to the ballad-tradition, however, 'The Ancient Mariner' is, as generations of critics have argued,[54] more richly complex thematically and a more highly wrought technical accomplishment than any ballad written before or since. It is 'the acknowledged *chef d'œuvre* of the whole genre'.[55]

Unlike Bürger and Lewis, Coleridge employs supernatural beings not for the gratuitous effects of *terror gratia terroris* but in order to project symbolically states and moods of the Mariner's inner being. The spectral figures are organic and functional, therefore, and not merely shocking and decoratively macabre; they are the leering and accusing incarnations of his own guilt and remorse, whom the Mariner confronts on his journey into the mirror and out again.

Leaving character and theme aside, however, it is equally apparent that there is nothing comparable in earlier ballads to the sophisticated technical virtuosity of 'The Ancient Mariner'. Working with the traditional ballad-stanza, for example, Coleridge is able to achieve almost miraculous effects with the usual rhetorical devices of alliteration, internal rhyme, and repetition — as in the memorable account in Part II of the becalming of the Mariner's ship:

> The fair breeze blew, the white foam flew,
> The furrow followed free;

We were the first that ever burst
Into that silent sea.

Down dropt the breeze, the sails dropt down,
'Twas sad as sad could be;
And we did speak only to break
The silence of the sea!

All in a hot and copper sky,
The bloody Sun, at noon,
Right up above the mast did stand,
No bigger than the Moon.

Day after day, day after day,
We stuck, nor breath nor motion;
As idle as a painted ship
Upon a painted ocean.

Water, water, every where,
And all the boards did shrink;
Water, water, every where,
Nor any drop to drink.

The very deep did rot: O Christ!
That ever this should be!
Yea, slimy things did crawl with legs
Upon the slimy sea.

About, about, in reel and rout
The death-fires danced at night;
The water, like a witch's oils,
Burnt green, and blue and white.

And some in dreams assuréd were
Of the Spirit that plagued us so;
Nine fathom deep he had followed us
From the land of mist and snow.

(103—34)

In these thirty-two lines there are twelve significant (sometimes multiple) instances of alliteration, three striking examples of internal rhyme, and six major instances of verbal repetition. But what makes the passage so impressive is not its accumulation of such devices but rather the subtle and effective way in which rhetorical invention is varied and modulated — and the artful way in which it subserves a narrative end. Tumbled joyfully into the Pacific Ocean on a gust of rhyme and alliteration, the ship falls in the second stanza into the immobilising grip of an ocean-calm, and the torpor that afflicts body and soul is reflected in the phasing out of rhetorical effects in stanzas 2 and 3: alliteration drops off and then disappears entirely; the strong rhythm and internal rhymes of the opening stanza fall with the wind, leaving only the 'sight'-rhyme of 'speak'-'break' (line 109) as the tacit vestige of former activity; and the quick-paced assonance of the ship running before the breeze, overwhelmed by a series of long *o*-vowels, grows torpid and heavy under the influence of the fixed tropical sun. In stanzas 4 and 5, where the tedium of inertia is reinforced in languorous repetitions, there are also the beginnings of a counter-movement — a quickening of the pulse that grows, paradoxically, out of these very repetitions. The calm begins, through repetition, to evoke an emotional response and to acquire, as a result, a vitality of its own: lassitude (stanza 4) gives way to anguish (stanza 5), which, in its turn, prompts revulsion (stanza 6) that is transformed into an unconscious admiration of the calm's bewitching beauty (stanza 7). Thus, although the deadly calm maintains its hold on the Mariner's body, he experiences internally an emotional awakening, which builds through a crescendo of repetition and returning alliteration, and which opens out suddenly in the last two stanzas into an ominous universe governed by spirits of the air and water. In these eight stanzas, then, Coleridge suspends our disbelief and transports us in the Mariner's wake from the world of ordinary ships and men into the mysterious realm of the subconscious where the Polar Spirit dwells — and he accomplishes this, it must be stressed, within the framework of the traditional ballad-stanza and with the tools (for the most part) of traditional balladry.

But the technical brilliance of 'The Ancient Mariner' does not depend only on Coleridge's manipulation of traditional forms and devices. There is an important measure of innovation as well. For illustration, one need look no further than his use of the ballad-stanza itself. While most ballads employ the customary four-line stanza used throughout 'Sir Patrick Spence' and Taylor's translation

of Bürger's 'Lenore', Coleridge often relieves the monotony of this
measure by extending his stanzas to five or six (and in one case
nine) lines.[56] Such expansion, which is more frequent in the supernatural parts of the story, serves a variety of functions. Sometimes
it is used to heighten the emotional impact of an incident by
drawing out its dramatic quality:

> With throats unslaked, with black lips baked,
> We could nor laugh nor wail;
> Through utter drought all dumb we stood!
> I bit my arm, I sucked the blood,
> And cried, A sail! a sail!
>
> (157–61)

Sometimes, as in the case of the sailors' contradictory responses to
the Mariner's deed, expansion by incremental repetition is used to
fix a scene in the memory:

> And I had done a hellish thing,
> And it would work 'em woe:
> For all averred, I had killed the bird
> That made the breeze to blow.
> Ah wretch! said they, the bird to slay,
> That made the breeze to blow!
>
> Nor dim nor red, like God's own head,
> The glorious Sun uprist:
> Then all averred, I had killed the bird
> That brought the fog and mist.
> 'Twas right, said they, such birds to slay,
> That bring the fog and mist.
>
> (91–102)

And sometimes expansion provides the means of intensifying a
moment of lyric impulse, as when the 'troop of spirits blest' in Part
V raise their matin hymn:

> Around, around, flew each sweet sound,
> Then darted to the Sun;
> Slowly the sounds came back again,
> Now mixed, now one by one.

Sometimes a-dropping from the sky
I heard the sky-lark sing;
Sometimes all little birds that are,
How they seemed to fill the sea and air
With their sweet jargoning!

And now 'twas like all instruments,
Now like a lonely flute;
And now it is an angel's song,
That makes the heavens be mute.

It ceased; yet still the sails made on
A pleasant noise till noon,
A noise like of a hidden brook
In the leafy month of June,
That to the sleeping woods all night
Singeth a quiet tune.

                              (354–72)

The stanzas just quoted illustrate forcefully what is perhaps the
major difference between 'The Ancient Mariner' and the traditional ballads on which it is modelled. One has only to compare the
terse narrative and stark economy of imagery in such a poem as 'Sir
Patrick Spence' to be immediately aware of the lyric and pictorial
elaborateness of Coleridge's poem. While the anonymous medieval
bard stresses action and situation almost to the exclusion of
transition and explanation, Coleridge throws the emphasis onto
the intricate elaboration of atmosphere, the careful description of
time and setting, and the significance of moral edification in the
narrative progression. In an intensely personal way he reworks the
forms and rhetorical techniques of the old ballads and polishes
them to a Regency brilliance. Archaic diction (drawn from
Chaucer and Spenser as well as from ballad tradition), alliteration,
repetition and the ballad-stanza itself are all brought to maturity in
'The Ancient Mariner' and made to support the moral pattern of
sin and expiation that lies at the heart of the poem. Similarly, the
crude superstitious animism of the typical medieval ballad, like the
gratuitously horrific supernatural of the later ballads of the Gothic
revival, is spiritualised, internalised, and transformed into a
powerful imaginative instrument to probe the dark recesses of the
Mariner's troubled psyche. Unlike 'Sir Patrick Spence' or Bürger's

'Lenore', which are tales of deeds and actions, 'The Ancient Mariner' is in the final analysis a poem of the inner life. For all its affinities with earlier ballads, Coleridge's poem remains a work apart − a psychological ballad, a moral ballad, and (not to be forgotten) a lyrical ballad.

SOURCES AND INFLUENCES

τὰ ἀρχαῖα παρῆλθεν, ἰδοὺ γέγονεν καινά:
the old things are passed away; behold,
they are become new.
                  (Lowes, *Road to Xanadu*, p. 311)

The sources of 'The Ancient Mariner' are many and varied. Some of them have been encountered already in earlier sections of this chapter: the formal origin of the poem in hints from John Cruikshank's dream of a skeleton ship and Wordsworth's suggestion of the killing of an albatross as the cause of spectral persecution; Coleridge's early interest in the Wandering Jew (*CN*, I no. 45) and the origin of evil (*CN*, I no. 161; *CL*, I 396), and the propaedeutic influence of his own earlier literary studies of guilt and remorse in works such as *Osorio* and 'The Wanderings of Cain'; and, of course, his indebtedness to the traditions of folk and Gothic ballads. Hundreds of other influences, most of them from books which Coleridge either knew or is supposed to have known, have been proposed by critics from the middle of the nineteenth century to the present day. Yet in this climate of diversity there is one crucial point of agreement: all concur that whatever Coleridge touches he transmutes; whatever he borrows, or imitates, from earlier writers is transformed, as by the touch of Prospero's wand, into something rich and strange.

John Livingston Lowes, who has traced in minute detail the influence on 'The Ancient Mariner' of numerous early explorers' accounts of their voyages, has shown, for example, how Coleridge has time and again fashioned stanzas out of images, scraps of nautical information, superstitious shipboard lore, and observation of exotic natural phenomena that lie scattered through the yellowing leaves of old navigators' memoirs. Coleridge loved these old tomes and the simple, daring men who wrote them. Their adventures among savages in the Southern Ocean, their awed encounters with the terrors and beauties of the unknown, their hard experiences for weeks on end among the unforgiving splendour of fields of Arctic ice — these and much else besides sank into the very marrow of his being, were retained in his tenacious memory, and ultimately stirred into new imaginative life. More perhaps than by any others Coleridge was fascinated by the vivid accounts of those intrepid captains — Frederick Martens, William Barents, Thomas James of Bristol, David Crantz, and a host of others — who charted the Arctic seas and inhospitable northern lands of mist and snow, where icebergs rose like mountains and the growling pack-ice could roar and split with a noise like thunder — a desolate, lifeless world of jagged, broken shapes like those depicted by Caspar David Friedrich in *Das Eismeer* (Plate 10).

Here are the very words of some of the men who endured such rigours, and whose accounts and descriptions Coleridge devoured with passion:

> In the night we saw the Moon very pale, as it used to look in the day time in our Country, with clear Sun-shine, whereupon followed mist and snow. . . . The Ice came a floating down apace . . . and it was very cold.   (Frederick Martens)

> We had Ice not farre off about us, and some pieces, as high as our Top-mast-head. . . . We continued on our course, blinded with foggie and durtie weather; and that, intermixt with snow, and frost; amongst disperst pieces of Ice: many of them higher then our Top-mast head . . . mountainous Ice; farre higher then our Top-mast head.   (Thomas James)

> Nor do [the] Figures and Shape [of the ice] alone surprize, but also their Diversity of Colours pleases the Sight; for some are like white Chrystal, others as blue as Saphires, and others again green as Emeralds.   (John Harris)

> There was such a frightful rumbling, and cracking of the ice, as if many cannons had been fired at once, and then ensued a violent noise, like the roaring of a cascade.   (David Crantz)

> The men were worn out with fatigue in defending the ships with their ice-poles from being engulphed; and now nothing but

scenes of horror and perdition appeared before their eyes. But the Omnipotent . . . caused . . . the ice to part in an astonishing manner, rending and cracking with a tremendous noise, surpassing that of the loudest thunder. At this very instant the whole continent of ice . . . moved together in various directions, splitting and dividing into vast bodies.   (Commodore Phipps)

Wee might heare the Ice cracke in the Sea . . . which made a huge noyse. . . . We were taken with a great swounding and dazeling in our heads . . . [but] when the doores were open, we all recovered our healths againe, by reason of the cold Ayre . . . otherwise without doubt, we had dyed in a sudden swound, after that the Master . . . gave every one of us a little Wine to comfort our hearts.   (Gerrit de Veer)[57]

Consciously or unconsciously, vestiges of these or similar passages remembered from the old navigators dovetailed in Coleridge's mind to give a graphic and memorable picture of the Mariner's ship in the grip of polar ice:

> And now there came both mist and snow,
> And it grew wondrous cold:
> The ice, mast high, came floating by
> As green as emerald. . . .
>
> The ice was here, the ice was there,
> The ice was all around:
> It cracked and growled, and roared and howled,
> Like noises in a swound!
> (51—4, 59—62)

Although the narratives of the explorers certainly inspired Coleridge and provided him with many nautical facts and images, not everything in 'The Ancient Mariner' may be traced to sources in books. 'Things read have blended with things seen', as Lowes himself has said.[58] The bassoon, for instance, which causes the Wedding-Guest to beat his breast (lines 31—2) probably owes its origin to 'the Bassoon and the Music' that Tom Poole arranged to be sent in December 1797 to the church at Nether Stowey; and the striking image of the lonely flute (line 364) may well be traced to Coleridge's tour of Wales with John Hucks in 1794, when the two travellers encountered a solitary flute-player in the romantic ruins of Denbigh Castle.[59] Similarly, the Mariner's hypnotic power and 'glittering eye' owe a good deal to the lively interest generated in London and Bristol in the 1780s and 1790s by F. A. Mesmer's experiments with hypnosis or, as it was then called, 'animal magnetism'.[60] And even in the case of the explorers themselves, whose histories Coleridge so avidly consumed, there is strong evidence of a connection closer than books: William Wales, who had visited Hudson's Bay and later had sailed, as astronomer and meteorologist, aboard the *Resolution* with Captain Cook in 1772, was the mathematics master at Christ's Hospital during Coleridge's time at the school.[61] It is impossible not to believe that the experiences of this former world-navigator circulated widely through the school in many forms, from the canonical pronouncements of William Wales himself all the way down to those unauthorised − and gloriously embellished − versions that were doubtless passed from boy to whispering boy in the darkened dormitories after curfew.

In addition to personal observation and the pervasive influence of the voyagers, possible sources for lines and images in 'The Ancient Mariner' have been found in poems and plays from Aristophanes's *The Frogs* and Virgil's *Aeneid* to Robert Blair's *The Grave* (1743) and William Cowper's *The Task* (1785).[62] Usually the connections proposed are verbal parallels, which are occasionally quite striking − as in the case of the oft-noticed correspondence[63] between stanza 49 of Sir John Davies's *Orchestra* (1594) −

> For loe the Sea that fleets about the Land,
>   And like a girdle clips her solide wast,
> Musick and measure both doth vnderstand:
> For his great Christall eye is alwayes cast
> Vp to the Moone, and on her fixed fast
>   And as she daunceth in her pallid spheere,
>   So daunceth he about the Center heere.

− and lines 414−19 of 'The Ancient Mariner':

> 'Still as a slave before his lord,
> The ocean hath no blast;
> His great bright eye most silently
> Up to the Moon is cast −
>
> If he may know which way to go;
> For she guides him smooth or grim. . . .'

Deeper but less tangible than any such verbal parallels, however, is the powerful influence exerted on Coleridge's imagination by the great metaphorical voyages of Homer, Virgil and Dante. The *Odyssey*, the *Aeneid* and the *Divina Commedia* — all of them using a physical voyage as structural scaffolding for spiritual exploration — lie behind Coleridge's miniature epic in which the cycle of departure and return is a metaphor for spiritual growth and where the setting and events of the story give substance to the inner realities of the Mariner's guilt-haunted psyche. 'The Ancient Mariner' is, as G. Wilson Knight has said, 'a little poem greatly conceived', an epic *in petto*, in which 'the experience is of fearful fascination; a feverish horror that is half positive delight, mental pre-eminently; and the return is a return to earth, the hermit's cell and mossy stone, a return to reality and sanity'.[64] The Mariner's return, of course, is not an entire restoration: at an 'uncertain hour' the agony of his experience on the wide wide sea returns upon him, forcing him to retell a story whose significance and implications he only partially understands. But the basic pattern of the spiritual voyage from ignorance to self-knowledge is still there — a pattern inspired and sustained by the example of Homer, Virgil, and especially Dante.

Of the many other 'sources' and influences proposed for 'The Ancient Mariner' there are three which deserve special notice. H. W. Piper, in an important study entitled *The Active Universe* (1962), discusses in detail the influence on Coleridge of late eighteenth-century scientific and pseudo-scientific thought, particularly his debts to Joseph Priestley's *History of Electricity* (1767) and Erasmus Darwin's *The Botanic Garden* (1789—91). Behind the spirits and animated corpses of 'The Ancient Mariner', for example, lie an imaginative appreciation and substantial knowledge of Priestley's experiments with electricity and magnetism; and moreover, as Piper goes on to show, Priestley's peculiar brand of scientific Unitarianism, a neo-Newtonian system of rational theism employing empirical observation to underwrite spiritual truth, is implicit in the Mariner's active universe: 'It is a world in which natural forces — heat and cold, wind, seas, rain and lightning — work in strange yet coherent ways towards ends which are not physical but moral. It is a world in which the whole concert of nature plays its part in the mariner's spiritual history.'[65] Piper's argument that the Mariner's universe, although inhabited by spirits and other supernatural beings, is none the less governed by the rules of contemporary science is both qualified and extended in an interesting paper by Maren-Sofie Røstvig, who finds evidence in 'The Ancient Mariner' of the influence of syncretistic Neoplatonism and, in particular, of the writings of Robert Fludd, an early seventeenth-century Rosicrucian whose cosmic system anticipates (she argues) in significant ways Coleridge's presentation of a world where matter and spirit interpenetrate.[66] And finally − turning from scientific theology to a possible source in aesthetic theory − Daniel Stempel has argued with spirit in a recent essay that the 'dazzling interplay of the natural, the aesthetic, and the moral which constitutes the world of "The Ancient Mariner" is a literary analogue of the aesthetic theories of Friedrich Schiller's *Briefe über die ästhetische Erziehung des Menschen* (1795) and *Über naive und sentimentalische Dichtung* (1795−96)'.[67] Following the pattern of man's aesthetic education set down in Schiller's treatises, Stempel traces in the poem a tripartite process of enlightenment: the Mariner, beginning as 'sensual man' (the thoughtless slayer of the albatross), progresses to the attainment of *aesthetic* perception in his blessing of the water snakes, and then finally achieves *moral* understanding and so becomes an ordained preacher of Nature and One-Life unity. Since, for Schiller, 'the passage from sensation to thought, from the physical to the moral, takes place only through the mediation of the aesthetic', the Mariner's act of blessing the water snakes is both the turning-point and climax of the poem.[68] This is an attractive argument certainly, and Stempel presents his case with erudition, careful analysis, and enthusiastic conviction. One only wonders, as one often does in reading source-studies, whether Coleridge was himself aware of Schiller's theories in 1797−8 or had any knowledge of the two treatises around which his imagination is supposed to have crystallised.

CRITICAL APPROACHES TO 'THE ANCIENT MARINER'

We do not sufficiently understand the story to analyse it.   (Southey)

Poetry gives most pleasure when only generally and not perfectly understood.   (Coleridge)[69]

For its earliest critics 'The Ancient Mariner' frustrated interpretation because it defeated expectation. It was first published at a time when 'Germany was [being] poured forth into England, in all her flood of skulls and numsculls';[70] and, naturally enough, it was read against the background of Gothic supernaturalism made fashionable by Schiller and Bürger, 'Monk' Lewis and the horrid mysteries of Mrs Radcliffe's novels. In this context 'The Ancient Mariner' inevitably appeared an enigma and a failure: its complexity was comfortably construed to be obscurity, its departures from conventional expectation were adjudged defects, and its disturbing power was dismissed as extravagance. Robert Southey's curt depreciation in the *Critical Review* for October 1798 is entirely typical of early critical reaction:

> This piece appears to us perfectly original in style as well as in story. Many of the stanzas are laboriously beautiful; but in connection they are absurd or unintelligible. . . . We do not sufficiently understand the story to analyse it. It is a Dutch attempt at German sublimity. Genius has here been employed in producing a poem of little merit.[71]

Since 'The Ancient Mariner' could not be slotted neatly into any existing ballad-classification, the easiest solution was simply to invoke custom and convention to declare the work incomprehensible.

The only significant exception in this early stream of adverse criticism is Charles Lamb. 'I am sorry', Lamb wrote to Southey in November 1798, 'you are so sparing of praise to the "Ancient Marinere;" – so far from calling it, as you do, with some wit, but more severity, "A Dutch Attempt," &c., I call it a right English attempt, and a successful one, to dethrone German sublimity' (*LL*, I 142). This is an acute perception. Although he had objections to some (unspecified) 'unmeaning miracles' in the poem, Lamb was instinctively aware that Coleridge had struck a new note in English poetry. Two years later in a letter to Wordsworth (30 Jan 1801), Lamb continued his praise for 'The Ancient Mariner': 'For me, I was never so affected with any human Tale. After first reading it, I was totally possessed with it for many days. – I dislike all the miraculous part of it, but the feelings of the man under the operation of such scenery dragged me along like Tom Piper's magic Whistle' (*LL*, I 266). By 1801, of course, Wordsworth had come to think 'The Ancient Mariner' an albatross around the neck of his *Lyrical Ballads* and had appended to Coleridge's poem a long note on its 'great defects' (see above, p. 112). Lamb went on to refute Wordsworth's criticisms at some length and with some spirit, concluding 'You will excuse my remarks, because I am hurt and vexed that you should think it necessary, with a prose apology, to open the eyes of dead men that cannot see − − −' (*LL*, I 266). Wordsworth did not, however, excuse Lamb's remarks: 'The Post did not sleep a moment', Lamb told Thomas Manning. 'I received almost instantaneously a long letter of four sweating pages . . .' (*LL*, I 272).[72]

Lamb's comments on 'The Ancient Mariner' are equally interesting for what they say and what they do *not* say. He admires the poem, he is moved by it − but he does not attempt to interpret it. Indeed, the question of 'meaning' never raises its head: he talks only of his *experience* of the poem, of being 'totally possessed' by it for many days. Lamb's response, in fact, after the initial flurry of negative criticism of 1798–1801 had vented itself, set the tone for almost every critical assessment of 'The Ancient Mariner' during the nineteenth century. An acquaintance with the poem and admiration for it are critical presuppositions from about 1817 onward;[73] but for nineteenth-century readers it remained a work beyond the grasp of rational understanding:

> To speak of it at all is extremely difficult; above all the poems with which we are acquainted in any language, it is a poem to be felt, cherished, mused upon, not to be talked about, not capable of being described, analyzed, or criticised. It is the wildest of all the creations of genius, it is not like a thing of the living, listening, moving world, the very music of its words is like the melancholy mysterious breath of something sung to the sleeping ear, its images have the beauty, the grandeur, the incoherence of some mighty vision.[74]

The 'meaning' of the poem, that is to say, is experiential; it is not something detachable from its dramatic context but is, rather, inextricably bound up with the richness and terror of the Mariner's whole experience − an experience which the reader, like the fascinated Wedding-Guest, both understands and shares vicariously. In other words, the meaning of 'The Ancient Mariner' depends not upon the poem's events or characters but upon the *effect* of these events and characters on the reader: and the critical approach involved here amounts, in effect, to an unformulated version of reader-response theory.

The general reluctance − or inability − to find a definable meaning in 'The Ancient Mariner' began to disappear during the last two decades of the nineteenth century. In a hesitant trickle at first, which shortly became a respectable stream and grew eventually into a swollen torrent, excited readers found the enchanted fabric of the Mariner's world to be inwrought with figures dim. Patterns of meaning emerged, were captured and tamed into expository prose, were refined and developed and expanded by successive generations of interpreters. At last 'The Ancient Mariner' made sense − or at least 'sense' could be found in it. But as meanings proliferated, their very plurality became a problem. If 'The Ancient Mariner' had an ulterior meaning or purpose, then what was it? For some, it was a religious or ethical poem; for others, it was a psychological, even autobiographical, study of guilt and terror; and, for still others, it was concerned with philosophy, or aesthetic theory, or politics. But diversity is not necessarily self-defeating. Indeed, there have been able defences of a wide variety of possible interpretations, and what emerges most clearly from an overview of criticism during the last hundred years is not the failure of critics to agree on a single reading but the depth and complexity of the poem itself which can, without contradiction, embrace and harmonise and sustain such connotative diversity. Although it resists reductionism, 'The Ancient Mariner' encourages critical variety − as a glance at the main lines of interpretation will clearly show.

Undoubtedly the most popular approach holds that 'The Ancient Mariner' is, by design and intention, a spiritual allegory depicting human life as a sort of Pilgrim's Progress on the sea: 'the Ancient Mariner − who is at once himself, Coleridge and all humanity − having sinned, both incurs punishment and seeks redemption'.[75] Some critics (especially the earlier ones) develop this theme in a crudely allegoric fashion, drawing one-to-one correspondences between events and their significance: the slaying of the albatross = Original Sin; the Hermit = the idea of enlightened religion; etc.[76] Most recent critics, however, influenced by Robert Penn Warren's important essay (1946),[77] have turned from allegorical to symbolic readings of the poem's moral and spiritual dimensions. Nevertheless, at the heart of all these interpretations − whether allegoric or symbolic − lies the conviction that the poem is 'about' the orthodox Christian progression from sin and the recognition of sin, through repentance and punishment, to such redemption as is possible in this world.[78] Beyond this, however, there is little agreement. Robert Penn Warren, for example, who stresses that in Coleridge's sacramental conception of the universe (i.e. the 'One Life') a crime against Nature is a crime against God, finds in the Fall an analogy for the Mariner's symbolic killing of the albatross: 'what is at stake . . . is not the objective magnitude of the act performed − the bird is, literally, a trivial creature − but the spirit in which the act is performed, the condition of the will'.[79] Thus, although the Mariner's deed is unmotivated, he is none the less responsible for it, for, like Adam, he possesses free will.[80] But is this really so? J. A. Stuart, for one, does not think so: the Mariner is one of those predestined to election − a man who, having sinned, is led inexorably by the hand of indefectible grace through an Augustinian process of justification and sanctification.[81] Edward Bostetter, however, who rejects both Warren's sacramentalism and Stuart's predestinarianism, argues vigorously that the spiritual forces at work in the Mariner's authoritarian universe are despotic and unpredictable. It is a nightmare world of inconsequence, terror and meaningless suffering through which the Mariner moves, a world governed by chance, where caprice is the decisive factor − as the dice-game between Death and Life-in-Death for the Mariner and his shipmates makes clear. It is, in essence, the Chritian universe gone mad, and reveals, according to Bostetter, 'Coleridge's fundamental uncertainty and doubt about the universe of love and law'.[82] But James D. Boulger takes issue with Bostetter and with Warren as well. Stressing the dream-logic of the poem and the purely imaginative and mysterious dimensions of the Mariner's experience, Boulger presents a strong case for believing that the 'world of "The Rime of the Ancient Mariner" is neither a sacramental universe [Warren] nor a nightmare vision [Bostetter], but a parable of the uneasy Christian skepticism that has been with us since Newton and Kant'. Indeed, he argues, 'The Ancient Mariner' can lay claim to being 'the first modern religious poem in the sense that it asserts a mysterious religious universe but cannot give us even a partial explanation of its nature'.[83] Now, since Warren, Stuart, Bostetter and Boulger all throw light on the poem and articulate, though in exaggerated form, aspects of its religious theme which most readers would agree are present in one way or another, it seems obvious that it is an error to attempt to impose any rigorous theological structure on the poem: 'The Ancient Mariner' is religious in a broad sense. It is about man's attempt to understand the mystery surrounding the human soul in a universe moved by forces and powers at once immanent and transcendent.

The Mariner shares the *Angst* and strictly limited insights achieved by most post-Romantic spiritual travellers, and his voyage is symbolic of the visionary terrors experienced by many who have, by circumstance or desire, been exposed to the world beyond the humanly imposed fictions of time and space. He returns from his experience as a deeply shaken man possessed of a profound and simple truth which he is charged to impart to others, although he himself, being neither philosopher nor prophet, lacks adequate means and understanding to give it more than a simple, albeit highly dramatic, account.

Not surprisingly the Mariner is sometimes considered by critics to be symbolic of the poet himself, especially the Romantic poet. Robert Penn Warren maintains that the Mariner's paradoxical stature of being at once blessed and accursed makes him a figure of the *poète maudit*; his dilemma, that is, is that of the Romantic poet himself who is both a healer and bringer of truth and beauty *and* at the same time an outsider, an outcast, a wanderer cut off from the society of men.[84] But Warren's aesthetic interpretation goes well beyond a simple identification of the Mariner as poet, for he believes that 'The Ancient Mariner' is a poem 'about poetry itself' and, in particular, about the poetic imagination. Warren's desire to find a single unified meaning in the poem leads him to posit the existence of two interwoven themes: the 'primary' or moral theme of sacramental vision and the 'One Life', which centres on the story of the Mariner's crime, punishment and reconciliation; and the 'secondary' or aesthetic theme of Imagination, which reveals its presence in the symbolic operation of the poem's major images (particularly the sun and the moon). Having declared that 'the good events' in the poem 'take place under the aegis of the moon, the bad events under that of the sun', Warren tries to establish that there is a coherent image-cluster (involving the moon, albatross, wind, Polar Spirit and water snakes) that symbolises the Imagination, and an antithetical image-cluster of sun, spectre-bark, and so on, that represents the Understanding or 'mere reflective faculty' — and that the Mariner's redemption (primary theme) is effected through Imagination (secondary theme), so that the moral and aesthetic themes are fused into a single experiential curve of meaning and intent.[85] This interpretation, although it has influenced the views of many later critics, has satisfied very few of them. In the first place, Coleridge's moon-imagery in 'The Ancient Mariner' and his other writings is by no means always beneficent or always to be associated with the healing power of Imagination: the Mariner's shipmates in Part III, for example, die beneath 'the star-dogged Moon' (lines 210–15). And the sun in Coleridge's poetry can as easily be associated with Reason (the mind's highest power) as with the merely empirical Understanding.[86] In other words, Warren's symbolic equations are too rigid and lean toward allegory; the poem's symbols need to be granted a freer, wider, less exact frame of reference. In the second place, as Humphry House points out, Warren's '"theme of the imagination" is something narrower and more technical than the poem can carry'. 'The Ancient Mariner' rather than being a poem 'about' the creative imagination is, more properly, 'part of the exploration, . . . part of the experience which led Coleridge into his later theoretic statements . . . [and not] a symbolic adumbration of the theoretic statements themselves'.[87]

Closely related to the theological concern with the question of free will *versus* determinism in the Mariner's universe is the problem of whether the poem reflects Coleridge's early infatuation with empiricism and philosophic necessity or his later devotion to transcendental metaphysics. S. F. Gingerich, who was the first critic to isolate the philosophic dimension of 'The Ancient Mariner', firmly established the direction of most early philosophic interpretations by finding in favour of the former. According to Gingerich, 'The Ancient Mariner' is the 'logical outcome' both philosophically and theologically of beliefs expressed in such poems as 'Religious Musings' and 'The Destiny of Nations', which set out Coleridge's Unitarian and Necessitarian convictions of the mid 1790s. The Mariner, he argues, is a naïve but engaging Unitarian who, not acting but consistently acted upon, is also a complete Necessitarian: 'He has no will of his own; he is passive to the powers outside himself and the new law of life revealed to him; that is, he is a true Necessitarian.'[88] Dorothy Waples, in another early philosophic interpretation, takes Gingerich's argument for empirical necessity a step further by attempting to demonstrate that 'The Ancient Mariner' is a 'complete exemplification' of David Hartley's mechanistic stimulus–response theory of association.[89] Such views are reductive, of course, and make their cases largely by ignoring what they do not wish to see. And most recent philosophic interpretations come close to reversing the empirical, mechanistic and necessitarian emphases of Gingerich and Waples. John Beer, for example, stresses the visionary and transcendent nucleus of

1 St Mary's Church, Ottery St Mary, Devon

2 Whittington Library, Christ's Hospital, 1790

3   Coleridge in 1795, by Peter Vandyke

4 Coleridge's cottage in Lime Street, Nether Stowey, built prior to 1753. The north wall, shown above, was not the original front. The cottage at one time faced east. The end building, on the right, is a later addition

5 Coleridge's cottage after repairs and decoration, which were carried out during the late 1970s

6　Alfoxden (Wordsworth's house in 1797–8) and the Quantock Hills

7 *Höhle mit Grabmal* (1813–14) by Caspar David Friedrich

In Xannadù did Cubla Khan
A stately Pleasure Dome decree;
Where Alph, the sacred River, ran
Thro' Caverns measureless to Man
Down to a sunless Sea.
So twice six miles of fertile ground
With Walls and Towers were compass'd round:
And here were Gardens bright with sinuous Rills
Where blossom'd many an incense-bearing Tree,
And here were Forests ancient as the Hills
Enfolding sunny spots of Greenery.
But o! that deep romantic Chasm, that slanted
Down a green Hill athwart a cedarn Cover,
A savage Place, as holy and inchanted
As e'er beneath a waning Moon was haunted
By Woman wailing for her Demon Lover.
From forth this Chasm with hideous Turmoil seething,
As if this Earth in fast thick Pants were breathing,
A mighty Fountain momently was forc'd,
Amid whose swift half-intermitted Burst
Huge Fragments vaulted like rebounding Hail,
Or chaffy Grain beneath the Thresher's Flail,
And mid these dancing Rocks at once & ever
It flung up momently the sacred River.
Five miles meandring with a mazy Motion
Thro' Wood and Dale the sacred River ran,
Then reach'd the Caverns measureless to Man
And sank in Tumult to a lifeless Ocean;
And mid this Tumult Cubla heard from far
Ancestral Voices prophesying War.
      The Shadow of the Dome of Pleasure
      Floated midway on the Wave
      Where was heard the mingled Measure
      From the Fountain and the Cave
      'Twas a miracle of rare Device
      A sunny Pleasure Dome with Caves of Ice!

      A Damsel with a Dulcimer

8 & 9   Crewe Manuscript of 'Kubla Khan', recto and verso

In a vision once I saw:
It was an Abyssinian Maid,
And on her Dulcimer she play'd
Singing of Mount Amara.
Could I revive within me
Her Symphony & Song,
To such a deep delight 'twould win me,
That with Music loud and long
I would build that Dome in Air,
That sunny Dome! those Caves of Ice!
And all, who heard, should see them there,
And all should cry, Beware! Beware!
His flashing Eyes! his floating Hair!
Weave a circle round him thrice,
And close your Eyes in holy dread,
For He on Honey-dew hath fed
And drank the Milk of Paradise.——

This fragment with a good deal more, not
recoverable, composed, in a sort of Reverie brought
on by two grains of Opium, taken to check a
dysentery, at a Farm House between Porlock &
Linton, a quarter of a mile from Culbone Church,
in the fall of the year, 1797.——

S. T. Coleridge

10 *Das Eismeer* (1823—4) by Caspar David Friedrich

11   Coleridge in 1799, from a pastel by an unknown German artist

12   Derwentwater in 1784, from an engraving by S. Middimans

13 Greta Hall, Keswick, one-time home of Coleridge, now part of Keswick School

14   Coleridge in 1804, by James Northcote

15 *Carceri d'Invenzione* by Giambattista Piranesi, 2nd edn (1760)

16   Coleridge in 1814, by Washington Allston

17 No. 3, The Grove, Highgate, Coleridge's residence from 1823 until his death in 1834

18 Coleridge's 'Bed- and Book-room' in the attic of No. 3, The Grove, Highgate, from a lithograph by George Scharf the Elder

Neoplatonic metaphysics that lies at the poem's heart: external events and physical phenomena are symbolic of inner truths and metempirical realities. In 'The Ancient Mariner', as in Coleridge's other major poems, the material universe both masks and is the medium for apprehending the noumenal realms of spiritual and psychological reality. The supernatural is not separate from the natural, but the inner essence of it; and the Mariner's experiences, at once physical and metaphysical, constitute an imaginative exploration of the links between the material and the spiritual, the natural and the supernatural. But Beer, unlike both Gingerich and Waples, is not dogmatic in his application of philosophic ideas to the poem; indeed, his central point is that 'The Ancient Mariner' reflects an acute conflict in Coleridge's thinking between mechanical and transcendental explanations of the universe. By 1797–8, when the poem was composed, Coleridge had grown beyond his hard youthful commitment to empiricism, but he had not yet embraced, despite some serious reading in Neoplatonic works, the transcendental metaphysic that he was to develop out of his later immersion in Germany philosophy. 'The Ancient Mariner', then, belongs to a period of philosophic uncertainty, a kind of limbo between Hartley and Kant, when Coleridge was between philosophic creeds; and the poem is explorative and experimental, a probing with the help of the mystics and the Neoplatonists into transcendental speculation that anticipates Coleridge's later metaphysical commitments.[90]

For a large number of twentieth-century readers biographical and psychological analyses have provided important keys to understanding the richness and emotional power of 'The Ancient Mariner'. It has become virtually a critical axiom, for example, that the Mariner reflects a good deal of Coleridge himself and that there are striking parallels between the experiences of the poet and those of the old navigator. Precisely what these connections are, however, is another matter entirely. Hugh l'Anson Fausset finds the poem to be

an involuntary but inevitable projection into imagery of [Coleridge's] own inner discord. The Mariner's sin against Nature in shooting the Albatross imaged his own morbid divorce from the physical: and the poem was therefore moral in its essence, in its implicit recognition of creative values and of the spiritual death which dogs their frustration.[91]

Other readers propose other parallels: for D. W. Harding, the poem reflects a pathological depression resulting from Coleridge's repudiation of ordinary social ties; for Douglas Angus, it reveals the poet's abnormal need for love and sympathy; for Lynn Grow, it is a symbolic exculpation of Coleridge's failure to answer the question, 'What is real?'; for Molly Lefebure, it is a proleptic vision of Coleridge's future struggles with the horrors of opium-addiction; and, for L. D. Berkoben, it reflects an inner spiritual struggle leading to apostasy and eventually to a return to religious orthodoxy.[92] About the only shared conviction in this plurality of opinions is the initial premise, common to all, that Coleridge unconsciously wrote a great deal of himself into his Ancient Mariner. And, as George Whalley has shown in an important essay, there *is* much in Coleridge's life and in his poem to support the conviction that the Mariner's spiritual and emotional experiences amount almost to a self-portrait of the poet. The 'haunting quality' and vivid fascination of 'The Ancient Mariner', Whalley argues convincingly, grow

> from our intimate experience in the poem of the most intense personal suffering, perplexity, loneliness, longing, horror, fear. This experience brings us, with Coleridge, to the fringes of madness and death, and carries us to that nightmare land that Coleridge inhabited, the realm of Life-in-Death. . . . Whether or not he recognised this process at the time, Coleridge enshrined in 'The Ancient Mariner' the quintessence of himself, of his suffering and dread, his sense of sin, his remorse, his powerlessness.[93]

The Mariner, whose passivity and mesmeric eye are salient features of Coleridge himself, mirrors his maker's existential anxieties and profound sense of 'aloneness'. During his time on Malta (1804–6), when his hopeless addiction to opium exacerbated his neuroses almost beyond bearing, Coleridge realised vividly his kinship with the Mariner, and Coleridge's consciousness of this connection may be traced in the revisions of 1817 and, especially, in the famous 'Moon gloss', where the note of personal allegory, of pain and despair and utter isolation, comes closest to the surface. As composed in 1798 'The Ancient Mariner was

> both an unconscious projection of Coleridge's early sufferings and a vivid prophecy of the sufferings that were to follow. The

poem was probably not originally intended to be a personal allegory: but that is what, in Coleridge's eyes, it became later as the prophecy was slowly, inexorably, and lingeringly fulfilled.[94]

Generally attempts to carry parallels between the experiences of the poet and those of his poem further than a recognition of broad similarities are severely strained and unconvincing. It has been suggested, for example, that Coleridge presents himself as the listening Wedding-Guest (surely an unnatural posture for a compulsive talker such as Coleridge), that the Hermit who 'singeth loud his godly hymns / That he makes in the wood' represents Wordsworth, and that Life-in-Death is to be identified as Mrs Coleridge, with whom the poet was no longer in love because he had fallen in love with someone else (probably Dorothy Wordsworth!).[95] Ingenious speculation of this sort, with its potential for enthusiastically espoused absurdity, has also left its mark on much of the Freudian criticism of the poem. Instead of remaining content with half-truths, the Freudians crave specific relationships and tend, therefore, to reduce complex symbols to simple (often biographical) correspondences. Kenneth Burke links the albatross with Sara Coleridge and the poet's marital troubles, cheerfully declares that the blessing of the water snakes symbolises Coleridge's capitulation to opium, and reads the Pilot's Boy (who goes crazy) as the fictive scapegoat for Coleridge's opium guilt.[96] Other Freudian analysts have found in the poem evidence of Coleridge's unresolved incestuous conflicts, or latent homosexuality, or sadomasochism, or exhibitionism, or rejection of genital sexuality, or Oedipal fantasies concerned with the father—son relationship.[97] Or something else to be traced back into Coleridge's overburdened psyche. The most useful of the Freudian interpretations is David Beres's carefully developed argument that 'The Ancient Mariner' is Coleridge's unconscious attempt to resolve in art his feelings of hostility and guilt toward his mother — but even Beres falls prey to over-precision, as when he asserts, for example, that the 'silly buckets' which fill with dew (lines 297—9) 'symbolize the mother's breasts, previously empty and cruel, now full and forgiving'.[98]

Although the critical approaches summarised above constitute the major lines of analysis, there are, of course, other interpretations of 'The Ancient Mariner'. Maud Bodkin and Mark Littmann have proposed mythic readings, exploring the poem in the light of Jung's archetypes of rebirth and initiation.[99] A number of readers have argued for the existence of a political dimension in the poem.[100] Still others have discussed the function and significance of the frame story of the wedding and the role of the Wedding-Guest, analysing the ways in which the wedding-feast provides a framework of reality for the Mariner's strange tale of the supernatural and the manner in which the Wedding-Guest serves as a foil for the hypnotic Mariner and as a bridge for the reader into the Mariner's nightmare world.[101] And finally, despite the widespread (indeed, almost universal) conviction that 'The Ancient Mariner' is a 'symbolic' statement of some kind, whether religious or philosophic or psychological or political or whatever, there remain some few voices proclaiming, in the tradition of Charles Lamb and his nineteenth-century heirs, that the poem is not *about* anything: it is a work of pure imagination to be experienced but not plundered for meaning, a poem to be 'understood' only when understanding is suspended and the rationalising powers of the mind are asleep.[102]

What, then, can one say finally about 'The Ancient Mariner'? The anti-symbolists are surely right in objecting to those rigid interpretations that use symbolism to explain away the poem; and, yet, one inevitably feels cheated by the anti-symbolists who counsel a flight from meaning, for the poem speaks to the head as well as to the heart. The answer, it seems clear, must lie in a middle course between the extremes. John Beer expresses the solution thus:

> The relationship between the energies of the inquiring mind that an intelligent reader brings to the poem and the poem's refusal to yield a single comprehensive interpretation enacts vividly the everlasting intercourse between the human mind, with its instinct to organise and harmonise, and the baffling powers of the universe about it.[103]

Less theoretically, the same point is made by Father Barth:

> There is room for precision in the articulation of symbol, as long as it does not claim to be all. There is room for indefiniteness, as long as it does not abdicate the search for meaning. The Nicene definition of the consubstantiality of the Son with the Father does not deny the ultimate mystery of the Trinity, nor does the confession of the mystery negate the validity of the definition. As in 'The Ancient Mariner', we articulate what we can, in faithfulness to the revelation (or the poem) set before us; the rest is mystery.[104]

Poetry, as Coleridge himself succinctly reminds us, 'gives most pleasure when only generally and not perfectly understood' (*AP*, p. 5).

A NOTE ON THE 'MORAL' OF 'THE ANCIENT MARINER'

Pain from having cursed *a gnat that was singing about my head.* (*CN*, II no. 2666)

Doubtless the most celebrated anecdote about 'The Ancient Mariner' is Coleridge's retort to Mrs Barbauld's criticisms of the poem, as recorded in Coleridge's *Table Talk* (31 May 1830):

> Mrs Barbauld once told me that she admired *The Ancient Mariner* very much, but that there were two faults in it — it was improbable, and had no moral. As for the probability, I owned that that might admit some question; but as to the want of a moral, I told her that in my own judgement the poem had too much; and that the only, or chief fault, if I might say so, was the obtrusion of the moral sentiment so openly on the reader as a principle or cause of action in a work of such pure imagination. It ought to have had no more moral than the *Arabian Nights'* tale of the merchant's sitting down to eat dates by the side of a well, and throwing the shells aside, and lo! a genie starts up, and says he *must* kill the aforesaid merchant, *because* one of the date shells had, it seems, put out the eye of the genie's son.
>
> (*TT*, p. 106)[105]

One should approach this anecdote with considerable caution, for its intention is by no means as transparent as is often assumed. It is, after all, an after-dinner comment divorced from its after-dinner context of port and cigars, which has tended to invest it with a seriousness and rigidity that may well have been absent in the original telling. And this raises some interesting points. In the first place, Coleridge was certainly not opposed to didactic poetry, although he believed that morality should be delivered obliquely: 'the communication of pleasure may be the immediate purpose, . . . [but] truth, either moral or intellectual, ought to be the *ultimate* end' (*BL*, II 9). It may be supposed, therefore, that 'the *obtrusion* of the moral sentiment *so openly* on the reader' (emphasis added) refers to the blunt moral maxims of the Mariner at the end of the poem:

> Farewell, farewell! but this I tell
> To thee, thou Wedding-Guest!
> He prayeth well, who loveth well
> Both man and bird and beast.
>
> He prayeth best, who loveth best
> All things both great and small;
> For the dear God who loveth us,
> He made and loveth all.
>
> (610–17)

But, if Coleridge felt these stanzas to be obtrusively moralistic, why did he not alter or excise them? He had plenty of opportunity. Yet, from 1798 through the major revisions of 1800 and 1817 and into the later editions of 1828, 1829 and 1834, these stanzas stand unchanged. Presumably, then, Coleridge thought them to be integral to his poem. But this leaves us still with the problem of explaining (a) how they might be integral to the poem, and (b) why he should have labelled them 'the only, or chief fault . . . in a work of such pure imagination'.

One possible and, I think, highly probable solution to the latter problem is that the charge of obtrusive morality is levelled, with witty irony, against Mrs Barbauld herself. Mrs Barbauld was a professional moralist and third-rate poet, who devoted herself in print to the inculcation of virtue and who often inveighed against the sin of being cruel to animals, particularly birds:[106]

A naughty boy will not feed a starving and freezing robin; in fact he even pulls the poor bird's tail! It dies. Shortly after that, the boy's parents leave him because he is cruel, and he is forced to beg for food. He goes into a forest, sits down and cries, and is never heard of again; it is believed that bears ate him.

And then there is her 'Epitaph on a Goldfinch':

                    Reader,
    if suffering innocence can hope for retribution,
            deny not to the gentle shade
                of this unfortunate captive
        the natural though uncertain hope
                of animating some happier form,
        or trying his new-fledged pinions
                in some humble Elysium,
        beyond the reach of Man,
                the tyrant
        of this lower universe.

Mrs Barbauld complained that 'The Ancient Mariner' had no moral. *Au contraire*, riposted Coleridge, it has too much! – a dexterous turning of the tables and a witty rebuke to a lady to whom *imaginative* writing was as foreign as imported brandy. The origin, too, of an amusing postprandial anecdote.

The story, of course, has its serious side as well, for the moral stanzas at the end of the poem clearly do draw attention to themselves by their jingling prosody and Sunday-school sentiment. Most of the early critics, unable to account for so apparently awkward an intrusion of sententious godliness as the spiritual dénouement of the Mariner's tale, found themselves forced, like John Livingston Lowes, to deplore 'the Mariner's valedictory piety, which does, I fear, warrant Coleridge's (and our own) regret'.[107] More recent readers, however, have defended the moral stanzas in terms of their dramatic propriety: the valedictory piety, in other words, is the Mariner's simple-minded summary of what his terrible experience has taught him, but it does not necessarily follow that Coleridge stops with the Mariner. According to Lionel Stevenson, 'the "morality" of the poem . . . is not Coleridge's, but that of a primitive seaman who has evolved a creed for himself on the basis of terrific experiences, and is therefore fanatically devoted to it'.[108] For George Watson,

> the Mariner's moral is a centrally Christian one, . . . [but the reader] is no more required to believe [it] to be Coleridge's than to accept phrases like 'To Mary Queen the praise be given' as evidence of the poet's mariolatry during his unitarian years. The truth of the poem . . . is a dramatic truth, and the Mariner may well be wrong.[109]

As attractive as is the general notion of distinguishing between Coleridge and his Mariner, however, both Stevenson and Watson go too far in insisting upon a radical divorce. Distinction does not necessitate division. And, in any case, there is a great deal of evidence to put beyond doubt the fact that not only Coleridge but the Wordsworths as well would heartily approve of the Mariner's 'piety'. Coleridge, who in verse could pity a tethered donkey, was also someone who in real life could be *pained* 'from having *cursed* a gnat' that disturbed his rest (*CN*, II no. 2666). Wordsworth, too, learned moral lessons out of a guilty response to his thoughtless plunder of a raven's nest (*The Prelude* (1805) I 333–41). And, perhaps most revealing of all is Dorothy Wordsworth's unmotivated uprooting of a wild strawberry-plant:

> I found a strawberry blossom in a rock. The little slender flower had more courage than the green leaves, for *they* were but half expanded and half grown, but the blossom was spread full out. I uprooted it rashly, and I felt as if I had been committing an outrage, so I planted it again. It will have but a stormy life of it, but let it live if it can.   (31 Jan 1802; *JDW*, p. 83)

It is as if the Mariner, having felt *on his own* the moral imperative of the universe, were able to reanimate the albatross. But the Mariner must be brought to an understanding of his deed by external forces which, as it happens, are not really external at all, since they are projections from his own troubled psyche.

The point, quite simply, is this: the Mariner's moral is not, as is sometimes claimed, either a 'sham moral' or an ironic *non sequitur*,[110] for it expresses a faith in the 'One Life' that Coleridge himself espoused and which, in the poem, is a legitimate lesson for the Mariner to learn. 'The Ancient Mariner' is not a tract on the prevention of cruelty to albatrosses; it is an imaginative and profoundly moving exploration of the moral integrity of the universe, which concludes – and *here* is the problem – with an unsettlingly naïve expression of this leading idea in the form of two sentimental quatrains. The major problem with the 'moral stanzas', then, is an artistic one. Are they a banal excrescence, a platitudinous restatement of the poem's 'theme', or are they organically and dramatically defensible? There are almost as many answers, or shades of opinion, as there are commentators who have addressed themselves to the question. Humphry House argues that the Mariner's moralising, 'coming in context, after the richness and terror of the poem', is both justified and meaningful because its meaning '*has been lived*'.[111] John Beer, on the other hand, finds it anticlimactic and unsatisfying: 'Successful as the occasional nursery-rhyme diction is within the scope of *The Ancient Mariner*, one recognises it as another (albeit more successful) attempt to deal with the check that [Coleridge] had elsewhere felt obliged to impose (as in *The Eolian Harp*) upon his more adventurous speculations.'[112] But Gayle Smith, who argues well that the 'moral stanzas' belong to the frame story rather than to the central narrative, defends them as an intentionally insipid choric summary of the action which, like the rhyming endings in Shakespeare's tragedies or the banal epi-grammatic conclusions or Sophocles and Euripides, provides the 'perspective of the moral commonplace upon the moral sublime'.[113]

But one need not go so far afield as Sophocles or Shakespeare to find analogies for the Mariner's moralising. Coleridge's own Con-versation Poems, although lyric rather than narrative, share the Mariner's moralising strain. Indeed, the similarities can be quite striking. It is not often enough remarked, for example, that 'The Ancient Mariner' is built upon the same structural pattern of departure and return as the Conversation Poems. Setting out from his home harbour, the Mariner is swept outward and upward into a world of *rêverie* and imaginative experience from which he is returned, at the poem's close, to the same harbour from which he had first sailed. As in the Conversation Poems, however, the 'return' is not a simple coming-back: the self who returns is not the same as the self who had set out; he has been fundamentally altered by his experiences. Sometimes, too, the moral lessons of the Conversation Poems are expressed, as in 'The Ancient Mariner', in the form of an explicit and detachable maxim that neatly sums up the poem's didactic drift. Such is clearly the case, for example, at the close of 'This Lime-Tree Bower':

> Henceforth I shall know
> That Nature ne'er deserts the wise and pure;
> No plot so narrow, be but Nature there,
> No waste so vacant, but may well employ
> Each faculty of sense, and keep the heart
> Awake to Love and Beauty!
> (59—64)

In essence, this is the Mariner's message as well, except that he, having learned in terror and suffering that no sound is dissonant which tells of Life, is constrained to preach his lesson against a backdrop of profound personal guilt and a less-than-perfect reconciliation. 'The Ancient Mariner', in other words, is both more complex and less optimistic than the Conversation Poems; and its sermonising conclusion – the Mariner's stumbling effort to articulate what he has learned – is at one and the same time an accurate inference and a hopelessly inadequate expression of what befell him on the wide wide sea.

5 'Dejection: An Ode'

COMPOSITION, REDACTIONS AND PUBLICATION HISTORY

Coleridge's health and spirits were matters of grave concern to his friends in the spring of 1802. Five years earlier he had been happy and carefree, impetuous and bubbling over with good humour. On his visit to Racedown in June 1797 (as Wordsworth long remembered) he had vaulted over a gate and bounded across an open field to greet William and Dorothy. But now, in the spring of 1802, he was a sadly altered man. Much of his natural ebullience had been sapped by a concatenation of personal troubles: a debilitating succession of physical illnesses in the winter of 1801–2, a growing reliance upon opium, a conviction that he had lost his shaping power of imagination, the terrible realisation that he could not live *with* his wife or *without* his children, and his hopeless love for Sara Hutchinson. All of these had exacted their toll; and all were known (or suspected) by his close friends in the Grasmere circle. On a blustery Friday afternoon in mid March he arrived at Dove Cottage during a heavy rainstorm: 'His eyes', Dorothy confided to her Journal, 'were a little swollen with the wind. I was much affected with the sight of him — he seemed half-stupified' (*JDW*, p. 105). That evening Coleridge and Wordsworth disputed about Ben Jonson and, after Coleridge had retired to bed, the Wordsworths stayed up until four o'clock in the morning discussing their friend's plight — his domestic unhappiness and, perhaps, his use of opium. 'My spirits', Dorothy wrote, 'were agitated very much.'

Coleridge remained at Grasmere for two days and, when he departed, the Wordsworths promised to pay a visit to Keswick the following week. Over the next few days they talked and worried a good deal about him, and anguished when no letters arrived from

169

him. They were occupied with other matters too, notably William's engagement to Mary Hutchinson and his resolve to visit Annette Vallon and their daughter Caroline in France before his marriage. But there was still time for poetry. On Friday 26 March, five days after Coleridge's return to Keswick, Wordsworth composed 'The Rainbow'. The following morning, at breakfast, he wrote part of the 'Ode: Intimations of Immortality from Recollections of Early Childhood' and then spent the rest of the morning digging into the garden the dung sent by Mr Olliff. The afternoon and evening were given up to meditation and quiet conversation in the orchard behind Dove Cottage. Wordsworth, it seems, did no more work on his ode that day. In all probability his breakfast-table labours had resulted in a draft of the opening four stanzas of the 'Ode' — lines in which the poet, while still responsive to natural beauty, recognises that for him 'there hath past away a glory from the earth'. The precise nature and extent of the loss was at this point unclear, the remedy unknown; and the draft ended with unanswered (probably then unanswerable) questions:

> Whither is fled the visionary gleam?
> Where is it now, the glory and the dream?

There has been a change in his view of nature, and this change, it is true, has involved a concomitant loss; but while much has been taken, much abides. The winds still visit him from the fields of sleep, and he is still able to respond to joy and beauty: 'I hear, I hear, with joy I hear'.

The next day (Sunday, 28 March) the Wordsworths went to Keswick to spend a week with the Coleridges at Greta Hall. During this visit Wordsworth and Coleridge (sometimes accompanied by Dorothy Wordsworth and Sara Coleridge) went on a number of short walking-excursions in the vicinity of Keswick. The two men spent a good deal of time together and at some point Wordsworth recited his recent compositions, including the beginning of his ode, to his friend. Undoubtedly they discussed the source and character of the 'loss' experienced by Wordsworth and so vividly described in his poem. The mood of the fragmentary 'Ode' spoke to Coleridge's condition: he too felt that his creative power — a power both to see and to record what he had seen — had deserted him.

But Coleridge's situation was more critical than was Wordsworth's, and it was more complex as well. Wordsworth's loss was temporary and could find relief in a 'timely utterance' such as 'To the Cuckoo' or 'The Rainbow' (both composed in the same week as the first four stanzas of the 'Ode'); moreover, Wordsworth's domestic life was happy and untroubled: he was engaged to be married and was surrounded by three women — his sister, his future wife and Sara Hutchinson (Coleridge's beloved Asra) — who reverenced his genius and encouraged his poetic endeavours. Coleridge, on the other hand, was experiencing an 'intellectual *exsiccation*' (*CL*, II 713) more severe and more permanent than Wordsworth's vague sense of imaginative loss; and, since, in pointed contrast to his friend, his domestic life was fraught with strife and tension, Coleridge did not have at Greta Hall any of the solicitude and intellectual companionship that characterised Wordsworth's life at Dove Cottage. Mrs Coleridge did not understand her husband and she was unable — not unwilling, but unable — to give him the sympathy and encouragement that he so desperately needed: 'She would', Dorothy Wordsworth had declared in 1801, 'have made a very good wife to many another man, but for Coleridge! Her radical fault is want of sensibility and what can such a woman be to Coleridge?' (*LW: EY*, pp. 330–1). The Coleridges' marital problems, moreover, while grounded in mutual dyspathy, were exacerbated by the near presence of the Wordsworths and the Hutchinsons. Mrs Coleridge did not entirely approve of the unconventional life-style of the Wordsworths and, with some justice, she resented relationships (from which she was largely excluded) which consumed so much of her husband's time and attention.[1] For Coleridge himself, however, the Grasmere circle was essential; the Wordsworths and the Hutchinson sisters furnished him with the hope, warmth, love, admiration, and understanding that he could not find at home.

Yet Grasmere was a bane as well as a blessing. Dove Cottage was an idyllic environment into which he could occasionally escape but which, since he was bound with fetters of steel to Greta Hall, he knew that he could neither possess nor wholly share. And then, too, there were emotions that ran deeper than friendship, for Coleridge was deeply in love with Sara Hutchinson. His love for her, however, although requited, was fated to remain unfulfilled, for he would not contemplate divorce: 'Carefully have I *thought thro'* the subject of marriage', he told Southey in October 1801, '& deeply am I convinced of it's indissolubleness' (*CL*, II 767). He no longer loved his wife, but neither would he leave her for another woman. Tantalus himself was not more sorely tried.

On Sunday, 4 April 1802, the Wordsworths were still at Keswick. Their week's visit, however, was drawing to a close and they were preparing to leave the following day to spend a few days with the Clarksons at Eusemere near the foot of Ullswater. That Sunday, as evening deepened into night over Derwentwater and the encamped army of tent-like mountains around Greta Hall, Coleridge sat alone in his study and began to compose a long verse-letter to Sara Hutchinson.[2] His thoughts were full of her, of the pain he had caused her recently in a complaining letter of love for her and unhappiness with his wife. He thought, too, of his declining poetic powers and his discussions with Wordsworth earlier in the week about the visionary glory that had passed away from his perception of the natural world. He was haunted by his friend's uncompleted ode; its phrases tolled through his memory like a knell declaring his own departed powers. His conversational verse-letter assumed the shape of an ode — consciously or unconsciously it was an imitation of Wordsworth's poem and served as Coleridge's despairing answer to his friend's question: 'Where is it now, the glory and the dream?'

The themes of lost imagination and lost love mingled in his mind. As he wrote to Sara — both the object and the victim of his passion — he found himself analysing their relationship, his unhappy marriage, and his poetic failure. Although subconsciously hampered by self-censureship and a measure of self-pity, he made an honest attempt to lay bare and articulate the causes of his dejection. Love was certainly a major factor, but at the root of his problem was the harrowing contrast between himself and Wordsworth. The verse-letter is, as Ernest de Selincourt (who discovered it in 1936) has said,

> a psychological analysis, as acute as it is tragic, of his own mental and emotional state viewed throughout in conscious and deliberate contrast with that of his poet friend. The lines bewailing his own domestic woes are conceived with the perfect affection and harmony of Dove Cottage vividly present in his mind; even the lines more definitely addressed to Sara are written with a sense — and herein lies much of their pathos — that though she returned his love, she yet belonged intrinsically, not to him, but to that happy company of friends, Mary and Dorothy and William, from which, despite their sympathy with him, his own misery seemed more and more to shut him out.[3]

On Monday, 5 April, the Wordsworths set out for Eusemere. Coleridge, without apparently mentioning the poem he had begun the previous evening, accompanied them along the Penrith road as far as Threlkeld before turning back to Keswick. In all probability he spent the next week or so completing the verse-letter. The Wordsworths did not learn of it until later in the month, when Coleridge arrived unexpectedly at Dove Cottage. Looking pale but otherwise well, he reached Grasmere on Tuesday, 20 April. Dorothy's Journal entry for the following day reads,

> William and I sauntered a little in the garden. Coleridge came to us and repeated the verses he wrote to Sara. I was affected with them and was on the whole, not being well, in miserable spirits. The sunshine − the green fields and the fair sky made me sadder; even the little happy sporting lambs seemed but sorrowful to me.   (*JDW*, p. 113)

Dorothy's response indicates not only the depth of her concern for Coleridge but also her instinct that the verse-letter had, in part, been prompted by her brother's ode, for her reference to 'the little happy sporting lambs' has its source in the third stanza of Wordsworth's 'Ode: Intimations of Immortality':

> Now, while the birds thus sing a joyous song,
>   And while the young lambs bound
>   As to the tabor's sound,
> To me alone there came a thought of grief. . . .

Over the next four months (May–September 1802) Coleridge's verse-letter to Sara Hutchinson, gradually restructured, revised, and purged of intimate personal references, became 'Dejection: An Ode'. With the aid of Coleridge's surviving letters from this period we can plot this development in some detail. On 7 May he wrote to Thomas Poole saying, 'I have neither been very well, nor very happy; but I have been far from idle'; he spoke of his plan to compose a long poem 'next year' and then, after copying out two of Wordsworth's recent lyrics to avoid leaving too much of the sheet blank (since postage charges were paid by the recipient not the sender), he concluded, 'I ought to say for my own sake that on the 4th of April last I wrote you a letter in verse; but I thought it dull & doleful − & did not send it' (*CL*, II 799, 801). This is, of course, a patent falsehood. The verse-letter was addressed to Sara Hutchinson, not to Poole; but Coleridge was anxious to let his friend know that he had been thinking of him and he was anxious, too, to evade the charge of indolence. In any case, the process of objectification and distancing had begun as early as the first week of May.

In the original verse-letter the themes of lost imaginative power and lost love had been intricately interwoven as the major causes of Coleridge's dejection-crisis. Few people outside the Grasmere circle, however, knew of his love for Sara Hutchinson or of his domestic unhappiness. In writing to correspondents who knew little or nothing of these matters it was necessary, therefore, to suppress the more personal sections of the original poem. The inevitable result was a marked change in emphasis: when these elements were edited out, the poem became less accurate as an autobiographical record and became, indeed, an altogether different poem – a poem 'about' poetry and the intermission of Coleridge's imaginative power. It may be added, too, that physical illness and Coleridge's intense metaphysical investigations (both given as contributory causes of dejection in the verse-letter) became more prominent factors in the later versions of the poem once the themes of love and domestic discord had been deleted.

The metamorphosis of the verse-letter into 'Dejection: An Ode' can be traced in two letters of July 1802, one to William Sotheby (a new friend whom Coleridge was anxious to impress) and one to Robert Southey. And still more light is shed on the evolution of the poem in Coleridge's important letter to Sotheby of 10 September 1802.

On 19 July Coleridge wrote to tell Sotheby that he had undertaken a translation of Salomon Gessner's prose romance *Der erste Schiffer*, 'partly, because I could not endure to appear *irresolute & capricious* to you', and partly, too,

> because I wished to force myself out of metaphysical trains of Thought – which, when I trusted myself to my own Ideas, came upon me uncalled – & when I wished to write a poem, beat up Game of far other kind – instead of a Covey of poetic Partridges with whirring wings of music, or wild Ducks *shaping* their rapid flight in forms always regular (a still better image of Verse) up came a metaphysical Bustard, urging it's slow, heavy, laborious, earth-skimming Flight, over dreary & level Wastes. . . . Sickness

& some other & worse afflictions, first forced me into *downright metaphysics* / for I believe that by nature I have more of the Poet in me / In a poem written during that dejection to Wordsworth, & the greater part of a private nature — I thus expressed the thought /   (*CL*, II 814–15)

— and he goes on to quote (with some omissions) the lines about turning to 'abstruse research' and about the suspension of his 'shaping Spirit of Imagination'. 'Thank Heaven!' he continues, 'my better mind has returned to me — and I trust, I shall go on rejoicing'; and, having 'nothing better' with which to fill up the sheet, he transcribes large sections of the verse-letter (lines 1–51, 296–340), omitting the entire middle section dealing with Sara Hutchinson and his wife, altering all the personal references from Sara to Wordsworth, and explaining that the opening lines 'allude to a stanza in the Ballad of Sir Patrick Spence' (*CL*, II 815). 'I have', he goes on after the transcription, 'selected from the Poem which was a very long one, & truly written only for "the solace of sweet Song", all that could be interesting or even pleasing to you — except indeed, perhaps, I may annex as a *fragment* a few Lines on the Eolian Lute, it having been introduced in it's Dronings in the 1st Stanza' (*CL*, II 818) — whereupon he copied out lines 184–215 (with appropriate alterations) of the verse-letter composed in April.

This letter to Sotheby is more revealing than it may at first sight appear to be, for in it we are given an opportunity to watch a poet at work recollecting an experience in tranquillity and transforming one kind of poetic statement into another. With Coleridge, of course, there is always the problem of deception — either self-deception or misleading (not to say false) statements designed to speak to a correspondent's preconceptions. Some of what he tells Sotheby (as, for instance, that the poem was originally addressed to Wordsworth) is demonstrably false. Yet, such obvious disingenuousness aside, there is much that is revealed.

Coleridge says, for instance, that the poem is addressed to Wordsworth. Now, however wrong this may be as a factual statement, it has a clear *poetic* relevance and appropriateness, for the original verse-letter to Sara Hutchinson was prompted by and was, in some sense, Coleridge's answer to Wordsworth's 'Ode: Intimations of Immortality'. As described to Sotheby, the poem is not a love-letter but a verse-epistle to a brother poet, and its tone is much less intensely personal than it had been in the original draft; indeed, as David Pirie has pointed out,

> In the original poem [Wordsworth] was the centre of a complex of interdependent human relationships, which were both precious and tragic to Coleridge. In the new version [sent to Sotheby] he is abstracted into a 'Calm stedfast Spirit, guided from above', and seems to have no more intimate relationship to Coleridge's unhappiness than Shakespeare.[4]

More important still, however, is the fact that the version sent to Sotheby and Coleridge's comments on it give a clear indication of his intentions. He transcribes three sections of the original verse-letter: (1) the section on the suspension of his imaginative power and his enmeshment in 'abstruse research', in order to explain to Sotheby the nature of his dejection; (2) a long passage comprising the first fifty and the last forty-five lines of the original poem — an extract which (he tells Sotheby) is all that is 'of a sufficiently general nature to be interesting to you'; and (3) the storm and Aeolian-harp sequence, which is annexed specifically 'as a *fragment*'. Two conclusions may be drawn from these facts. First, Coleridge was engaged in transforming a poetic statement, the 'greater part' of which was 'of a private nature', into a poem 'of a sufficiently general nature' to be interesting to a wider readership. Second, although he had excised the purely private sections dealing with Sara Hutchinson and his marital troubles and had begun the task of recasting what remained, he had not yet determined how to integrate the unexpurgated sections into a unified and coherent poem. In the letter to Sotheby the 'poem' exists as three related, yet distinct, fragments; however, with some revision, it is precisely these three sections which are brought together to form 'Dejection: An Ode', in which the passage on the suspension of imagination becomes stanza 6, the 'fragment' on the storm and Aeolian harp becomes stanza 7, and the eighty-five lines deemed 'sufficiently general' to be of interest to Sotheby become stanzas 1–5 and provide at least the starting-point for stanza 8. Thus, by mid July 1802, Coleridge had isolated the portions of the April verse-letter that he would use in constructing his ode, but he had not yet succeeded in welding the component parts into a unified whole.

On 29 July 1802, ten days after the letter to Sotheby, Coleridge wrote to Robert Southey, spawning plans like a herring. He told Southey that he had written 'more than half' of a book on the use of the definite article in the Greek New Testament and that he was contemplating publishing a two-volume work entitled 'Concerning Poetry, & the characteristic Merits of the Poets, our Contemporaries – one Volume Essays, the second Selections' (*CL*, II 829). Then, turning to Wordsworth's Preface to *Lyrical Ballads* – a Preface which he quite legitimately terms 'half a child of my own Brain' – he advises Southey that he is, none the less, 'far from going all lengths with Wordsworth':

> On the contrary, I rather suspect that some where or other there is a radical Difference in our theoretical opinions respecting Poetry – / this I shall endeavor to go to the Bottom of – and acting the arbitrator between the old School & the New School hope to lay down some plain, & perspicuous, tho' not superficial, Canons of Criticism respecting Poetry.   (*CL*, II 830)

From literary critical theory Coleridge turns to poetry and his own claim to the title of poet. He transcribes from the verse-letter the lines about suspension of imagination and the influence of abstruse research, prefaced with this statement:

> As to myself, all my poetic Genius, if ever I really possessed any *Genius*, & it was not rather a mere general *aptitude* of Talent, & quickness in Imitation / is gone – and I have been fool enough to suffer deeply in my mind, regretting the loss – which I attribute to my long & exceedingly severe Metaphysical Investigations – & these partly to Ill-health, and partly to private afflictions which rendered any subject, immediately connected with Feeling, a source of pain & disquiet to me.   (*CL*, II 831)

This statement and the transcription from the verse-letter are followed by an analysis of Coleridge's marriage which provides an insight into the domestic situation and dejection that had led four months earlier to the composition of the verse-letter to Sara Hutchinson. At that time he had resolved upon a separation from his wife ('a very aweful Step'). The decision, however, had affected Coleridge's physical and mental health to such a degree and had so alarmed his wife that a reconciliation had been effected; both husband and wife had subsequently amended their behaviour – a 'happy Revolution in our domestic affairs' which Coleridge hoped would be permanent. Thus, although the 'stern Match-maker' had perhaps never brought together 'two minds so utterly contrariant in their primary and organical constitution', Coleridge was able to report to Southey that 'now for a long time there has been more Love & Concord in my House, than I have known for years before' (*CL*, II 832).

July to September 1802 was for Coleridge a period of improved health and domestic calm. During these months he spent a good deal of time thinking, not about metaphysics, but about literary theory. While he would continue to write poems, he had come to believe that his true vocation (at least as far as literature was concerned) lay in poetic theory rather than in original composition. A year earlier such a thought had been too painful for rational contemplation: 'Into a *discoverer* I have sunk from an *inventor*' (*CN*, I no. 950). He had often spoken of abandoning poetry and of his loss of imaginative power (e.g. *CL*, I 623, 656, 658), but all these early statements somehow protest too much; it was not until the summer of 1802 that he could, with equanimity, face the prospect of poetry as an avocation rather than a vocation. This is not to say that Coleridge ceased to be a poet in 1802, but merely that in mid 1802 he consciously turned his attention in literary matters from poetic practice to poetic theory. The primary motivation for this change of emphasis seems to have been the publication of the third edition of *Lyrical Ballads* with its expanded Preface and an Appendix on poetic diction. (Copies of this new edition, published in London in April 1802, did not reach the Wordsworths until the end of June.[5]) Coleridge was uneasy about Wordsworth's pronouncements on the nature of poetry and the poet in the revised Preface of 1802 and he was startled, too, when reading some of his friend's recent verse, by 'a daring Humbleness of Language & Versification, and a strict adherence to matter of fact, even to prolixity' (*CL*, II 830). He gave a good deal of thought to these matters and discussed them at length with Wordsworth — but Wordsworth did not resolve his doubts. 'On the contrary,' as he told Southey, 'I rather suspect that some where or other there is a radical Difference in our theoretical opinions respecting Poetry.'

In July 1802, Coleridge had set out to get to the bottom of their theoretical differences. The first-fruits of this labour were presented to William Sotheby in a letter dated 10 September 1802.

It is, perhaps, the most important letter about critical theory that Coleridge ever wrote. Coleridge's 'abstruse research' in British empiricism and German transcendentalism after his return from Germany had convinced him that neither a purely empirical epistemology (such as the systems of Locke or Hume) nor a rigidly associationist psychology (such as Hartley's) were tenable philosophic positions. He had come to believe that the human mind was active in cognition, that perception was a bilateral activity involving a blending of self and non-self, and that, therefore, 'any system built on the passiveness of the mind must be false, as a system' (*CL*, II 709). Wordsworth, however, still accepted a mechanical theory of mind grounded on Hartley's doctrine of the association of ideas, and this theory lay at the heart of his critical Preface in *Lyrical Ballads*: 'The principal object then which I proposed to myself in these Poems was to make the incidents of common life interesting by tracing in them, truly though not ostentatiously, the primary laws of our nature: chiefly as far as regards the manner in which we associate ideas in a state of excitement' (*PWW*, I 122). It was here, Coleridge began to see, that the fundamental divergence between his own and his friend's poetic theory was to be found. For Wordsworth, in so far at least as his *theory* was concerned, the poetic process involved no more than presenting new and refined combinations of 'ideas' already existing in the mind. But such a theory did not, in Coleridge's view, explain what was best and most enduring in Wordsworth's poetic achievement. On the contrary, Wordsworth's poetry was pre-eminently the product of a shaping and modifying power, a power that fused and blended past and present impressions with thought and feeling, not simply of an associative faculty governed by blind, mechanical laws. At the same time, however, it was clear that *some* poetry was the product of association, though often this poetry was of a lower order. Clearly, then, there were two faculties at work in the composition of poetry, one passive and associative, the other active and poietic. Both find appropriate expression in poetry, but the latter is more characteristic of great poetry than is the former. This is, essentially, what Coleridge told Sotheby in September 1802 in a letter in which, using Bowles rather than Wordsworth as his example, he formulated for the first time his distinction between fancy and imagination:

Nature has her proper interest; & he will know what it is, who believes & feels, that every Thing has a Life of it's own, & that we are all *one Life*. A Poet's *Heart & Intellect* should be *combined*, *intimately* combined & *unified*, with the great appearances in Nature — & not merely held in solution & loose mixture with them, in the shape of formal Similies. I do not mean to *exclude* these formal Similies — there are moods of mind, in which they are natural — pleasing moods of mind, & such as a Poet will often have, & sometimes express; but they are not his highest, & most appropriate moods. They are 'Sermoni propiora' which I once translated — '*Properer for a Sermon.*' The truth is — Bowles has indeed the *sensibility* of a poet; but he has not the *Passion* of a great Poet. His latter Writings all want *native* Passion — Milton here & there supplies him with an appearance of it — but he has no native Passion, because he is not a Thinker — & has probably weakened his Intellect by the haunting Fear of becoming extravagant / Young somewhere in one of his prose works remarks that there is as profound a Logic in the most daring & dithyrambic parts of Pindar, as in the Ὄργανον of Aristotle — the remark is a valuable one /. . . . It must occur to every Reader that the Greeks in their religious poems address always the Numina Loci, the Genii, the Dryads, the Naiads, &c &c — All natural Objects were *dead* — mere hollow Statues — but there was a Godkin or Goddessling *included* in each — In the Hebrew Poetry you find nothing of this poor Stuff — as poor in genuine Imagination, as it is mean in Intellect — / At best, it is but Fancy, or the aggregating Faculty of the mind — not *Imagination*, or the *modifying*, and *co-adunating* Faculty. This the Hebrew Poets appear to me to have possessed beyond all others — & next to them the English. In the Hebrew Poets each Thing has a Life of it's own, & yet they are all one Life. In God they move & live, & *have* their Being — not *had*, as the cold System of Newtonian Theology represents / but *have*. (*CL*, II 864–6)

This letter is usually overlooked in critical discussions of 'Dejection: An Ode'. I do not know why this is so. Surely it is significant that Coleridge, less than a month before the first publication of his Dejection ode, should have penned such an affirmation of the integrity and unity of all life, and that he should have insisted on the 'profound Logic' of Pindar's odes when he was in the final stages of transforming his April verse-letter into an irregular ode in the tradition of English 'Pindaricks'. One cannot so easily divorce his poetry from his poetic theory, especially in so important an instance. When we read 'Dejection: An Ode', we should bear in mind Coleridge's comments about the unity of life, about the *'native* Passion' of great poetry and great poets, about the subtle logic of seemingly wild, disorganised odes — and, as well, his distinction between fancy and imagination. It is a poem of paradox, of great loss and partial restoration, and of crises in love, faith and imagination. Although itself the very antithesis of all that 'the cold System of Newtonian Theology' represents, it nevertheless records an experience, later recollected in tranquillity, when the poet had felt excluded from life and bereft of 'passion' — a time of severe depression when he had no inner strength to respond or interact with the natural beauty of earth and sea and sky.

In September and October 1802 Coleridge published a number of epigrams and some longer poems in the *Morning Post*. (The paper's owner—editor Daniel Stuart was a personal friend, and between 1798 and 1802 Coleridge had written a large volume of essays on contemporary political events for the paper.) Many of these poetic contributions, published over the transparent pseudonym ΕΣΤΗΣΕ,[6] were slight and 'never meant for any thing else but the peritura charta [ephemeral pages] of the M. Post' (*CL*, II 857). Some, however, were more substantial productions — notably, 'Dejection. An Ode', which appeared on 4 October 1802. The date is certainly an interesting one: it was the day that Wordsworth married Mary Hutchinson and it was, as well, the seventh anniversary of Coleridge's own ill-fated marriage to Sara Fricker. It is often suggested that the date was deliberately chosen, but this seems unlikely. Daniel Stuart, not Coleridge, decided when and what should appear in the paper, and there is no evidence to suggest that Coleridge asked that the poem be printed on that particular day. It seems a case of pure coincidence. The version of 'Dejection: An Ode' published in the *Morning Post* in October 1802 is essentially a restructured rendering of the version sent to Sotheby in the letter of July 19 and it is close to the *textus receptus* (1817) of the poem.[7] The *Morning Post* version contains 139 lines, as compared with the 340 lines of the original verse-letter; the poem is now addressed, neither to Sara Hutchinson nor to Wordsworth, but to 'Edmund' — which is (as de Selincourt points out) 'a transparent sobriquet for Wordsworth'.[8] It is a more formal work, prefaced by four lines from the 'Ballad of Sir Patrick Spence' and divided into seven numbered stanzas.[9] Apart from the exclusion of seven lines about the effect of 'abstruse research' (87–93) — lines which, three weeks later, Coleridge quoted to Wedgwood for their 'Truth & not for [their] Poetry' (*CL*, II 875) — the poem is a recasting of the three 'fragments' sent to Sotheby: all the personal references of the April verse-letter have been deleted; the first four stanzas reproduce with variations of detail the bulk of the lines sent to Sotheby; the section on the suspension of imagination becomes stanza 5; the storm and Aeolian-harp section becomes stanza 6; and the last stanza — and this is the most significant change — expands from eight to twenty lines the blessing of Edmund—Wordsworth, who is seen to possess 'joy' that is denied to Coleridge himself.

After 1802 the poem was not published in its entirety until *Sibylline Leaves* (1817), although Coleridge quoted a long passage from it in the third of his essays 'On the Principles of Genial Criticism' (*BL*, II 240—1) and two lines of it in chapter 22 of *Biographia Literaria* (*BL*, II 131). Between 1802 and 1806, however, he frequently transcribed parts of the poem in his letters: he wrote out the opening stanzas for the Beaumonts (after Dorothy Wordsworth in the same letter had copied her brother's 'Resolution and Independence') in August 1803, breaking off abruptly at the end of the fifth stanza with the words 'I am so weary of this doleful Poem that I must leave off' (*CL*, II 973); and in three letters between 1802 and 1806 he quoted the seven-line section on abstruse research (87—93) that he had omitted from the *Morning Post* version.[10] There are no quotations from or references to the poem in the letters of 1807—17.

Entitled 'Dejection: An Ode', the poem was published (its second appearance in print) in *Sibylline Leaves* (1817), this version being the *textus receptus*. While there are a large number of minor variations between the *Morning Post* and *Sibylline Leaves* versions, the major variants may be reduced to five. First, the poem is addressed, not to Edmund—Wordsworth, but to an unnamed 'Lady' who may or may not be Sara Hutchinson. Second, the poem contains eight stanzas rather than seven: this has been achieved by dividing stanza 4 of the 1802 version into two stanzas numbered 4 and 5. Third, four lines (17—20) have been added to the end of the first stanza; these lines were probably written in 1803, for they first appear in the version of the poem which Coleridge transcribed for the Beaumonts in August of that year (see *CL*, II 971). Fourth, the seven lines on 'abstruse research' (87—93), which Coleridge had omitted from the *Morning Post* version but had so often quoted in letters of 1802—6, become the closing lines of stanza 6 in the 1817 text. And, finally, the twenty-line concluding stanza of 1802 has been reduced to fourteen lines and has been refashioned so that what, in 1802, had been a description of Edmund's actual possession of 'joy' has become a *wish* that the Lady may possess a similar joy, though the poet himself is still excluded from it. With these five changes (and one minor alteration in wording)[11] the 1817 version was reprinted in Coleridge's *Poetical Works* of 1828, 1829 and 1834.

'A LETTER TO –' (4 APRIL 1802)[12]

Perhaps the best introduction to Coleridge's April verse-letter to Sara Hutchinson is provided by two of his Notebook entries (*CN*, I nos 1064—5) dating from December 1801:

> To write a *series* of Love Poems — truly Sapphic, save that they shall have a large Interfusion of moral Sentiment & calm Imagery on Love in all the moods of the mind — Philosophic, fantastic, in moods of high enthusiasm, of simple Feeling, of mysticism, of Religion — / comprize in it all the practice, & all the philosophy of Love —

> A lively picture of a man, disappointed in marriage, & endeavouring to make a compensation to himself by virtuous & tender & brotherly friendship with an amiable Woman — the obstacles — the jealousies — the impossibility of it. — Best advice that he should as much as possible withdraw himself from pursuits of morals &c — & devote himself to abstract sciences —

These two contrapuntal statements — the first calm and detached, the second anguished and advising withdrawal — form an interesting prelude to the poem he composed four months later. That poem combines honest self-criticism with despairing self-pity. It attempts, on the one hand, sincere psychological self-analysis and Coleridge endeavours to anatomise his relationship with his wife and with Sara Hutchinson and the Grasmere circle; yet, on the other hand, the poet's overwhelming anxiety and depression will scarcely permit such dispassionate inquiry, and the result is that objective analysis is frequently swept under by the violent rip-tide of ungovernable emotion.

Coleridge had first met Sara Hutchinson − or 'Asra', as he affectionately called her − in late 1799. 'It was', as George Whalley has said,

> a case of love at first sight; but Coleridge was already married, and divorce in those days was virtually impossible − even if he had been prepared (as he was not) to consider such a course. Coleridge certainly expressed his love, and his addresses were not rejected. It was at first a light-hearted matter, and later a sorrowful and agonising relation for both of them; it continued intermittently until 1810, when, on the occasion of a bitter quarrel between Coleridge and Wordsworth, Sara withdrew herself from Coleridge's attentions and continued to live for the rest of her life − as she had done off and on since 1808 − with the Wordsworths.[13]

Their love, it seems certain, was never consummated; and it is probable (as the Wordsworths supposed) that Coleridge was in love as much with the idea of love as he was with Sara Hutchinson. Certainly, in the poems written to or about her − many of which were composed in 1801−2 − she is an idealised figure.

By January 1802 Coleridge had come to 'the heart-withering Conviction − that I could not be happy without my children, & could not but be miserable with the mother of them' (*CL*, II 784). His domestic unhappiness was aggravated by constant ill health (he was bedridden for much of 1801 and the early months of 1802) and by the opium he took to escape from physical pain and, no doubt, in part to escape from himself as well. Repeatedly in the letters of 1801 he expressed the belief that he was dying, that his only chance of survival was to move (without his wife) to a warmer climate, perhaps the Azores. The vicious succession of bodily sicknesses and scenes of domestic strife with his wife led him to seek relief in 'austerest reasonings' which 'so denaturalized [his] mind' that he became incapable of feeling and sentiment (*CL*, II 725); and he was tortured, too, by what he described as a lack of *moral will* − a 'want of steadiness & self-command' that was as much a cause as an effect of his physical ailments (*CL*, II 783). For all these ills Asra was the imagined cure. Yet, while he clung to her and to the *idea* of her as panacea, he knew that he could never possess her. Moreover, with Wordsworth's engagement to Mary Hutchinson, Coleridge saw the Wordsworths and the Hutchinsons becoming a single, tightly knit family unit, from which he was more and more excluded − or, at least, felt himself to be so − by reason of his unhappiness and loss of sensibility. Isolation, a sense of personal inadequacy, hopeless love, marital discord, physical illness, and opium: all these were factors in Coleridge's dejection-crisis; and there were other, less tangible, less conscious factors, too, such as Coleridge's repressed envy of Wordsworth's happiness and poetic productivity.

Apart from a visit to Tom Poole at Nether Stowey, Coleridge spent most of the cold winter of 1801−2 in London working for Daniel Stuart at the *Morning Post*. On 1 March he set off for the North − but he did not go directly home. Instead, he spent two weeks with the Hutchinsons at Gallow Hill and did not reach Keswick until 15 March. A month earlier he had written to his wife from London,

> I attribute my amendment [in health] to the more tranquil state of my mind − & to the chearfulness inspired by the thought of speedily returning to you in love & peace. . . . And it is my frequent prayer, & my almost perpetual aspiration, that we may meet to part no more − & live together as affectionate Husband & Wife ought to do. (*CL*, II 785−6)

This − and then a fortnight's stay with Sara Hutchinson. It is not difficult to imagine the bitter scenes and recriminations that must have attended his arrival at Greta Hall. Two weeks later he began to compose his despairing verse-letter to Asra.

The letter − 340 lines of predominantly blank-verse divided into twenty stanzas of varying length − is the most anguished utterance outside of Coleridge's private Notebooks. The poem begins quietly enough in a relaxed, genial, conversational idiom reminiscent of 'This Lime-Tree Bower' −

> Well! if the Bard was weatherwise, who made
> The grand old Ballad of Sir Patrick Spence,
> This Night, so tranquil now, will not go hence
> Unrous'd by winds . . .

— but there are ominous portents, too, 'foretelling / The coming-on of Rain & squally Blast'. In stanzas 2 and 3 (lines 17–57) the poet describes his mood of dejection and its characteristics:

> A stifling, drowsy, unimpassion'd Grief
> That finds no natural Outlet, no Relief
>   In word, or sigh, or tear

— a 'heartless Mood' in which he sees, but cannot *feel*, the beauties of the natural world. His *dejection* is, as David Pirie notes, 'not conventional misery, any more than Joy later in the poem is conventional happiness. The former exists below, the latter above, the normal capacity for feeling'.[14] Seeking some outlet for grief and isolation, Coleridge ranges back in memory, first, to the secret yearning of youth and his time at Christ's Hospital (stanza 4, lines 58–73), and, second, to a projected image of Asra in the 'weather-fended Wood' or sitting on 'the sod-built Seat of Camomile' that he had constructed with the Wordsworths in 1800 (stanza 5, lines 74–91). The evocation of Sara leads, in stanza 6 (lines 92–8), to a temporary release and a feeling of contact in the belief that she, at that very moment, might be gazing on the same sky as he is:

> I feel my spirit moved —
> And wheresoe'er thou be,
> O Sister! O Beloved!
> Those dear mild Eyes, that see
> Even now the Heaven, *I* see —
> There is a Prayer in them! It is for *me* —
> And I, dear Sara — *I* am blessing *thee*!

Stanza 7 (lines 99–110) prolongs the contact by returning, in memory, to the 'brief Happiness' of an evening he had spent at Gallow Hill with Sara and her sister Mary.[15]

In stanzas 8 and 9 (lines 111–29) Coleridge laments a 'complaining Scroll' that he had recently sent to Sara and anguishes over the grief that it has caused her. This self-chastisement yields in stanza 10 (lines 130–68) to some sober reflection on the way in which his misery excludes him from the happy Dove Cottage circle —

> While *ye* are *well & happy*, 'twould but wrong you
> If I should fondly yearn to be among you —

Wherefore, O wherefore! should I wish to be
A wither'd branch upon a blossoming Tree?

He imagines at the beginning of stanza 11 (lines 169−215) the
agony of being deprived of Sara's company altogether but quickly
turns his attention from this 'dark distressful Dream' to the sounds
of the wind that 'long has rav'd unnotic'd' and of the tortured
Aeolian harp in his study-window − tragic sounds that tell of 'the
Rushing of an Host in Rout' or, in a minor key, of a lost child on a
'heathy Wild' who 'now moans low in utter grief & fear − / And
now screams loud, & hopes to make it's Mother hear!' The lost
child is an image of Coleridge's own isolation, its helpless cries an
echo of his own bewildered spirit.

In stanza 12 (lines 216−30) he calls down the blessings of Nature
on Sara and hopes to hear good tidings from her, for 'I am not the
buoyant Thing, I was of yore'. There *was* a time, he says in stanza
13 (lines 231−42) echoing Wordsworth's Immortality ode, when
he possessed the resilience to transform and transcend misfortune
− a time when, as in the halcyon Somerset years with Wordsworth, 'Hope grew round me, like the climbing Vine, / And
Leaves & Fruitage, not my own, seem'd mine' − but now, four
years later, the steady exhaustion of marital incompatibility has
sapped his natural ebullience to the extent that each visitation of
ill tidings suspends his 'shaping Spirit of Imagination'. And stanza
14 (lines 243−8) is a blunt and resigned statement of his marriage
failure:

> I speak not now of those habitual Ills
> That wear out Life, when two unequal Minds
> Meet in one House, & two discordant Wills −
>   This leaves me, where it finds,
> Past cure, & past Complaint − a fate austere
> Too fix'd & hopeless to partake of Fear!

In stanza 15 (lines 249−71) he turns again for relief to Asra − 'My
Comforter! A Heart within my Heart!' − and the Grasmere circle
who, 'tho' few ye be, / Make up a world of Hopes & Fears for me';
but he is fearful that his 'coarse domestic Life', in which he has
known

> No habits of heart-nursing Sympathy,
> No Griefs, but such as dull and deaden me,
> No mutual mild Enjoyments of it's own,
> No Hopes of it's own Vintage,

has unfitted him for companionship with the Wordsworths and Hutchinsons — for, to escape the pain of *feeling*, he has buried himself in 'abstruse Research', with the result that he has virtually lost the ability to respond with imaginative sympathy to any situation. There are even moments, he confides in stanza 16 (lines 272–85), when he has 'half-wish'd' that his children had never been born; he cannot see them — despite his love and joy at the sight — without being reminded that things would have been different if he had married Sara Hutchinson: 'sad Thoughts they always bring, / And like the Poet's Philomel, I sing / My Love-song, with my breast against a Thorn'. And this same bittersweet conjunction of joy and sadness characterises, not only his attitude to his children, but also his perception of the mountains, vales and woods of the Lake District — for, as he says in stanza 17 (lines 286–95), again echoing Wordsworth's ode, these natural beauties 'are not to me now the Things, which once they were'.

At this point there is a major break in the poem. Having explored the causes of his dejection and the complexities of his relationship with Sara Hutchinson, Coleridge as it were steps back from his immediate situation to state the general philosophic truths to which he has been led by consideration of his own particular case. Stanza 18 (lines 296–307) sets out a doctrine of *active* perception —

> O Sara! we receive but what we give,
> And in *our* Life alone does Nature live.
> Our's is her Wedding Garment, our's her
> Shroud

— and in stanza 19 (lines 308–23) this 'beautiful & beauty-making Power' is identified as *joy*:

> JOY, Sara! is the Spirit & the Power,
> That wedding Nature to us gives in Dower
> A new Earth & new Heaven. . . .

The final stanza (lines 324–40) achieves a precarious balance. Since these lines were much altered both in phrasing and in intention in the later redactions, it is worth quoting them in full:

Sister & Friend of my devoutest Choice!
Thou being innocent & full of love,
And nested with the Darlings of thy Love,
And feeling in thy Soul, Heart, Lips & Arms
Even what the conjugal & mother Dove
That borrows genial Warmth from those, she warms,
Feels in her thrill'd wings, blessedly outspread –
Thou free'd awhile from Cares & human Dread
By the Immenseness of the Good & Fair
     Which thou see'st every where –
Thus, thus should'st thou rejoice!
To thee would all Things live from Pole to Pole,
Their Life the Eddying of thy living Soul –
O dear! O Innocent! O full of Love!
A very Friend! A Sister of my Choice –
O dear, as Light & Impulse from above,
Thus may'st thou ever, evermore rejoice!

For David Pirie, these lines (together with the two preceding stanzas) represent Coleridge's transcendence of dejection: 'In describing Joy, Coleridge finally achieves it, and the movements towards Sara and towards Joy are one.'[16] I do not think the transformation is this simple or this complete. Coleridge is able at the end of the poem to apprehend *joy* intellectually, he is able to wish that others may experience it, and he knows that *sometimes* (even if only vicariously) he himself can share it. But he still belongs to Greta Hall, while Sara 'nested with the Darlings of [her] Love' belongs to the world of Dove Cottage – a world of which, indeed, she is (for him) the religious symbol of 'the conjugal & mother Dove'. Beneath her healing wings he can take sanctuary, but the relief she offers in this idealised form is purely spiritual. By the end of the poem Coleridge has come to terms with his grief, but he has not abolished it; the albatross has dropped away but the memory of it is not so easily erased. The poem is the record of great loss and partial restoration, and the poet (like Milton's Adam) is sent forth from the experience 'though sorrowing, yet in peace' (*Paradise Lost*, XI 117). An even better Miltonic emblem is provided by the closing lines of *Samson Agonistes* — a poem which Coleridge had been reading only a month earlier (*CN*, I no. 1155) — in which a 'new acquist / Of true experience', though purchased with great pain, allows the Hebrew Chorus to depart 'With peace and consolation . . . / And calm of mind, all passion spent' (lines 1757–8).

Since its discovery in 1936 Coleridge's verse-letter to Sara Hutchinson has attracted a good deal of critical comment. Reactions to it as a piece of literature, while varied, have generally been qualified, and Coleridge's readers have as a rule preferred the final ode to the verse-letter. William Walsh speaks for most: 'There are those . . . who prefer the more exposed and fluent letter to the formal ode and it may be that there is more of the naked nerve in the letter. In my own response I see a decided preference for the ode.'[17] Until quite recently Walsh's view could be considered normative. In 1970, however, David Pirie published a long paper in which he argued vigorously that the verse-letter is one of Coleridge's best poems and that in the various redactions between May and October 1802 one can trace 'its gradual disintegration through various revisions until it became *Dejection: An Ode*'.[18] Of the verse-letter Pirie concludes,

> *A Letter* is a poem of great unity, yet it conceals its art beneath an impression of spontaneity. It is held together by a complex series of cross references, and yet flows with all the ease of immediate expression. Its style ranges from a colloquial opening, which never seems trivial, to an incantatory end, which never sounds pompous. Each passage draws on what has gone before for its effect, and prepares the way for what follows, and yet there is no obtrusive contrivance. The problems of philosophy and of poetic creation become part of a statement of loneliness, and the resolution is that of a great love poem. The unity of the poem thus depends on passages which were, as Coleridge told Sotheby, 'of a private nature'. . . .[19]

Pirie argues his case with great conviction and considerable success; and, while most readers would not be willing to go to all lengths with him, he has none the less demonstrated that the verse-letter is a more successful and unified production than was previously thought.

The April verse-letter has elicited comment, too, from a number of psychological analysts, for whom it is a fascinating document.

Beverly Fields, for example, who offers a close reading of the letter in terms of Freudian psychodynamics, finds revealed in it Coleridge's covert hostility to Sara Hutchinson and a latent homosexual impulse (coupled with fear and envy) towards Wordsworth. The world of Dove Cottage, she argues, is 'made up of a man − a father surrogate − and three phallic women, all of whom represent to [Coleridge] the strongest possible danger'; he is crippled by a castration complex and his neurotic despair 'results from the unconscious wish to be androgynous and the consequent inability to fulfill himself in either direction'.[20] For Mary Jane Lupton, the cause of Coleridge's repressed hostility toward Sara Hutchinson, which emerges 'in the guise of solicitude over Sara's health', is to be found in the unresolved Oedipal conflict brought about by the early death of his father. Coleridge, she argues, 'went to great lengths in sublimating his sexual drive' for Sara Hutchinson − and one way of doing this was to establish a reaction-formation against this drive: 'If Sara embodies the seductive mother, then one way not to love her is to hate her, punish her, get rid of her. At the same time Coleridge displays excessive concern over her illness, thus covering up his aggressive feelings.'[21] While these readings go well beyond the evidence in unwarranted speculation and must be handled with circumspection, it is also true, as Max Schultz has said that,

> There are gleanings helpful to our understanding of 'Dejection' to be gathered from these psychoanalytical exegeses: the emotional implications in the language Coleridge uses and the emotional discrepancies that exist between the two versions [i.e. the April verse-letter and the final version of 'Dejection: An Ode']; but for the most part the poem is less the goal of these studies than a bridge to the poet.[22]

THE WORDSWORTH−COLERIDGE 'DIALOGUE'

It is now universally accepted that Coleridge's verse-letter of April 1802 was prompted by and is, in some sense, an answer to the first four stanzas of Wordsworth's 'Ode: Intimations of Immortality'; and it is widely believed that these two poems form part of a larger dialogue carried on between the poets in a number of poems written between 1802 and 1807. The subject of this poetic dialogue is the nature of poetic creation and the relationship between the perceiving mind and the external world of nature.

The starting-point of this dialogue is provided by the second stanza of Coleridge's poem 'The Mad Monk',[23] which was first published in the *Morning Post* in October 1800:

> There was a time when earth, and sea, and skies,
> The bright green vale, and forest's dark recess,
> With all things, lay before mine eyes
> In steady loveliness:
> But now I feel, on earth's uneasy scene,
> Such sorrows as will never cease; –
> I only ask for peace;
> If I must live to know that such a time has been!
> (9–16; *CPW*, I 348)

These lines, as Stephen Prickett points out, were 'taken up by Wordsworth for the opening of the *Immortality Ode*, and . . . used by him as the initial schema from which he can move towards a more precise analysis of his own sense of loss, and of its relation to his development':[24]

> There was a time when meadow, grove, and stream,
> The earth, and every common sight,
> To me did seem
> Apparelled in celestial light,
> The glory and the freshness of a dream.
> It is not now as it hath been of yore; –
> Turn wheresoe'er I may,
> By night or day,
> The things which I have seen I now can see no more.
> (1–9)

In the three stanzas which follow Wordsworth develops further his conviction that 'there hath passed away a glory' from his perception of the natural world; he can still respond to Nature's universal springtime joy –

> My heart is at your festival,
> My head hath its coronal,
> The fulness of your bliss, I feel – I feel it all
> (39–41)

but he is aware of an undefined 'something that is gone'; and he closes the introductory section with the queries,

> Whither is fled the visionary gleam?
> Where is it now, the glory and the dream?
>
> (56−7)

As I said at the beginning of this chapter (pp. 170−2), it was probably at this point − the end of stanza 4 − that Wordsworth broke off the composition of his ode on Saturday, 27 March 1802, and it was probably, therefore, this opening section only that Coleridge heard recited during the following week when the Wordsworths were visiting Keswick. Coleridge, too, had experienced a loss, but it was more profound, more crippling, and more enduring than that described by Wordsworth. And on Sunday, 4 April, while the Wordsworths were still at Keswick, Coleridge undertook to explore the nature and extent of his loss in the long verse-letter to Sara Hutchinson. Wordsworth's ode was much in his thoughts and he echoed his friend's poem on a number of occasions;[25] indeed, there is one section in the middle of the letter where, contrasting what he *was* with what he now *is*, he seems to be gauging the distance between Wordsworth's qualified loss and his own more severe imaginative failure:

> For, oh! beloved Friend!
> I am not the buoyant Thing, I was of yore −
> When like an own Child, I to JOY belong'd;
> For others mourning oft, myself oft sorely wrong'd,
> Yet bearing all things then, as if I nothing bore!
>
> Yes, dearest Sara! yes!
> There *was* a time when tho' my path was rough,
> The Joy within me dallied with Distress;
> And all Misfortunes were but as the Stuff
> Whence Fancy made me Dreams of Happiness:
> For Hope grew round me, like the climbing Vine,
> And Leaves & Fruitage, not my own, seem'd mine!
> But now Ill Tidings bow me down to earth /
> Nor care I, that they rob me of my Mirth /
> But oh! each Visitation
> Suspends what Nature gave me at my Birth,
> My shaping Spirit of Imagination!
>
> (226−42; *CL*, II 796)

The loss described in Wordsworth's ode is that of a *je ne sais quoi* 'visionary gleam' — a loss of a *degree* of perceptual insight rather than that of the ability to perceive at all. For Coleridge, on the other hand, it is precisely this inability to feel, to respond sympathetically to natural joy, that lies at the heart of his dejection: 'He felt', in Stephen Prickett's words, 'his whole imaginative intercourse with the created world — his whole capacity for open response — to be threatened.'[26]

On Wednesday, 21 April 1802, Coleridge 'repeated the verses he wrote to Sara' to the Wordsworths in the garden behind Dove Cottage. The recitation left Dorothy (and, we may assume, William as well) 'in miserable spirits' (*JDW*, p. 113). Wordsworth himself, although doubtless aware of echoes of his own unfinished ode in his friend's lines, was prompted to respond to Coleridge's despairing view of what was happening to him, not by completing his 'Ode: Intimations of Immortality' (he did not return to finish it until March 1804), but rather by composing an altogether new poem. On Monday evening, 3 May 1802, less than a fortnight after hearing Coleridge recite his verse-letter to Sara Hutchinson, Wordsworth began to write 'Resolution and Independence' — or, as it was then called, 'The Leech Gatherer' — and the next morning before breakfast 'he wrote several stanzas in bed' (*JDW*, p. 120). Later that day, while they were out walking, the Wordsworths ran into Coleridge near the shore of Thirlmere; the trio found 'a moss covered Rock' rising out of the bed of Wyth Burn, where they ate dinner while 'Wm and C. repeated and read verses' (ibid.). By Friday, 7 May, Wordsworth had finished the first draft of the poem, but (as usual) he spent more time in revision than in original composition. Thus, on Sunday, 9 May, we hear that 'William worked at the Leech gatherer almost incessantly from morning till tea-time', while Dorothy copied it and some other poems for Coleridge; and it is not until two months later (4 July) that we are told that 'Wm finished the Leech gatherer today', with Dorothy transcribing the revised version for Coleridge on the following day (*JDW*, pp. 122–3, 145).

'Resolution and Independence', based on an incident recorded in Dorothy's Journal in October 1800 (*JDW*, p. 42), tells of the poet's chance meeting with an old but resolutely persevering leech-gatherer on the moors. It had been, we are told, a night of wind and storm, but 'now the sun is rising calm and bright' and 'All things that love the sun are out of doors'. The poet, however, finds that he is out of tune with Nature's joy:

But, as it sometimes chanceth, from the might
Of joy in minds that can no further go,
As high as we have mounted in delight
In our dejection do we sink as low;
To me that morning did it happen so;
And fears and fancies thick upon me came;
Dim sadness — and blind thoughts, I knew not,
        nor could name.

                                    (22–8)

He thinks of Chatterton and Robert Burns (both cultic figures of
ignored genius), concluding that 'We Poets in our youth begin in
gladness; / But thereof come in the end despondency and madness' (48–9). In the midst of these self-pitying reflections on the
poet's lot, the narrator comes upon the old man stirring wayside
pools with his foot in search of leeches:

'Once I could meet with them on every side;
But they have dwindled long by slow decay;
Yet still I persevere, and find them where I may.'

                                    (124–6)

The old man's sufferings and patient resolution put the poet's situation in perspective, and the leech-gatherer assumes a didactic
and symbolic function:

And the whole body of the Man did seem
Like one whom I had met with in a dream;
Or like a man from some far region sent,
To give me human strength, by apt admonishment.

                                    (109–12)

This 'moral' is often thought to have been aimed at Coleridge.
According to George Meyer, for example, 'Resolution and Independence' was inspired 'not so much by [Wordsworth's] own
mood . . . as by what he was currently observing in Coleridge.
Wordsworth considered the tragedies of Chatterton and Burns,
made them represent the fate of poets in general, and attributed to
his ideal poet fears and self-recriminations that he regarded as
appropriate to Coleridge'; and Coleridge, like the poem's persona,
was expected to respond to the leech-gatherer, that 'living example

of resolution and independence [who] rouses the poet from his melancholy trance, points up the absurdity of his own despair, and drives him to pray for resolution and independence of his own'.[27]

It is clear from Dorothy Wordsworth's Journal, as we have seen, that Coleridge was well informed about the progress of 'Resolution and Independence' from early May to early July 1802 and that he was sent transcriptions of the poem in an early version (9 May) and in a later, much revised form (4 July); it is also clear from Dorothy's Journal that Coleridge and the Wordsworths paid each other visits in May–June 1802 and that, when they were apart, there was a flourishing correspondence (now lost) between Greta Hall and Dove Cottage during these months. There was ample opportunity, then, for the two men to compare their respective 'losses' and to propose, if possible, solutions or ways of compensating for what had been lost. Now, if (as seems highly probable) Coleridge's verse-letter to Sara Hutchinson was triggered by the first four stanzas of Wordsworth's 'Ode: Intimations of Immortality', and if, in turn, 'Resolution and Independence' was offered as a 'solution' for Coleridge's dejection, then it seems to follow that 'Dejection: An Ode' is Coleridge's *answer* to Wordsworth's two poems. This hypothesis is supported by two significant facts. In the first place, on 19 July 1802, two weeks after Dorothy had transcribed the revised 'Resolution and Independence' for him, Coleridge sent about a third of his April verse-letter in a letter to William Sotheby: these lines, which are very close to the poem printed two and a half months later in the *Morning Post*, are addressed *to Wordsworth* and they stress (since intimate details of his marriage and his love for Asra have been omitted) Coleridge's suspension of imagination and his inability to respond to nature. They read, indeed, very much like a reply to Wordsworth − an explanation that his creative loss is more profound than the leech-gatherer's and that, in the words of the Black Knight in Chaucer's 'Book of the Duchess', 'I have lost more than thow wenest'. In the second place, the close relationship which the Wordsworth–Coleridge circle felt to exist between 'Resolution and Independence' and 'Dejection: An Ode' is apparent in the fact that the two poems were transcribed (the first by Dorothy Wordsworth, the second by Coleridge himself) in a letter to the Beaumonts of August 1803 (*CL*, II 966–73). The conjunction of *these* two poems and, indeed, the appearance of two separate hands in the transcription reinforces the sense of a deliberate dialogue.

The place of stanzas 5–11 of Wordsworth's 'Ode: Intimations of Immortality' in this 'dialogue' between the poets is difficult to ascertain, primarily because we do not know exactly when these stanzas were composed. Dorothy tells us that on 17 June 1802 'William added a little to the Ode he is writing' (*JDW*, p. 137), but we do not know what or how much he added and there are no further references to the 'Ode' before Dorothy's Journal stops in January 1803; it was not until 1804, probably in early March, that Wordsworth took up and completed his ode (*WW*, II 20). In any case, the last six stanzas of the 'Ode' provide the philosophical answer to the question raised at the end of stanza 4: 'Whither is fled the visionary gleam?' The answer, based on the Platonic doctrine of anamnesis or 'recollection',[28] is that the gradual dulling of our intuitive responses to nature in childhood is compensated for by a more mature perception that allows us to find in even the meanest flower that blows 'Thoughts that do often lie too deep for tears'. This amounts to a flat denial of Coleridge's view in 'Dejection: An Ode' that (in Harold Bloom's words) 'human process is irreversible: imaginative loss is permanent, and nature intimates to us our own mortality always'.[29] For Wordsworth, however, imaginative love is transformed but never wholly lost; and, if we accept that Wordsworth formulated this position after Coleridge had revised his verse-letter into 'Dejection: An Ode', then it is reasonable also to accept Stephen Prickett's view that 'Wordsworth's final affirmation of strength from the memory of childhood moments of guilt and fear [in the completed 'Ode: Intimations of Immortality'] is a *reply* to Coleridge's lament that isolation suspended his Imagination.'[30]

Most scholars would, I think, accept the argument thus far (at least in broad outline) and would agree that Coleridge's ode together with Wordsworth's ode and 'Resolution and Independence' 'form a kind of dialogue'.[31] Some readers extend the 'dialogue' to other poems. Thus, Milton Teichman, for example, believes that 'Wordsworth's reply to Coleridge overflows "Resolution and Independence" into a poem Wordsworth wrote immediately afterward, "Stanzas Written in My Pocket-Copy of Thomson's 'Castle of Indolence'"';[32] and Harold Bloom argues (I think convincingly) that Coleridge continues the dialogue in 'To William Wordsworth' (1807), where 'the debate of *Dejection* is carried on . . . again, five years after the earlier poem'.[33]

'DEJECTION: AN ODE' (1817)

According to Samuel Johnson's *Dictionary of the English Language* (1755), 'the ode is either of the greater or less kind. The less is characterised by sweetness and ease; the greater by sublimity, rapture, and quickness of transition.' The distinction that Johnson is making is that between the literary heirs of Horace and those of Pindar. Gilbert Highet distinguishes the two traditions in this way:

> Among the lyricists who follow classical inspiration, consciously or unconsciously, some are descendants of Pindar, some of Horace. The Pindarics admire passion, daring, and extravagance. Horace's followers prefer reflection, moderation, economy. Pindaric odes follow no pre-established routine, but soar and dive and veer as the wind catches their wing. Horatian lyrics work on quiet, short, well-balanced systems. Pindar represents the ideals of aristocracy, careless courage and the generous heart. Horace is a *bourgeois*, prizing thrift, care, caution, the virtue of self-control. Even the music we can hear through the odes of the two poets and their successors is different. Pindar loves the choir, the festival, the many-footed dance. Horace is a solo singer, sitting in a pleasant room or quiet garden with his lyre.[34]

In English literature the Pindaric tradition attracted such practitioners as Milton in 'On the Morning of Christ's Nativity' and Dryden in 'Alexander's Feast', and the publication in 1656 of Abraham Cowley's *Pindarique Odes* spawned a shoal of lesser fry in a stream that tumbles eventually into the calmer waters of Gray and Collins in the middle of the eighteenth century. The Horatian tradition, which found perhaps its most able exponent in Andrew Marvell, begins with Ben Jonson and passes, through Pope, to such mid-century poets as Mark Akenside, Matthew Prior, and William Collins.[35]

By 1802 Coleridge had composed a number of odes, ranging from the turgid 'Pindarick' sublime of 'Ode to the Departing Year' (1796) to the meditative Horatian accents of 'Ode to Tranquillity', which appeared in the *Morning Post* of 4 December 1801. From its first publication in October 1802, Coleridge called his 'Dejection' an ode. It is, like Wordsworth's 'Ode: Intimations of Immortality', an irregular English Pindaric. And yet it has always existed somewhat uneasily within the confines of this generic description. On the one hand, it is one of the most regular odes in the language: 'five-sixths of its lines', as John Jump has pointed out, 'are either iambic pentameters or alexandrines, nearly four-fifths of them iambic pentameters'.[36] In addition, it shares a significant number of characteristics with Coleridge's Conversation Poems; and some critics — notably G. M. Harper and (with reservations) George Watson[37] — are inclined to group it generically with these earlier poems, while M. H. Abrams (imitating the Augustan distinction between 'greater' and 'lesser' odes) prefers to assign both the best of the Conversation Poems and 'Dejection: An Ode' to a new lyric category which he denominates 'the greater Romantic lyric'.[38] On the other hand, however, there is the fact that Coleridge persistently referred to 'Dejection' as an ode[39] and the fact that the poem is (despite other influences) recognisably part of the English Pindaric tradition. While no one, I think, would deny that Coleridge's 'conversational' mode has left its mark on the poem and is largely responsible for its being so different in many ways from earlier Pindarics in English, it is equally apparent that 'Dejection: An Ode' cannot properly be called a Conversation Poem. Its tone, for one thing, while genial and (at least superficially) familiar, is not intimate and is exalted and dignified to a degree that has no parallel in the Conversation Poems of 1795–8. Its form and style, moreover, are radically unlike those of the earlier poems: it is divided into formal stanzas rather than into apparently artless verse-paragraphs; and, while iambic pentameter provides the prosodic base, there is no blank verse in the poem at all — rhyme is employed throughout and line-lengths are varied. In short, 'Dejection: An Ode' is a sort of middle thing between a traditional Pindaric and a Coleridgean Conversation Poem; and I would agree with A. H. Fairbanks that the poem 'has fair claim to status as the first distinctively Romantic ode' — a status achieved by the 'synthesis of the magnitude and dynamics of the ode with the personal style and immediacy of the conversation poem'.[40]

'Dejection: An Ode' is a poem of paradox, of balanced opposites — the formal and the informal, imaginative loss and imaginative power — held in delicate equilibrium. The magnificent opening stanza (lines 1–20), which merits citation in full, subtly establishes the antitheses that the poem develops as it progresses:

Well! If the Bard was weather-wise, who made
   The grand old ballad of Sir Patrick Spence,
   This night, so tranquil now, will not go hence
Unroused by winds, that ply a busier trade
Than those which mould yon cloud in lazy flakes,
Or the dull sobbing draft, that moans and rakes
Upon the strings of this Æolian lute,
   Which better far were mute.
   For lo! the New-moon winter-bright!
   And overspread with phantom light,
   (With swimming phantom light o'erspread
   But rimmed and circled by a silver thread)
I see the old Moon, in her lap, foretelling
   The coming-on of rain and squally blast.
And oh! that even now the gust were swelling,
   And the slant night-shower driving loud and fast!
Those sounds which oft have raised me, whilst they awed,
   And sent my soul abroad,
Might now perhaps their wonted impulse give,
Might startle this dull pain, and make it move and live!

These lines, relaxed and colloquial, giving a sense of ambling, meandering thought, are unobtrusively but firmly controlled by a formal rhyme-scheme that never threatens or interferes with the illusion of genial spontaneity. The formality of rhyme and stanza-form are modulated by an abundance of enjambment and by varied metrical patterns that imitate the ebb and flow of thought and of the rising and falling breeze. The imagery, too, moves effortlessly from the external world to the internal demesne of the poet's mind, blending outness with inscape: the lute, for example, is both an actual Aeolian harp and a metaphor of mind, and the rising wind is both real and a symbol of inspiration. And there is in the stanza, as William Walsh points out, 'a constant transition from particular to general and from general to particular: reflection feeds on the concrete and the concrete holds within it the impulse of the general'.[41] Thus, the moon, while mysteriously overspread with a vague 'phantom light', is yet defined with mathematical precision as 'rimmed and circled by a silver thread'. The surety of the present moment and the present scene are counterbalanced by contingency and a deep-set apprehension of what the future holds; the rising wind, while invoked, is yet feared − for it

strikes a deeper chord that reverberates through the stanza from
the ominous prolepsis of the epigraph:

> And I fear, I fear, my Master dear!
> We shall have a deadly storm.

Will the wind, when it comes, be creative or destructive? And the
moon, too — the new moon with the old moon in her arms — is
similarly ambiguous: does it signify rebirth or death, what is yet to
come or what has passed away? Poised between expectation and
foreboding, between vivid awareness of the world and an apathetic
inability to respond to it, the opening stanza establishes the para-
doxes which the following stanzas will explore.

In the second stanza (lines 21–38), which develops the disparity
between internal and external nature, Coleridge comes to the
heart of his dejection:

> A grief without a pang, void, dark, and drear,
>   A stifled, drowsy, unimpassioned grief,
>   Which finds no natural outlet, no relief,
>   In word, or sigh, or tear. . . .

Essentially, the crisis has its root in a failure of perception; and,
while this failure is initially described in a weary piling-up of
epithets ('void, dark, and drear', etc.), it eventually finds a *natural*
outlet in a powerfully realised response to nature, a response which
(paradoxically) laments the inability to respond:[42]

> And those thin clouds above, in flakes and bars,
> That give away their motion to the stars;
> Those stars, that glide behind them or between,
> Now sparkling, now bedimmed, but always seen:
> Yon crescent Moon, as fixed as if it grew
> In its own cloudless, starless lake of blue;
> I see them all so excellently fair,
> I see, not feel, how beautiful they are!

The failure of his 'genial spirits'[43] — a loss to which he is now
resigned — leads in stanza 3 (lines 39–46) to the conclusion: 'I may
not hope from outward forms to win / The passion and the life,

whose fountains are within'. Something has died at the centre of his being and the loss is irreparable.

Stanzas 4 and 5 are marked by an outward-turning cadence, as the poet addresses himself directly to the 'Lady', and there is a corresponding shift from the particular to the general − a shift, that is to say, from the poet's personal loss to an examination of the general truths implied by individual experience. In stanza 4 (lines 47−58) Coleridge states, as a universal truth, that true perception depends upon interaction between the self and the non-self, that (if the world is to be other than inanimate and cold, then) 'from the soul itself must issue forth / A light, a glory, a fair luminous cloud / Enveloping the Earth'; and in stanza 5 (lines 59−75), still speaking universally, he explains that this 'beautiful and beauty-making power' both *is* and *results in* 'joy':[44]

> Joy, virtuous Lady! Joy that ne'er was given,
> Save to the pure, and in their purest hour,
> Life, and Life's effluence, cloud at once and shower,
> Joy, Lady! is the spirit and the power,
> Which wedding Nature to us gives in dower
> A new Earth and new Heaven. . . .

Stanza 6 (lines 76−93) turns inward again, back to the poet himself and his own particular loss. There was a time, he says, when he possessed enough 'joy' to withstand 'misfortunes', but now affliction has robbed him of this power and suspended his 'shaping spirit of Imagination'. As a last recourse, he had sought relief from his sorrows in 'abstruse research':

> This was my sole resource, my only plan:
> Till that which suits a part infects the whole,
> And now is almost grown the habit of my soul.

What has happened in these three stanzas (4−6)? What conclusions have been reached? Although it is not possible to say *exactly*, there are three observations that may be useful. First, for Coleridge *perception* involves both receptivity and projection. The poem laments the loss of the latter power (the drying up of the 'fountains within') and, as well, the resulting atrophy of the power to shape and develop perceptual experience. With the aid of Coleridge's later terminology one might put the case this way: an impairment of the Primary Imagination results in the suspension of the Secondary (or poetic) Imagination. Second, Coleridge's loss of 'joy' is as much a moral as a metaphysical problem. Joy, he says, is given *only* 'to the pure, and in their purest hour'. In his own case he is mightily aware of the depth of *im*purity, caused primarily by his illicit (if idealised) passion for Sara Hutchinson and probably as well by the failure of his 'moral will' to cope with the evil of opium: 'For the good that I would I do not: but the evil which I would not, that I do' (Romans 7 : 19). So heartfelt a conviction of sin and personal guilt must necessarily be crippling to one who believes, with Ben Jonson and Milton, that a good poet must also be a good man.[45] Third, there is the problem of what Coleridge means by saying that he had allowed 'abstruse research to steal / From my own nature all the natural man'. Is this a good or a bad thing, an escape or a revelation? 'Is the state being described [in stanza 6] one of sickness, or maturity?' asks Stephen Prickett; and he concludes that

> there is a feeling of qualitative mental change in Coleridge following on his 'loss' of the creative (Secondary) Imagination that he certainly regrets, but is not quite sure whether to regard as a disaster or a development. If, on the one hand, he talks of it as if it is an unmitigated disaster, on the other, *Dejection* itself is one of his greatest insights into the workings of his own creativity — and he is always aware of this.[46]

In the much-discussed seventh stanza (lines 94–125) the poet, by an effort of will, thrusts from him the 'viper thoughts, that coil around my mind', and turns his attention outward again to the wind that 'long has raved unnoticed'. The wind, demonic and demented, tortures 'a scream / Of agony' from the Aeolian harp in the window. There follow three apostrophes where the wind is called, first, a 'Mad Lutanist' that disturbs the nascent springtime of buds and peeping flowers 'with worse than wintry song', then, an 'Actor, perfect in all tragic sounds', and finally, a 'mighty Poet' telling now 'of the rushing of an host in rout, / With groans, of trampled men, with smarting wounds'[47] and now (after 'a pause of deepest silence')

> It tells another tale, with sounds less deep and loud!
> A tale of less affright,
> And tempered with delight,

As Otway's self had framed the tender lay, —
    'Tis of a little child
    Upon a lonesome wild,
Not far from home, but she hath lost her way:
And now moans low in bitter grief and fear,
And now screams loud, and hopes to make her mother hear.[48]

In this stanza, as Walter Jackson Bate has said, 'the imagination turns out to be far from dead or suspended. It is only too active. If joy is creative, the poem exemplifies that dejection can be equally so.'[49] The inspiration prayed for in the opening stanza of the poem has come — but it has brought, not images of joy and solace, but images of horror, of isolation, of loss. And in the last stanza (lines 126–39) the poet wishes for the Lady the peaceful sleep and 'joy' that are (at least on this night of storm) denied to him:

    To her may all things live, from pole to pole,
    Their life the eddying[50] of her living soul!
      O simple spirit, guided from above,
    Dear Lady! friend devoutest of my choice,
    Thus mayest thou ever, evermore rejoice.

'The blessing' — to cite Bate again — 'is possible, more than possible, but it is not for him.'[51]

There are two persistent critical problems associated with 'Dejection: An Ode', especially with the last two stanzas. First, there is the question of unity. 'I think', wrote Humphry House in the early 1950s, 'it is the opinion of many readers of the Ode, that brilliantly successful as most of it is, as *parts*, yet it fails to achieve complete artistic unity.'[52] House's view is based on his belief that the finished ode is a flawed public rendering of the original verse-letter to Sara Hutchinson; both poems, he maintains, are 'about unhappiness and about love and about joy' — rather than about 'modes of perception' — and the finished ode suffers from the exclusion of the love theme and is, as a result, 'not a whole poem'.[53] William Walsh, however, considers 'Dejection' 'one of the finest of all Romantic poems' and says that 'the formal, distancing qualities of the ode, while they strengthen the arrangement of the poem, do not subdue the intense and feeling part of it. In fact they help towards a steadiness of honesty and a continuity and patience of attention all too rare in Coleridge.'[54]

The second major problem that has vexed critics of the poem is *whether* or *to what extent* the dejection with which the poem begins is alleviated, or transcended, or come to terms with. For some readers there is no spiritual or psychological advance at all. Walter Jackson Bate, for example, states flatly that the poem is 'no triumphant assertion of the "creative imagination". . . . It is a cry of despair'; and Max F. Schulz concurs, saying of stanza 7 that 'Sharpness of feeling has returned to the poet, but it is not the imaginatively creative, life-giving wholeness of joy; it is still the death-dealing fragmentation of dejection.'[55] F. M. Smith, comparing Coleridge's poem with Wordsworth's 'Ode: Intimations of Immortality', is even blunter: 'In Wordsworth's *Ode* grief finds relief and ends in joy; in Coleridge's, grief finds no relief and ends in dejection.'[56] In diametric opposition to these views is the position of R. H. Fogle, who argues that the poem illustrates Coleridge's 'rebirth of imagination' − a position supported, in recent years, by such readers as J. L. Simmons and P. R. Broughton, the latter of whom asserts that the poem 'remains an ode about *dejection*, but it is not an apostrophe to dejection' and that, as Coleridge learns (or sees) by stanza 6, 'Dejection understood . . . is dejection controlled.'[57]

Still other readers, however, prefer to say that the poem's conclusion is essentially ambivalent. M. H. Abrams states the case admirably:

The poetic meditation is set in April, which turns out, as in Eliot's *Waste Land*, to be the cruelest month because, in breeding life out of the dead land, it painfully revives emotional life in the observer, mixing memory and desire. . . . In implicit parallel with the wind-harp, the poet also responds to the storm with mounting vitality . . . until, in a lull of the wind, the poem rounds on itself and ends where it began, with a calm both of nature and of mind. But the poet has moved from the calm of apathy to one of peace after passion. By the agency of the wind storm it describes, the poem turns out to contradict its own premises: the poet's spirit awakes to violent life even as he laments his inner death, achieves release in the despair at being cut off from all outlet, and demonstrates the power of imagination in the process of memorializing its failure.[58]

6　*Biographia Literaria*

Until you understand a writer's ignorance, presume yourself ignorant of his understanding.　(*BL*, I 160)

EVOLUTION AND COMPOSITIONAL HISTORY

The story of *Biographia Literaria* begins many years before the book was published in 1817. Its origins, indeed, may be traced back nearly two decades to Coleridge's German tour of 1798–9 and a projected biography of the dramatist and critic Gotthold Ephraim Lessing. The first we hear of the Lessing project is in a letter to Poole of January 1799, where the work is described as 'a Life of Lessing – & interweaved with it a true state of German Literature, in its rise & present state' (*CL*, I 455). Coleridge had chosen the 'Life of Lessing', he told Josiah Wedgwood in May 1799, because 'it would give me an opportunity of conveying under a better name, than my own ever will be, opinions, which I deem of the highest importance' (*CL*, I 519). The Lessing project had as its object, not biography *per se*, but the explication and dissemination of general truths which Lessing had articulated in a manner and with an authority that Coleridge considered beyond his own capacity.

The relevance of the Lessing scheme to *Biographia Literaria* will become apparent if we pursue the evidence a little further. Coleridge left Germany, the biography unwritten, in July 1799. Toward the end of July 1800 he settled finally, after a year of wandering, at Greta Hall, Keswick, twelve miles from the Wordsworths' cottage at Grasmere. Lessing, however, was not forgotten during this period. In January 1800, busy with political articles for the *Morning Post*, Coleridge was nevertheless expecting 'in April' to return to 'my greater work — the Life of Lessing' (*CL*, ɪ 559); in July, indeed on the very day on which he moved into Greta Hall, he told Josiah Wedgwood that 'I am now working at my introduction to the life of Lessing which I trust will be in the press before Christmas — that is, the Introduction which will be published first I believe' (*CL*, ɪ 610—11); and finally, on 9 October, in an important letter to Humphry Davy, he declared that

> The works which I gird myself up to attack as soon as money-concerns will permit me, are the Life of Lessing — & the Essay on Poetry. The latter is still more at my heart than the former — it's Title would be an Essay on the Elements of Poetry / it would in reality be a *disguised* System of Morals & Politics. . . .
>
> (*CL*, ɪ 632)

The most noticeable feature of these three statements is the shift in emphasis from the biography of Lessing to the prefatory essay designed (originally) to introduce it. Between January and October 1800 Coleridge's interest and energies focused more and more on the introductory 'Essay on Poetry', which he came eventually to see as a volume in its own right. This shift in interest is not difficult to explain. Coleridge was outgrowing Lessing. As he meditated on the nature of poetry and the principles of poetic composition — an investigation facilitated and furthered by his renewed association with Wordsworth in the summer of 1800 — Coleridge began seriously to develop his own ideas, to evolve his own theories. More and more he wished to state *his* views, not Lessing's; and, as a consequence, the introductory 'Essay on Poetry' lay more at his heart than the proposed biography. After October 1800, indeed, we hear nothing more about a 'Life of Lessing' at all.

Why then did Coleridge not publish his 'Essay on Poetry' in 1800? The simple answer is that the essay — at least in its aesthetic aspect — was eventually written, not by Coleridge, but by Wordsworth, who published it as the Preface to the second edition (1800) of *Lyrical Ballads*. We now know, from statements by both Coleridge and Wordsworth, that the idea of introducing the poems with an analytic preface was Coleridge's and that it was originally intended that the preface (replacing the short 'Advertisement' of the 1798 *Lyrical Ballads*) should have been written by him. In a marginal comment of 1839 in Barron Field's *Memoirs of Words-worth*, Wordsworth declared,

> In the foregoing there is frequent reference to what is called Mr W[s] theory, & his Preface. I will mention that I never cared a straw about the theory − & the Preface was written at the request of Mr Coleridge out of sheer good nature. I recollect the very spot, a deserted Quarry in the Vale of Grasmere where he pressed the thing upon me, & but for that it would never have been thought of.[1]

(Wordsworth *did*, of course, care about the theory or he would not have defended it so lustily in subsequent additions to his 1800 Preface.) Coleridge, for his part, described his role in a letter of July 1802: 'It is most certain, that that Preface arose from the heads of our mutual Conversations &c − & the first passages were indeed partly taken from notes of mine / for it was at first intended, that the Preface should be written by me' (*CL*, ii 811).

The Coleridgean 'notes' on which the first part of the Preface was based have, it seems, been lost − unless, that is, a vestige of them survives in a faded, almost illegible Notebook entry of August or September 1800 containing the tantalising phrase 'recalling of passion in tranquillity' (*CN*, i no. 787).[2] In any case, what is clear from these statements is that Coleridge was the 'only begetter' of the 1800 Preface, that (for reasons which remain obscure) it was eventually written by Wordsworth, who used some of Coleridge's notes at least in the initial sections, and that (as Coleridge later reported) 'The Preface contains our joint opinions on Poetry'(*CL*, i 627). Whenever Wordsworth took over the writing of the Preface, it was finished by the end of September, when Dorothy copied out 'the last sheet' of it for the printer's copy (*JDW*, p. 41).

Once the Preface had been written, once their 'joint opinions on Poetry' had been set down by Wordsworth, Coleridge's motivation to articulate his own position became less pressing − but it did not entirely disappear. In September–October 1800 Coleridge was still planning, even after Wordsworth had finished the Preface, to press on with the Lessing project and his 'Essay on the Elements of Poetry' (see *CL*, i 623, 632). Why were these projects, especially the latter, never brought to fruition? Indolence, no doubt, was partly to blame; so, too, was illness and Coleridge's immersion in 'abstruse researches'. And there was also, I suspect, another reason: Coleridge had not yet worked out to his own satisfaction the underlying 'principles' or 'elements' of poetry; he needed more time to think and study, more time to mature and explore the hints and half-revealed theories on which he was meditating. All that *could* be said in 1800 *had* been said by Wordsworth in the Preface. For the moment, Coleridge could go no further.

In January 1801 Coleridge spoke warmly of Wordsworth's 'valuable Preface' (*CL*, II 665), but then we hear no more about the matter until July 1802. The intervening eighteen months, however, had seen a dramatic reversal in his views. On 13 July 1802 Coleridge wrote to William Sotheby expressing his doubts about Wordsworth's theories of poetic diction and metre: 'Indeed, we have had lately some little controversy on this subject − & we begin to suspect, that there is, somewhere or other, a *radical* Difference in our opinions' (*CL*, II 812). It was, almost certainly, the publication of the third edition of *Lyrical Ballads* (1802) with its revised and expanded Preface and an Appendix on poetic diction that focused Coleridge's growing uneasiness about Wordsworth's theory and prompted in him a renewed interest, in July–September 1802, in literary theory − a renewal of interest which led to the revision of 'Dejection: An Ode' and to the initial formulation of the fancy–imagination distinction. Coleridge received a copy of the new edition of *Lyrical Ballads* in làte June or early July 1802. Within a fortnight he had written to Sotheby about 'a *radical* Difference' between his own and Wordsworth's theories of poetry. At the end of the month, in a letter to Robert Southey (29 July), he was more explicit − and he was planning, he said, to set down his own views in a series of critical essays on contemporary poets, including Wordsworth:

> The object is not to examine what is good in each writer, but what has ipso facto pleased, & to what faculties or passions or habits of the mind they may be supposed to have given pleasure / Of course, Darwin & Wordsworth having given each a defence of *their* mode of Poetry, & a disquisition on the nature & essence of Poetry in general, I shall necessarily be led rather deeper.
>
> (*CL*, II 829–30)

He went on to say that he had been 'startled' in reading some of Wordsworth's recent poetry to discover 'here & there a daring

Humbleness of Language & Versification, and a strict adherence to matter of fact, even to prolixity'; and, as for the poetic theory, he declared himself 'far from going all lengths with Wordsworth'. The Appendix in the new edition of *Lyrical Ballads* he thought 'valuable', but parts of the revised Preface were 'obscure beyond any necessity'; and he was resolved 'to go to the Bottom' of the differences between his own and Wordsworth's theoretical opinions on poetry and, by 'acting the arbitrator between the old School & the New School, . . . to lay down some plain, & perspicuous, tho' not superficial, Canons of Criticism respecting Poetry' (*CL*, II 830).

There are three things to notice in this statement to Southey. First, the major areas of disagreement with Wordsworth centre on poetic diction and versification and on an even more fundamental difference (which he *feels* but does not yet understand) growing out of some underlying tension between Wordsworth's theory and his actual practice as a poet. The nature of this discrepancy, as Coleridge began to see in September, was that his friend's theory (based on Hartleian associationism) took account of the poetry of fancy but not of the poetry of imagination; and the best and most characteristic of Wordsworth's own poetry was imaginative, not fanciful (see above, pp. 179–81). All of these issues – poetic diction, versification, fancy-imagination – are, of course, matters of central importance in the later *Biographia Literaria*. Second, it is apparent from his ruminations in the letter to Southey that Coleridge, immersed in abstruse philosophical and psychological researches that were leading him 'rather deeper' into the nature and essence of poetic experience than Wordsworth found it necessary to go, was concerned with the general underlying *principles* of composition and poetic pleasure: 'not to examine what is good in [an individual] writer, but what has ipso facto pleased'. This, too, foreshadows the method of *Biographia Literaria*:

> it was Mr Wordsworth's purpose to consider the influences of fancy and imagination as they are manifested in poetry, and from the different effects to conclude their diversity in kind; while it is my object to investigate the seminal principle, and then from the kind to deduce the degree. My friend has drawn a masterly sketch of the branches with their *poetic* fruitage. I wish to add the trunk, and even the roots as far as they lift themselves above ground, and are visible to the naked eye of our common consciousness.

> (ch. 4; *BL*, I 64)

Finally, in July 1802 Coleridge still expected to proceed bio-graphically, not autobiographically. Although Lessing had yielded place to contemporary English poets (especially Words-worth), Coleridge's plan was still to refract 'opinions, which I deem of the highest importance', through the writings of other men. The title for the proposed work, he told Southey, was to be 'Concerning Poetry, & the characteristic Merits of the Poets, our Contem-poraries – one Volume Essays, the second Selections' (*CL*, II 829).

The centrality of Wordsworth in the evolution and early plan-ning of what was eventually to become the *Biographia Literaria* is something that must be insisted upon. We begin with Lessing but come quickly to Wordsworth; and, as George Whalley has said, 'The various modifications of the Lessing scheme, the talks with Wordsworth that produced the 1800 Preface, and the attempts to resolve the "radical difference" that he mentioned to Southey in July 1802, made the need for a personal statement imperative.'[3] In a letter to Thomas Wedgwood (20 Oct 1802) Coleridge was still wrestling with the problem of poetic diction, convinced that poetry required 'a certain *Aloofness* from the language of real Life, which I think deadly to Poetry'; he was working, he told Wedgwood, on elaborating in full his opinions 'on the subject of Style both in prose & verse', first, in an analysis of English prose from Bishop Hall to Dr Johnson, and then, this completed, 'I shall . . . put together my memorandum Book on the subject of poetry' (*CL*, II 877). Then in September or October 1803 the biographical thread that had begun with Lessing became an autobiographical one: 'Seem to have made up my mind', Coleridge confided in his pocket-book, 'to write my metaphysical works, as *my Life*, & *in* my Life – inter-mixed with all the other events / or history of the mind & fortunes of S. T. Coleridge' (*CN*, I no. 1515).[4] How or why he came to this determination we shall probably never know. Nevertheless, what is important (as D. M. Fogel points out) is that by the end of 1803 'Coleridge possessed the main elements of the *Biographia*, both in its intense concern with speculation arising from his experience of Wordsworth and in its autobiographical intention'.[5]

For more than a decade, however, nothing happened. Between October 1803 and March 1815 the plan for a literary autobiography drops completely out of sight; it is not mentioned anywhere in Coler-idge's letters or Notebooks or marginalia or published works. This does not mean, of course, that he ceased to speculate and to sharpen his views about the nature of poetry and poetic composition, about

Wordsworth as poet and critic, about the metaphysical and psychological foundations of aesthetic theory. Quite the reverse, indeed, is true. Coleridge's writings of this period are full of ideas (in various states of development) that turn up later in *Biographia Literaria* − but the 'idea' of *Biographia Literaria* itself is absent.

In March 1815, in great financial distress, Coleridge asked some of his Bristol friends to advance him money in the form of a loan, using his manuscripts as security.[6] His first approach, on 7 March, was to Joseph Cottle (*CL*, IV 546−7); but within three days, anticipating Cottle's refusal, he had applied to William Hood, another Bristol friend (*CL*, IV 551). The result was that Hood, after consulting John Gutch and a Mr Le Breton (both former schoolfellows of Coleridge), accepted the proposal and sent Coleridge a loan to cover his immediate debts. (Later in the year they paid his life-insurance premium, advanced him further money, and also arranged for the printing at Bristol of his poems and *Biographia*, on the understanding that the printing-expenses and Coleridge's personal debt would be recovered by the sale of these works to a London publisher.) By the end of March 1815, as we know from a letter to Lord Byron, Coleridge was planning a collective edition of his poems which was to include 'all the poems composed by me from the year 1795 to the present Date, that are sanctioned by my maturer Judgement, all that I would consent to have called mine if it depended on my own will'. This edition, he went on to say, would contain two prefaces:

> A general Preface will be pre-fixed, on the Principles of philosophic and genial criticism relatively to the Fine Arts in general; but especially to Poetry: and a particular Preface to the Ancient Mariner and the Ballads, on the employment of the Supernatural in Poetry, and the Laws which regulate it.
>
> (*CL*, VI 1033−5)

He expected to have the work ready for the press by the first week of June. In the event, however, as we shall shortly see, the affair was to be both more complicated and more protracted than Coleridge originally expected. Eventually, the edition of his poems appeared as *Sibylline Leaves*, the 'general Preface' became *Biographia Literaria* − both finally published in 1817 − and the proposed preface on 'the Supernatural in Poetry' (while promised at the end of the first volume of *Biographia Literaria* − *BL*, I 202) was never, in fact, written.

In April—May 1815 Coleridge was busy collecting and polishing poems for his new edition, and on 30 May he informed Wordsworth that he had 'only to finish a Preface which I shall have done in two or at farthest three days' (*CL*, IV 567) in order to complete the work. Then, for two months, we hear nothing — either because Coleridge wrote few letters (as is probable) or because they have not survived. But when the silence is broken, in a letter of 29 July to R. H. Brabant, the revelation is both surprising and dramatic:

> The necessity of extending, what I first intended as a preface,[7] to an Autobiographia literaria, or Sketches of my literary Life & opinions, as far as Poetry and *poetical* Criticism is concerned, has confined me to my Study from 11 to 4, and from 6 to 10, since I last left you. — I have just finished it, having only the correction of the *Mss.* to go thro'. — I have given a full account (raisonné) of the Controversy concerning Wordsworth's Poems & Theory, in which my name has been so constantly included — I have no doubt, that Wordsworth will be displeased[8] — but I have done my Duty to myself and to the Public, in (as I believe) compleatly subverting the Theory & in proving that the Poet himself has never acted on it except in particular Stanzas which are the Blots of his Compositions. — One long passage — a disquisition on the powers of association, with the History of the Opinions on this subject from Aristotle to Hartley, and on the generic difference between the faculties of Fancy and Imagination — I did not indeed altogether insert, but I certainly extended and elaborated, with a view to your perusal — as laying the foundation Stones of the Constructive or Dynamic Philosophy in opposition to the merely mechanic —.
>
> (*CL*, IV 578—9)

Between 30 May, when he wrote to Wordsworth, and this statement to Brabant at the end of July, Coleridge abandoned (or, rather, extended) his plan to write a 'general Preface' for his collected poems and composed, instead, an 'Autobiographia literaria'. Now, if we accept (as we must, given the complete absence of documentary evidence) that we cannot know exactly *when* during these two months (June—July 1815) Coleridge changed his plans, we are left still with two important questions, both of which can be answered at least conditionally: first, what prompted him to metamorphose his proposed preface into a literary autobiography?; and, second, how much (and which parts) of the *Biographia Literaria* had he in fact composed when he wrote to Brabant at the end of July 1815?

While other factors are involved, a partial solution to the first question is provided by Coleridge himself: 'in consequence of information received from various Quarters,' he told Gutch in September 1815,

> I concluded, that a detailed publication of my opinions concerning Poetry & Poets, would excite more curiosity and a more immediate Interest than even my Poems. – Therefore instead of Poems *and* a Preface I resolved to publish 'Biographical Sketches of my LITERARY LIFE, Principles, and Opinions, chiefly on the Subjects of Poetry and Philosophy . . .'. (*CL*, IV 584).

Supposed commercial prospects, then, exercised a determining influence; but there were other factors too, the most important of which may be summarised in a single word – Wordsworth.

For well over a decade, as we have seen, the long-meditated project of setting down his critical opinions on poetry had been intimately connected with Wordsworth, and the early motivation for such a work had been provided by his conviction of a '*radical* Difference' between his views and those of his friend. In the spring of 1815 Coleridge was still concerned about Wordsworth's theory and its (often) deleterious effect on his poetry. In comparing *The Excursion* (published in July 1814) with *The Prelude* (which he had heard recited in 1807), Coleridge was prompted to tell Lady Beaumont in April 1815 that Wordsworth, 'having . . . *himself* convinced *himself* of Truths, which the generality of persons have either taken for granted from their Infancy, or at least adopted in early life, . . . has attached all their own depth and weight to doctrines and words, which come almost as Truisms or Commonplace to others' (*CL*, IV 564).[9] Wordsworth's penchant for *matter-of-factness*, which Coleridge first censured in 1802 (above, p. 210) and later numbered among Wordsworth's 'defects' in *Biographia* chapter 22 (*BL*, II 101–9), seems to have been the focal point of Coleridge's uneasiness and continuing sense of a radical theoretical difference with Wordsworth in early 1815.

Before long, however, a new and influential factor emerged which forced Coleridge's hand, gave firm focus to his understanding of Wordsworth's strengths and weaknesses, and provided the final spur needed to transform the proposed preface to his poems into the *Biographia Literaria*. This event was the publication of Wordsworth's *Poems, including Lyrical Ballads* (March 1815) in two octavo volumes. This edition, which was in Coleridge's possession by May 1815 (though we do not know exactly when he received it), was no mere reprint of earlier publications: it contained, as Mary Moorman has said,

> all the poems and sonnets written since 1807, and the whole was divided into classes according to Wordsworth's peculiar and original plan. A new Preface described this arrangement to the reader, while at the end of the first volume stood an *Essay, Supplementary to the Preface*, and at the end of the second the preface to the 1800 edition of *Lyrical Ballads* was reprinted. It was therefore a very complete exposition of Wordsworth's poetic theory and achievements which was now offered to the world.
>
> (*WW*, II 269–70)

Coleridge could no longer remain silent. Not only had Wordsworth reprinted the 1800 Preface to *Lyrical Ballads* – a preface about which Coleridge had had serious reservations since 1802 – but, more grievously, he had in the introductory Preface to the volumes perverted the Coleridgean distinction between fancy and imagination, declaring (*inter alia*) that 'To aggregate and to associate, to evoke and to combine, belong as well to the Imagination as to the Fancy' (*PWW*, III 36). To blur the distinction in this fashion, to say that both imagination and fancy are aggregative and associative, was to strike at the heart of Coleridge's theory. Wordsworth's statements made the necessity for a response imperative, for his 1815 Preface rested on a fundamental misinterpretation that could not remain unchallenged, uncorrected, unanswered. And so, probably early in June 1815, Coleridge abandoned the idea of a simple preface and set about composing the *Biographia Literaria*, motivated largely (in John Shawcross's words) by 'the desire . . . to state clearly, and defend adequately, his own poetic creed' (*BL*, I xcii).

To say that Coleridge set about composing the *Biographia Literaria* in June–July 1815, is, perhaps, a little misleading. His plan during these months was to publish two volumes – the first an extended 'preface' in the form of a literary autobiography, the second an edition of his collected poems. Doubtless this plan was much indebted to (if not wholly inspired by) the format of Wordsworth's 1815 *Poems* with its various prefaces. The analogy between the two works is borne out by a comment (early August 1815) of Mary Morgan which has been preserved in one of Mary Lamb's letters to Sara Hutchinson. (In 1815 Coleridge was domiciled with the Morgan family at Calne in Wiltshire, where John Morgan served as his 'friendly Amanuensis' in the onerous business of preparing works for the press.) Mrs Morgan informed the Lambs (according to Mary Lamb's transcription) that

> Your old friend Coleridge is very hard at work at the preface to a new Edition which he is just going to publish in the same form as Mr Wordsworth's — at first the preface was not to exceed five or six pages it has however grown into a work of great importance. I believe Morgan has already written nearly two hundred pages. The title of it is '*Auto biographia Literaria*': to which are added '*Sybilline Leaves*', a collection of Poems by the same Author.
>
> (*LL*, III 192)

It was not finally until mid September that Coleridge came to regard *Biographia Literaria* as a work separate from his edition of his poems: 'the Biographical Sketches', he told John Gutch on 17 September 1815, 'are not a *Preface* or any thing in the Nature of a Preface, but a Work per se' (*CL*, IV 585). How are we to account for this change in emphasis? The answer is closely involved with the answer to the second of the two questions posed a moment ago (p. 214): how much (and which parts) of *Biographia Literaria* had Coleridge composed when he wrote to Dr Brabant at the end of July 1815?

In July he told Brabant that the 'Autobiographia literaria' was finished and that he had 'only the correction of the *Mss.* to go thro' (*CL*, IV 579). At that stage the work, still thought of as a Preface to his poems, comprised (a) sketches of his own opinions on poetry and criticism, (b) a full account of the controversy over Wordsworth's poems and poetic theory, and (c) a 'long passage' on the history of associationist doctrine from Aristotle to Hartley and, as well, on the generic difference between fancy and imagination. The work, however, was not 'finished', as we know from a letter (10 Aug 1815) from John Morgan to William Hood, written a fortnight after Coleridge's letter to Brabant. Morgan wrote, 'At length

I am enabled to send you 57 sides of C's work — the rest (full 100 sides) is finished, and not finished — that is, there is a metaphysical part of about 5 or 6 sheets which must be revised or rather re-written — this I trust will be done in a few days (*CL*, IV 585 n. 2). In the event, the rewriting of the 'metaphysical part' occupied Coleridge through August and into September, the complete manuscript being mailed to Gutch at Bristol on 19 September.

Now then, what conclusions may be drawn from this evidence? We may, with considerable confidence I think, say that June–July 1815 saw the composition of the material in chapters 1–3 (the '57 sides' sent off by Morgan on 10 August) and chapters 14–21 together with part[10] at least of chapter 22 (the critique of Wordsworth). To this same period (June–July) belong both chapter 4 on the generic difference between fancy and imagination and, in an early form, the historical survey of associationism in chapter 5. Then, in August–September, intending at first only to revise the 'metaphysical part of about 5 or 6 sheets' (i.e. chapter 5), Coleridge ended up composing the material in chapters 6–13, the philosophic core of the work. It is probable, as D. M. Fogel has suggested, that it was the 'new stress on philosophy' in August–September 1815, when Coleridge was busy enlarging the metaphysical section, that led him to see that the work was in no sense a Preface, but rather 'a Work per se'.[11] Such a hypothesis is supported, indeed made compelling, by statements in Coleridge's letters where a shift in thematic emphasis parallels the emerging sense of the *Biographia* as a work in its own right. In July, when still conceived of as being a Preface for *Sibylline Leaves*, it was described as 'an Autobiographia literaria, or Sketches of my literary Life & opinions, as far as Poetry and *poetical* Criticism is concerned' (*CL*, IV 578–9); but in September, when the work was no longer 'a *Preface* or any thing in the Nature of a Preface, but a Work per se', it was described as being concerned with 'my LITERARY LIFE, Principles, and Opinions, chiefly on the Subjects of Poetry and Philosophy, and the Differences at present prevailing concerning both' (*CL*, IV 584–5).[12]

There is one further point — bearing on the vexed issues of plagiarism and the gnomic definitions of Imagination and Fancy (chs 12 and 13, respectively) — that needs to be made about the composition of the philosophical section of the *Biographia Literaria*. This part (chs 6–13) of the work grew, as we have seen, out of Coleridge's decision in early August to revise and extend the philosophical discussion begun in chapters 4 and 5. But Gutch, the printer, was anxious to have the whole manuscript so that he could begin setting the work for the press, and there was, consequently, fierce pressure put on Coleridge to finish as quickly as possible. On 10 August Morgan sent Gutch '57 sides of C's work' as a palliative, promised the rest of the manuscript (whose scope and length both he and Coleridge then badly underestimated) 'in a few days', and assured Gutch that Coleridge was working hard on the project (*CL*, IV 585 n. 2). And he *was* working hard: in the six weeks between Morgan's letter (10 August) and the sending to Gutch of the completed manuscript (19 September) Coleridge wrote and/or dictated to Morgan the equivalent of 128 printed pages (*BL*, I 74–202). Moreover, early in chapter 12, in a footnote, we find the following remarkable statement: 'I had never heard of the correspondence between Wakefield and Fox till I saw the account of it this morning (16th September 1815) in the Monthly Review' (*BL*, I 165). Only *three days later* the complete manuscript was mailed to Gutch! Now, whether this means (as Fogel implies) that chapters 12 and 13 were written in three days or whether it means that the footnote only was written on 16 September (three days before the manuscript was sent off), it remains true that chapters 12–13 'were turned out at white heat'.[13] The entire *Biographia*, written as it was in under four months, shows signs of hasty composition; but nowhere has this haste left more clearly defined marks than in chapters 12 and 13, the last to be composed, in September 1815.

As has long been known, chapter 12 of the *Biographia Literaria* consists largely of extended passages of translation, some of them verbatim and none of them acknowledged, from F. W. J. Schelling's *Abhandlungen zur Erläuterung des Idealismus der Wissenschaftslehre* and *System des transcendentalen Idealismus*.[14] Chapter 12 is not the only place, nor is Schelling the only German philosopher from whom Coleridge plagiarises in the course of *Biographia Literaria*; but the fact remains that the bulk of unacknowledged borrowings in the book appear in this chapter, which Coleridge must have composed with Schelling's works open before him.[15] Speed of execution will not, of course, excuse such behaviour (the case for exculpation rests on other and more complex proofs),[16] but it surely does go a long way toward explaining why the borrowings are so extensive at this particular point.

The same necessity may legitimately be claimed, in extenuation, for the faltering performance of chapter 13, 'On the imagination, or esemplastic power' — a chapter promising much more than it delivers, though still it delivers a good deal. The ruse of a letter addressed to himself, the deferral of a full discussion to a later work at a later time, the terse and cryptic — albeit brilliant — paragraphs distinguishing fancy from primary and secondary imagination are all expedients dictated by the pressures of time and an impatient printer. In September 1815 there was no time for reflection or meditation; none for working out complex philosophical arguments without external supports, or for polishing their exposition into clarity and originality of expression; none even, in the case of chapter 13, for providing other than a fleeting glimpse, adumbrated in its oracular conclusion, of the promised deduction of the imagination.

Finally, then, in mid September 1815 the complete manuscript of *Biographia Literaria* and *Sibylline Leaves* was at last transmitted to the Bristol printer. The agreed plan was that the work should be printed in two octavo volumes — the first volume containing the *Biographia*, the second volume the poems. 'The *Autobiography*', Coleridge told Gutch, 'I regard as the *main* work', and (since it was no longer considered in any sense a 'preface' to the poems) 'I would fain have it printed in *Chapters*' (*CL*, IV 585). Coleridge had himself divided the larger part of the manuscript (chapters 4–22) into chapters, and he gave Gutch instructions on how to divide the '57 sides' (sent by Morgan on 10 August) in his possession into three chapters (*CL*, IV 584). Then, as far as Coleridge was concerned, the task was finished — a conviction conveyed, with relief and pride, to numerous correspondents in the autumn of 1815 (see *CL*, IV 588, 591, 597–8, 607–8). Gutch, too, was satisfied: he began printing the *Biographia* in October and *Sibylline Leaves* in November 1815.[17] By 12 October the first proof-sheets of *Biographia* reached Coleridge at Calne (*CL*, IV 593); in April 1816 Coleridge, now seeing his *Christabel* volume through the press in London, took up what was to prove a lifelong residence with the Gillmans in Highgate, in an effort to control his opium habit; and meanwhile, back in Bristol, the printing of the earlier work was proceeding smoothly: by May 1816 the first twelve chapters of *Biographia Literaria* and almost the whole of *Sibylline Leaves* had been printed. All was well — or so, at least, it seemed.

The storm broke in July 1816.[18] Two months earlier, with the printing well under way, Gutch had discovered that the planned two volumes would be disproportionate in size, the *Biographia* volume being much longer than the *Sibylline Leaves* volume. (Why this problem was not spotted before the spring of 1816 remains a mystery.) It was decided, in any event, to solve the difficulty by publishing *Biographia Literaria* in *two* volumes (*CL*, IV 646n.) and *Sibylline Leaves* separately as a third volume. This decision, made in early May 1816, was based on Gutch's 'positive assurance' (*CL*, IV 660) that the manuscript as it stood contained enough material for two volumes. Coleridge, though 'incredulous', agreed (after consultation with Morgan and John Murray, the London publisher) to split the *Biographia* into two volumes, the first to contain chapters 1–13, the second chapters 14–22. There was *not*, however, enough material in Chapters 14–22 to make a second volume. Gutch, realising that a blunder had been made in estimating copy, informed Coleridge in July 1816 that more material was required to flesh out the second volume of *Biographia*. Coleridge, who had since September 1815 considered the work finished and had, consequently, turned his energies to other projects, was angered and perplexed by the news: 'I have no way to remedy it,' he exclaimed in exasperation, 'but by writing *a hundred and fifty pages* additional – on *what*, *I* am left to discover' (*CL*, IV 661). By mid July the printing of the second volume had progressed as far as page 14 of chapter 22. The additional material, therefore, would have to be tacked on to the end of a completed work, most of which had already been printed. What, indeed, could he be expected to do at this point? What could be added without distortion, without destroying the structural and thematic integrity of the book he had already written? And how, having recently agreed with the firm of Gale and Fenner to write a lay sermon and prepare a new edition of *The Friend*, was he to find the time to compose such extensive additions?

Relations with Gutch deteriorated rapidly through the summer and autumn of 1816. There were threats and angry words on both sides. Gutch stopped the printing of *Biographia* midway through chapter 22 and, in December 1816, sent Coleridge a bill for the printing costs, refusing to surrender any of the printed sheets until the account was paid and threatening to denounce Coleridge publicly for failure to complete the work unless a speedy settlement was reached. At this point Coleridge's London publishers, Gale and Fenner, took over the correspondence. After months of contentious negotiations, a financial compromise was reached and, in April 1817, Gutch released the printed sheets and the manuscript of the work to the London firm. It was not, however, until May 1817 that a final settlement was achieved and the rights to *Biographia Literaria* and *Sibylline Leaves* passed to Gale and Fenner.

In the meantime Coleridge was still left with the problem of what to use in fleshing out the second volume of *Biographia Literaria*. Although he spoke of getting on with this task as early as September 1816 (*CL*, IV 679), he seems to have made no constructive steps until the spring of 1817. Partly, he was too discouraged and the fate of the work too much in doubt to justify supplying new material in 1816; partly, he was prevented by the pressure of other work, for in the period September 1816–March 1817 he was hard at work composing and seeing through the press his *Statesman's Manual* (published in December 1816) and his *Lay Sermon* (published in March 1817); and partly, too, there was ill health – a 'sinking down of my Health that made it so perplexing for me to remedy' the printer's blunder (*CL*, IV 704). At length, however, in February 1817 he addressed himself seriously to the problem of how to 'fill the Gap'. At first, although reluctantly, he planned to use his play *Zapolya*; but, by 14 March, he had decided to substitute his 'German Letters' (*CL*, IV 709), which had first appeared in *The Friend* in 1809.[19] But the addition of these letters (entitled 'Satyrane's Letters') still left the second volume short of the required length. Consequently, Coleridge supplied some other items: (a) a reprint of his review of C. R. Maturin's *Bertram* from *The Courier*,[20] which became chapter 23 of the *Biographia Literaria*; (b) a concluding chapter (24), written in the spring of 1817, in which he answered the critics of his 'Christabel' and *Statesman's Manual*[21] and stated his own beliefs 'concerning the true evidences of Christianity'; and (c) *perhaps* a revision, padded out with quotations, of the last two-thirds of chapter 22 (see n. 10).

With these additions – most of them mere makeweights – the work was at last ready for the press. By May 1817 Gale and Fenner had secured the publication rights from Gutch. The printing of the second volume of *Biographia Literaria* was resumed at page 145, incorporating the new materials supplied by Coleridge. At long last, in July 1817, twenty-three months after Coleridge had transmitted the manuscript to Gutch in Bristol, *Biographia Literaria* and *Sibylline Leaves* were released for sale. 'It sometimes happens', Coleridge observed, 'that we are punished for our faults by incidents, in the causation of which these faults had no share: and this I have always felt the severest punishment' (*BL*, II 207).

THE STRUCTURE OF *BIOGRAPHIA LITERARIA*

'I can assert,' Thomas DeQuincey declared in 1834, 'upon my long and intimate knowledge of Coleridge's mind, that logic, the most severe, was as inalienable from his modes of thinking, as grammar from his language.'[22] What, then, is the 'logic' of the *Biographia Literaria*? How, and on what principles, is the work structured — or, indeed, has it any structure at all?

Adverse criticism begins (as is not unusual) with Coleridge himself, who deprecatingly refers to *Biographia Literaria* as an 'immethodical miscellany' and a 'semi-narrative' (*BL*, I 64, 110). Early reviewers took the author at his word: the kindest epithet any of them could manage for the work was 'strange medley', and usually they were searing in their condemnation of its rambling structure. The legacy of these early reviewers persisted unchallenged until well into the present century. T. S. Eliot, for example, saw reflected in *Biographia Literaria* the 'state of lethargy' produced by 'the disastrous effects of long dissipation and stupefaction of [Coleridge's] powers in transcendental metaphysics'; and Maurice Carpenter, for whom the book was 'a long monologue' of incorrigible heterogeneity, felt justified as late as 1954 in dismissing it as 'the most exasperating book in the English language'.[23] The first serious attempt to dispel the prevailing notion of *Biographia* as 'a whimsical and absent-minded improvisation, a mushroom growth in which toughness of fibre is scarcely to be expected', was made by George Whalley in 1953.

Whalley's defence of the structural integrity of *Biographia Literaria* proceeds along two lines. First, he refutes the view that it was a hasty improvisation by pointing out that the issues which it explores had been in Coleridge's mind for well over a decade and that the work 'has many indelible marks of prolonged, patient, and mature consideration'.[24] Second, he stresses the centrality of Wordsworth, both in the early development and in the final execution of *Biographia Literaria*. The original motivation to compose the work was rooted in Coleridge's desire to explain the novel power of Wordsworth's art and the related desire to solve the 'radical Difference' between his own and Wordsworth's theoretical opinions about poetry. Both these desires come to fruition in *Biographia Literaria* and, in the final analysis, it is Coleridge's view of Wordsworth that imparts unity and purpose of design to this *soi-disant* 'immethodical miscellany'. A substantial portion of the work, of course, is devoted to a critical appraisal and exposition of Wordsworth's theory and poetic achievement. Most of the second volume (chs 14–22) deals directly with these matters. The largely philosophic first volume, on the other hand, prepares the ground for the literary analysis to follow and deals, sometimes directly, sometimes by implication, with Wordsworth. Certainly, the philosophical chapters are not gratuitous metaphysical embroidery unrelated to the book's central concerns, and (as Whalley observes) it is not often enough remembered that 'the centre of the philosophical critique – the distinction between Fancy and Imagination – arose from Wordsworth's poetry and was intended to elucidate it'.[25] In short, then, Wordsworth is omnipresent; and Whalley argues convincingly that, with the long examination of Wordsworth's work in chapters 14–22, 'the *Biographia Literaria* comes full circle, spun upon the firm centre of Coleridge's poetic and philosophic life, his admiration for Wordsworth's work, his need to utter forth an intuition [fancy–imagination] that had long haunted and enlightened his thinking'.[26]

Although dissenting voices may still be heard,[27] Whalley's position has been endorsed – sometimes enthusiastically[28] – by most recent commentators. Subsequent readers have often wished to modify or qualify Whalley's conclusions, or to adjust the emphasis of the argument by focusing on other unifying threads in *Biographia Literaria*. Thus, J. E. Barcus, for example, argues that 'if the *Biographia Literaria* is read in the light of Coleridge's own literary principles, it becomes a practical demonstration of the principles he was propagating';[29] and George Watson, although part of his argument is untenable,[30] finds in the work a 'peculiarly Coleridgean' unity in the fact that here Coleridge

> succeeds for the first and (so far) for the last time in English criticism in marrying the twin studies of philosophy and literature, not simply by writing about both within the boards of a single book or by insisting that such a marriage should be, but in discovering a causal link between the two in the century-old

preoccupation of English critics with the theory of the poet's imagination.   (*BL*[W], p. xix)

What Whalley has taught us to see (wherever we may choose to place the emphasis) is that *Biographia Literaria* is not without method or purpose. The point no longer is whether or not the book is unified, but rather to identify the nature (and degree) of its thematic and structural organisation.

Coleridge's success is, of course, debatable: some critics (most notably J. A. Appleyard) regard the *Biographia* as 'a remarkable failure, an important fragment';[31] others, such as Lynn M. Grow, find it to be 'a coherent expression . . . a cogent and compelling statement'.[32] These opposing arguments, in their elaboration, often show the defects of their qualities; and a true assessment lies in a middle ground where these extremes meet.

In the opening paragraph of *Biographia Literaria* Coleridge states, clearly and concisely, the scope and purpose of his book:

It will be found, that the least of what I have written concerns myself personally. I have used the narration chiefly for the purpose of giving a continuity to the work, in part for the sake of the miscellaneous reflections suggested to me by particular events, but still more as introductory to the statement of my principles in Politics, Religion, and Philosophy, and an application of the rules, deduced from philosophical principles, to poetry and criticism. But of the objects, which I proposed to myself, it was not the least important to effect, as far as possible, a settlement of the long continued controversy concerning the true nature of poetic diction; and at the same time to define with the utmost impartiality the real *poetic* character of the poet, by whose writings this controversy was first kindled, and has since been fuelled and fanned.   (*BL*, i 1–2)

The book is not, then, an *autobiography* in any usual sense of the term. Rather, autobiography is a thread used to give continuity to the central themes and concerns of the work: (a) a statement of Coleridge's principles in politics, religion, philosophy, and literary theory;[33] (b) a philosophic investigation of the *principles*[34] governing poetry and criticism; and (c) the practical application of these principles, once established, to the poetry and poetic theory of Wordsworth. At the heart of the book stands, not Coleridge himself, but Coleridge's principles — the general laws which underlie and direct his judgement. *Biographia Literaria*, then, is not an expository outline of its author's life and times, but an exploration of the formative stages of his intellectual development. It is, too, a *selective* history of mental and moral growth, concentrating on poetry; however, the homogeneity of the principles to which he has been guided (and which he hopes to explicate and to illustrate) allows him without being irrelevant to explore their exfoliation into the fields of politics, theology and philosophy. But this procedure is not without its difficulties and drawbacks. It involves Coleridge, for example, in a paradox — for he finds himself engaged simultaneously in the two quite different activities of exploring and expounding fundamental principles. That is, he sees his task as the philosophic deduction of principles; yet, at the same time, he is concerned with *applying* to politics and religion and (especially) literary theory the very principles that he is involved in deducing. 'One has the sense', as M. G. Cooke observes, 'of his reporting his universe in order to be able to see it.'[35] The dilemma of *Biographia Literaria* is that it is both process and product. Whether or not Coleridge is able to reconcile these methodological difficulties, and the degree of his success, are debatable issues.

Although *Biographia Literaria* is concerned primarily with Coleridge's response to Wordsworth, the introductory chapters deal with preliminary matters and acknowledge debts predating his association with Wordsworth.

The opening chapter emphasises the formative influence exerted on Coleridge's understanding of poetry by James Boyer and William Lisle Bowles. From Boyer, his headmaster at Christ's Hospital, Coleridge learned that poetry was fundamentally and formally distinct from other modes of writing and that it possessed 'a logic of its own, as severe as that of science; and more difficult, because more subtle, more complex, and dependent on more, and more fugitive causes' (*BL*, I 4). From Bowles, whom he considered the first modern poet to combine 'natural thoughts with natural diction', he learned that poetry could (and should) bring together thought and feeling, that it should reconcile the workings of both the head and the heart. In the poetry of Bowles he first caught the accents of the true voice of feeling, and what he heard led him to appreciate that the epigrammatic couplets of fashionable eighteenth-century verse were artificial and were characterised 'not so much by poetic thoughts, as by thoughts *translated* into the language of poetry' (*BL*, I 11). These insights from Boyer and Bowles originated in Coleridge's mind the whole question of the nature of poetry, and they prompted him to labour at establishing 'a solid foundation, on which permanently to ground my opinions, in the component faculties of the human mind itself, and their comparative dignity and importance' (*BL*, I 14). From the outset, then, philosophy and psychology were intimately connected with poetry and poetic experience in the search for aesthetic principles and an individual poetic vision.

In chapters 2 and 3, which superficially appear gratuitously digressive, Coleridge exposes the malicious inadequacy of the pseudo-criticism of anonymous reviewers, whose views, unsupported by sound principles, are both wrongheaded and uncritical. Since Coleridge's purpose in *Biographia Literaria* is to establish sound critical principles as the basis for literary judgement, these chapters are far from irrelevant.

In chapter 4 Coleridge returns to the early formation of his poetic creed and to the third (and most important) influence upon it — the poetry of Wordsworth. Boyer and Bowles provided indispensable preliminary insights, but Wordsworth struck him with the disturbing force of radical revelation. While still at Cambridge, Coleridge had read Wordsworth's *Descriptive Sketches*, and 'seldom, if ever,' (he declared) 'was the emergence of an original poetic genius above the literary horizon more evidently announced' (*BL*, I 56). The full revelation of Wordsworth's genius and power, however, came two years later in September or October 1795, when, at their first meeting, Wordsworth recited his manuscript poem 'Guilt and Sorrow'. The effect of this reading on Coleridge was instant, profound and revolutionary: what made 'so unusual an impression on my feelings immediately, and subsequently on my judgement' was

the union of deep feeling with profound thought; the fine balance of truth in observing, with the imaginative faculty in modifying the objects observed; and above all the original gift of spreading the tone, the *atmosphere*, and with it the depth and height of the ideal world around forms, incidents, and situations, of which, for the common view, custom had bedimmed all the lustre, had dried up the sparkle and the dew drops. (*BL*, I 59)

Here was the seminal insight, though Coleridge found it difficult to define its nature precisely. To a degree unknown in English literature since Milton, Wordsworth had unified thought and feeling in poetic utterance, had both realised and idealised the commonplace, had made the reader see man and nature as if he were seeing them for the first time. Wherein lay the source of this 'freshness of sensation'? What was it in Wordsworth's poetry, what power there manifested itself, that distinguished his poetry from that of eighteenth-century writers? 'Repeated meditations', says Coleridge, anticipating yet laying the ground-work for arguments and illustrations to follow,

> led me first to suspect, (and a more intimate analysis of the human faculties, their appropriate marks, functions, and effects matured my conjecture into full conviction,) that fancy and imagination were two distinct and widely different faculties, instead of being, according to the general belief, either two names with one meaning, or, at furthest, the lower and higher degree of one and the same power. (*BL*, I 60–1)

The desynonymisation of fancy and imagination lies at the heart of *Biographia Literaria* and is, in a very real sense, its *raison d'être*. Coleridge's object in the work is 'to investigate the seminal principle' of imagination and, in so doing, 'to present an intelligible statement of my poetic creed; not as my *opinions*, which weigh for nothing, but as deductions from established premises' (*BL*, I 65). The *terminus a quo* of this investigation is largely Wordsworth, whose 'Guilt and Sorrow' first directed Coleridge's attention to the subject of poetic imagination; the *terminus ad quem*, which will follow the philosophic deduction of the imagination, is a mature assessment of Wordsworth's poetic achievement.

Chapters 5–13 constitute the philosophic core of the *Biographia Literaria* – and the major stumbling-block for the majority of its readers. They are, certainly, difficult reading; but they are integral to the book's purpose and meaning. They trace the growth of Coleridge's philosophic consciousness, his rejection of empirical epistemology and the influence on his thought of German idealism, and they lead, in chapter 12, to an outline (heavily dependent on Schelling) of his own 'dynamic' philosophy — an outline intended as the metaphysical substratum from which was to arise the promised (but undelivered) deduction of a theory of imagination. Chapters 5–7 are devoted to a detailed refutation of associationist psychology, especially that of David Hartley, among whose fervent adherents Coleridge had once (and Wordsworth still) counted himself; chapter 8 deals, briefly but effectively, with the problem of Cartesian dualism and the inadequacy of post-Cartesian materialism; and chapter 9 sketches Coleridge's intellectual obligations, in breaking free of materialism and associationism, to the mystics (such as Jacob Boehme) who 'contributed to keep alive the *heart* in the *head*', to Immanuel Kant who 'took possession of me as with a giant's hand', and to the post-Kantian idealists, especially Schelling, in whose work 'I first found a genial coincidence with much that I had toiled out for myself, and a powerful assistance in what I had yet to do' (*BL*, I 98–9, 102). There is, as J. A. Appleyard observes, an imbalance in these chapters (5–9) that is not easily explained and is, in the final analysis, unsatisfactory:

> This ninth chapter disappoints the reader who hopes to find in the *Biographia* some clue to the extent of the idealist influence on Coleridge's thinking. What he gives by way of comment amounts to not much more than a hasty outline, a cartoon that will not do where a finished painting is demanded. . . . The fact is that Coleridge devotes most of four chapters to a long and very circumstantial refutation of associationist psychology, but only one short chapter to the influence of the whole idealist tradition on his thought.[36]

To say that there is a structural imbalance in these chapters is not, however, to say that they are irrelevant. Indeed, both their relevance and their peculiar emphasis on philosophical positions that Coleridge rejects rather than on those he accepts may be explained — though perhaps not excused — by bearing in mind two things. First, Coleridge's theory of the imagination as a vital, active, *poietic* ('making') power was achieved only after he had exploded the doctrine of passive perception on which the associationist hypothesis depended. In England the prevailing epistemology was stolidly empirical, holding that the human mind was merely a passive receiver of external impressions through the senses; and

Coleridge, for whom perception involved an active and vital interchange between the perceiver and the perceived, was only too conscious that he was swimming against the current. Given the intellectual climate of the day and the philosophic preconceptions of English readers (who knew little or nothing of German transcendentalism), it is not surprising that Coleridge considered a detailed confutation of associationism more important than a lengthy acknowledgement of his obligations to obscure or unknown foreign thinkers. In the second place, the emphasis on associationism in Chapters 5–8 is partly to be explained as an answer to Wordsworth's indistinct but essentially Hartleian doctrine of association in the Preface to *Lyrical Ballads*. Since 1802 Coleridge had regarded this tenet of his friend's theory as inadequate and jejune; it formed part of the '*radical* Difference' that he perceived and came gradually to understand between their theoretical views on poetry. In later chapters of the *Biographia* Coleridge would deal with the other areas of his disagreement with Wordsworth's theory (namely, the problems of poetic diction and metre); but here, on the threshold of the proposed deduction of imagination, it was necessary to explore in detail the failure of associationism – a doctrine which had encumbered Wordsworth's theory in the Preface to *Lyrical Ballads* and which, in Wordsworth's 1815 Preface, had led him to muddle and misconstrue Coleridge's fancy-imagination distinction. Obviously, such a doctrine could not go unchallenged.

Chapters 10 and 11 are confessedly digressive. Like the 'Landing-Place' essays in *The Friend*, they are largely anecdotal interludes interposed for amusement, retrospect and perparation. They shift our attention in an engaging manner from Coleridge's intellectual history to more personal episodes in his biography, narrating with relish such events as his trials with enrolling subscribers for his early periodical *The Watchman* and the now legendary 'Spy-Nosy' incident belonging to his Somerset years with Wordsworth. They stress, too, with respect to his political and theological thinking especially – and this is not often enough noticed – his lifelong commitment to the 'establishment of *principles* . . . by [which] all *opinions* must be ultimately tried' (*BL*, i 124). More is meant, more is implied in these apparently unassuming chapters, than meets the eye of a purely casual reader. They are digressive, it is true, but not without purpose – for they pursue and consolidate insights already gained, applying them to other of Coleridge's myriad-minded interests, and so prepare the ground indirectly for insights still to come.

Chapters 12 and 13, the most difficult and perplexing in the book, resume the discussion of Imagination. No summary of their contents is possible, although some rudimentary signposts and milestones may help the belabyrinthed traveller keep his bearings and hold the journey's end in sight. Chapter 12, heavily indebted to Schelling's *Abhandlungen* and *System des transcendentalen Idealismus*,[37] is concerned with establishing the postulates of the *dynamic* (as opposed to mechanistic) philosophy upon which Coleridge's theory of imagination depends. The chapter is very heavy reading, full of what James Joyce would call 'abstruosities'. From anyone familiar with Carlyle's comically vindictive portrait of Coleridge snuffling about 'sum-m-mject' and 'om-m-mject', it elicits an involuntary shudder of recognition:

> I have heard Coleridge talk, with eager musical energy, two stricken hours, his face radiant and moist, and communicate no meaning whatsoever to any individual of his hearers. . . . He began anywhere: you put some question to him, made some suggestive observation: instead of answering this, or decidedly setting out towards an answer of it, he would accumulate formidable apparatus, logical swim-bladders, transcendental life-preservers and other precautionary and vehiculatory gear, for setting out; perhaps did at last get under way. . . . He had knowledge about many things and topics, much curious reading; but generally all topics led him, after a pass or two, into the high seas of theosophic philosophy, the hazy infinitude of Kantean transcendentalism, with its 'sum-m-jects' and 'om-m-mjects'.[38]

In chapter 12 Coleridge (*via* Schelling) postulates the existence and the simultaneous reality of two diverse states of being, which he distinguishes as SUBJECT and OBJECT. By *subject* he means human intelligence, the self and *self*-consciousness, the I AM; by *object* he means external Nature, the non-self, the IT IS. The *existence* and *reality* of these polarities are assumed (on the basis of experience) as axioms, and the problem is to discover the *relationship* between the subjective and the objective in any act of knowledge.[39] If the perceiving subject and the perceived object are equally 'real' yet equally distinct, then (a) what is *a perception* (the product of their union), and (b) how does it come about? To the first question Coleridge answers, satisfactorily enough, that in all acts of perception there is an interpenetration of self and non-self resulting in a *tertium aliquid* or third entity partaking of both. Perceptions, then, are modifications of self-consciousness: the perceiver knows himself in and through the objects which he perceives. This hypothesis yields, as Coleridge says, the paradox that true idealism 'is only so far idealism, as it is at the same time, and on that very account, the truest and most binding realism' (*BL*, I 178). So far, so good — but *how* (turning to the second question) does this fusion of subject and object take place? Coleridge does not say. At the crucial point of his argument he defers 'the demonstrations and constructions of the Dynamic Philosophy' to the third treatise of his projected 'Logosophia' and is content to restate, in the categorical form of ten 'theses' (largely appropriated from Schelling), the main conclusions already reached. Now, we know from chapter 7 (esp. I 85–6) of *Biographia Literaria*, as well as from elsewhere in his writings, that Coleridge proposed to defend his 'true and original realism' and explain the relationship between *thoughts* and *things* by positing the existence of 'an intermediate faculty [of the mind], which is at once both active and passive'. This faculty is, of course, the imagination. Why, then, does he draw up short in chapter 12, asking us to '*assume* such a power as [a] principle' (*BL*, I 188) so that he can deduce from it in his next chapter what is, after all, merely another aspect or degree (i.e. the *poetic* imagination) of the very power he wishes us to assume as an axiom? Perhaps he was too short of time with the printer snapping at his heels to elaborate such a complex argument; perhaps, in a work concerned with his *literary* opinions, he felt it improper to develop in the detail required so purely philosophical a proposition; perhaps, as Father Appleyard maintains, he was himself confused by his own arguments and found it necessary (in 1815) to resort to Schelling in order 'to bolster a not very satisfactory theory which he had obligated himself to explain'.[40] Perhaps all of these factors were involved.

Chapter 13, 'On the imagination, or esemplastic power',[41] is fragmentary and disappointing, and its failure is doubtless to be explained as a flow-on from the untidy and inconclusive arguments of chapter 12. After a brief excursus into Kant and Schelling, Coleridge abruptly breaks in with a 'letter from a friend' advising him to postpone his deduction of imagination to fuller

consideration in his 'Logosophia'. (This letter, as Coleridge told
Thomas Curtis in April 1817, he had written himself 'without
taking my pen off the paper except to dip it in the inkstand' — *CL*,
IV 728). Chapter 13 stops (rather than ends) by 'stating the main
result' of the unwritten chapter in the celebrated definitions of
Primary Imagination, Secondary Imagination, and Fancy.

This is not the place to enter into a discussion of the meaning
and critical utility of these distinctions. However, one or two brief
explanatory notes will not be out of place. From a structural point
of view, the three definitions constitute a watershed between the
philosophy of chapters 5—13 and the literary criticism of chapters
14—22. In opposition to the empirical philosophies of the followers
of Locke and Hume, for whom the mind was like an inert block of
wax or a blank sheet of paper on which external objects imprint
themselves, Coleridge asserts that the mind is *active* in perception.
This activity, which is subconscious and is the common birthright
of all men, is the work of the Primary Imagination, which may be
defined as the inborn power of perceiving that makes it possible to
know things. This vital, synthesising power effects a coalescence of
subject (self) and object (non-self), yielding, as its product, a
modified combination of the percipient and the thing-perceived;
by blending and fusing 'thoughts' and 'things', self and non-self,
Man and Nature, this *esemplastic* power generates new realities in
which opposites are reconciled, unity is drawn from diversity, and
parts are shaped into wholes. Moreover, since the Primary Imagination is 'a repetition in the finite mind of the eternal act of creation
in the infinite I AM' (*BL*, I 202), it has a theological as well as a
philosophical dimension: Coleridge insists, as he had done for over
a decade (see *CL*, II 1034), that the activity of the perceiving mind
is an analogue, at a finite level, of the eternally generative activity
of God. And finally, by denominating the power of perception as
'primary Imagination', Coleridge establishes *at one stroke* the
intimate relationship between philosophy and poetry: like the
poetic or Secondary Imagination, the Primary Imagination is
poietic — that is to say, *seeing* is *making*.[42]

The Secondary Imagination is, in effect, the poetic imagination. It differs from the Primary Imagination in *degree*, but not
in kind. While all men possess the Primary Imagination, only some
men possess the heightened degree of that universally human
power to which the poet lays claim. Secondary Imagination differs
in two important respects from Primary Imagination. First,

Primary Imagination is subconscious, while Secondary Imagination coexists 'with the conscious will' and involves, therefore, elements of conscious and subconscious activity. Poetic 'making' – I take it that this is Coleridge's meaning – blends conscious selection with subconscious infusion: a poem is both predetermined and preterdetermined, some elements intentionally chosen while others are mysteriously given or supplied from the deep well of the poet's subconscious mind. Indeed, the two impulses may (and probably do) operate simultaneously in many instances: for example, a poet may consciously choose a particular image or expression without being consciously aware of its full implications – such an image or expression, therefore, being both voluntary and involuntary. Second, the Secondary Imagination is described as a power that 'dissolves, diffuses, dissipates, in order to recreate' (*BL*, I 202). Dissolves *what*? Presumably, it dissolves the original union of subject and object effected by the Primary Imagination, a union which most of us take for granted, and then reintegrates the components in a new way that draws attention to their coalescence. In works of genius, this idealising and unifying power operates (as Coleridge had noted in chapter 4) by producing 'the strongest impressions of novelty, while it rescues the most admitted truths from the impotence caused by the very circumstance of their universal admission' (*BL*, I 60). Through the agency of the Secondary Imagination, as Shelley (in a very Coleridgean moment) observes, poetry

> reproduces the common universe of which we are portions and percipients, and it purges from our inward sight the film of familiarity which obscures from us the wonder of our being. It compels us to feel that which we perceive, and to imagine that which we know. It creates anew the universe, after it has been annihilated in our minds by the recurrence of impressions blunted by reiteration.[43]

Fancy, on the other hand, is distinguished from Imagination (both Primary and Secondary) because it is not *poietic*. Fancy differs from Imagination in *kind*.[44] Imagination is coadunative, blending Man and Nature in modified educts participating in, and bridging the gap between, the divided and distinguished worlds of spirit and matter. Imaginative writing is characterised by its seamless fusion of perception, intellect, feeling (or passion),

memory, association and language. Fancy, however, is merely
aggregative and associative; it is a 'mode of Memory' receiving 'all
its materials ready made from the law of association' (*BL*, I 202).
In other words, Fancy joins without blending, yokes together pre-
existing sensations without creating anything organically new,
fabricates without refashioning the elements which it combines.

An image or illustration may be useful in clarifying these
abstractions. Take two metal rods, one of tin, the other of copper.
If we simply *weld* these two rods together, then we produce a single
rod which is half tin and half copper, in which the elements are
joined yet still separate: this is an emblem of the operation of
Fancy. If, however, we put the two rods (one copper, one tin) into
a crucible together and melt them down, we shall end up producing a *bronze* rod in which the original elements of copper and tin
have coadunated to form a third form (a *tertium aliquid*) which is
both and yet neither: this is an emblem of the blending, synthesising power of Imagination. Fancy, which manifests itself in poetry
chiefly through *formal similes*, is (Coleridge would argue) inferior
to Imagination, which operates primarily through *symbols*.[45]
However − and this is important − he would maintain that both
Fancy and Imagination are appropriate to poetry and that both
modes may coexist in a single poet or an individual poem; but
Imagination is the higher mode and the most predominant
characteristic of 'great' poetry.[46] 'A Poet's *Heart & Intellect*', he
told William Sotheby in September 1802,

> should be *combined*, *intimately* combined & *unified*, with the
> great appearances in Nature − & not merely held in solution &
> loose mixture with them, in the shape of formal Similies. I do
> not mean to *exclude* these formal Similies − there are moods of
> mind, in which they are natural − pleasing moods of mind, &
> such as a Poet will often have, & sometimes express; but they are
> not his highest, & most appropriate moods.   (*CL*, II 864)

The bridge between philosophy and aesthetics provided in the
fancy-imagination distinction is followed, in chapters 14−22, by a
detailed examination − an analysis promised from the beginning
− of Wordsworth's theory and art. Coleridge's method in these
chapters is interesting. Basically, as R. H. Fogle has pointed out,

> Coleridge establishes an ideal Wordsworth, or an idea of
> Wordsworth, and finds him at fault when he does not measure

up to this ideal. . . . That is to say, Coleridge attempts to provide not a Wordsworth of literal actuality, but rather an interpretation in which something of himself is infused. Along with
an idea of Wordsworth go an idea of poetry and an idea of
criticism. The ideal poetry is characterized by universality, and
the ideal criticism is a reconciliation of a deduction from critical
principles with an induction or intuitive apprehension of the
body of poetry to be criticized.[47]

In other words, Coleridge's object in these chapters is, by using
Wordsworth as an example and an ideal, to establish the ground-
rules or fixed principles of poetic criticism generally. Such a procedure allows Coleridge (a) to articulate what poetry should
ideally be and on what fundamental criteria it should be judged or
assessed; (b) to measure Wordsworth's poetry and poetic theory
against the ideal on the basis of these criteria; (c) to identify and
explore discrepancies between Wordsworth's theory and actual
poetry, and to mark out clearly Coleridge's disagreement with
aspects of Wordsworth's theory and its poetic application; and (d)
to demonstrate how Wordsworth's critics have erred because they
have not assessed his achievement in the light of fixed canons of
criticism. The movement in these chapters is from the general to
the particular, from the establishment of critical principles to
their application to Wordsworth's poetry. Coleridge's concern is
not to provide 'recipes' for writing poems or 'rules' to be used in
passing judgement on them; rather, he proposes, like Aristotle in
the *Poetics* or Sidney in his *Apologie for Poetrie*, to deduce from an
existing body of poetry the principles of its construction.[48]

In chapter 14 Coleridge outlines his poetic creed. All the major
issues to be discussed are raised here. He begins by recalling how
conversations with Wordsworth on 'the two cardinal points of
poetry' (namely, 'the power of exciting the sympathy of the reader
by a faithful adherence to the truth of nature, and the power of
giving the interest of novelty by the modifying colors of imagination' − *BL*, ii 5) had originated the plan of the *Lyrical Ballads*;
and he describes how their different contributions to the volume
were intended as explorations of different ideas about poetry. He
then turns to Wordsworth's Preface to *Lyrical Ballads*, declaring
that with 'many parts' of it he had 'never concurred; but on the
contrary objected to them as erroneous in principle, and as contradictory (in appearance at least) both to other parts of the same

preface, and to the author's own practice in the greater number of the poems themselves' (*BL*, I 8). While it is necessary for Coleridge to state where he differs from Wordsworth, it is imperative first to state the essential tenets of his own position. This he accomplishes in the famous definitions of *poem* and *poet*. Both definitions describe an ideal against which to set particular examples. A *poem* he defines as an organic construct which, unlike works of science, proposes 'for its *immediate* object pleasure, not truth' (*BL*, I 10).[49] In other words, while truth is the *ultimate* end of poetry, pleasure is its *immediate* end: Coleridge is reversing the emphasis in the Christian humanist poetic dictum *docere cum delectatione*, 'to teach with delight', in which the didactic element is pre-eminent both as immediate and ultimate end, while pleasure or delight is a kind of sugar-coating to help the moral pill go down. Coleridge's second definition, that of the ideal poet, is characterised by its emphasis on imagination (and it repeats in formal terms his earlier description, in chapter 4, of the impact of Wordsworth on him in 1795):

> The poet, described in *ideal* perfection, brings the whole soul of man into activity, with the subordination of its faculties to each other, according to their relative worth and dignity. He diffuses a tone and spirit of unity, that blends, and (as it were) *fuses*, each into each, by that synthetic and magical power, to which we have exclusively appropriated the name of imagination. This power, first put in action by the will and understanding, and retained under their irremissive, though gentle and unnoticed, controul (*laxis effertur habenis*) reveals itself in the balance or reconciliation of opposite or discordant qualities. . . .
>
> (*BL*, I 12)

In a final image, poetic genius is described in the organic metaphor of a human figure in which the various elements are united in 'one graceful and intelligent whole': Imagination (the unifying power) is the omnipresent soul, Good Sense (sound logic, meaning, and judgement) forms the body, and Fancy provides the superficial drapery in which this living, moving figure is clothed.

Chapter 15, substantially a reproduction of Coleridge's 1811 lecture on Shakespeare's early narrative poems (see *CN*, III no. 4115), at first seems wantonly excursive. But it is not. In fact, two important things are happening. First (and most obviously), the discussion of Shakespeare's *Venus and Adonis* and selected sonnets allows Coleridge to apply the critical principles of chapter 14 to the greatest of English poets and to demonstrate how his poetic genius manifested itself in even his earliest productions before he turned to dramatic writing. Second, there is an oblique admonition of Wordsworth's theory and practice that both anticipates and prepares the ground for the criticism in the following chapters. At the end of chapter 15 Coleridge distinguishes two imaginative modes: the centrifugal imagination of Shakespeare and the centripetal imagination of Milton. While Shakespeare (especially in his dramatic works) 'darts himself forth, and passes into all the forms of human character and passion', Milton 'attracts all forms and things to himself, into the unity of his own IDEAL' (*BL*, II 20).[50] The Miltonic mode is explained in more detail in Coleridge's *Table Talk* (18 Aug 1833):

> In the *Paradise Lost* − indeed in every one of his poems − it is Milton himself whom you see; his Satan, his Adam, his Raphael, almost his Eve − are all John Milton; and it is a sense of this intense egotism that gives me the greatest pleasure in reading Milton's works. The egotism of such a man is a revelation of spirit.   (*TT*, pp. 267−8)

Now, in Coleridge's view, Wordsworth's particular genius was Miltonic, not Shakespearean; his strength lay, as *The Prelude* had demonstrated, in impressing the stamp of his own mind and character on all that he chose to write about. The 'egotistical sublime' (as Hazlitt and Keats later depricatingly denominated it) was the mark of his mind and the proper province of his poetic voice. In *The Excursion*, however, which Coleridge had criticised in letters to Lady Beaumont and Wordsworth himself (*CL*, IV 564, 572−4), Wordsworth had adopted unsuccessfully a pseudo-Shakespearean mode of refracting his own personality through externalised, theoretically 'dramatic' characters. Some of the *Lyrical Ballads* had also suffered from Wordsworth's 'undue predeliction for the *dramatic* form'. And Coleridge's dicta on Shakespeare in chapter 15 are, as U. C. Knoepflmacher has demonstrated convincingly, 'as integral to the explanation of [Coleridge's] reservations about Wordsworth's theories as they are to his wider efforts to reclaim Wordsworth from practicing forms of poetry unsuited to a peculiarly Miltonic genius'.[51]

Chapter 16 is transitional. In it, by detailing some of the 'striking points of difference between the Poets of the present age and
those of the 15th and 16th centuries', Coleridge prepares the
ground for examining the specific qualities of Wordsworth. In
chapters 17–20 Coleridge concentrates on those aspects of Wordsworthian theory in the Preface to *Lyrical Ballads* with which he
disagrees – specifically, the theories of poetic diction and metre.
Both are misguided, because both falsify Wordsworth's true incli-
nations, aptitude, and actual practice in the best of his poetry. In
these four technical chapters Coleridge believed, as he told R. H.
Brabant in July 1815, that 'I have done my Duty to myself and to
the Public, in (as I believe) compleatly subverting the Theory & in
proving that the Poet himself has never acted on it except in particular Stanzas which are the Blots of his Compositions' (*CL*,
IV 579). His purpose in refuting Wordsworth's theories of poetic
diction and metre was twofold: on the one hand, he wished to
make clear his own position and to settle 'the long continued controversy' (*BL*, I 1) between himself and Wordsworth on these
issues; on the other hand, he wished (as Nathaniel Teich has said)
'to restore critical perspective and rescue Wordsworth from the
incomplete and misleading theorizing that left him vulnerable to
attack and ridicule' in the contemporary journals.[52] While not all
recent commentators would accept that Coleridge is entirely fair
or accurate in his analysis of Wordsworth's theory,[53] most (if not
all) readers would accept R. H. Fogle's general assessment of
Coleridge's critique. According to Coleridge's account, Fogle says,

> Wordsworth's defects both of theory and of practice are defects
> of his positive qualities. His faults of theory are truths that have
> been carried beyond their proper limits; his faults of practice
> are virtues inadequately controlled and realized. They arise
> from imperfect knowledge of the craft of poetry, and from
> imperfect knowledge of himself as a poet. Coleridge would not
> have said of Wordsworth, as he did of Shakespeare, that his
> judgment was equal to his genius.[54]

Having admonished in chapter 21 the journals (in particular the
Edinburgh Review) for their want of critical principles and their
wanton *ad hominem* vituperation, Coleridge turns in chapter 22
to 'a fair and philosophical inquisition into the character of
Wordsworth, as a poet, on the evidence of his published works'

(*BL*, II 85). His examination, based on the fixed principles established in earlier chapters, takes the form of an illustrated exploration of Wordsworth's *characteristic* poetic defects and strengths. Of the five 'defects' listed, the two most important are (1) '*matter-of-factness*', which reveals itself either 'in a laborious minuteness and fidelity in the representation of objects' or in 'a *biographical* attention to probability, and an *anxiety* of explanation and retrospect' (*BL*, II 101, 103); and (2) a form of '*mental* bombast' in which thoughts or images — such as the panegyric on the child-philosopher in stanzas 7 and 8 of the 'Ode: Intimations of Immortality' — are 'too great for the subject' (*BL*, II 109). Wordsworth's poetic excellences, which set his work apart from all other contemporary poets, are six in number: (1) 'an austere purity of language' in which there is 'a perfect appropriateness of the words to the meaning' (*BL*, II 115), (2) a fine balancing of 'Thoughts and Sentiments, won — not from books, but — from the poet's own meditative observation' (*BL*, II 118), (3) 'the frequent *curiosa felicitas* of his diction' (*BL*, II 121), (4) 'the perfect truth of nature in his images and descriptions, as taken immediately from nature' (*BL*, II 121), (5) 'a meditative pathos, a union of deep and subtle thought with sensibility; a sympathy with man as man' (*BL*, II 122), and (6) lastly and pre-eminently, 'the gift of IMAGINATION in the highest and strictest sense of the word' — although in 'the play of *Fancy*, Wordsworth, to my feelings, is not always graceful, and sometimes *recondite*' (*BL*, II 124). One has only to set this assessment against that of any other contemporary or, for that matter, modern commentator on Wordsworth to appreciate the sensitivity and acuity of Coleridge's criticism. On Wordsworth in particular, and on poetry in general, Coleridge first said what most of us now take for granted.

Chapter 22 is followed by 'Satyrane's Letters' and the critique of Maturin's *Bertram*, both of which (as makeweight materials) we may disregard. Chapter 24, the 'Conclusion', however, merits a word, although it was not part of the book conceived and written in the summer and early autumn of 1815. This chapter was added in the spring of 1817, shortly before printing of the volumes was completed by Rest Fenner, Coleridge's London publisher. It is partly exculpation, partly explanation, partly assertion. Coleridge declares that the long delay in publication has not been due to any laziness or neglect on his part; he defends 'Christabel' and laments the 'malignity and spirit of personal hatred' by which it had been assailed in the *Edinburgh Review* without motive, without substance, without principle; and he laments, too, that much that has appeared under his name in print has been 'condemned beforehand, as predestined metaphysics' (*BL*, II 212). *The Statesman's Manual* had excited such motiveless malignity, even before its publication, from the pen of William Hazlitt.

What then is to be done? Nothing, nothing more. Coleridge has prompted the age to quit its clogs, to judge by principles in geniality of spirit, but the age has chosen to ignore him. The truths which he has sought to propagate are, however, none the less true — in politics, in philosophy, in literary criticism, and, most of all, in religion; and he closes by asserting that Christianity,

> though not discoverable by human Reason, is yet in accordance with it; . . . that Religion passes out of the ken of Reason only where the eye of Reason has reached its own Horizon; and that Faith is then but its continuation: even as the Day softens away into the sweet Twilight, and Twilight, hushed and breathless, steals into the Darkness.   (*BL*, II 218)

Truth, known in the pulses of the heart and corroborated by the activity of the head, is a goal and a refuge beyond the reach of scorners, beyond the quills of Hazlitt, beyond the myopic temporising of the unimaginative and the unprincipled.

Notes

Where a work has been published in two or more editions, unless specifically stated to the contrary the *most recent* of the editions has been cited.

NOTES TO CHAPTER ONE: COLERIDGE: A BIOGRAPHICAL SKETCH

1. The major biographies are the following: (a) James Dykes Campbell, *Samuel Taylor Coleridge: A Narrative of the Events of his Life* (London and New York, 1894; repr. Highgate, 1970); (b) E. K. Chambers, *Samuel Taylor Coleridge: A Biographical Study* (Oxford, 1938; repr. 1967); (c) Lawrence Hanson, *The Life of S. T. Coleridge: The Early Years* (London and Oxford, 1938; repr. New York, 1962); and (d) Walter Jackson Bate, *Coleridge* (Masters of World Literature Series) (New York, 1968; London, 1969; repr. 1973).
2. See *CL*, I 310, 354. Coleridge's relations with his mother are both baffling and complex: see, for example, Thomas McFarland, 'Coleridge's Anxiety', in *Coleridge's Variety: Bicentenary Studies*, ed. John Beer (London, 1974; Pittsburgh, 1975) pp. 134–65.
3. See, for example, the Introduction to my *Imagination in Coleridge* (London, 1978) pp. 1–26.
4. Charles Lamb, 'Christ's Hospital Five and Thirty Years Ago', in *Prose of the Romantic Period*, ed. Carl R. Woodring (Boston, Mass., 1961) pp. 193–204; the quotation is from p. 203. For Coleridge's recollections of Christ's Hospital, see (especially) his letter of 19 February 1798 to Thomas Poole (*CL*, I 387–9) and his tribute to James Boyer in *Biographia Literaria*, ch. 1 (*BL*, I 4–6).
5. See George Whalley, 'Coleridge and Southey in Bristol, 1795', *RES*, n.s. I (1950) 324–40.
6. Coleridge has left a vivid description of his Midlands tour in *Biographia Literaria*, ch. 10: see *BL*, I 114–19.
7. Charles Lloyd, an emotionally unstable young man who wished to be a poet and philosopher, had fallen under Coleridge's spell in January 1796. In August, Lloyd asked Coleridge to take him in as a pupil, and Coleridge, at the request of Lloyd's father, went to Birmingham to discuss the proposal. Consent was obtained, the terms were fixed at £80 a year, and Lloyd returned with Coleridge to Bristol.
8. Lloyd, in fact, spent only three or four weeks in all with the Coleridges in

Nether Stowey. After an unexpected series of epileptic fits in the autumn of 1796, Lloyd returned to his parents in Birmingham and did not finally join the Coleridges until 22 February 1797. By 23 March at the latest Lloyd had left Stowey and was shortly afterwards placed under the care of Dr Erasmus Darwin in a sanatorium at Lichfield.

9. The biographical background and compositional history of 'Kubla Khan', 'The Ancient Mariner' and the Conversation Poems of 1797–8 are discussed in detail in the chapters which follow.

10. William Hazlitt, 'My First Acquaintance with Poets' (1823), in *Prose of the Romantic Period*, pp. 279–94.

11. Both Wordsworth and Coleridge were thought by many of their neighbours to be dangerous Jacobins, and a government agent was sent down from London to spy on their activities: see Coleridge's amusing account in *Biographia Literaria*, ch. 10 (*BL*, I 126–8).

12. For an account of John Chester, a Stowey neighbour who idolised Coleridge, see Hazlitt, in *Prose of the Romantic Period*, pp. 291, 293.

13. See George Whalley, *Coleridge and Sara Hutchinson and the Asra Poems* (Toronto, 1955).

14. For a vivid account of Coleridge's nightmares, see 'The Pains of Sleep' (*CPW*, I 389–91), which Coleridge told Southey was 'a true portrait of my nights' (*CL*, II 984).

15. See Ch. 5 below.

16. See Donald Sultana, *Samuel Taylor Coleridge in Malta and Italy* (Oxford and New York, 1969); and Alethea Hayter, *A Voyage in Vain: Coleridge's Journey to Malta in 1804* (London, 1973).

17. See 'To William Wordsworth', in *CPW*, I 403–8.

18. See Ch. 6 below.

19. Thomas Carlyle, 'The Life of John Sterling' (1851), in *Thomas Carlyle's Works*, 18 vols (London, 1905) II 45.

20. Quoted in Chambers, *Coleridge: A Biographical Study*, p. 330.

NOTES TO CHAPTER TWO: THE CONVERSATION POEMS

1. G. M. Harper, 'Coleridge's Conversation Poems', *Quarterly Review*, CCXLIV (1925) 284–98.

2. Harper (ibid.) includes both 'Dejection' and 'To William Wordsworth' in his list of Conversation Poems. Among recent critics only George Watson still argues for 'Dejection': see *Coleridge the Poet* (London, 1966) p. 74. 'To William Wordsworth' has attracted a number of supporters: see R. H. Fogle, 'Coleridge's Conversation Poems', *TSE*, V (1955) 103; Watson, *Coleridge the Poet*, pp. 80–2; and Max F. Schulz, *The Poetic Voices of Coleridge* (Detroit, 1963; rev. edn 1964) p. 73. The case for 'Lines Written at Shurton Bars' is argued vigorously by Geoffrey Little, '*Lines Written at Shurton Bars . . .*: Coleridge's First Conversation Poem?', *Southern Review* (Adelaide), II (1966) 137–49.

3. On the general characteristics of the Conversation Poems, see (in addition to the works cited in note 2 above) the following: R. A. Durr, '"This Lime-Tree Bower my Prison" and a Recurrent Action in Coleridge', *ELH*, XXVI (1959)

514–30; M. F. Schulz, 'Oneness and Multeity in Coleridge's Poems', *TSE*, ix (1959) 53–60; A. S. Gérard, 'The Systolic Rhythm: the Structure of Coleridge's Conversation Poems', *EIC*, x (1960) 307–19, enlarged and repr. as ch. 2 in Gérard's *English Romantic Poetry: Ethos, Structure, and Symbol in Coleridge, Wordsworth, Shelley, and Keats* (Berkeley, Calif., and London, 1968) pp. 20–39; J. D. Boulger, 'Imagination and Speculation in Coleridge's Conversation Poems', *JEGP*, lxiv (1965) 691–711; F. Garber, 'The Hedging Consciousness in Coleridge's Conversation Poems', *TWC*, iv (1973) 124–38.

4. More complex structural patterns are proposed by Gérard and by Schulz: see above, n. 3. Gérard argues that a heart-beat rhythm of systole and diastole is the fundamental pattern in all the Conversation Poems. Schulz, in a rather similar way, sees a centripetal–centrifugal action developed in two calm–exaltation–calm parabolas as the poems' basic structural pattern.

5. The original version of 'Frost at Midnight' (1798) ended with a six-line coda which Coleridge dropped in all later printings because, he said, the lines destroyed 'the rondo, and return upon itself of the Poem' and because 'Poems of this kind of length ought to be coiled with its' tail round its' head': quoted in B. Ifor Evans, 'Coleridge's Copy of "Fears in Solitude"', *TLS*, 18 Apr 1935, p. 255.

  For the history of the *ouroboros* emblem (i.e. a coiled serpent with its tail in its mouth), see H. B. de Groot, 'The Ouroboros and the Romantic Poets: a Renaissance Emblem in Blake, Coleridge and Shelley', *English Studies* (Amsterdam), l (1969) 553–64.

6. Humphry House, *Coleridge: The Clark Lectures 1951–52* (London, 1953; repr. 1969) p. 79.

7. Before Coleridge's close relationship with the Wordsworths, which began in the late spring of 1797 (by which time 'The Eolian Harp' and 'Reflections on Having Left a Place of Retirement' had already been composed), perhaps the most important influence on Coleridge was Charles Lamb: see George Whalley, 'Coleridge's Debt to Charles Lamb', *E&S*, xi (1958) 68–85.

  In 1796–7 there was a flourishing correspondence between Lamb and Coleridge. Lamb's letters are mostly about poetry, and their general thrust is well summarised in the letter of 8 November 1796: 'Cultivate simplicity, Coleridge, or rather, I should say, banish elaborateness; for simplicity springs spontaneous from the heart, and carries into daylight its own modest buds and genuine, sweet, and clear flowers of expression. I allow no hot-beds in the gardens of Parnassus' (*LL*, i 60–1). For Coleridge, whose poetry in these years was tainted either by elaborate Miltonising or the insipid sentimentalising of Bowles, Lamb's advice was salutary and his stress on the virtues of compression and simplicity was an influence entirely in favour of the conversational mode with its easy intimacy, its directness, and its flowing rhythms. 'I have seen your last very beautiful poem in the Monthly Magazine', Lamb wrote of 'Reflections' in December 1796, '– write thus . . . and I shall never quarrel with you about simplicity' (*LL*, i 65).

8. Samuel Johnson, 'Life of Denham', in *Lives of the English Poets*, 2 vols (London, 1906; repr. 1964) i 58.

9. M. H. Abrams, 'Structure and Style in the Greater Romantic Lyric', in *Romanticism and Consciousness*, ed. Harold Bloom (New York, 1970) pp. 201–29. On the tradition of Augustan loco-descriptive poetry, see

244   *Notes to pp. 22–30*

Robert A. Aubin's compendious survey, *Topographical Poetry in XVIII-Century England* (New York, 1936).

10. Abrams, in *Romanticism and Consciousness*, p. 224.

11. For the 1803 text of 'The Eolian Harp', see *Coleridge's Verse: A Selection*, ed. William Empsom and David Pirie (New York, 1973) pp. 103–4.

12. Coleridge's image of 'Music slumbering on its instrument' is perhaps an echo of Keats's description of Poetry as 'might half slumbering on its own right arm' in 'Sleep and Poetry', line 237: see John Barnard, 'An Echo of Keats in "The Eolian Harp"', *RES*, xxviii (1977) 311–13.

13. In 1828, line 33 reads, 'Is Music slumbering on *her* instrument' (emphasis added).

14. For detailed analysis, see: H. J. W. Milley, 'Some Notes on Coleridge's "Eolian Harp"', *MP*, xxxvi (1938–9) 359–75; M. H. Abrams, 'Coleridge's "A Light in Sound": Science, Metascience, and Poetic Imagination', *PAPS*, cxvi (1972) 458–76; and W. H. Scheuerle, 'A Reexamination of Coleridge's "The Eolian Harp"', *SEL*, xv (1975) 591–9.

15. Abrams, in *PAPS*, cxvi 474.

16. H. Nidecker, 'Notes marginales de S. T. Coleridge en marge de Kant et de Schelling, transcrites et annotées', *Revue de littérature comparée*, vii (1927) 529.

17. John Beer, *Coleridge the Visionary* (London, 1959; repr. 1970) p. 92. See also Beer's *Coleridge's Poetic Intelligence* (London, 1977) p. 67.

18. Abrams, in *PAPS*, cxvi 459–60.

19. Coleridge's *joy* is not simply a reading of our own feelings into nature. 'It is rather', as Dorothy Emmet says, 'the possibility of entering into a deep *rapport* with something in the world beyond us, seeing it with such loving sympathy that we make, as Coleridge says, the "external internal, the internal external" and out of this comes the possibility of the creation of imaginative symbolism. But the first condition of such creation is that we should be able not only to look, but to love as we look' – 'Coleridge on the Growth of the Mind', in *Coleridge: A Collection of Critical Essays*, ed. Kathleen Coburn (Englewood Cliffs, NJ, 1967) p. 173.

20. House, *Coleridge*, p. 77; Watson, *Coleridge the Poet*, p. 66.

21. See Geoffrey Yarlott, *Coleridge and the Abyssinian Maid* (London, 1967) pp. 95–6; and Ronald C. Wendling, 'Coleridge and the Consistency of "The Eolian Harp"', *SIR*, viii (1968–9) 26–42.

22. Harold Bloom, *The Visionary Company: A Reading of English Romantic Poetry* (New York, 1961; rev. edn Ithaca, NY, and London, 1971) p. 200.

23. Beer, *Coleridge's Poetic Intelligence*, pp. 66–7.

24. House, *Coleridge*, p. 76.

25. Horace, *Satires* i iv 41–2: *neque, si qui scribat uti nos / sermoni propiora putes hunc esse poetam* ('nor would you consider anyone a poet who writes, as I do, lines nearer to prose'). Although Horace uses the proper form *propiora*, Coleridge always used the 'fractured' form *propriora*, perhaps to facilitate a punning translation (apparently originating with Charles Lamb): 'Charles Lamb translated my motto *Sermoni propriora* by – *properer for a sermon!*' (*TT*, p. 191). In a letter of 1802 Coleridge claimed this witty translation as his own (*CL*, ii 864). The phrase is discussed by Richard T. Martin, who in 'Coleridge's Use of "*sermoni propriora*"', *TWC*, iii (1972) 71–5,

argues that Coleridge's use of the term was influenced by its appearance in John Foster's *Essay on . . . Accent and Quantity* (1762).

26. The querulous egotism of the poem is discussed by Jill Rubenstein in 'Sound and Silence in Coleridge's Conversation Poems', *English*, xxi (1972) 54—60, esp. pp. 56—7.

27. See Wordsworth's later pantheistic treatments of the theme in the Simplon Pass and Mount Snowdon episodes of *The Prelude* (1805) vi 549—72 and xiii 29—119.

28. Richard Haven, *Patterns of Consciousness: An Essay on Coleridge* (Amherst, Mass., 1969) p. 56.

29. Another copy of the poem was sent in a letter of July 1797 to Charles Lloyd; this letter was known to Ernest Hartley Coleridge (*CPW*, i 178n.), who quotes from it, but it has since been lost. In October 1797 Coleridge quoted lines 38—43 of 'This Lime-Tree Bower' in a letter to John Thelwall: *CL*, i 350.

30. For an analysis of the significance of the changes between 1797 and 1800, see Haven, *Patterns of Consciousness*, pp. 64—8.

31. Michael Schmidt, 'Coleridge: "This Lime-Tree Bower my Prison"', *Critical Survey*, vi (1973) 47.

32. Donald Davie, *Articulate Energy: An Inquiry into the Syntax of English Poetry* (London, 1955; repr. 1976) pp. 72—3.

33. *Biographia Literaria*, ch. 22 (*BL*, ii 103). In the Fenwick note to 'Lines Written in Early Spring' Wordsworth describes what (in all probability) was the precise location of Coleridge's dell: 'The brook fell down a sloping rock so as to make a waterfall considerable for that country, and across the pool below had fallen a tree, an ash, if I rightly remember, from which rose perpendicularly boughs in search of the light intercepted by the deep shade above. The boughs bore leaves of green that for want of sunshine had faded into almost lily-white; and from the underside of this natural sylvan bridge depended long and beautiful tresses of ivy which waved gently in the breeze that might poetically speaking be called the breath of the waterfall' (*WPW*, iv 411—12).

34. See Coleridge's note of September 1803 on *Gentiana major* — 'It's *blue* Flower, the Colour of Hope' — in line 57 of 'Hymn Before Sunrise': *CL*, ii 966.

35. Durr, in *ELH*, xxvi 526—7.

36. In September 1796 Mary Lamb, in a fit of insanity, had killed her mother and wounded her father with a kitchen-knife. Charles Lamb sent Coleridge word of the tragedy and asked him to write 'as religious a letter as possible' (*LL*, i 44); Coleridge did so on 28 September, imploring his friend, 'if by any means it be possible, [to] come to me' (*CL*, i 239).

37. Durr, in *ELH*, xxvi 525—6.

38. Cf. Coleridge's Notebook entry of August 1803: 'As I write this, I turn my head, & close by me I see a Birch, so placed as among a number of Trees it alone is in full sunshine, & the Shadows of its Leaves playing on its silver Bark, an image that delighted my Boyhood, when I had no waterfalls to see' (*CN*, i no. 1449, f.4ᵛ). While much of the natural description in 'This Lime-Tree Bower' derives ultimately from actual scenery known to Coleridge (see also above, n. 33), it should be pointed out that this topography is also

indebted to Coleridge's reading. There are, for example, a number of Miltonic echoes (especially in lines 22–37); and, as Mario L. D'Avanzo has suggested, the lime-tree bower itself (although certainly a description of Poole's arbour at Stowey) is also an adaptation of Prospero's 'lime grove' in Act v of Shakespeare's *The Tempest*: see 'Coleridge's "This Lime-tree Bower my Prison" and *The Tempest*', *TWC*, I (1970) 66–8.

39. Durr, in *ELH*, XXVI 530.
40. Quoted by B. Ifor Evans, in *TLS*, 18 Apr 1935, p. 255.
41. House, *Coleridge*, p. 82.
42. E. H. Coleridge quotes these variants in full: see *CPW*, I 240–1.
43. I have discussed Coleridge's view of perception and its relation to imagination (and fancy) in the Introduction to my *Imagination in Coleridge* (London, 1978) esp. pp. 1–3 and 21–3.
44. House, *Coleridge*, p. 79.
45. In a footnote to line 15 Coleridge explains that 'In all parts of the kingdom these films are called *strangers* and supposed to portend the arrival of some absent friend'. See also Cowper's *The Task*, IV 291–5: quoted above, p. 40.
46. Garber, in *TWC*, IV 130–1.
47. On Coleridge's affection for his sister and his grief at her death, see the two sonnets concerning her composed in 1791: *CPW*, I 20–1.
48. There is an early version of this image in a Notebook entry belonging (probably) to the winter of 1797–8:

> The reed-roof'd Village, still bepatch'd with snow
> Smok'd in the sun-thaw.
>
> (*CN*, I no. 329)

49. Schulz, *The Poetic Voices of Coleridge*, p. 94.
50. *Biographia Literaria*, ch. 4 (*BL*, I 59).
51. Reeve Parker, *Coleridge's Meditative Art* (London and Ithaca, NY, 1975) p. 127.
52. Robert Langbaum, *The Poetry of Experience: The Dramatic Monologue in Modern Literary Tradition* (London and New York, 1957; repr. 1972) p. 46.
53. Walter de la Mare, 'Night', from *Memory and Other Poems* (1938): *The Complete Poems of Walter de la Mare* (London, 1969) p. 378.
54. Carl R. Woodring, *Politics in the Poetry of Coleridge* (Madison, Wis., 1961) p. 192.
55. E. P. Thompson, 'Disenchantment or Default? A Lay Sermon', in *Power and Consciousness*, ed. C. C. O'Brien and W. D. Vanech (London and New York, 1969) p. 167.
56. Quoted ibid.
57. Ibid., p. 168.
58. Ibid., pp. 168–9.
59. *Coleridge: The Critical Heritage*, ed. J. R. de J. Jackson (London, 1970) pp. 47–8.
60. Schulz, *The Poetic Voices of Coleridge*, p. 98; Watson, *Coleridge the Poet*, p. 71; Reginald Watters, *Coleridge* (London, 1971) p. 26.
61. Coleridge makes a similar statement in a marginal note (probably of 1807) to lines 159–75 of 'Fears': these lines 'are neither poetry, nor anything — as eloquence for instance which approximates to it. They are *Prose* that in a

frolic has put on a masquerade Dress of metre & like most Masquerades, blundered in the assumed character': quoted by B. Ifor Evans, in *TLS*, 18 Apr 1935, p. 255.
     On *sermoni propriora* see above, n. 25.

62. Woodring, *Politics in the Poetry of Coleridge*, p. 189.

63. Under the pseudonym Nicias Erythraeus, Coleridge had published 'Lewti' in the *Morning Post*, 13 Apr 1798. In fact, 'Lewti' was actually set up in type and some copies of *Lyrical Ballads* containing the cancelled sheets of 'Lewti' were mistakenly issued before 'The Nightingale' was substituted for it. For the printing history (which is quite complex) of the volume, see D. F. Foxon, 'The Printing of *Lyrical Ballads*, 1798', *The Library*, 5th ser. IX (1954) 221–41. Not all readers would accept that the substitution of 'The Nightingale' for 'Lewti' was made in order to preserve the anonymity of *Lyrical Ballads*: see John E. Jordan, *Why the Lyrical Ballads?* (London and Berkeley, Calif., 1976) pp. 42–5.

64. *Coleridge: The Critical Heritage*, p. 58.

65. Watson, *Coleridge the Poet*, p. 71.

66. These three lines and the four lines that follow them are found in a Notebook entry probably belonging to early 1798: see *CN*, I no. 231. For a discussion of this Notebook entry in its context, see George Whalley, 'Coleridge's Poetic Sensibility', in *Coleridge's Variety: Bicentenary Studies*, ed. John Beer (London, 1974; Pittsburgh, 1975) pp. 4–7.

67. '– Hartley fell down & hurt himself – I caught him up crying & screaming – and ran out of doors with him. – The Moon caught his eye – he ceased crying immediately – & his eyes & tears in them, how they glittered in the Moonlight!' (*CN*, I no. 219).

68. Schulz, *The Poetic Voices of Coleridge*, p. 89.

69. Watson, *Coleridge the Poet*, pp. 72–3.

70. Many modern readers have confidently identified the castle of the poem as Enmore Castle (the seat of Lord Egmont in north Somerset) and the 'gentle Maid' as Ellen Cruikshank, whose father was Lord Egmont's agent. There is no good reason, however, for so dogmatic an identification. Indeed, the description of the maiden would seem to fit Dorothy Wordsworth more closely than anything we know about Ellen Cruikshank. Dorothy's Alfoxden Journal describes many night-time walks, some of them with Coleridge, in the spring of 1798. Her entry for 27 April, for example, reads, 'Coleridge breakfasted and drank tea . . . went with him in the evening through the wood, afterwards walked on the hills: the moon, a many-coloured sea and sky'; and even more interesting (cf. 'The Nightingale', lines 64–9) is the entry for 6 May: 'Went with [Coleridge] to Stowey; heard the nightingale; saw a glow-worm' (*JDW*, p. 14). However, since Dorothy is presented in 'The Nightingale' as 'our Sister' (line 40), it seems unlikely that she should reappear transformed in the guise of a 'gentle Maid' only a few lines later. The maiden of the poem is probably no *particular* individual but rather a conflation of Ellen (and/or Mary?) Cruikshank, Dorothy Wordsworth, and (as well) the lady Christabel; the castle, if one *must* identify it, is probably Enmore Castle.

71. Robert Mayo, 'The Contemporaneity of the *Lyrical Ballads*', *PMLA*, LXIX (1954) 494. In a footnote (ibid., n. 12) Mayo gives a brief list of nightingale poems in the magazine verse of the 1790s.

72. R. H. Hopkins, 'Coleridge's Parody of Melancholy Poetry in "The Nightingale: a Conversation Poem, April 1798"', *English Studies* (Amsterdam), XLIX (1968) 436–41; the quotation is from p. 438.
73. *Coleridge: The Critical Heritage,* p. 57.
74. Alun Jones, 'Coleridge and Poetry: the Conversational and other Poems', in *S. T. Coleridge* (Writers and their Background series), ed. R. L. Brett (London, 1971) pp. 104–5.
75. Watson, *Coleridge the Poet*, p. 72.
76. Derek Roper argues that Coleridge probably found the form 'blosmy' (line 84) – so spelled in all editions of the poem until 1828 – in Chaucer's *Troilus and Criseyde* (II 821) or 'Parlement of Foules' (line 183): *Lyrical Ballads 1805*, ed. D. Roper (London, 1968) p. 325. George Watson thinks that Coleridge probably found the word 'joyance' (line 43) in Spenser's *Faerie Queene* (III xii 18) and reintroduced it into English poetry: *Coleridge the Poet*, p. 72.
77. I am grateful to my colleague Dr C. J. Wortham for bringing this parallel to my attention. T. S. Eliot uses the phrase in Part II of *The Waste Land* (line 103).
78. Watson, *Coleridge the Poet*, p. 72.
79. In March 1797 Dorothy Wordsworth wrote to Mrs Marshall, 'You ask to be informed of our system respecting Basil. . . . We teach him nothing at present but what he learns from the evidence of his senses. He has an insatiable curiosity which we are always careful to satisfy to the best of our ability. It is directed to everything he sees, the sky, the fields, trees, shrubs, corn, the making of tools, carts, &c &c &c. He knows his letters, but we have not attempted any further step in the path of *book learning*. Our grand study has been to make him *happy* in which we have not been altogether disappointed . . .' (*LW: EY*, p. 180).

NOTES TO CHAPTER THREE: 'KUBLA KHAN'

1. John Livingston Lowes, *The Road to Xanadu: A Study in the Ways of the Imagination* (Boston, Mass., 1927; rev. edn, 1930; repr. 1964); Elisabeth Schneider, *Coleridge, Opium and 'Kubla Khan'* (Chicago, 1953; London, 1954; repr. New York, 1970); John Beer, *Coleridge the Visionary* (London, 1959; repr. 1970); Marshall Suther, *Visions of Xanadu* (New York and London, 1965); E. S. Shaffer, *'Kubla Khan' and the Fall of Jerusalem: The Mythological School in Biblical Criticism and Secular Literature 1770–1880* (London, 1975).
2. George Watson, 'The Meaning of "Kubla Khan"', *REL*, II (1961) 21–9. In fairness, I hasten to add that, in the revised version of this paper which appears as chapter 8 in Mr Watson's *Coleridge the Poet* (London, 1966), he begins by saying that 'this chapter is bound to be speculative' and by confessing that 'some aspects of "Kubla Khan" remain inexplicable' (p. 117).
3. Quoted in Morchard Bishop, 'The Farmhouse of *Kubla Khan*', *TLS*, 10 May 1957, p. 293.
4. Although these references will be discussed individually later in the present chapter, it may be useful to have them listed briefly here: (a) a cryptic

reference in Dorothy Wordsworth's Hamburgh Journal (October 1798); (b) allusions to 'Kubla Khan' in a poem by 'Perdita' Robinson (Oct 1800); (c) an account (*c*. 1811–12) of Coleridge reciting his poem, reported by John Payne Collier in his diary; (d) Leigh Hunt's record in his *Autobiography* of Coleridge reciting 'Kubla Khan' to Lord Byron in 1816; (e) Charles Lamb's comments on the poem in a letter to Wordsworth (26 Apr 1816); and (f) Mrs Coleridge's terse remark about the poem's forthcoming publication, in one of her letters to Thomas Poole (24 May 1816): 'He has been so unwise as to publish his fragments of "Christabel" & "Koula-Khan" . . . we were all sadly vexed when we read the advertisement of these things.'

5. Quoted and discussed in Lowes, *Road to Xanadu*, pp. 321–4.
6. *Journals of Dorothy Wordsworth*, ed. E. de Selincourt, 2 vols (London, 1941; repr. 1959) I 34.
7. H. M. Margoliouth, *Wordsworth and Coleridge, 1795–1834* (London, 1953; repr. New York, 1966) p. 49. Margoliouth's conjecture is supported by Mary Moorman (*WW*, I 412–13) and, with reservations, by Elisabeth Schneider (*Coleridge, Opium and 'Kubla Khan'*, esp. p. 305). At one time it was assumed that Dorothy was referring to a manuscript copy of 'Kubla Khan', but that interpretation no longer has any currency. Jean Robertson, in *RES*, n.s. XVIII (1967) 438–9, offers a third interpretation: she proposes that Dorothy, whose German was weak, may have intended to write *Kübel* ('a vat, tub, milking-pail or bucket') or a diminutive form *Küblein* — but this solution seems far-fetched and more ingenious than the original problem.
8. Schneider, *Coleridge, Opium and 'Kubla Khan'*, pp. 216–18, 298–305.
9. J. D. Campbell, *Samuel Taylor Coleridge: A Narrative of the Events of his Life* (London and New York, 1894; repr. Highgate, 1970) p. 89.
10. Malcolm Elwin, *The First Romantics* (London, 1947) pp. 226–32.
11. Lawrence Hanson, *The Life of S. T. Coleridge: The Early Years* (London and New York, 1938; repr. New York, 1962) pp. 259–60, 282 and 487 n. 115.
12. E. K. Chambers, *Samuel Taylor Coleridge: A Biographical Study* (Oxford, 1938; repr. 1967) p. 101; Schneider, *Coleridge, Opium and 'Kubla Khan'*, pp. 158–61.
13. Ibid., p. 165.
14. Hanson, *Coleridge: The Early Years*, p. 260.
15. Schneider, *Coleridge, Opium and 'Kubla Khan'*, p. 236.
16. Ibid., p. 200.
17. Ibid., p. 186.
18. Ibid., p. 214.
19. To my knowledge only two other serious attempts have been made to defend a 1799–1800 date: Warren Ober, 'Southey, Coleridge, and "Kubla Khan"', *JEGP*, LVIII (1959) 414–22; and Jean Robertson, in *RES*, n.s. XVIII 438–9.
20. Schneider, *Coleridge, Opium and 'Kubla Khan'*, p. 236.
21. Alice Snyder, 'The Manuscript of "Kubla Khan"', *TLS*, 2 Aug 1934, p. 541.
22. Chambers, *Coleridge: A Biographical Study*, pp. 100–3.
23. Wylie Sypher, 'Coleridge's Somerset: a Byway to Xanadu', *PQ*, XVIII (1939) 353–66; E. L. Griggs, *CL*, I 348–9; Mary Moorman, *WW*, I 346 ('late September or October 1797'); Molly Lefebure, *Samuel Taylor Coleridge: A Bondage of Opium* (London, 1974; repr. 1977) pp. 251–2.

24. '[From Porlock] we kept close to the shore about four miles. Our road lay through wood, rising almost perpendicularly from the sea, with views of the opposite mountains of Wales: thence we came by twilight to Lynmouth, in Devonshire. The next morning we were guided to a valley at the top of one of those immense hills which open at each end to the sea, and is from its rocky appearance called the Valley of Stones. We mounted a cliff at the end of the valley, and looked from it immediately on to the sea' (*LW: EY*, p. 194).

25. Mark Reed, *Wordsworth: The Chronology of the Early Years, 1770–1799* (Cambridge, Mass., and London, 1967) pp. 208–9 n. 33.

26. John Beer, 'Coleridge and Poetry: I. Poems of the Supernatural', in *S. T. Coleridge* (Writers and their Background series), ed. R. L. Brett (London, 1971) pp. 53–4 n. 1.

27. Sypher, in *PQ*, XVIII 364–5.

28. Bishop, in *TLS*, 10 May 1957, p. 293.

29. D. H. Karrfalt, 'Another Note on "Kubla Khan" and Coleridge's Retirement to Ash Farm', *N&Q* n.s. XIII (1966) 171–2. See also Beer, in *S. T. Coleridge*, p. 60; and Walter Jackson Bate, *Coleridge* (Masters of World Literature series) (New York, 1968; London, 1969; repr. 1973) p. 76 n. 7.

30. See *Coleridge's Lectures and Notes on Shakespeare*, ed. T. Ashe (London, 1897) p. 17; and *The Autobiography of Leigh Hunt*, ed. Roger Ingpen, 2 vols (London, 1903) II 58.

31. Skeat's note: 'This has sometimes been read as "Mr Southey" but "M^{rs}" is a much more probable reading.'

32. T. C. Skeat, 'Kubla Khan', *British Museum Quarterly*, XXVI (1963) 78.

33. Snyder, in *TLS*, 2 Aug 1934; E. H. W. Meyerstein, 'A Manuscript of "Kubla Khan"', *TLS*, 12 Jan 1951, p. 21; John Shelton, 'The Autograph Manuscript of "Kubla Khan" and an Interpretation', *REL*, VII (1966) 30–42. Shelton provides both a photocopy of the Crewe Manuscript and a transcription of it.

34. Alethea Hayter, *Opium and the Romantic Imagination* (London, 1968; repr. 1971) pp. 29–30.

35. E. L. Griggs, 'Samuel Taylor Coleridge and Opium', *Huntington Library Quarterly*, XVII (1954) 357–78. See also *CL*, II 731.

36. Molly Lefebure, for example, vigorously maintains on entirely circumstantial evidence (which few scholars have accepted) that Coleridge was a confirmed addict as early as 1796–7: 'Everything about S. T. C. at this period of time conforms to the classical portraiture of the narcotics addict' (*Coleridge: A Bondage of Opium*, p. 252). Elisabeth Schneider, whose voice on this topic is always one to be reckoned with, is purposely vague: 'The habit, at any rate, was permanently fixed by 1801, and perhaps much earlier. He had used the drug more than once as early as 1791; by 1803 (probably by the preceding year) he knew only too well that it was an evil, at least for himself' (*Coleridge, Opium and 'Kubla Khan'*, p. 62).

37. As Alethea Hayter points out, 'We have the testimony of both Coleridge and DeQuincey that the closest visual equivalent they had ever seen to their opium visions was one of the *Carceri d'Invenzione* engravings by Piranesi' (*Opium and the Romantic Imagination*, p. 93). Miss Hayter discusses the relationship in some detail on pp. 93–8.

38. For a similar image, not explicitly connected with opium but closer in time to the fall 1797 composition-date of 'Kubla Khan', see *CN*, I no. 220: 'Some

wilderness-plot, green & fountainous & unviolated by Man.' Kathleen Coburn dates this Notebook entry in June–September 1797.

39. J. M. Robertson, *New Essays towards a Critical Method* (London and New York, 1897) p. 138; M. H. Abrams, *The Milk of Paradise: The Effect of Opium Visions on the Works of DeQuincey, Crabbe, Francis Thompson, and Coleridge* (Cambridge, Mass., 1934) p. 4. See also R. C. Bald, 'Coleridge and *The Ancient Mariner*: Addenda to *The Road to Xanadu*', in *Nineteenth-Century Studies*, ed. H. Davis, W. C. De Vane, and R. C. Bald (Ithaca, NY, 1940) pp. 1–45.

40. Schneider, *Coleridge, Opium and 'Kubla Khan'*, pp. 35, 40–1. Miss Schneider goes on to argue (pp. 71–2) that Coleridge (unlike DeQuincey, from whom most of the myths about opium and imagination have sprung) 'seems never to have suggested that opium stamped a peculiar or unique character of its own upon his creative imagination; his own statements, if read without the exaggeration encouraged by the subsequent tradition, are not as far as has been supposed from conformity to scientific modern knowledge'.

41. Hayter, *Opium and the Romantic Imagination*, pp. 331, 334–5.

42. Hanson, *Coleridge: The Early Years*, p. 260.

43. Lowes, *Road to Xanadu*, pp. 367, 331.

44. F. W. Bateson, *The Scholar-Critic: An Introduction to Literary Research* (London, 1972) p. 56.

45. Thomas Love Peacock, 'An Essay on Fashionable Literature', in *The Works of Thomas Love Peacock*, ed. H. F. B. Brett-Smith and C. E. Jones, 10 vols (London, 1924–34; repr. New York, 1967) VIII 290.

46. Schneider, *Coleridge, Opium and 'Kubla Khan'*, pp. 88–9. 'Coleridge', Miss Schneider goes on to say (p. 90), 'may have been in a sort of "reverie" as the note says. . . . No doubt he had been taking opium; perhaps, too, the euphoric effect of opium rendered his process of composition more nearly effortless than usual. But he was wide enough awake, we may suppose, to write down his poem more or less as he composed it, and there is no reason to think that it was printed without revision and polishing. There is reason to suspect that the whole was not composed at one sitting. Finally, we cannot suppose that opium created the particular character of the poem.'

47. Watson, in *REL*, II 21.

48. Norman Fruman, *Coleridge: The Damaged Archangel* (New York, 1971; London, 1972) p. 343.

49. As Alethea Hayter remarks, the 'vision' recorded in 'Kubla Khan', while unlike Coleridge's recorded *dreams*, is very like his *daydreams*: 'We know from his Notebooks and from many references all through his works that a wilderness-plot, green and fountainous, far away beyond a desert, was an image that . . . would at any time have been a likely starting-point for a reverie of his': Hayter, *Opium and the Romantic Imagination*, pp. 216–17. On 'Kubla Khan' as a 'daydream poem', see also Schneider, *Coleridge, Opium and 'Kubla Khan'*, pp. 90–1; Max F. Schulz, *The Poetic Voices of Coleridge* (Detroit, 1963; rev. edn 1964) pp. 114–24; and Fruman, *Coleridge: The Damaged Archangel*, pp. 348–9.

50. Lefebure, *Coleridge: A Bondage of Opium*, p. 255.

51. Beer, *Coleridge the Visionary*, pp. 201–6.

52. Schneider, *Coleridge, Opium and 'Kubla Khan'*, pp. 26–7. See also ibid., pp. 87–8.

53. Ober, in *JEGP*, VIII 414. For a similar view, see R. Smith, 'Spontaneous Overflow', *LiNQ: Literature in North Queensland*, II (1973) 25–8.

54. Fruman, *Coleridge: The Damaged Archangel*, p. 335.

55. Bate, *Coleridge*, p. 84.

56. Edward Bostetter, *The Romantic Ventriloquists: Wordsworth, Coleridge, Keats, Shelley, Byron* (Seattle and London, 1963; rev. edn 1965) p. 85.

57. Alicia Martinez, 'Coleridge, "Kubla Khan", and the Contingent', *Concerning Poetry*, X (1977) 59.

58. Bernard Breyer, 'Towards an Interpretation of *Kubla Khan*', in *English Studies in Honor of James Southall Wilson*, ed. Fredson Bowers (Charlottesville, Va, 1951) pp. 286–7.

59. Paul Magnuson, for example, argues that 'the Preface need not be accepted or rejected on the grounds of its literal truth; it can be taken seriously as Coleridge's attempt to explain one process of poetic creation and the inadequacies of that process which led to an inevitable loss. Both the Preface and the poem have creativity as their subjects; both trace, not only the creative process, but also the loss of creativity': *Coleridge's Nightmare Poetry* (Charlottesville, Va, 1974) p. 40.

60. Irene Chayes, '"Kubla Khan" and the Creative Process', *SIR*, VI (1966) 1–21. The sentence quoted is on p. 4.

61. Elisabeth Schneider, 'The "Dream" of *Kubla Khan*', *PMLA*, LX (1945) 784–801. The findings of this paper were later incorporated into Schneider's important book, *Coleridge, Opium and 'Kubla Khan'*.

62. Beer, *Coleridge the Visionary*, p. 200.

63. Shaffer, *'Kubla Khan' and the Fall of Jerusalem*, pp. 89–90. Shaffer goes so far, indeed, as to say (p. 90) that 'In the new secular theory of inspiration, then − and this was its triumph − there was no difference between the brief note on the Crewe MS of "Kubla Khan" and the later, more elaborate prefatory "Vision in a Dream".'

64. James Hoyle, '"Kubla Khan" as an Elated Experience', *Literature and Psychology*, XVI (1966) 27–39.

65. *Minnow among Tritons: Mrs S. T. C.'s Letters to Thomas Poole*, ed. Stephen Potter (London, 1934) p. 13.

66. E. H. W. Meyerstein, 'Completeness of *Kubla Khan*', *TLS*, 30 Oct 1937, p. 803. Also Humphry House, *Coleridge: The Clark Lectures 1951–52* (London, 1953; repr. 1969) p. 114: 'If Coleridge had never published his Preface, who would have thought of "Kubla Khan" as a fragment?'

67. Bate, *Coleridge*, p. 76.

68. Other critics who argue for 'Kubla Khan' as a complete and completed poem include: George Watson, in *REL*, II, esp. p. 23; S. K. Heninger, Jr, 'A Jungian Reading of "Kubla Khan"', *Journal of Aesthetics and Art Criticism*, XVIII (1959–60) 358–67, esp. p. 367; Harold Bloom, *The Visionary Company: A Reading of English Romantic Poetry* (New York, 1961; rev. edn Ithaca, NY, and London, 1971) pp. 217–20; Kenneth Burke, '"Kubla Khan", Proto-Surrealist Poem', in his *Language as Symbolic Action: Essays on Life, Literature, and Method* (Berkeley and Los Angeles, Calif., and London, 1966) pp. 202–22, esp. pp. 217–18; Norman Mackenzie, '"Kubla

Khan": a Poem of Creative Agony and Loss', *English Miscellany*, xx (1969) 229—40.

69. See, for example, Breyer, in *English Studies in Honor of Wilson*, pp. 285—6.
70. R. H. Fogle, 'The Romantic Unity of "Kubla Khan"', *College English*, XIII (1951) 13—19; repr. ibid., XXII (1960—1) 112—16. The prototype of Fogle's view may be found in N. B. Allen, 'A Note on Coleridge's "Kubla Khan"', *MLN*, LVII (1942) 108—13.
71. Alan Purves, 'Formal Structure in "Kubla Khan"', *SIR* I (1962) 187—91; the quotation is on p. 191.
72. See also Carl Woodring, 'Coleridge and the Khan', *EIC*, IX (1959) 361—8. Woodring argues (p. 361) that the 'Germanic idea of organic unity' (which Coleridge himself propagated in the *Biographia Literaria* and elsewhere) 'discourages a complacent acceptance of anything imperfected'. For Woodring, 'Kubla Khan' is 'imperfect' in the sense that it *is* a fragment, as Coleridge claimed; but that fact does not necessarily imply that the poem lacks a total meaning. Ironically, 'Kubla Khan' has become the victim of the success of Coleridge's own doctrine of organic unity.
73. T. S. Eliot, *The Use of Poetry and the Use of Criticism: Studies in the Relation of Criticism to Poetry in England* (London, 1933; repr. 1975) p. 146.
74. See, for example, Lowes, *Road to Xanadu*, pp. 312—88 *passim*; Bostetter, *Romantic Ventriloquists*, p. 84; Lefebure, *Coleridge: A Bondage of Opium*, p. 258; Fruman, *Coleridge: The Damaged Archangel*, esp. pp. 331, 346; Shaffer, *'Kubla Khan' and the Fall of Jerusalem*, pp. 89—95; and L. D. Berkoben, *Coleridge's Decline as a Poet* (Paris and The Hague, 1975) pp. 108—20.
75. Schneider, *Coleridge, Opium and 'Kubla Khan'*, pp. 252, 246—8. John Beer comes to a similar conclusion: 'Coleridge's own assertion that the poem was unfinished was probably sincere, for his notebooks contain various notes on Kubla Khan and the Tartars which were no doubt collected with a continuation in mind. One can continue a poem in the middle, however, as well as at the end: and it is likely that this was his plan. Certainly it is difficult to see how the poem could be carried on after the last stanza: the argument is there brought to an end with overwhelming finality' (*Coleridge the Visionary*, p. 275).
76. Lowes, *Road to Xanadu*, p. 375.
77. The case for biblical influences on 'Kubla Khan' from the books of Ezekiel and Revelation is well argued by H. W. Piper, 'The Two Paradises in *Kubla Khan*', *RES*, n.s. XXVII (1976) 148—58. On the possible influence of the apocryphal book of Tobit, see T. Copeland, 'A Woman Wailing for her Demon Lover', *RES*, XVII (1941) 87—90.
78. R. H. Milner, 'Coleridge's "Sacred River"', *TLS*, 18 May 1951, p. 309; Robert F. Fleissner, *'Hwæt! Wē Gardēna*: "Kubla Khan" and those Anglo-Saxon Words', *TWC* (1974) 50.
79. Robert F. Fleissner, '"Kubla Khan" and "Tom Jones": an Unnoticed Parallel', *N&Q*, n.s. VII (1960) 103—5.
80. Susan M. Passler, 'Coleridge, Fielding and Arthur Murphy', *TWC*, V (1974) 55—8; the quotation is on p. 57.
81. See, for example, Sypher in *PQ*, XVIII 353—66; Geoffrey Grigson, 'Kubla Khan in Wales: Hafod and the Devil's Bridge', *Cornhill Magazine*, no. 970 (Spring 1947) 275—83; George Whalley, 'Romantic Chasms', *TLS*, 21 June 1947,

p. 309; Eugene L. Stelzig, 'The Landscape of "Kubla Khan" and the Valley of Rocks', *TWC*, VI (1975) 316–18.

82. Collinson's *Somerset* (1791), as quoted by Sypher, in *PQ*, XVIII 364.

83. Lane Cooper, 'The Abyssinian Paradise in Coleridge and Milton', *MP*, III (1906) 327–32; Howard Parsons, 'The Sources of Coleridge's "Kubla Khan"', *N&Q*, CXCVI (1951) 233–5; Schneider, *Coleridge, Opium and 'Kubla Khan'*, pp. 264–77; Beer, *Coleridge the Visionary*, pp. 233–7; and Piper in *RES*, n.s. XXVII 148–58. Perhaps it is not surprising that Lowes, who was in quest of rarer game than Milton, should have virtually ignored the influence of *Paradise Lost* on 'Kubla Khan'.

84. See above, pp. 72–3.

85. Lowes, *Road to Xanadu*, pp. 345–6.

86. Schneider, *Coleridge, Opium and 'Kubla Khan'*, p. 245.

87. Lamb, letter to Wordsworth (26 Apr 1816): *LL*, III 215.

88. *Coleridge: The Critical Heritage*, ed. J. R. de J. Jackson (London, 1970) pp. 246, 235.

89. Lamb to Wordsworth, *LL*, III 215; Leigh Hunt, 'Sketches of the Living Poets', *Examiner*, 21 Oct 1821, as repr. in *Coleridge: The Critical Heritage*, p. 475.

90. Hazlitt's review of the *Christabel* volume in the *Critical Review*, May 1816, as repr. in *Coleridge: The Critical Heritage*, p. 208.

91. Algernon Swinburne, *Essays and Studies*, 5th edn (London, 1901) p. 263. For a survey of other Victorian assessments, see R. Hoffpauir, '"Kubla Khan" and the Critics: Romantic Madness as Poetic Theme and Critical Response', *English Studies in Canada*, II (1976) 402–22, esp. pp. 405–9.

92. Lowes, *Road to Xanadu*, pp. 367, 374, 377.

93. William Walsh, *Coleridge: The Work and the Relevance* (London, 1967) p. 111; Hanson, *Coleridge: the Early Years*, p. 260.

94. Schneider, *Coleridge, Opium and 'Kubla Khan'*, p. 285.

95. Peacock, in *Works*, VIII 291.

96. Watson, *Coleridge the Poet*, p. 122.

97. For example, Bloom, *The Visionary Company*, pp. 217–20; H. H. Meier, 'Ancient Lights on Kubla's Lines', *English Studies* (Amsterdam), XLVI (1965) 15–29, esp. pp. 26–7.

98. For example, Beer, *Coleridge the Visionary*, esp. pp. 222–9; Watson, *Coleridge the Poet*, pp. 117–30.

99. House, *Coleridge*, p. 116; Chayes, in *SIR*, VI 17; Bostetter, *Romantic Ventriloquists*, p. 84. Bostetter's view has enjoyed wide popularity in the criticism of the last two decades: see, for example, Mackenzie, in *English Miscellany*, XX 229–40; Magnuson, *Coleridge's Nightmare Poetry*, p. 40; and Berkoben, *Coleridge's Decline*, pp. 108–20.

100. On *pleasure*, see *Biographia Literaria*, ch. 14 (*BL*, II 9–10), and the following critics: Breyer, in *English Studies in Honor of Wilson*, pp. 278–9; and Fogle in *College English*, XIII 115–16. On *genius*, see *Biographia Literaria*, ch. 2 (*BL*, I 20–1), and the following critics: Breyer, in *English Studies in Honor of Wilson*, pp. 289–90; and Beer, *Coleridge the Visionary*, pp. 226–9. On the *reconciliation of opposites*, see *Biographia Literaria*, ch. 14 (*BL*, II 12), and the following critics: Fogle in *College English*, XIII 112–16; Chayes, in *SIR*, VI 11–14; Charles Moorman, 'The

Imagery of "Kubla Khan"', *N&Q*, n.s. VI (1959) 321–4; and D. B. Schneider, 'The Structure of *Kubla Khan*', *American Notes and Queries*, I (1963) 68–70. On *fancy–imagination*, see *Biographia Literaria*, ch. 13 (*BL*, I 202), and the critics listed below in nn. 102–4.

101. Schneider, *Coleridge, Opium and 'Kubla Khan'*, p. 286.
102. Watson, *Coleridge the Poet*, pp. 124–6.
103. Purves, in *SIR*, I 189–90.
104. Chayes, in *SIR*, VI 8–11, 15–17.
105. Robert Graves, *The Meaning of Dreams* (London, 1924) pp. 156–9.
106. I. A. Richards, *Principles of Literary Criticism* (London, 1925; repr. New York, 1968) p. 30.
107. Douglas Angus, 'The Theme of Love and Guilt in Coleridge's Three Major Poems', *JEGP*, LIX (1960) 655–68; Eugene Sloane, 'Coleridge's *Kubla Khan*: the Living Catacombs of the Mind', *American Imago*, XXIX (1972) 97–122; and Gerald Enscoe, 'Ambivalence in "Kubla Khan": the Cavern and the Dome', *Bucknell Review*, XII (1964) 29–36.
108. James Bramwell, '*Kubla Khan* – Coleridge's Fall?', *Neuphilologische Mitteilungen*, LIII (1952) 449–66; and Eli Marcovitz, 'Bemoaning the Lost Dream: Coleridge's "Kubla Khan" and Addiction', *International Journal of Psycho-analysis*, XLV (1964) 411–25 (the passage quoted is on p. 422).
109. Most of these interpretations (including the outrageous hypothesis about miscegenation) are either proposed or discussed in Fruman, *Coleridge: The Damaged Archangel*, pp. 395–401. See also the critics cited in nn. 107–8 and 110–11.
110. H. S. and D. T. Bliss, 'Coleridge's "Kubla Khan"', *American Imago*, VI (1949) 261–73; the quotation is on p. 267.
111. James F. Hoyle, '"Kubla Khan" as an Elated Experience', *Literature and Psychology*, XVI (1966) 27–39; the passages quoted are on p. 37.
112. Kathleen Raine, 'Traditional Symbolism in *Kubla Khan*', *Sewanee Review*, LXXII (1964) 626–42; the quotation is on p. 638.
113. Maud Bodkin, *Archetypal Patterns in Poetry: Psychological Studies of Imagination* (Oxford, 1934) pp. 90–115; the quotations are from pp. 96 and 114.
114. See, for example, Burke, *Language as Symbolic Action*, esp. pp. 220–2; and N. L. Goldstein, 'Coleridge's "Kubla Khan": Mythic Unity and an Analogue in Folklore and Legend', *Queen's Quarterly*, LXXV (1968) 642–50.
115. See Raine, in *Sewanee Review*, LXXII 640: 'Coleridge's Abyssinian maid comes from the heights, and her song is of "Mount Abora"; yet the poet knows that the song he hears arises from the depths and heights of his own being. He has only to recollect her music. . . . He has but to *remember* in order to re-create in his poetry an image of the sphere and harmony of heaven. That is what the poem is about – that forever unfinished poem.' For Plato's doctrine of recollection, see *Phaedo*, 72e–76, and *Phaedrus*, 247c–252c.
116. See Heninger, in *Journal of Aesthetics and Art Criticism*, XVIII 358–67; and H. M. Brown, 'Archetypal Patterns in "Kubla Khan"', *Proceedings of the Conference of College Teachers of English of Texas*, XXXIII (1968) 13–17. Jungian *individuation* is 'the process by which the self becomes

consciously larger through assimilating to the conscious more of the aspects of the unconscious part of the self' (ibid., p. 15) – thus, the Abyssinian maid, for example, is a symbol of the Jungian *anima* (the feminine personification of the unconscious) who sings to the poet about the depths of his own soul.

117. Robert F. Fleissner, '"Kubla Khan" as an Integrationist Poem', *Negro American Literature Forum*, VIII (1974) 254–6. In essence, the argument is this: 'Since the [Abyssinian maid] is Black, the final love and inspiration suggests the harmony of integration. . . . The basic disharmony in the poem is that the speaker cannot reach the "Vision" of the dulcimer damsel and thereby become her spirit-lover. Though he is cut off from her, the inherent unconscious urge, a communal and anti-racist longing, persists' (pp. 255–6).

118. Schneider, *Coleridge, Opium and 'Kubla Khan'*, pp. 277–82.

119. Schulz, *Poetic Voices of Coleridge*, pp. 114–24.

120. Woodring, in *EIC*, IX (1959) 361–8; and Norman Rudich, 'Coleridge's "Kubla Khan": his Anti-political Vision', in *Weapons of Criticism: Marxism in America and the Literary Tradition*, ed. N. Rudich (Palo Alto, Calif., 1976) pp. 215–41.

121. Beer, *Coleridge the Visionary*, pp. 207–76, with summaries on pp. 222, 266–67; and Piper, in *RES*, n.s. XXVII 148–58.

122. Keats, letter of 21 Dec 1817: see *Letters of John Keats*, ed. R. Gittings (London, 1970) p. 43.

NOTES TO CHAPTER FOUR: 'THE ANCIENT MARINER'

1. The history of the origin of 'The Ancient Mariner' is well documented. The evidence, moreover, is remarkably consistent, so that minor errors (e.g. Wordsworth's dating of the poem in the spring of 1798 instead of the autumn of 1797, in the Fenwick note to 'We Are Seven') are usually self-correcting in the light of substantial documentary evidence from other sources. The first five paragraphs of this chapter draw freely on seven separate accounts, which I shall list in chronological order: (1) a fragment of Dorothy Wordsworth's letter, probably to Mary Hutchinson, dated 'Alfoxden. Nov 20 1797' (*LW: EY*, p. 194); (2) Coleridge's note in *Sibylline Leaves* (1817) to lines 226–7 of 'The Ancient Mariner' (*CPW*, I 196); (3) Henry Crabb Robinson's report (13 Jan 1836) of a conversation with Wordsworth (*HCR*, II 481); (4) Wordsworth's Fenwick note (1843) to 'We Are Seven' (*WPW*, I 360–2); (5) Mrs Davy's account of a dinner conversation between a Mr Price and Wordsworth in July 1844 (*PWW*[G] III 442); (6) Christopher Wordsworth's record of his uncle's words in *Memoirs of William Wordsworth*, published in 1851 (*PWW*, III 374); and (7) the Revd Alexander Dyce's report of a statement by Wordsworth, first published in the 1852 edition of Coleridge's *Poems* and quoted in John Livingston Lowes, *The Road to Xanadu: a Study in the Ways of the Imagination* (Boston, Mass., 1927; rev. edn 1930; repr. 1964) pp. 203–4. One other contemporary account, by a witness (however) whose testimony is not always reliable, appeared in DeQuincey's first essay in *Tait's Magazine*, Sept 1834): see Thomas DeQuincey, *Recollections of the Lakes*

and the Lake Poets, ed. David Wright (Harmondsworth, 1970) pp. 38–9. For detailed modern commentary, see (for example) Mary Moorman, *WW*, I 346–8; Lowes, *Road to Xanadu*, pp. 202–8; and E. K. Chambers, 'Some Dates in Coleridge's *Annus Mirabilis*', *E&S*, XIX (1934) 85–111.

2. 'The Ancient Mariner' was not their first attempt at collaboration in 1797. 'The Three Graves' (also a ballad) was begun by Wordsworth in 1796 and taken over by Coleridge in June 1797; and, more significantly still, it was probably on a walking-tour to the Valley of the Rocks in early November 1797 (that is, only a fortnight or so before the planning of 'The Ancient Mariner' that Wordsworth and Coleridge proposed to join forces on a prose tale in the manner of Gessner's *Der Tod Abels* – an attempt at collaboration which, according to Coleridge in 1828, 'broke up in a laugh: and the Ancient Mariner was written instead' (*CPW*, I 287). Coleridge's light-hearted account of 1828, however, as Mary Moorman has pointed out (*WW*, I 346–7), is a conflation of two separate tours of November 1797 and the two quite separate attempts at collaboration associated with them.

3. 'It is an enormous blunder', asserted Coleridge later in life, 'to represent the An. M. as an old man on board ship. He was in my mind the everlasting wandering Jew – had told this story ten thousand times since the voyage, which was in his early youth and 50 years before' (*CN*, I, no. 45n).

4. The relevant passage from Shelvocke's *Voyage* is quoted in Lowes, *Road to Xanadu*, p. 206: 'we had not had the sight of one fish of any kind, . . . nor one sea-bird, except a disconsolate black *Albitross*, who accompanied us for several days, hovering about us as if he had lost himself, till *Hatley*, (my second Captain) . . . imagin'd, from his colour, that it might be some ill omen. That which, I suppose, induced him the more to encourage his superstition, was the continued series of contrary tempestuous winds, which had oppress'd us ever since we had got into this sea. But be that as it would, he, after some fruitless attempts, at length, shot the *Albitross*, not doubting (perhaps) that we should have a fair wind after it.'

5. Wordsworth's words, as recorded by Miss Fenwick: see n. 1 above.

6. *PWW*[G], III 442: see n. 1 above.

7. Wordsworth's words, as recorded by Miss Fenwick: see n. 1 above.

8. On the origin and development of the *Lyrical Ballads*, see Moorman, *WW*, I 369–74; and Mark Reed, 'Wordsworth, Coleridge, and the "Plan" of the *Lyrical Ballads*', *UTQ*, XXXIV (1965) 238–53.

9. It is perhaps significant that, until many years later, neither Coleridge nor the Wordsworths ever gave a title to the poem intended for the *Monthly Magazine*; they referred to it in every recorded instance between November 1797 and March 1798 simply as the 'ballad'. The earliest (apparent) reference to it as 'The Ancient Mariner' occurs in Coleridge's letter to Cottle of 28 May 1798 (*CL*, I 412). If the ballad composed for the *Monthly Magazine* remained untitled, and if the title 'The Ancient Mariner' should properly be applied only to the revised and much expanded version of that early ballad, then Coleridge's later statement that he had composed 'The Ancient Mariner' in partial fulfilment of his obligation with respect to *Lyrical Ballads* is perfectly accurate and perfectly comprehensible: 'it was agreed, that my endeavours should be directed to persons and characters supernatural. . . . With this view I wrote "The Ancient Mariner"' (*BL*, II 6).

10. See *CL*, I 399–400, 402–3, 411–12; Joseph Cottle, *Reminiscences of Samuel Taylor Coleridge and Robert Southey* (London, 1847; repr. Highgate, 1970) pp. 174–80. A useful guide through the labyrinth of negotiations leading to the *Lyrical Ballads* is provided in Mark Reed's *Wordsworth: The Chronology of the Early Years, 1770–1799* (Cambridge, Mass., and London, 1967) pp. 238, 318–20.

11. Cottle, *Reminiscences*, p. 178.

12. These lines were cancelled in all subsequent editions of the poem. The full text of the 1798 version of 'The Ancyent Marinere' is readily available in *Lyrical Ballads*, ed. R. L. Brett and A. R. Jones (London, 1963; rev. 1965) pp. 9–35; and (on facing pages with the 1834 *textus receptus*) in *The Rime of the Ancient Mariner: A Handbook*, ed. R. A. Gettmann (San Francisco, 1961) pp. 2–41; and also in *CPW*, I 528–46.

13. As quoted in *Coleridge: The Critical Heritage*, ed. J. R. de J. Jackson (London, 1970) p. 52.

14. Southey in the *Critical Review*, Oct 1798, and Burney in the *Monthly Review*, June 1799: as quoted in *Coleridge: The Critical Heritage*, pp. 53, 56.

15. Robert Mayo, 'The Contemporaneity of the *Lyrical Ballads*', *PMLA*, LXIX (1954) 486–522; the quotations are from pp. 490, 492.

16. The deletions and alterations in the 1798 text are listed (and quoted) in E. H. Coleridge's notes to 'The Ancient Mariner': see *CPW*, I 186–209. For a fine and detailed study of Coleridge's changes to the poem, see B. R. McElderry, Jr, 'Coleridge's Revision of "The Ancient Mariner"', *SIP*, XXIX (1932) 68–94; the discussion of the revisions of 1800 is on pp. 70–9.

17. As quoted in *Coleridge: The Critical Heritage*, pp. 57–8.

18. Although Mary Moorman believes that 'Coleridge . . . must have seen the note and given his full consent to its inclusion' (*WW*, I 491), Max F. Schulz has argued convincingly that the note on 'The Ancient Mariner' was an afterthought, written and posted to the printer without Coleridge's knowledge: 'Coleridge, Wordsworth, and the 1800 Preface to *Lyrical Ballads*', *SEL*, v (1965) 619–39; see esp. pp. 630–1.

19. Reproduced from *Lyrical Ballads*, ed. Brett and Jones, pp. 276–7. For a discussion, see below, pp. 133–4.

20. The subtitle 'A Poet's Reverie' is most frequently discussed by critics who wish to argue for the influence of opium on 'The Ancient Mariner'. The case, however, is not a strong one. Since there is no solid evidence, the argument for opium influence is inferential and conjectural. The most vigorous exponents of the case *for* opium influence are M. H. Abrams, *The Milk of Paradise* (Cambridge, Mass., 1934) pp. 36–9, and R. C. Bald, 'Coleridge and *The Ancient Mariner*: Addenda to *The Road to Xanadu*', in *Nineteenth-Century Studies*, ed. H. Davis, W. C. De Vane, and R. C. Bald (Ithaca, NY, 1940) pp. 24–45. The most vigorous opponents of such a view are Lowes, *Road to Xanadu*, pp. 381–8; E. H. Coleridge, 'The Genesis of *The Ancient Mariner*', *Poetry Review*, IX (1918) 271–7, esp. pp. 276–7; and Molly Lefebure, *Samuel Taylor Coleridge: A Bondage of Opium* (New York, 1974; repr. London and New York, 1977) pp. 60–4.

21. After 1800, the 'Argument' was omitted altogether in all subsequent versions of 'The Ancient Mariner'. The subtitle 'A Poet's Reverie' was retained when

the poem was published in the third and fourth editions (1802, 1805) of *Lyrical Ballads*, but was omitted in all versions after 1805.

22. See Coburn's notes in *CN*; I have cited the relevant Notebook entries in this and the following paragraph. Patricia Adair offers a convincing and detailed study of the influence of the Malta voyage on the 1817 revisions: see her *The Waking Dream: A Study of Coleridge's Poetry* (London, 1967) pp. 75–94.

23. Adair, ibid., p. 79. The most striking illustration in the notebooks of Coleridge's self-identification with the Ancient Mariner occurs in the entry for 13 May 1804, which records the unmotivated thoughtlessness of sailors shooting at a hawk, and does so in terms that inevitably recall the strange impulse which slew the albatross: 'Hawk with ruffled Feathers resting on the Bowsprit − Now shot at & yet did not move − how fatigued − a third time it made a gyre, a short circuit, & returned again / 5 times it was thus shot at / left the Vessel / flew to another / & I heard firing, now here, now there / & nobody shot it / but probably it perished from fatigue, & the attempt to rest upon the wave! − Poor Hawk! O Strange Lust of Murder in Man! − It is not cruelty / it is mere non-feeling from non-thinking' (*CN*, II no. 2090).

24. For a detailed analysis of these revisions, see McElderry, in *SIP*, xxIx 79–87.

25. Some hints about the probable content of this proposed essay may also be gleaned from Coleridge's review of M. G. Lewis's *The Monk* in the *Critical Review* for February 1797 (*IS*, p. 192), from some comments on 'Asiatic supernatural beings' in a lecture of March 1818 (*MC*, 191–4), and from a late Notebook entry on the supernatural in poetry (*IS*, p. 191).

26. J. R. Barth, *The Symbolic Imagination: Coleridge and the Romantic Tradition* (Princeton, NJ, 1977) p. 90.

27. In both the Notebook entry and the motto to 'The Ancient Mariner', Coleridge abridges Burnet while adding two short phrases of his own: see *CN*, I no. 1000H(n). For helpful critical discussions of the motto, see S. C. Wilcox, 'The Arguments and Motto of *The Ancient Mariner*', *MLQ*, xxII (1961) 264–8, and J. Twitchell, 'The World above the Ancient Mariner', *Texas Studies in Literature and Language*, xvII (1975) 103–17.

28. R. C. Bald, 'The Ancient Mariner', *TLS*, 26 July 1934, p. 528.

29. McElderry, in *SIP*, xxIx 87–92; the quotation is from p. 91. McElderry also makes the interesting point (p. 91) that, since 'The Ancient Mariner' is Coleridge's 'one completed masterpiece', the composition of the prose gloss to accompany it would have given the poet a nostalgic opportunity 'to relive the creative joy of his youth; and by reliving "The Ancient Mariner" who could tell but that one day he might achieve something worthy to stand beside it?'

30. See Empson's Introduction in *Coleridge's Verse: A Selection*, ed. W. Empson and David Pirie (London, 1972) esp. pp. 42–54; and also L. J. Forstner, 'Coleridge's "The Ancient Mariner" and the Case for Justifiable "Mythocide": an Argument on Psychological, Epistemological and Formal Grounds', *Criticism*, xvIII (1976) 211–29. In essence, Empson and Forstner object to the gloss and to most of the other 1817 revisions because they emphasise the 'greasy injustice' of a specifically moral and Christian theme. Empson discards the gloss, arguing (perversely) that it provides an entirely mistaken frame of reference for the poem, since it was composed by a poet who had

rejected his earlier political and theological ideals and had grown more conventional and orthodox in his old age.

31. Huntington Brown, 'The Gloss to *The Rime of the Ancient Mariner*', *MLQ*, vi (1945) 319–24; the quotation is from p. 320. Brown's thesis, which is now widely accepted, has been developed further by a number of more recent critics: see, for example, George Watson, *Coleridge the Poet* (London, 1966; repr. 1970) pp. 89–94; Sarah Dyck, 'Perspective in "The Rime of the Ancient Mariner"', *SEL*, xiii (1973) 591–604; and Raimonda Modiano, 'Words and "Languageless" Meanings: Limits of Expression in *The Rime of the Ancient Mariner*', *MLQ*, xxxviii (1977) 40–61, esp. pp. 44–6.

32. Thomas McFarland, 'The Symbiosis of Coleridge and Wordsworth', *SIR*, xi (1972) 263–303; the quotation is from p. 263. See also H. M. Margoliouth, *Wordsworth and Coleridge 1795–1834* (London, 1953); A. M. Buchan, 'The Influence of Wordsworth on Coleridge (1795–1800)', *UTQ*, xxxii (1962–3) 346–66; and Stephen Prickett, *Coleridge and Wordsworth: The Poetry of Growth* (Cambridge, 1970).

33. See, for example, the anti-Wordsworthian argument of Malcolm Elwin, *The First Romantics* (London, 1947) pp. 194–6, and the pro-Wordsworthian arguments of L. S. Boas, 'Coleridge's "The Ancient Mariner", Part iv', *Explicator*, ii (1944) item 52; and L. H. Harris, 'Coleridge's "The Ancient Mariner"', *Explicator*, vi (1948) item 32.

34. Sheridan's suggestion that Coleridge should compose 'a tragedy on some popular subject' for Drury Lane was transmitted to Coleridge in early February 1797 (*CL*, i 304), and in compliance with this request Coleridge began to plan *Osorio*. On 16 March, although his plot was 'chaotic' and not yet fully worked out, he described it as 'romantic & wild & somewhat terrible' (*CL*, i 318). At the end of March Wordsworth paid a brief visit to Coleridge at Nether Stowey – their first meeting since 1795 – but Coleridge was in ill health and not even Wordsworth's conversation could rouse him much (*CL*, i 319–20), so that it is unlikely that there was discussion of their respective tragedies. On 10 May Coleridge announced to Cottle that he had completed '*1500* lines of *my Tragedy*' (*CL*, i 324); and a month later, when he visited Wordsworth at Racedown, he sounded surprised to discover that Wordsworth, too, had written a tragedy (*CL*, i 325). *Osorio*, then, seems to have been well under way well before Coleridge had any knowledge or, at least, any substantial knowledge of Wordsworth's *Borderers*.

35. For the full text of 'The Three Graves', see *CPW*, i 269–84. Until comparatively recently it was thought that Coleridge composed all four parts of the projected six-part ballad that were written, but it is now clear that the working draft (all that survives) of Parts i and ii are by Wordsworth, while Coleridge contributed Parts iii and iv. The projected conclusion of the work (Parts v and vi) was never written. In 1809 Coleridge published Parts iii and iv (his parts of the ballad) in *The Friend* (*CC*, iv ii 89–96); Parts i and ii, by Wordsworth, were not published until 1893, when they were wrongly attributed to Coleridge. See *WW*, i 388.

36. Charles Smith, 'Wordsworth and Coleridge: the Growth of a Theme', *SIP*, liv (1957) 53–64; the quotation is from pp. 53–4.

37. Barron Field, *Memoirs of Wordsworth*, ed. Geoffrey Little (Sydney, 1975) pp. 100–1.

38. Wordsworth's own later account in the Fenwick note to 'We Are Seven' is rather different, for it omits any reference to the supernatural: 'we began to talk of a Volume, which was to consist, as Mr Coleridge has told the world, of Poems chiefly on natural subjects taken from common life, but looked at, as much as might be, through an imaginative medium' (*WPW*, I 361). This statement constitutes an important piece of evidence to support the contention that Wordsworth either misunderstood or rejected Coleridge's theory of the supernatural.

39. In his 1800 note to 'The Thorn' Wordsworth likens the poem's garrulous narrator to 'a Captain of a small trading vessel', who is 'prone to superstition' and who, 'having little to do' since his retirement from seafaring, has 'become credulous and talkative from indolence'. Wordsworth's merchant captain, selected 'to exhibit some of the general laws by which superstition acts upon the mind', looks suspiciously like a domesticated version of Coleridge's Ancient Mariner, whose glittering eye and compelling tale mesmerise his auditors.

40. For an interesting analysis of the place of 'The Thorn' in the developing aesthetic rift between the two poets see Stephen Parrish, 'The Wordsworth-Coleridge Controversy', *PMLA*, LXXIII (1958) 367–74.

41. See, for example, in addition to *WW*, I 392–4, the following: Smith in *SIP*, LIV 60–3; Kathleen Coburn, 'Coleridge and Wordsworth and "the Supernatural"', *UTQ*, XXV (1956) 121–30, esp. pp. 122–6; and Anya Taylor, *Magic and English Romanticism* (Athens, Ga, 1979) pp. 138–43.

42. Coburn, in *UTQ*, XXV 124.

43. For example, Wordsworth's various notes to 'The Thorn' (*WPW*, II 512–13), his 1819 Dedication in 'Peter Bell' (*WPW*, II 331; quoted in part on p. 131 above), and his statement about the 'plan' of *Lyrical Ballads* made to Miss Fenwick in 1843 (see above, n. 38).

44. Coburn, in *UTQ*, XXV 125.

45. Keats's friend John Hamilton Reynolds published his 'Peter Bell: A Lyrical Ballad' in 1819 in advance of Wordsworth's poem. Shelley's 'Peter Bell the Third', written in October 1819, was not published until the second edition of his *Poetical Works* in 1839.

46. Line references are to the Reading Text of the two-part *Prelude*: see *The Prelude, 1798–1799*, ed. Stephen Parrish (Ithaca, NY, 1977) pp. 43–67.

47. Adair, *The Walking Dream*, p. 63.

48. On 'The Ancient Mariner' as 'epic', see the following: A. A. Mendilow, 'Symbolism in Coleridge and the Dantesque Element in "The Ancient Mariner"', *Scripta Hierosolymitana*, II (1955) 25–81, esp. pp. 48–50; K. Kroeber, '"The Rime of the Ancient Mariner" as Stylized Epic', *Transactions of the Wisconsin Academy of Sciences, Arts, and Letters*, XLVI (1957) 179–87; and Warren Stevenson, '*The Rime of the Ancient Mariner* as Epic Symbol', *Dalhousie Review*, LVI (1976) 542–7. For readings of it as a dramatic monologue, see Lionel Stevenson, '"The Ancient Mariner" as a Dramatic Monologue', *The Personalist*, XXX (1949) 34–44; and E. E. Gibbons, 'Point of View and Moral in "The Rime of the Ancient Mariner"', *University Review* (Kansas City), XXXV (1968) 257–61. Anca Vlasopolos, inspired by M. H. Abrams's paper 'Structure and Style in the Greater Romantic Lyric', in *Romanticism and Consciousness*, ed. Harold Bloom (New York, 1970)

pp. 201–29, proposes an entirely new generic category in '*The Rime of the Ancient Mariner* as Romantic Quest', *TWC*, x (1979) 365–9.

49. W. P. Ker, *Form and Style in Poetry* (London, 1928; repr. New York, 1966) p. 98.
50. Anne H. Ehrenpreis, *The Literary Ballad* (London, 1966) p. 11.
51. Joseph Addison, in *Spectator*, no. 70 (21 May 1711).
52. The translation is by William Taylor, from the *Monthly Magazine*, Apr 1796; repr. in Ehrenpreis, *The Literary Ballad*, pp. 68–76.
53. The ballad 'Alonzo the Brave' first appeared in Lewis's notorious (but extremely popular) Gothic novel, *The Monk* (1796); it is reprinted in Ehrenpreis, *The Literary Ballad*, pp. 64–7.
54. On the thematic complexity of 'The Ancient Mariner', see the section on critical approaches below. Various aspects of Coleridge's technical success and virtuosity are analysed in detail in the following: C. W. Stork, 'The Influence of the Popular Ballad on Wordsworth and Coleridge', *PMLA*, xxix (1914) 299–326; Tristram P. Coffin, 'Coleridge's Use of the Ballad Stanza in "The Rime of the Ancient Mariner"', *MLQ*, xii (1951) 437–45; R. H. Fogle, 'The Genre of *The Ancient Mariner*', *TSE*, vii (1957) 111–24; Alice Chandler, 'Structure and Symbol in "The Rime of the Ancient Mariner"', *MLQ*, xxvi (1965) 401–13; and Richard Payne, '"The Style and Spirit of the Elder Poets": the *Ancient Mariner* and English Literary Tradition', *MP*, lxxv (1978) 368–84.
55. Ehrenpreis, *The Literary Ballad*, p. 10.
56. For a discussion of Coleridge's use of extended stanzas, see Coffin, in *MLQ*, xii 437–45, who also provides a useful chart of the 'distorted stanzas' in 'The Ancient Mariner'. It should be pointed out that some of the old ballads – namely 'Chevy Chase' and 'Sir Cauline' – with which Coleridge was familiar from Percy's *Reliques* contain stanzas of five or (more often) six lines, but these extended stanzas in the old ballads lack the technical sophistication and architectural power that Coleridge achieves.
57. All of these passages are quoted and discussed in Lowes, *Road to Xanadu*, pp. 129–30, 134–5. Whatever objections one may raise to Lowes's method and assumptions (see above pp. 87–8), he has demonstrated the influence of the explorers' narratives on 'The Ancient Mariner' beyond doubt, and his case is both stronger and broader than that which he makes in his later chapters for 'Kubla Khan'. A number of other critics since Lowes have argued (not often with great success) for the influnce on 'The Ancient Mariner' of specific travel-books: see, for example, B. Martin, *The Ancient Mariner and the Authentic Voyage* (London, 1949; repr. 1970); Bernard Smith, 'Coleridge's *Ancient Mariner* and Cook's Second Voyage', *Journal of the Warburg and Courtauld Institutes*, xix (1956) 117–54; and Warren Ober, '"The Rime of the Ancient Mariner" and Pinckard's "Notes on the West Indies"', *N&Q*, ccii (1957) 380–2.
58. Lowes, *Road to Xanadu*, p. 198.
59. Discussed by Lowes, ibid., pp. 195–7. Lowes devotes an entire chapter (pp. 178–200) to detailing the influence of Coleridge's friendships and personal experiences on the poem. For additional suggestions, see E. H. Coleridge, in *Poetry Review*, ix 271–7; and Elwin, *The First Romantics*, pp. 197–8.

60. See Lane Cooper, 'The Power of the Eye in Coleridge', in *Studies in Language and Literature in Celebration of the Seventieth Birthday of James Morgan Hart* (New York, 1910) pp. 78–121. The essay is also reprinted in Cooper's *Late Harvest* (Ithaca, NY, 1952) pp. 65–95.

61. See Bernard Smith's useful essay 'Coleridge's *Ancient Mariner* and Cook's Second Voyage', *Journal of the Warburg and Courtauld Institutes*, XIX (1956) 117–54.

It has also been suggested that Fletcher Christian and the thrilling story of the mutiny aboard HMS *Bounty* in 1789 may have influenced 'The Ancient Mariner'. In 1795–6 Coleridge included in a list of projected works one on the 'Adventures of CHRISTIAN, the mutineer –' (*CN*, I no. 174); and, as Lowes has pointed out (*Road to Xanadu*, pp. 26–7), this hint may imply that the famous mutineer provided in some way a source for the adventures and guilt-haunted soul of Coleridge's Ancient Mariner. Lowes's suggestion, which is reasonable and possible, is made guardedly and presented as, in fact, no more than an interesting possibility. But in the hands of some more recent source-hunters, the suggestion has lost its aura of tantalising conjecture and been precipitated into the arena of historical certainty: C. S. Wilkinson, for example, insists that Coleridge's Mariner is modelled on Fletcher Christian, and speculates that Christian instead of dying on Pitcairn Island returned as a fugitive to England where he was in contact with Wordsworth ('schoolmate, relative, and family friend of Fletcher Christian'), who subsequently related Christian's adventures to Coleridge, who, of course, wrote 'The Ancient Mariner': see *The Wake of the Bounty* (London, 1953) esp. pp. 123–4. Wilkinson's imaginative conjectures have been enthusiastically endorsed by N. B. Houston, 'Fletcher Christian and "The Rime of the Ancient Mariner"', *Dalhousie Review*, XLV (1966) 431–46, and have been just as enthusiastically disputed by R. C. Leitz III, 'Fletcher Christian and *The Ancient Mariner*: a 'Refutation', *Dalhousie Review*, L (1970) 62–70. On Wordsworth's connections with Fletcher Christian and his family, see J. R. MacGillivray, 'An Early Poem and Letter by Wordsworth', *RES*, n.s. V (1954) 62–6.

62. The most comprehensive collection of such parallels is to be found in Lowes's *Road to Xanadu, passim*; but other interesting connections have been made, *inter alia*, by the following later critics: E. G. Ainsworth, Jr, 'Another Source of the "Lonesome Road" Stanza in *The Ancient Mariner*', *MLN*, XLIX (1934) 111–12 (on Blair's 'The Grave'); C. O. Parsons, 'The Mariner and the Albatross', *Virginia Quarterly Review*, XXVI (1950) 102–23 (on Peter Longueville's *The Hermit: or . . . Adventures of Mr Philip Quarll*); E. Schanzer, 'Shakespeare, Lowes, and "The Ancient Mariner"', *N&Q*, n.s. II (1955) 260–1; R. Huang, 'William Cowper and "The Rime of the Ancient Mariner"', *University of Windsor Review*, III (1968) 54–6; and M. Jacobus, 'William Huntington's "Spiritual Sea-Voyage": Another Source for "The Ancient Mariner"', *N&Q*, n.s. XVI (1969) 409–12.

63. See, for example, *Coleridge's Poetical Works*, ed. J. D. Campbell (London, 1893) p. 598; or (most recently) W. Nelson, 'A Coleridge "Borrowing"', *TLS*, 11 June 1954, p. 377.

64. G. Wilson Knight, *The Starlit Dome: Studies in the Poetry of Vision* (Oxford, 1941; repr. London, 1964) p. 90. Knight's general thesis is that

'Christabel', 'The Ancient Mariner' and 'Kubla Khan' 'may be grouped as a little *Divina Commedia* exploring in turn Hell, Purgatory, and Paradise' (p. 83). The influence of Dante on 'The Ancient Mariner' has been discussed by a number of readers: see, for example, Lowes, *Road to Xanadu*, esp. pp. 263–4, 480–3; Mendilow, in *Scripta Hierosolymitana*, ii 25–81; Adair, *The Waking Dream*, esp. pp. 93–4; and E. Moses, 'A Reading of "The Ancient Mariner"', *Costerus*, viii (1973) 101–7.

65. H. W. Piper, *The Active Universe: Pantheism and the Concept of Imagination in the English Romantic Poets* (London, 1962) p. 85.

66. Maren-Sofie Røstvig, '"The Rime of the Ancient Mariner" and the Cosmic System of Robert Fludd', *Tennessee Studies in Literature*, xii (1967) 69–81.

67. Daniel Stempel, 'Coleridge's Magical Realism: a Reading of *The Rime of the Ancient Mariner*', *Mosaic*, xii (1978) 143–56; the quotation is from p. 145.

68. Ibid., p. 151.

69. Epigraphs: (a) from Robert Southey's review of *Lyrical Ballads* in the *Critical Review*, Oct 1798: see *Coleridge: The Critical Heritage*, p. 53; (b) *AP*, p. 5.

70. *Coleridge: The Critical Heritage*, p. 403.

71. Ibid., p. 53. Southey's public opinion was also his private opinion: 'The ballad I think nonsense', he declared to C. W. W. Wynn in a letter of December 1798 – *New Letters of Robert Southey*, ed. Kenneth Curry, 2 vols (New York and London, 1965) i 177. Coleridge, for his part, was stung by Southey's comments and long remembered them, citing phrases in 1809 and 1811 to illustrate his harsh treatment at the hands of the reviewers: see *CL*, iii 203, 316.

72. In fairness to Wordsworth it should be said that his letter (which has not survived) appears largely to have been concerned not with what Lamb had said about 'The Ancient Mariner' but what he had said about Wordsworth's poems in the 1800 edition of *Lyrical Ballads* – although (Lamb declares) 'Devil a hint did I give that it [i.e. the 1800 *Lyrical Ballads*] had *not pleased me*' (*LL*, i 272).

73. An anonymous review in the *Edinburgh Magazine*, Oct 1817, for example, begins with these words: 'Every reader of modern poetry is acquainted of course with "The Ancient Mariner" . . . which, when once read, can never afterwards be entirely forgotten' – *Coleridge: The Critical Heritage*, p. 392.

74. J. G. Lockhart in *Blackwood's Edinburgh Magazine*, Oct 1819: *Coleridge: The Critical Heritage*, p. 436. See also Richard Haven's useful essay, 'The Ancient Mariner in the Nineteenth Century', *SIR*, xi (1972) 360–74.

75. G. H. Clarke, 'Certain Symbols in *The Rime of the Ancient Mariner*', *Queen's Quarterly*, xl (1933) 27–45; the quotation is from pp. 29–30.

76. See, for example, Gertrude Garrigues, 'Coleridge's "Ancient Mariner"', *Journal of Speculative Philosophy*, xiv (1880) 327–38; A. W. Crawford, 'On Coleridge's *Ancient Mariner*', *MLN*, xxxiv (1919) 311–13; and Newton P. Stallknecht, 'The Moral of the *Ancient Mariner*', *PMLA*, xlvii (1932) 559–69.

77. Robert Penn Warren, 'A Poem of Pure Imagination: an Experiment in Reading', *Kenyon Review*, viii (1946) 391–427; rev. and expanded in *Selected Essays of Robert Penn Warren* (New York, 1958) pp. 198–305. (All my references are to this latter version.)

78. Among the best of the symbolic religious interpretations are the following: Clarke, in *Queen's Quarterly*, xl 27–45; Warren, *Selected Essays*, pp. 198–305; C. M. Bowra, *The Romantic Imagination* (Cambridge, Mass., 1949; repr. New York, 1961) pp. 51–75; R. L. Brett, *Reason and Imagination: A Study of Form and Meaning in Four Poems* (Oxford, 1960; repr. 1968) pp. 78–107; and J. W. R. Purser, 'Interpretation of *The Ancient Mariner*', *RES*, viii (1957) 249–56.

79. Warren, *Selected Essays*, pp. 227–33; the quotation is from pp. 232–3. The view that 'the great constitutive idea' of *The Ancient Mariner* is 'the concept of the fall and of man's damaged nature' has been argued by a number of critics: e.g. William Walsh, *Coleridge: The Work and the Relevance* (London, 1967; New York, 1973) pp. 118–21. See also W. H. Auden, *The Enchafèd Flood, or the Romantic Iconography of the Sea* (Charlottesville, Va, 1950; repr. New York, 1967) pp. 72–3: 'But for the Fall (the shooting of the Albatross), Adam (The Ancient Mariner) would never have consciously learned through suffering the meaning of Agapé, i.e., to love one's neighbour as oneself without comparisons or greed (the blessing of the snakes), so that the Ancient Mariner might well say in the end, *O felix culpa*.'

80. Adam's transgression, however, while perhaps unmotivated, is by no means a sin committed (like the Mariner's) in ignorance. Adam was specifically interdicted the eating of the apple; the hapless Mariner received no such warning about shooting birds.

81. J. A. Stuart, 'The Augustinian "Cause of Action" in Coleridge's *Rime of the Ancient Mariner*', *Harvard Theological Review*, lx (1967) 177–211. See also George Bellis, 'The Fixed Crime of *The Ancient Mariner*', *EIC*, xxiv (1974) 243–60.

82. Edward Bostetter, 'The Nightmare World of *The Ancient Mariner*', *SIR*, i (1962) 241–54; rev. in Bostetter's *The Romantic Ventriloquists: Wordsworth, Coleridge, Keats, Shelley, Byron* (Seattle and London, 1963; rev. edn, 1965) pp. 108–18; the quotation is from p. 115.

83. James D. Boulger, 'Christian Skepticism in *The Rime of The Ancient Mariner*', in *From Sensibility to Romanticism: Essays Presented to Frederick A. Pottle*, ed. F. W. Hilles and Harold Bloom (New York, 1965) pp. 439–52; the quotations are from pp. 451 and 444.

84. Warren, *Selected Essays*, pp. 257–60. Although many critics would agree that the Mariner symbolises the figure of a poet, not everyone accepts Warren's case for his being a *poète maudit*: Boulger, for example, argues that 'he is a parable of the creative poet, of course, working in the modern rationalistic world, but he is not *maudit*, but rather a necessarily suffering being' (in *From Sensibility to Romanticism*, p. 450).

85. Warren, *Selected Essays*, pp. 233–50.

86. See, for example, John Beer's analysis of Coleridge's sun and moon imagery in *Coleridge the Visionary* (London, 1959; repr. 1970) pp. 158–74 *passim*.

87. Humphry House, *Coleridge: The Clark Lectures 1951–52* (London, 1953; repr. 1969) pp. 110–13.

88. S. F. Gingerich, 'From Necessity to Transcendentalism in Coleridge', *PMLA*, xxxv (1920) 1–59; the quotation is from p. 14.

89. Dorothy Waples, 'David Hartley in *The Ancient Mariner*', *JEGP*, xxxv

(1936) 337–51. See also G. O. Carey, 'Ethics in "The Mariner"', *English Record*, XVII (1966) 18–20.

90. See Beer, *Coleridge the Visionary*, pp. 133–74, and his chapter on 'The Ancient Mariner' ('An Exploring Fiction') in *Coleridge's Poetic Intelligence* (London, 1977) pp. 147–84. Also helpful is Adair *The Waking Dream*, esp. pp. 44–55. Other examinations of the relationship between empiricism and transcendentalism in the poem include the following: Irene Chayes, 'A Coleridgean Reading of "The Ancient Mariner"', *SIR*, IV (1965) 81–103; Ralph Freedman, 'Eyesight and Vision: Forms of the Imagination in Coleridge and Novalis', in *The Rarer Action: Essays in Honor of Francis Fergusson*, ed. A. Cheuse and R. Koffler (New Brunswick, NJ, 1970), pp. 202–17; and George Bellis, 'The Fixed Crime of *The Ancient Mariner*', *EIC*, XXIV (1974) 243–60.

91. Hugh l'Anson Fausset, *Samuel Taylor Coleridge* (London, 1926; repr. 1972) p. 166.

92. D. W. Harding, 'The Theme of "The Ancient Mariner"', *Scrutiny*, IX (1941) 334–42; Douglas Angus, 'The Theme of Love and Guilt in Coleridge's Three Major Poems', *JEGP*, LIX (1960) 655–68; Lynn M. Grow, '*The Rime of the Ancient Mariner*: Multiple Veils of Illusion', *Notre Dame English Journal*, IX (1973) 23–30; Lefebure, *Coleridge: A Bondage of Opium*, pp. 259–66; L. D. Berkoben, *Coleridge's Decline as a Poet* (Paris and The Hague, 1975) pp. 73–92.

93. George Whalley, 'The Mariner and the Albatross', *UTQ*, XVI (1947) 381–98. Reprinted in *Coleridge: The Ancient Mariner and Other Poems*, ed. A. R. Jones and W. Tydeman (London, 1973) pp. 160–83; the quotation is from pp. 161–2.

94. Ibid., p. 177. For other important discussions of the Mariner's and Coleridge's shared experience of alienation and depression, see the following: A. M. Buchan, 'The Sad Wisdom of the Mariner', *SIP*, LXI (1964) 669–88; Adair, *The Waking Dream*, pp. 39–94; and Richard Haven, *Patterns of Consciousness: An Essay on Coleridge* (Amherst, Mass., 1969) pp. 18–42.

95. H. Parsons, 'Coleridge as "The Wedding Guest" in the "Rime of the Ancient Mariner"', *N&Q*, CXCV (1950) 251–2; Hoxie N. Fairchild, *Religious Trends in English Poetry*, 6 vols (New York, 1949; repr. 1956) III 294; Mendilow, in *Scripta Hierosolymitana*, II 48–62.

96. Kenneth Burke, *The Philosophy of Literary Form: Studies in Symbolic Action* (Baton Rouge, La, 1941; 2nd edn, 1967) pp. 71–3, 287–8.

97. For a broad sample of Freudian readings, see the following: Beverly Fields, *Reality's Dark Dream: Dejection in Coleridge* (Kent, Ohio, 1968) pp. 84–91; H. S. Visweswariah, 'Motive-finding in *The Rime of the Ancient Mariner*', *Literary Criterion* (Mysore), VIII (1969) 27–38; M. J. Lupton, '"The Rime of the Ancient Mariner": the Agony of Thirst', *American Imago*, XXVII (1970) 140–59; Leon Waldoff, 'The Quest for Father and Identity in "The Rime of the Ancient Mariner"', *Psychoanalytic Review*, LVIII (1971) 439–53; and Norman Fruman, *Coleridge: The Damaged Archangel* (New York, 1971; London, 1972) pp. 403–12.

98. David Beres, 'A Dream, a Vision, and a Poem: a Psycho-Analytic Study of the Origins of *The Rime of the Ancient Mariner*', *International Journal of Psycho-Analysis*, XXXII (1951) 97–116; the quotation is from p. 109.

99. Maud Bodkin, *Archetypal Patterns in Poetry: Psychological Studies of Imagination* (Oxford, 1934; repr. New York, 1958) pp. 25–58; and Mark Littmann, '*The Ancient Mariner* and Initiation Rites', *Papers on Language and Literature*, IV (1968) 370–89.

100. The most attractive argument for a political undercurrent in the poem is John Beer's suggestion that the Mariner's anguish and subsequent restoration through blessing the water snakes reflects the process of political disillusionment through which young idealists such as Coleridge and Wordsworth passed when the French Revolution soured into the Reign of Terror and necessitated their effort to rediscover an idealistic vision in the reinterpretation of Nature rather than in the world of political events: see *Coleridge's Poetic Intelligence* (London, 1977) pp. 149–51, 161–4, 175.

   Other critics have seen reflected in the poem Coleridge's strong opposition to the slave-trade and his objections to exploitative colonial expansion: see Malcolm Ware, 'Coleridge's "Spectre-bark": a Slave Ship?', *PQ*, XL (1961) 589–93; William Empson, 'The Ancient Mariner', *Critical Quarterly*, VI (1964) 298–319 – a highly idiosyncratic and question-begging essay; and J. R. Ebbatson, 'Coleridge's Mariner and the Rights of Man', *SIR*, XI (1972) 171–206.

101. See, for example, House, *Coleridge*, p. 96; Ward Pafford, 'Coleridge's Wedding-Guest', *SIP*, LX (1963) 618–26; Boulger, in *From Sensibility to Romanticism* esp. pp. 446–50; M. L. D'Avanzo, 'Coleridge's Wedding-Guest and Marriage-Feast: the Biblical Context', *University of Windsor Review*, VIII (1972) 62–6; and Modiano, in *MLQ*, XXXVIII 40–61.

102. See, for example, E. E. Stoll, 'Symbolism in Coleridge', *PMLA*, LXIII (1948) 214–33; Lionel Stevenson, in *The Personalist*, XXX, esp. pp. 34–40; I. A. Richards, Introduction to *The Portable Coleridge* (New York, 1950; repr. Harmondsworth, 1977) p. 34; and Watson, *Coleridge the Poet*, esp. pp. 94–100.

103. Beer, *Coleridge's Poetic Intelligence*, p. 180.

104. Barth, *The Symbolic Imagination*, p. 99.

105. Henry Nelson Coleridge, the editor of his uncle's *Table Talk* (1835), first reported this anecdote a year earlier in the *Quarterly Review*, LII (Aug 1834) 28: 'Mrs. Barbauld, meaning to be complimentary, told our poet, that she thought the "Ancient Mariner" very beautiful, but that it had the fault of containing no moral. "Nay, madam," replied the poet, "if I may be permitted to say so, the only fault in the poem is that there is *too much*! In a work of such pure imagination I ought not to have stopped to give reasons for things, or inculcate humanity to beasts. 'The Arabian Nights' might have taught me better." They might – the tale of the merchant's son who puts out the eyes of a genii by flinging his date-shells down a well, and is therefore ordered to prepare for death – might have taught this law of imagination . . .' – quoted in T. M. Raysor, 'Coleridge's Comment on the Moral of "The Ancient Mariner"', *PQ*, XXXI (1952) 88.

106. Both the prose passage (from Mrs Barbauld's *Lessons for Children of Three Years Old*, pt I) and 'Epitaph on a Goldfinch' are quoted from Frances Ferguson, 'Coleridge and the Deluded Reader: "The Rime of the Ancient Mariner"', *Georgia Review*, XXXI (1977) 626.

107. Lowes, *Road to Xanadu*, p. 277.

108. Lionel Stevenson, *The Personalist*, XXX 42.
109. Watson, *Coleridge the Poet*, p. 99.
110. See Irving Babbitt, 'Coleridge and the Moderns', *The Bookman*, LXX (1929) 120; E. M. Bewley, 'The Poetry of Coleridge', *Scrutiny*, VIII (1940) 406–11; Bostetter, *Romantic Ventriloquists*, pp. 116–17; and Chayes, in *SIR*, IV (1965) 81–103, esp. pp. 101–3.
111. House, *Coleridge*, p. 92.
112. Beer, *Coleridge's Poetic Intelligence*, p. 182.
113. Gayle Smith, 'A Reappraisal of the Moral Stanzas in *The Rime of the Ancient Mariner*', *SIR*, III (1963) 42–52; the quotation is from p. 50.

NOTES TO CHAPTER FIVE: 'DEJECTION: AN ODE'

1. Coleridge spent a good deal of time at Dove Cottage; Mrs Coleridge, however, seldom visited the Wordsworths. It may be added that, while the Wordsworths frequently came to Keswick, their visits were usually short and somewhat strained: 'we are never comfortable there', Dorothy remarked, 'after the first 2 or 3 days' (*WL: EY*, p. 330).

2. While it is sometimes assumed that Coleridge composed the whole of this verse-letter between sunset and midnight of 4 April, there are two pieces of information that militate against the supposition that it was finished on the same day on which it was begun. First, although the Wordsworths were still at Keswick on 4 April and although he accompanied them as far as Threlkeld (about four miles) on their walk to Eusemere the following day, Coleridge did not read or (as far as we know) even mention the poem to them until two and a half weeks later, when he recited 'the verses he wrote to Sara' to them at Dove Cottage on Wednesday, 21 April (*JDW*, p. 113). Second, the wind which figures so prominently in the poem's imagery does not seem to have sprung up for almost a week; Dorothy's Journal says nothing about the weather on 4 April, but her entries for 9–12 April have a good deal to say about the change in the weather and the sharp windy nights (*JDW*, p. 108). A more probable conjecture, then, is that Coleridge began to compose the verse-letter on Sunday, 4 April, that he worked on it over the next week or so, and that he sent it to Sara Hutchinson sometime before Tuesday, 20 April, when he arrived at Grasmere and recited it to the Wordsworths on the following day.

3. E. de Selincourt, 'Coleridge's *Dejection: An Ode*', *Essays and Studies*, XXII (1936) 14.

4. David Pirie, '*A Letter to [Asra]*', in *Bicentenary Wordsworth Studies in Memory of John Alban Finch*, ed. J. Wordsworth (Ithaca, NY, and London, 1970) p. 329.

5. See *JDW*, p. 141 (22 June 1802): 'I wrote to Mary H. and put up a parcel for Coleridge. The LB arrived.' Doubtless the parcel for Coleridge included a copy of *Lyrical Ballads*.

6. ΕΣΤΗΣΕ (ESTESE) is, as Coleridge said in 'A Character' (1834), 'Punic Greek for "he hath stood"' (*CPW*, I 453). Literally, ἔστησε means 'he has placed', not 'he has stood', as Coleridge well knew; but he was interested in the pun on his own initials STC. (See *CL*, II 867.)

7. For more detailed accounts of the stages through which the poem passed from April to October 1802, see Pirie, in *Bicentenary Wordsworth Studies*, pp. 325–35, and also C. S. Bouslog's statistical analysis of deletions from the April verse-letter in 'Structure and Theme in Coleridge's "Dejection: An Ode"', *MLQ*, xxiv (1963) 48.

8. De Selincourt, in *Essays and Studies*, xxii 8.

9. The stanzas, while there are only seven of them (as compared with eight in the *textus receptus* of 1817), are numbered 1–5, then follow three rows of asterisks with the note 'The Sixth and Seventh Stanzas omitted', and finally the last two stanzas (numbered 8 and 9). 'It is', as Pirie remarks, 'hard to know what Coleridge meant by this claim [of two deleted stanzas]. No form of the poem contains two other stanzas at this point. . . . The most likely explanation is that Coleridge was aware of creating a clumsy transition, and decided that a little deceit would make it more acceptable' (*Bicentenary Wordsworth Studies*, p. 333). Pirie's explanation is, perhaps, as plausible as any that is possible; but one still wonders whether Coleridge *did* propose to add something at this point but never got around to doing it.

10. See the letter to Thomas Wedgwood of 20 October 1802 (*CL*, ii 875), and the letters to George Coleridge of 2 October 1803 and 30 November 1806 (*CL*, ii 1008, 1201).

11. In line 5 'clouds' (1817) is altered to 'cloud' in the texts of 1828 and following.

12. The verse-letter to Sara Hutchinson is readily available in a number of places. It is printed in full in *CL*, ii 790–8; by de Selincourt, in *Essays and Studies*, xxii 16–25; by George Whalley in *Coleridge and Sara Hutchinson and the Asra Poems* (London, 1955) pp. 155–64; by Humphry House in *Coleridge: The Clark Lectures 1951–52* (London, 1953; repr. 1969) pp. 157–65; by William Empson and David Pirie in *Coleridge's Verse: A Selection* (London and New York, 1972) pp. 187–97; and by George Dekker (who also reprints the *Morning Post* version) in *Coleridge and the Literature of Sensibility* (London, 1978) pp. 250–8.

13. Whalley, *Coleridge and Sara Hutchinson*, pp. 1–2.

14. Pirie, in *Bicentenary Wordsworth Studies*, p. 305.

15. Coleridge's poem 'A Day-Dream', which was probably written before the verse-letter (see Whalley, *Coleridge and Sara Hutchinson*, p. 125), describes this same incident: *CPW*, i 385–6.

16. Pirie, in *Bicentenary Wordsworth Studies*, p. 325.

17. Walsh, *Coleridge: The Work and the Relevance* (London, 1967) pp. 131–2.

18. Pirie, in *Bicentenary Wordsworth Studies*, p. 294. Dekker argues – although there is no evidence to support his view – that 'the essential components of *Dejection: An Ode* existed as actual stanzas of poetry *before* the verse letter to Sara Hutchinson was drafted' (*Coleridge and the Literature of Sensibility*, p. 47).

19. Pirie, in *Bicentenary Wordsworth Studies*, p. 325.

20. Beverly Fields, 'The First Draft of *Dejection*: an Explication', ch. 7 (pp. 119–64) of her *Reality's Dark Dream: Dejection in Coleridge* (Kent, Ohio, 1968) pp. 150–1.

21. Mary Jane Lupton, 'The Dark Dream of "Dejection"', *Literature and Psychology*, xviii (1968) 44–5.

22. Max F. Schulz, 'Coleridge', in *The English Romantic Poets: A Review of*

Research and Criticism, ed. Frank Jordan, 3rd (rev.) edn (New York, 1972) p. 203.

23. 'The Mad Monk' was published in the *Morning Post*, 13 Oct 1800, over the pseudonym 'Cassiani, jun.' and was later reprinted under Coleridge's name in *The Wild Wreath* (1804), a collection edited by 'Perdita' Robinson's daughter Maria. There is some dispute as to whether 'The Mad Monk' was composed by Coleridge or by Wordsworth — or, perhaps, as a joint production by them both: see S. M. Parrish and D. V. Erdman, 'Who Wrote *The Mad Monk*?: a Debate', *Bulletin of the New York Public Library*, LXIV (1960) 209–37.

24. Stephen Prickett, *Coleridge and Wordsworth: The Poetry of Growth* (Cambridge, 1970) p. 152.

25. The verbal parallels are detailed in F. M. Smith, 'The Relation of Coleridge's *Ode on Dejection* to Wordsworth's *Ode on Intimations of Immortality*', *PMLA*, L (1935) 224–34.

26. Prickett, *Coleridge and Wordsworth*, pp. 161–2.

27. George Meyer, '*Resolution and Independence*: Wordsworth's Answer to Coleridge's *Dejection: An Ode*', *TSE*, II (1950) 69.

28. For two early views of Coleridge's 'Platonic' influence on Wordsworth's 'Ode', see J. D. Rea, 'Coleridge's Intimations of Immortality from Proclus', *MP*, XXVI (1928) 201–13; and N. P. Stallknecht, 'The Doctrine of Coleridge's *Dejection* and its Relation to Wordsworth's Philosophy', *PMLA*, XLIX (1934) 196–207.

29. Harold Bloom, *The Visionary Company: A Reading of English Romantic Poetry* (New York, 1961; rev. edn, Ithaca, NY, and London, 1971) p. 222.

30. Prickett, *Coleridge and Wordsworth*, p. 155.

31. L. G. Salingar, 'Coleridge: Poet and Philosopher', in *From Blake to Byron* (vol. V of the Pelican Guide to English Literature), ed. Boris Ford (Harmondsworth, 1957; rev. edn, 1962) p. 195.

32. Milton Teichman, 'Wordsworth's Two Replies to Coleridge's "Dejection: An Ode"', *PMLA*, LXXXVI (1971) 982–9.

33. Bloom, *The Visionary Company*, pp. 228–9.

34. Gilbert Highet, *The Classical Tradition: Greek and Roman Influences on Western Literature* (Oxford, 1949) pp. 226–7.

35. On the development of the English ode, see George N. Shuster, *The English Ode from Milton to Keats* (New York, 1940; repr. Gloucester, Mass., 1964). Carol Maddison's *Apollo and the Nine: A History of the Ode* (London, 1960) is a thorough and scholarly examination of the development of the ode on the Continent and in England, but her discussion ends with Cowley. Two useful introductory studies (both of which discuss Coleridge's 'Dejection: An Ode') are John Heath-Stubbs's *The Ode* (London, 1969), and John D. Jump's *The Ode* (London, 1974) in the Critical Idiom series.

36. Jump, *The Ode*, p. 43.

37. See Ch. 2, n. 2.

38. See Ch. 2, n. 9.

39. From the date of its first publication in the *Morning Post* Coleridge called the poem an ode: see, for example, his reference to 'the ode to dejection' in a letter of 20 October 1802 to Thomas Wedgwood (*CL*, II 875) and his title for the poem — 'Dejection, an Ode. — (Imperfect) *April 4th, 1802*' — in the letter of 13 August 1803 to the Beaumonts (*CL*, II 970).

40. A. H. Fairbanks, 'The Form of Coleridge's Dejection Ode', *PMLA*, xc (1975) 874—5. For a similar view, see Irene Chayes, 'Rhetoric as Drama: an Approach to the Romantic Ode', *PMLA*, LXXIX (1964) 67—79, esp. p. 69.
41. Walsh, *Coleridge: The Work and the Relevance*, p. 133.
42. 'The paradox that he is capable of rendering his impressions so precisely is more apparent than real. As R. D. Laing has shown in his book *The Divided Self*, in moments of "dissociation" (when a person is thinking "this seems unreal", "nothing seems to be touching me") the self is often excessively alert and may be observing and recording with exceptional lucidity. It is such an experience that the *Dejection Ode* seems to offer': Reginald Watters, *Coleridge* (London, 1971) p. 91.
43. The phrase 'my genial spirits fail' has been much discussed. In Milton's *Samson Agonistes*, lines 594—6, the blind hero refers at the nadir of his despair to a similar loss, believing that God has forsaken him:

> So much I feel my genial spirits droop,
> My hopes all flat, nature within me seems
> In all her functions weary of herself.

Since Coleridge had had *Samson Agonistes* much in mind in the spring of 1802 (see *CN*, I no. 1155) when he composed these lines, the echo is of considerable interest. It may also be the case that Coleridge had one eye on Wordsworth's 'genial spirits' in line 113 of 'Tintern Abbey'. For a recent discussion, see M. L. D'Avanzo, 'Wordsworth's and Coleridge's "Genial Spirits"', *TWC*, II (1971) 17—20.
44. On *joy* see Ch. 2, n. 19. See also Pirie, in *Bicentenary Wordsworth Studies*, pp. 303—4; and Dekker, *Coleridge and the Literature of Sensibility*, pp. 142—76.
45. See my *Imagination in Coleridge* (London, 1978) pp. 168—9.
46. Prickett, *Coleridge and Wordsworth*, pp. 110—11.
47. The germ of this image is to be found in a Notebook entry of October 1800: 'Oct. 21 — Morning — 2 °clock — Wind amid its [?brausen] makes every now & then such a deep moan of pain, that I think it my wife asleep in pain — A trembling Oo! Oo! like a wounded man on a field of battle whose wounds smarted with the cold' (*CN*, I no. 832).
48. It is often confidently asserted that the reference in these lines on the lost child is to Wordsworth's 'Lucy Gray', and this view is supported by the fact that the April verse-letter specifies Wordsworth rather than Otway as the framer of the 'tender lay' (see *CL*, II 795, line 210). While Wordsworth's Lucy probably lies behind the image, I do not think that the matter is simply one of allusion, for the lost child is (in part) Coleridge himself and, as we know from a letter of February 1801, he had adapted the image to describe the wind as well: 'O my dear dear Friend! that you were with me by the fireside of my Study here, that I might talk it over with you to the Tune of this Night Wind that pipes it's thin doleful climbing sinking Notes like a child that has lost it's way and is crying aloud, half in grief and half in hope to be heard by it's Mother' (*CL*, II 669). The image may also have recalled to Coleridge a traumatic experience from his youth, on which occasion he nearly died from exposure having stayed out all night during a dreadful storm: see *CL*, I 353—4.

49. Walter Jackson Bate, *Coleridge* (New York, 1968; London, 1969; repr. 1973) p. 109.
50. Of this 'crowning metaphor' of the eddy, M. H. Abrams has said: 'The figure implies a ceaseless and circular interchange of life between soul and nature in which it is impossible to distinguish what is given from what received': *The Mirror and the Lamp: Romantic Theory and the Critical Tradition* (New York, 1953; repr. 1958) p. 68.
51. Bate, *Coleridge*, p. 110.
52. House, *Coleridge*, p. 134.
53. For various other similar views, see Bouslog, in MLQ, XXIV 49−52; Max F. Schulz, *The Poetic Voices of Coleridge* (Detroit, 1963; rev. edn 1964) p. 206; A. R. Jones, 'Coleridge and Poetry: the Conversational and other Poems', in *S. T. Coleridge* (Writers and their Background series), ed. R. L. Brett (London, 1971) pp. 116−22; and Pirie, who concludes that 'The *Ode* is not merely an acceptable reworking of *A Letter*; it is a wholly different poem, and a good one in its own right . . . I should, however, like to suggest that the *Ode* is essentially the slighter achievement. . . . The *Ode* is impressive, *A Letter* had been moving as well' (*Bicentenery Wordsworth Studies*, pp. 338−9).
54. Walsh, *Coleridge: The Work and the Relevance*, pp. 131−2. See also Fairbanks, in *PMLA*, XC 879.
55. Bate, *Coleridge*, p. 108; Schulz, *Poetic Voices of Coleridge* p. 203. To these views may be added that of Michael J. Kelly, who believes that Coleridge's dejection of April 1802 was resolved, not in the later redactions of the verse-letter, but in another poem entirely (namely, 'The Picture, or the Lover's Resolution', which appeared in the *Morning Post*, 6 Sep 1802): See 'Coleridge's "Picture, or the Lover's Resolution": its Relationship to "Dejection" and its Sources in the *Notebooks*', *Costerus*, V (1972) 75−96.
56. Smith, in *PMLA*, L 224.
57. R. H. Fogle, 'The Dejection of Coleridge's Ode', *ELH*, XVII (1950) 71−7; J. L. Simmons, 'Coleridge's "Dejection: an Ode": a Poet's Regeneration', *University Review* (Kansas City), XXXIII (1967) 212−18; and P. R. Broughton, 'The Modifying Metaphor in "Dejection: An Ode"', *TWC*, IV (1973) 241−9 (the quotations are from pp. 242 and 245).
58. M. H. Abrams, 'The Correspondent Breeze: a Romantic Metaphor', in *English Romantic Poets: Modern Essays in Criticism*, ed. M. H. Abrams (New York, 1960; rev. edn 1975) pp. 38−9.

NOTES TO CHAPTER SIX: BIOGRAPHIA LITERARIA

1. Barron Field, *Memoirs of Wordsworth*, ed. Geoffrey Little (Sydney, 1975) p. 62, n. 101. It is impossible to know exactly when Coleridge first suggested the idea of the Preface to Wordsworth, but the most probable time would be either April 1800 (when Coleridge spent several weeks at Grasmere) or early July 1800 (when the Coleridges were at Dove Cottage for more than three weeks before their move into Greta Hall at the end of the month).
2. In her note to this entry Miss Coburn says, 'Possibly this was a memorandum for the Preface to the *Lyrical Ballads* (1800) when it was still the intention

that Coleridge should write it. Or for the "Essay on Poetry" still in his mind, 9 Oct [*CL*, ɪ 632].' While either of these suggestions is possible, I incline toward the first of them. In the first place, there is the similarity of theoretical ideas and even of phrasing (examined by Miss Coburn) between Coleridge's note and the Preface to *Lyrical Ballads*. In the second place, it should be noticed that, although Wordsworth mentions the Preface as early as 29 July (*LW: EY*, p. 290), he does not say *who* was writing it – and in mid August (writing *from Keswick*) he apologises to the printers: 'The preface is not yet ready: I shall send it in a few days' (*LW: EY*, p. 292). Procrastination and non-delivery are not Wordsworthian traits. I suspect that in July–August 1800 Coleridge was the intended author of the Preface and that Wordsworth took it over, probably sometime in the first two weeks of September, when it became clear that Coleridge was not getting on with the job. The first clear evidence we possess that Wordsworth was himself writing the Preface dates from mid September (*JDW*, p. 40).

3. George Whalley, 'The Integrity of *Biographia Literaria*', *E&S*, n.s. ᴠɪ (1953) 87–101; the quotation is from p. 92.

4. Whalley, followed by D. M. Fogel in 'A Compositional History of the *Biographia Literaria*', *SIB*, xxx (1977) 224, dates this Notebook entry 'August 1803'; Miss Coburn, however, dates it (provisionally) 'September–October 1803' in her edition of the Notebooks. The entry is discussed by Watson, *BL*[W], pp. xi–xii. It may be added that, while the Notebook entry focuses on metaphysics, Coleridge was still very much concerned with Wordsworth's theory and its adverse effect on his poetry in the autumn of 1803: 'I have seen enough,' he told Poole on 14 October, 'positively to give me feelings of hostility towards the plan of several of the Poems in the L. Ballads: & I really consider it as a misfortune, that Wordsworth ever deserted his former mountain Track to wander in Lanes & allies . . .' (*CL*, ɪɪ 1013).

5. Fogel, in *SIB*, xxx 224.

6. In unravelling the complex compositional history of the *Biographia Literaria* in this and the following paragraphs, I have relied heavily on two important discussions: first, E. L. Griggs's summary (and notes) in his edition of Coleridge's letters (*CL*, ɪɪɪ xlvii–lii), and, second, D. M. Fogel's paper in *SIB*, xxx. Fogel provides a useful tabular synopsis (pp. 221–2) of the probable evolution of *Biographia Literaria*.

7. The placement of this comma is crucial. Its omission in the transcript of the letter published in the *Westminster Review* in 1870 led early scholars such as John Shawcross (*BL*, ɪ xc–xci) to suppose that Coleridge's literary autobiography 'came to demand a preface' and that this hypothetical preface (i.e. the critique of Wordsworth in chs 14–22) mushroomed to such a size that it could no longer serve as a 'preface' and had to be appended to the 'Autobiographia literaria' (i.e. chs 1–12). This theory, which George Watson erroneously persists in maintaining (*BL*[W], pp. xiii–xiv), is untenable. Since the publication in 1959 of the correct text of the letter (*including* the comma after 'preface') in E. L. Griggs's edition of the *Letters*, it is clear that 'At no time did Coleridge propose a preface to his autobiography' (*CL*, ɪᴠ 578 n. 2). The problem is discussed in detail by Fogel, in *SIB*, xxx 226–8.

8. As we know from Crabb Robinson's diary, Wordsworth *was* displeased with

Biographia Literaria: 'Coleridge's book has given him no pleasure, and he finds just fault with Coleridge for professing to write about himself and writing merely about Southey and Wordsworth. With the criticism on the poetry too he is not satisfied. The praise is extravagant and the censure inconsiderate. I recollected hearing Hazlitt say that Wordsworth would not forgive a single censure mingled with however great a mass of eulogy' (4 Dec 1817; *HCR*, I 213). See also *CL*, IV 591, 598, and 620.

9. Two months later (30 May 1815) Coleridge elaborated this criticism in a letter to Wordsworth himself: *CL*, IV 572–6.

10. Chapter 22 presents problems. Since Coleridge was required to expand *Biographia Literaria* in 1816–17 to make it a work of two volumes (see above, pp. 219–21), and since the printing of the planned one-volume edition was stopped midway through chapter 22, the question naturally arises as to whether or not the expansion involved any rewriting and extension of the so far unprinted material forming the last half of chapter 22. Scholars are divided on this issue. Griggs (*CL*, IV 657) assumes that chapter 22 was complete in 1815 and underwent no revision or extension; Fogel (in *SIB*, xxx, p. 233) argues that, since chapter 22 was originally intended to conclude the *Biographia*, Coleridge would 'have had to revise at least the last page' of it before carrying on with the interpolation of 'Satyrane's Letters' and the other new material incorporated in chapters 23 and 24; and George Watson (*BL*[W], p. xvi), who notes the liberal use of long quotations in the last half of chapter 22, conjectures that this section was rewritten and heavily padded in the revisions of 1816–17.

11. Fogel, in *SIB*, xxx 230.

12. Several later statements (Sep–Oct 1815) express Coleridge's conviction that *Biographia* was 'a Work per se' and his sense of the book's essentially miscellaneous character — 'sketches of my own *literary* Life; and of my opinions on Religion, Philosophy, Politics, and Poetry': see *CL*, IV 588, 591 and 598.

13. Fogel, in *SIB*, xxx 232.

14. Coleridge's borrowings from Schelling were first noticed by Thomas DeQuincey in 1834. For the extent and nature of these borrowings see, for example, J. W. Beach, 'Coleridge's Borrowings from the German', *ELH*, IX (1942) 36–58; G. N. G. Orsini, *Coleridge and German Idealism* (London and Carbondale, Ill., 1969) esp. pp. 192–221; and Norman Fruman, *Coleridge: The Damaged Archangel* (New York, 1971; London, 1972) esp. pp. 69–107.

15. He also had before him some notes (probably made for his projected 'Logosophia' rather than for the *Biographia*) based on Schelling's *System*: see *CN*, III no. 4265 (and notes).

16. The *reasons* for Coleridge's resorting to 'plagiarism' are complex, fugitive, and deeply rooted in his psychological make-up. DeQuincey, with justification, was quite simply baffled by what he found. More recent commentators have been more dogmatic and less charitable: the case for the prosecution may be gathered from n. 14 above. The case for the defence, begun by Sara Coleridge in her edition (1847) of *Biographia Literaria*, has been ably continued by Thomas McFarland, who demonstrates that Coleridge's 'borrowings, though skirting and sometimes crossing the boundary of propriety, were not the thefts of a poverty-stricken mind, but the mosaic materials of a neurotic technique of composition' — *Coleridge and the*

Pantheist Tradition (Oxford, 1969) p. 32. See also E. S. Shaffer, 'The "Postulates in Philosophy" in the *Biographia Literaria*', *Comparative Literature Studies*, VII (1970) 297–313.

17. For a detailed account of the printing history of *Sibylline Leaves*, see Grigg's headnote in *CL*, IV 618. Coleridge returned the final proof-sheet of this volume to Bristol on 14 June 1816.

18. I have abbreviated the complex story of the protracted and acrimonious disputes concerning *Biographia Literaria* between July 1816 and May 1817. For a fuller account, see Griggs's comments in *CL*, III xlix–lii and IV 657–60.

19. Although the *Biographia* version is slightly revised, the letters – said to have been written by a 'friend' (actually Coleridge himself) whose pseudonym was 'SATYRANE, the Idoloclast, or breaker of Idols' – first appeared in nos 14, 16 and 18 of *The Friend* (1809): see *CC*, IV ii 187–96, 209–21, 236–47. 'Satyrane's Letters' were based on seven letters written to Tom Poole and Mrs Coleridge during Coleridge's stay in Germany in 1798–9: see *CL*, I nos 256, 258–9, 261–2, 269–70.

20. In August–September 1816 a series of five unsigned letters criticising Maturin's *Bertram* (a play accepted by Drury Lane Theatre in preference to Coleridge's *Zapolya*) were published in *The Courier*. The letters were written by Coleridge, who dictated them to John Morgan: *CL*, IV 664 n. 2 and 670. Part of the first and all of the last four of these letters were reprinted as *Biographia* ch. 23: see *CC*, III ii 435 n. 1.

21. In 1816–17 Coleridge was savaged by reviewers, especially by William Hazlitt in the *Examiner* and (later) in the *Edinburgh Review*. In vicious attacks on the *Christabel* volume (June 1816) and on *The Statesman's Manual* – both *before* and after it was published in December 1816 – Hazlitt aimed (in Griggs's phrase) 'a veritable campaign of hate' at Coleridge both as man and author. Hazlitt's attacks, while the most virulent, were not isolated. For a résumé, see Griggs's headnote in *CL*, IV 668. The reviews of Hazlitt (and others) are reprinted in *Coleridge: The Critical Heritage*, ed. J. R. de J. Jackson (London, 1970).

22. Thomas DeQuincey, *Recollections of the Lakes and the Lake Poets*, ed. David Wright (Harmondsworth, 1970) p. 46. DeQuincey's essay on Coleridge first appeared (in four instalments) in *Tait's Edinburgh Magazine*, Sep 1834–Jan 1835.

23. T. S. Eliot, *The Use of Poetry and the Use of Criticism* (London, 1933; repr. 1975) p. 67; and Maurice Carpenter, *The Indifferent Horseman: The Divine Comedy of Samuel Taylor Coleridge* (London, 1954) p. 304.

24. Whalley, in *E&S*, n.s. VI 92.

25. Ibid., p. 95.

26. Ibid., p. 100.

27. Jerome C. Christensen, for example, argues in a recent paper that no reading of *Biographia Literaria* could ever produce a unified reading of the text: 'It would likely produce a parody of such a reading. The *Biographia* is itself a parody, but not one which could accurately be called intentional or unintentional – just because the *Biographia* is the parody not of a particular book but a parody of the idea of [a] book, a parody of the kind of book it would like to be.' See 'The Genius in the *Biographia Literaria*', *SIR*, XVII (1978) 215–31; the quotation is from p. 231.

28. See, for example, Lynn M. Grow's chapter 'The Consistency of the *Biographia Literaria*' (pp. 128–47) in her book *The Prose Style of Samuel Taylor Coleridge* (Salzburg, 1976).

29. J. E. Barcus, 'The Homogeneity of Structure and Idea in Coleridge's *Biographia Literaria, Philosophical Lectures*, and *Aids to Reflection*', unpublished doctoral dissertation (University of Pennsylvania, 1968): see *Dissertation Abstracts*, XXIX (1969) 2205A–6A.

30. Watson argues that Coleridge 'set out to write a work of metaphysics to which he hoped the events of his life would give a continuity: he ended by producing a work of aesthetics to which such narrative as there is has failed to give continuity. But there is another unity, and it is peculiarly Coleridgean . . .' (*BL*[W], p. xix). Coleridge did *not*, however, set out to write a work of metaphysics: see above, n. 7; indeed, *Biographia Literaria* began as an aesthetic work (a preface to Coleridge's poems) and the metaphysical section was the last part of the book composed in 1815.

31. J. A. Appleyard, *Coleridge's Philosophy of Literature* (Cambridge, Mass., 1965) p. 169. Appleyard also stresses (*contra* Whalley) that *Biographia Literaria* was 'the result of little planning and foresight' (ibid.).

32. Grow, *The Prose Style of Coleridge*, p. 136.

33. See also *CL*, IV 591, 598.

34. It is impossible to overstate the importance for Coleridge of the establishment of right principles: 'It is my object', he declared in the first number of *The Friend* (June 1809), 'to refer men to PRINCIPLES in all things; in Literature, in the Fine Arts, in Morals, in Legislation, in Religion' (*CC*, IV ii 13). This was his lifelong conviction and his lifelong endeavour, which found its most mature expression in his 'Essays on the Principles of Method' in the much revised 1818 version of *The Friend*: see *CC*, IV i 448–524. With respect to literary critical principles, it should be pointed out that there is a direct and unbroken belief, stretching from 1802 to 1815 and beyond in Coleridge's thought, in the existence of such underlying criteria. The 'object' of the *Ur-Biographia* described to Southey in July 1802 had been 'not to examine what is good in [an individual poet], but what has ipso facto pleased, & to what faculties or passions or habits of the mind they may be supposed to have given pleasure' (*CL*, II 829–30); then, in chapter 18 of the *Biographia* itself, we meet the following restatement of the same conviction: 'The ultimate end of criticism is much more to establish the principles of writing, than to furnish *rules* how to pass judgement on what has been written by others; if indeed it were possible that the two could be separated' (*BL*, II 63).

35. M. G. Cooke, '*Quisque Sui Faber*: Coleridge in the *Biographia Literaria*', *PQ*, L (1971) 208–29; the quotation is from p. 225.

36. Appleyard, *Coleridge's Philosophy of Literature*, p. 187.

37. See above, p. 218 and nn. 14 and 16.

38. Thomas Carlyle, 'The Life of John Sterling', in *Thomas Carlyle's Works*, 18 vols (London, 1905) II 46–7.

39. Three points must be made about this sentence. First, it must be insisted upon that Coleridge is concerned with epistemology *not* with ontology, with 'knowing' *not* with 'being'. (*Being* – that is, the reality and existence of the subjective and the objective, of self and non-self, is ASSUMED.) That is why he

declares that 'We are not investigating an absolute principium essendi [principle of being] . . . but an absolute principium cognoscendi [principle of knowing]' (*BL*, ɪ 186). Second, Coleridge argues that any true theory of knowledge and knowing must begin from the subjective pole and *then* take into account the objective pole in order to arrive at the fullness of the human intelligence. Third, following Fichte (see *BL*, ɪ 101), Coleridge asserts that knowledge involves an *act*, that knowing is an active not a passive activity: 'in all acts of positive knowledge there is required a reciprocal concurrence' of both conscious intelligence (or subject) and unconscious nature (or object), and the 'problem is to explain this concurrence' (*BL*, ɪ 174).

40. Appleyard, *Coleridge's Philosophy of Literature*, p. 197. It may be added that the probability of confusion on Coleridge's part is supported by his own statement of mid 1834, only a month before his death: 'The metaphysical disquisition at the end of the first volume of the *Biographia Literaria* is unformed and immature; it contains the fragments of the truth, but it is not fully thought out. It is wonderful to myself to think how infinitely more profound my views now are . . .' (*TT*, p. 311).

41. Coleridge had defined the neologism 'esemplastic' in the opening sentences of *Biographia*, ch. 10: '"*Esemplastic*. The word is not in Johnson, nor have I met with it elsewhere.*"* Neither have I. I constructed it myself from the Greek words, εἰς ἕν πλάττειν, to shape into one; because, having to convey a new sense, I thought that a new term would both aid the recollection of my meaning, and prevent its being confounded with the usual import of the word, imagination' (*BL*, ɪ 107).

42. Appleyard would not accept this point; he believes that there is 'a fatal difficulty implicit in [Coleridge's] approach, a confusion of knowing and making' (*Coleridge's Philosophy of Literature*, p. 207). Appleyard's analysis of the 'weaknesses' of Coleridge's mingling of philosophy and aesthetics is well worth reading, esp. pp. 203–8.

43. Percy Bysshe Shelley, *A Defence of Poetry*, ed. J. E. Jordan (New York, 1965) pp. 74–5.

44. It was this point that Wordsworth had misunderstood in the Preface to his *Poems* (1815), where he had asserted that 'To aggregate and to associate, to evoke and to combine, belong as well to the imagination as to the fancy': see Coleridge's retort at the end of *Biographia*, ch. 12 (*BL*, ɪ 194).

45. Coleridge defines *symbol* in *The Statesman's Manual* (1816). A symbol, he says there, is characterised 'Above all by the translucence of the Eternal through and in the Temporal. It always partakes of the Reality which it renders intelligible; and while it enunciates the whole, abides itself as a living part in that Unity, of which it is the representative' (*CC*, vɪ 30).

46. The complementary relationship existing between the two distinct powers of fancy and imagination is stated clearly in a Coleridgean aphorism of 1833: 'Genius must have talent as its complement and implement, just as in like manner imagination must have fancy. In short, the higher intellectual powers can only act through a corresponding energy of the lower' (*TT*, p. 269).

47. R. H. Fogle, *The Idea of Coleridge's Criticism* (Berkeley and Los Angeles, Calif., 1962) p. 71.

48. Coleridge confronts these issues directly in chapter 18. First, 'The ultimate

end of criticism is much more to establish the principles of writing, than to furnish *rules* how to pass judgement on what has been written by others; if indeed it were possible that the two could be separated' (*BL*, ii 63). Second, in answer to the notion that poetry (Wordsworth's or anybody else's) could be produced by the formulaic application of external rules, he responds: 'Could a rule be given from *without*, poetry would cease to be poetry, and sink into a mechanical art. It would be μόρφωσις [a shaping power], not ποίησις [a making power]' *BL*, ii 65.

49. There are numerous early drafts (dating as early as 1809) of this definition: see *CN*, iii nos 3615, 3827, 4111, 4112; *SC*, i 148 and ii 41, 50–1, 68.

50. This is a favourite Coleridgean distinction: see, for example, *CL*, ii 810; *CN*, ii no. 2086 and iii nos 3247–8; *TT*, pp. 92–4 (12 May 1830) and 309–10 (23 June 1834).

51. U. C. Knoepflmacher, 'A Nineteenth-Century Touchstone: Chapter xv of *Biographia Literaria*', in *Nineteenth-Century Literary Perspectives*, ed. C. de L. Ryals (Durham, NC, 1974) pp. 3–16; the quotation is from p. 4. See also Fogle, *The Idea of Coleridge's Criticism*, pp. 97–104.

52. Nathaniel Teich, 'Coleridge's *Biographia* and the Contemporary Controversy about Style', *TWC*, iii (1972) 61–70; the quotation is from p. 65.

53. D. H. Bialostosky, 'Coleridge's Interpretation of Wordsworth's Preface to *Lyrical Ballads*', *PMLA*, xciii (1978) 912–24. Bialostosky argues that Coleridge frequently distorts or misinterprets Wordsworth's meaning: 'Not only has he variously and inconsistently identified the passages to which he objects, but he has misleadingly distinguished between what the Preface can legitimately be taken to mean and what it probably does mean' (p. 912).

54. Fogle, *The Idea of Coleridge's Criticism*, p. 79.

Index

An asterisk indicates that the author or work is quoted. Numbers in bold print indicate extended discussion or detailed references. Except in the case of the *first* reference to a work (where full bibliographical information is given), names in the Notes section are not included when they merely refer to an author already cited in the text; however, authors cited only in the notes or those cited in notes which do not connect them directly with the text are included in the index.